See more examples of
cutting-edge
journalism

VISIT THE AUTHOR'S BLOG AT **dynamicsofwriting.com**

DYNAMICS OF WRITING

Remembering that first journalism class: "I was scared out of my mind."

I was recently on a panel that discussed student media and self-censorship. Most, if not all, of the people on the panel were former journalists and several people in the audience had made the transition to the field to the classroom. One theme that came up repeatedly was the way in which students "these days" didn't have SOMETHING about them. It might be drive, it might be curiosity or it might be a skill. In any case, many of the people who spoke recalled that when THEY were students at THAT age, THEY had whatever it was that the students today seemed to lack in their estimation.

Search ...

Categories

Select Category

Shredded Tweets

Tweets by @DoctorOfPaper

Vincent Filak
@DoctorOfPaper

In the most over-the-top way possible? twitter.com/Poynter /status...

4h

Dynamics of News Reporting
and Writing

For my mom, Lynn, and my father, Frank, who made sure
I always worked as hard as possible; for my wife, Amy,
who makes every day worth it; and for my daughter, Zoe,
who always asks, "Are you writing another book?"

Yes, sweet pea. And, yes, I mentioned you in this one, too.

Sara Miller McCune founded SAGE Publishing in 1965 to support the dissemination of usable knowledge and educate a global community. SAGE publishes more than 1000 journals and over 800 new books each year, spanning a wide range of subject areas. Our growing selection of library products includes archives, data, case studies and video. SAGE remains majority owned by our founder and after her lifetime will become owned by a charitable trust that secures the company's continued independence.

Los Angeles | London | New Delhi | Singapore | Washington DC | Melbourne

Dynamics of News Reporting and Writing

Foundational Skills for a Digital Age

Vincent F. Filak

University of Wisconsin–Oshkosh

FOR INFORMATION:

CQ Press
An imprint of SAGE Publications, Inc.
2455 Teller Road
Thousand Oaks, California 91320
E-mail: order@sagepub.com

SAGE Publications Ltd.
1 Oliver's Yard
55 City Road
London EC1Y 1SP
United Kingdom

SAGE Publications India Pvt. Ltd.
B 1/I 1 Mohan Cooperative Industrial Area
Mathura Road, New Delhi 110 044
India

SAGE Publications Asia-Pacific Pte. Ltd.
3 Church Street
#10-04 Samsung Hub
Singapore 049483

Acquisitions Editor: Terri Accomazzo
Content Development Editor: Anna Villarruel
Editorial Assistant: Erik Helton
Production Editor: Bennie Clark Allen
Copy Editor: Jim Kelly
Typesetter: C&M Digitals (P) Ltd.
Proofreader: Jen Grubba
Indexer: Molly Hall
Cover Designer: Scott Van Atta
Marketing Manager: Jillian Oelson

ISBN: 978-1-5063-4474-4

Printed in Canada

21 10 9 8 7 6 5

BRIEF CONTENTS

DETAILED CONTENTS

PREFACE

Rarely a week goes by that I don't have a student, a student's parent, a friend or a random stranger asking me about the potential job prospects available to journalism students these days. Those queries can usually be boiled down to this: "Newspapers are dying, nobody believes what they see on TV anymore and everyone on Earth is randomly tweeting fake news, so how will I ever get a job?"

A grain of truth exists in each of these concerns, but what I have found is that many people, organizations and professions still value the underlying skills associated with journalism and still need what you can do. More than ever, we need people who can communicate effectively and provide clear and accurate information to audience members, who are desperate to be informed on issues that matter to them. This has been the core of journalism for generations and will continue to be the foundation of good reporting, regardless of where society or content-providing tools go in the next few months, years or decades.

The purpose of this book is to provide you with a broader view of reporting and writing today. Journalists have more storytelling options at their disposal than ever before, thanks to improving technology and opportunities for reporters to multitask. Journalists who once wrote a single story or collected video for a single on-air package are now asked to use Twitter and Facebook to update and promote a story, YouTube and Instagram to deliver visual components of a story and the web and print platforms to write stories and reach readers.

This book takes the skills associated with each of those elements, as well as others, and teaches them to you in a chapter-by-chapter approach. The analogy most frequently used here is that each chapter provides you with a "tool for your toolbox." The idea is that you learn each important aspect of reporting and writing across multiple platforms like you would learn how to use a hammer or a saw. Then, when you go out and ply your trade, you make choices about which tool best serves you and your audience in each task you are attempting to accomplish.

THE BENEFIT OF AUDIENCE CENTRICITY

In introducing the concept of audience centricity, many professionals, reviewers and scholars worried that this book and others like it would drive that self-feeding loop of just telling people what they want to hear. These concerns have merit, as many people insulate themselves in "media bubbles" and refer to content they dislike as "fake news." So, why would a reporting text in this environment encourage "audience-centric" content? "If we keep feeding the bubbles, are we really doing journalism?" they asked. It's a good thought and a fair question, but it misses the point.

In the older days of journalism, reporters relied on a series of news values to craft their copy. We still do this, and it's a crucial aspect of how we determine what matters and what doesn't. The theory behind these elements of news was that they held within them the things people desperately wanted to know about. The readers were assumed to be homogeneous and geared toward a single set of important ideals, and it was the reporters' job to go get that stuff and bring it to them. In short, we write, you read.

The difference between bubble-breeding and audience centricity is best explained by comparing pandering with catering. When you pander to an audience, you write stories that will confirm their preconceived notions, regardless of the accuracy of those notions. You look for ways to hype the material, painting in black and white instead of the textured grays that traditionally constitute our society. You do whatever it takes to get the next big headline, the next traffic spike and the next series of comments declaring you to be a genius.

Catering to an audience is more nuanced and still relies on the traditional news values to guide the reporter. However, it also requires the reporter to engage in critical thinking to determine what matters most to the readers and how best to give them that information. For example, a story about budget cuts that affect education will have a lot of interest for a variety of audiences in many ways. Potential audience members include parents, teachers, administrators, professors and college students. A good reporter would know what would matter most to certain readers and thus place a stronger emphasis on the elements of those cuts that matter most to that audience. A reporter at a rural newspaper might focus on the K-12 cuts to schools in outlying areas. A blogger for a teachers union might examine the issues pertaining to class sizes and salary freezes. A college journalist at a student paper might focus on how the cuts could affect tuition.

Reporters who have an audience-centric focus will take those sharply focused stories a step further and explain more specifically what the cuts mean to the individual reader. In the case of the student journalist covering tuition, for example, the writer wouldn't focus on how the budget cuts will lead to the whole university system's needing to collect another $45 million in tuition next year. The reporter instead would focus on her own university's chunk of that and then break it down so a student reading the paper knows how much his tuition would go up next year if the cuts continue.

In short, audience-centric reporters take the traditional tenets of journalism and use them to answer each reader's basic question: "So, what does this mean to me personally?"

DIFFERENT NEEDS, DIFFERENT TOOLS

At its core, this book approaches journalism with two underlying premises:

1. Skills matter more than anything else, and they will help you regardless of where you go or what you do in this field. Thus, everything you pick up in this book should be considered a "tool" for your "toolbox" of skills.

2. If you take the skills you learn and apply a heavy dose of critical thinking with regard to how best to tell a story and how to reach your audience, you will be successful in this business.

With these two things in mind, each chapter is meant to introduce you to a skill that will help you tell stories. These become the tools that go into the toolbox that you will take with you into the field of journalism. The chapters then go further by layering critical thinking onto these tools, with the goal of helping you use the tools in the right situations to meet the needs of your audience.

This is a paradigm shift away from traditional media texts and courses that taught you one tool and helped you figure out ways to use it to solve every problem. For example, in the old days of the print versus broadcast demarcation, a broadcast text would teach you how to use video and audio to do every story, ranging from a city budget story to a Fourth of July parade feature. A print-based textbook would teach you how to use text to tell those exact same stories. The problem with this is that a broadcast story on a budget will be visually boring and factually limited, while a text story will never capture the action and vibrancy of a Fourth of July parade.

In keeping with the tool analogy, those texts handed you a hammer and told you, "Here's how you can use a hammer to open a ketchup bottle, eat a steak, cut some wood and pound a nail." The tool has value, but only for one of those tasks (two, maybe, if you have a particularly difficult ketchup bottle).

This book provides you with a working knowledge of each of the storytelling tools you can use in journalism as well as their benefits and drawbacks. It then helps you think about how best to use each of those tools in a given situation to best inform your audience.

In other words: "Here are all the tools you have at your disposal. Use the right tool for the right job: a hammer for the nail, a saw for the wood, a set of silverware for the steak and a rubber grippy thing for the ketchup bottle."

CONTENT AND ORGANIZATION

Any effort to organize a text like this in a way that will satisfy every reader is like trying to catch yesterday's thunderstorm: No matter how you do it, you will never be successful. The reason the book is arranged in this fashion has to do with the critical-thinking and audience-centric mentality I wanted to drive home throughout the text.

Up front, I introduce the two key concepts that will imbue the entire book: how to write for an audience and how to think critically.

The next stage of the book focuses primarily on writing for text-based platforms, such as print, the web and social media. Once the reader understands what is required in the writing, it makes the reporting easier, which is why things like interviewing, basic news coverage and feature news reporting come next. The importance of visuals as a crucial reporting and story-telling tool require the foundation established in the text-based chapters, so this is why the broadcast elements come closer to the end.

Finally, the issues of law and ethics bring the book to a close in a reflective way, allowing the readers to see how what they have been doing as journalists fits into a bigger picture.

FEATURES

In keeping with the "right tool for the right job" approach to the book, a series of examples, breakout boxes and special features are included at various points in the text. Not every chapter will have every feature, while some chapters will have a couple of one kind but none of another. The use of these features depends greatly on whether the feature makes sense for the chapter. Here is a quick look at what these elements are and what they are attempting to do:

- **Thoughts From a Pro** Things can change pretty quickly in the field of journalism, so understanding what is going on in the world of the profession is crucial for reporting students. The "Thoughts From a Pro" feature in each chapter provides an up-close look at a specific aspect of reporting and writing from a professional who is plying his or her trade each day. The goal here wasn't to find perfect people to give you a look at lifestyles of the rich and famous, but rather to showcase journalists who can offer practical advice on realistic problems facing rookie reporters. The people who agreed to provide these insights come from various parts of the field and have worked in a wide array of disciplines, thus giving you a broader understanding of how reporting works. However, if you pay particular attention to their "One Last Thing" comments, you will also likely find a common thread that can be both helpful and inspirational to you as you learn the process of journalism and prepare for a job in the field.

- **Helpful Hints** From lists of vocabulary to shortcut options, the "Helpful Hints" feature is meant to cover things that will give you some ways to save time or pick up important info in an easy way. This feature tends to be the most random, in that the hints and tips come from various experiences journalists have shared over time. These lists can translate jargon into English for you as you read the chapter or get involved in student media. The tips can provide you a step-by-step approach for dealing with a crisis or solving a problem. The bulleted items can give you a few quick thoughts as to how to immediately improve a piece of copy or change your view on a topic of interest. Each of these boxes should just help place a few extra ideas into your head as you move deeper into the chapter.

- **Consider This** Journalism often requires you to look at situations from various angles. In most cases, you can make a valid case for several positions regarding ethical dilemmas, reporting procedures and storytelling options. Throughout the book, whenever a topic that could inspire debate arises, a "Consider This" element appears. These outline a few thoughts on a topic of interest, bat around some possible suggestions and then leave it up to you to decide how you want to view things. These can lead to some class discussions or some interesting internal debates for individuals.

REVIEW, DISCUSS AND PRACTICE

The book's pedagogical approach comes from my own experience with beginning writers, many of whom find themselves frustrated as they learn this new approach to telling stories. Each chapter provides not only content to learn and review, but also a chance to discuss the material and practice the craft. This approach allows students to learn on their own as well as in conjunction with their classmates. It also provides them with the ability to ply their trade and get better with each attempt they make. This allows them to experience success and growth over time while still learning in a variety of ways.

- **Thinking Ahead** Each chapter begins with some discussion of the purpose of the chapter and the broader ideas that will be discussed within. This approach gives the reader the opportunity to understand the overall value of the chapter and to know what will be coming throughout the chapter. This kind of roadmap makes it easier for the reader to work through the chapter and see how and why the information within is presented.

- **The Big Three** In an attempt to reach a distracted and busy audience, news organizations often use a few bullet points in a breakout box or at the top of a story to summarize the story. The goal is to give the readers the most important information in a quick and simple way. This book mirrors that approach with its summary section, "The Big Three," which is an attempt to pick out a few crucial things that will matter most to you. In other words, it's likely you won't remember everything you read in every chapter, and that's OK. However, it's important to make sure you take three crucial ideas with you as you move on to the next chapter. I hope that this is both a useful and user-friendly feature of the book that keeps you reading through to the end of each chapter.

- **Discussion Questions** At the end of each chapter, a set of discussion questions will give the readers a chance to work with others or to reflect privately on what they just read. The goal for these questions is to promote a broader understanding of the content based on varied interpretations of the students. Just as in journalism itself, there are no real "right" or "wrong" answers, but rather some better and some not-so-great ones.

- **Write Now! Exercises** The adage "Practice makes perfect" is at the heart of journalism and the core of this book. The "Write Now!" exercises give the students an opportunity to immediately practice what they have just learned. The exercises vary in approach based on the chapters and specifically do not include length or page limits in most cases. This will allow instructors to establish what they see as reasonable expectations for their own classes as well as the opportunity for students to focus more on doing good work as opposed to meeting an arbitrary content minimum set by the author. In addition, many of the exercises can be done multiple times, thus increasing the opportunity for additional practice attempts.

- *Dynamics of Writing: An Exercise Guide* A student workbook will be available in print. It will feature several exercises in each chapter to reinforce concepts taught in this book. These include quizzes, writing prompts and critical thinking exercises.

DIGITAL RESOURCES
CONSTANT DIGITAL UPDATES VIA DYNAMICS OF WRITING BLOG

Two of the major complaints about textbooks are that they are out of date before they even hit the shelves and that they lack the interactive elements students enjoy. In an effort to address these concerns, this text has an accompanying digital presence: the *Dynamics of Writing* blog (**dynamicsofwriting.com**).

The blog is updated almost daily with additional information, current examples of material discussed in the text and additional interactive elements that will keep students engaged and the material fresh. Professional journalists take part in the blog through interviews and discussions about current events in the media. Guest bloggers frequently post on topics of interest, such as improving local content or covering underrepresented groups. The author has also made the experience more interactive through the inclusion of digital elements, discussion-board opportunities and other web-based options.

This approach to content provision provides students with an opportunity to further their knowledge as they read these thought-provoking posts and seek direct feedback from the author.

SAGE edge offers a robust online environment featuring an impressive array of tools and resources for review, study, and further exploration, keeping both instructors and students on the cutting edge of teaching and learning. SAGE edge content is open access and available on demand. Learning and teaching has never been easier!

SAGE edge for Students provides a personalized approach to help students accomplish their coursework goals in an easy-to-use learning environment.

- Mobile-friendly **eFlashcards** strengthen understanding of key terms and concepts

- Mobile-friendly practice **quizzes** allow for independent assessment by students of their mastery of course material

- **Newswriting Assignments** allow students to broaden their reporting skills and practice writing

- Test your knowledge of AP Style with our **AP Style Quizzes and Exercises**

- **Video and multimedia links** that appeal to students with different learning styles

- EXCLUSIVE! Access to full-text **SAGE journal articles** that have been carefully selected to support and expand on the concepts presented in each chapter

SAGE edge for Instructors supports teaching by making it easy to integrate quality content and create a rich learning environment for students.

- **Test banks** provide a diverse range of pre-written options as well as the opportunity to edit any question and/or insert personalized questions to assess students' progress and understanding

- Editable, chapter-specific **PowerPoint® slides** offer complete flexibility for creating a multimedia presentation for the course

- **Newswriting Assignments** allow students to broaden their reporting skills and practice writing

- Test your students' knowledge of AP Style with our **AP Style Quizzes and Exercises**

- **Sample course syllabi** for semester and quarter courses provide suggested models for structuring one's course

- **Video and multimedia links** that appeal to students with different learning styles

- EXCLUSIVE! Access to full-text **SAGE journal articles** have been carefully selected to support and expand on the concepts presented in each chapter to encourage students to think critically

ACKNOWLEDGMENTS

This book needed a lot of help from a lot of great people, and I'm so grateful to the people who gave of their time and skills to make this happen.

Special thanks go out to Erik Petersen, Jill Geisler, Janelle Cogan, Tony Rehagen, Lauren Leamanczyk, Brandon Kinnard, Mac Slavin, Pat Borzi, Ryan Wood, Jaimi Dowdell, Brian Urbanek, Charles Davis and Andrew Seaman, who provided incredible insight as to the state of the field as well as some great guidance in this book. Thanks to Kyle Miller, Joe Dennis and Justine Stokes for their assistance with the broadcast chapters; Kate Nash and her students at the University of New Mexico for their incredible digital storytelling; and to Daxton "Chip" Stewart for his review of the law chapter.

I greatly appreciate the help and candor provided by the various educators and professionals who reviewed the various approaches and draft chapters I put together. The insights from the August 2016 focus group hosted at the Association for Education in Journalism and Mass Communication's national convention also played a crucial role in restructuring the purpose and tone of this book. Without that event, this book would have been diminished in scope and value.

The team at SAGE has been fantastic in every way I could ever want, especially my editorial partners Terri Accomazzo and Anna Villarruel. You both make me want to write better and stronger each time I work for you, while simultaneously beating every deadline you set for me. Also thanks to Matthew Byrnie, who helped bring me into the SAGE family.

Finally, a special thanks to Steve Lorenzo, whose green pen made me work harder than I thought possible; to Teryl Franklin, who used her position as my night editor to pick me up and put me back on the journalism horse; to George Kennedy, who once told me that when it came to the job I applied for, "everyone is more qualified than you," but who picked me anyway; and to the staffs of the Daily Cardinal, Ball State Daily News and Advance-Titan, who gave me a reminder of what student journalism can be. Thanks for helping me get to this point.

SAGE would like to thank the following instructors for their invaluable feedback during the development of this book:

Dave Cassady, *Pacific University*

Terry Heifetz, *Ball State University*

Kirstie Hettinga, *California Lutheran University*

Jeremy Kohler, *Washington University in St. Louis*

Stephanie Reese Masson, *Northwestern State University*

Ambrose Metzegen, *Colby-Sawyer College*

Dante Mozie, *South Carolina State University*

Rheanna R. Rutledge, *NOVA Southeastern University*

Kimberly Schumacher, *Coastal Carolina University*

Mary Lou Sheffer, *University of Southern Mississippi*

Kevin Tankersley, *Baylor University*

Nancy Whitmore, *Butler University*

ABOUT THE AUTHOR

Vincent F. Filak, PhD, is an award-winning teacher, scholar and college media adviser who serves as a professor of journalism at the University of Wisconsin Oshkosh, where he primarily teaches courses on media writing and reporting. Prior to his arrival at UWO, he served on the faculty at Ball State University and also taught courses at the University of Missouri and the University of Wisconsin–Madison. He also previously worked for the Wisconsin State Journal and the Columbia Missourian newspapers.

Filak has earned the Distinguished Four-Year Newspaper Adviser award from the College Media Association for his work with the Advance-Titan, UWO's student newspaper. CMA previously honored him as an Honor Roll Recipient for his work as the adviser of the Daily News at Ball State. The National Scholastic Press Association presented him with its highest honor, the Pioneer Award, "in recognition of significant contributions to high school publications and journalism programs."

As a scholar, Filak has received 13 top conference paper awards, including those from the Association for Education in Journalism and Mass Communication, the Broadcast Education Association and the International Public Relations Society of America. He has published more than 30 scholarly, peer-reviewed articles in top-tier journals, including Journalism and Mass Communication Quarterly, Journalism and Mass Communication Educator, Newspaper Research Journal, the Atlantic Journal of Communication, Journalism: Theory, Practice and Criticism, the Howard Journal of Communication, Educational Psychology and the British Journal of Social Psychology. He is also the winner of CMA's Nordin Research Award, which goes to the best research paper completed on a topic pertaining to media advisers within a given year.

He has published several textbooks in the field of journalism, including "Dynamics of Media Writing" (Sage), "Convergent Journalism" (Focal) and "The Journalist's Handbook to Online Editing" (with Kenneth Rosenauer; Pearson).

He lives in Omro, Wisconsin, with his wife, Amy, and their daughter, Zoe.

1

AUDIENCE-CENTRIC JOURNALISM

LEARNING OBJECTIVES

After completing this chapter you should be able to:

- Understand what makes today's readers different from news consumers in prior generations and how best to serve them based on those differences.

- Identify the tools you can use to define your audience and how each tool will provide specific value for you as a reporter.

- Know and apply the interest elements that attract readers: fame, oddity, conflict, immediacy and impact.

- Understand what we owe our audiences above all else, including accuracy, value, fairness and objectivity as well as why these matter to both us and them.

THINKING AHEAD: UNDERSTAND YOUR AUDIENCE

Why do you want to be a journalist?

If your answer was "Because I'm good at writing" or "I enjoy talking to people and hearing their stories" or even "I'm nosy," those are all valid answers. People who have these skills often find long and prosperous careers in various media fields. Good writing, good reporting and good nosiness are all crucial elements of being great in this field.

The main thing you need to understand about all of those skills is how to use them to benefit other people. If you just rely on those skills for your own interests, what you are

saying is akin to stating that you want to be a famous chef at a top-flight restaurant because you enjoy eating.

No matter what area of this field you enter or on what platform you work, you won't be writing for yourself, speaking for yourself or even being nosy for yourself. You will be doing your work for an audience, a large group of specific individuals who seek information from you on a daily basis. Just as the famous chef should enjoy cooking great food for other people, you should receive joy when you find important things that matter to specific readers and viewers. You should also want to convey that information to them in a way they can use and in a form they understand.

Audience centricity is the core of everything journalists do today, whether it's when they use Twitter to send out important breaking news or cameras to capture gripping video to help viewers see a situation as it unfolded. However, journalists these days also understand that not every reader or viewer uses the same platforms for the same reasons or wants the same information in the same ways. This is why understanding your audience is crucial to everything you do.

In this chapter, we will explore who uses the media today, how they use it and what they expect from their media sources. In addition, we will outline the ways in which you can use the tools outlined in the rest of this book to give your audience members what they crave in the way they want.

Unlike media users of the past, today's readers and viewers can access vast volumes of content anywhere and at any time thanks to their mobile devices. How we serve them and what platforms we use to serve them require us to know who is in our audience and what they want from us.

MEDIA AND MEDIA USERS TODAY

For decades, newspapers were the standard source of information. Reporters used a series of news values to define what was and was not news. Then, they wrote the content in a way they felt best met the needs of the sources, the readers and the newspaper. As radio and television became important news outlets, audience members sought information from trusted professionals like Walter Winchell, Edward R. Murrow and Walter Cronkite. In each of these cases, the journalists drove the content and presented it to a mass audience in whichever way they saw best.

Today, social media has become a dominant force in the field of news, with new platforms and new sources supplanting traditional journalists. According to a 2015 study from the Pew Research Center and the Knight Foundation, 63 percent of Facebook and Twitter users said they use those sites to get their news.[1] Of those users, nearly 60 percent said they use Twitter to follow breaking news, while 32 percent of the Facebook users said they engaged with political content on the site.

Journalists no longer have the luxury of providing "all the news that's fit to print" and assuming people will gratefully consume every last word. The idea of a mass medium has gone away and has been replaced with fractured audiences, **niche** publications and a glut of information. News consumers today have so many choices that they can afford to be picky, and they can decide which sources best serve their interests. Here are some things that make this generation of audience members different from those readers and viewers of previous era:

INFORMATION WHENEVER AND WHEREVER

Generations of journalists were taught in **"silos"** based on the fields they saw themselves entering. Students with an interest in newspapers went down one path, while those interested in broadcast went down another. When they became professional journalists, they became biased toward their own areas of the field and disparaged their competition. Even as digital media became a force within the field, research has shown that both professionals and students in the field of news see themselves based on their **platform** choices.[2]

In today's day and age, this approach to journalism makes no sense, as the audiences we serve aren't as tied to platform-based biases as we can be. A study by the Media Insight Project found that audience members of all generations are essentially platform neutral when it comes to how they get their news.[3] The once-held beliefs that older generations rely on print, while middle-aged media users rely on TV and young people gravitate to digital devices don't hold water. The survey found that most Americans have more of a buffet approach to their media use, relying on upward of six devices, including television, newspapers and radio, to get their news. In addition, it is the content that drives their choices, with users turning to print publications for news about education and their local government while using mobile devices to keep up with breaking news.

These and other research findings drive home an important and yet uncomfortable point for up-and-coming journalists: It's not about you or what you like. The readers are driving the bus now, and you have the choice to either present your information in a way they want in an engaging format or to accept when they go elsewhere. Journalists have to adjust their own perceptions when it comes to their platform-based biases and focus more on what audience members want.

THE "INFOTAINMENT" PHENOMENON

The idea of **"infotainment"** has gained traction in the past half decade and continues to be an issue for journalists. On one hand, **demolisticles** like those on BuzzFeed[4] and humorous news accounts like those on "The Daily Show" and "Last Week Tonight" draw people into the news. On the other hand, the line between serious news and sarcastic commentary has continued to blur, much to the detriment of news providers. In a 2009 speech at the Poynter Institute, veteran broadcaster Ted Koppel noted that the media dedicates too much time to stories that are heavy on hype but light on facts and information.[5]

Just because news journalists must now think more about an audience than they once did, it doesn't necessarily follow that they have to pander to the audience's basest desires. The wide array of platforms has made it possible for people to post almost any kind of information they want, ranging from fan fiction to videos of cats falling off of TV sets. Although these bits of information show up on the same platforms as coverage of Russia's attacks on Syria or the president's State of the Union address, it doesn't follow that these items are news.

U.S. President Barack Obama, left, talks to television personality Stephen Colbert on Colbert's late-night comedy show. The line between news and entertainment has continued to blur over the years, making it more difficult for journalists to help readers separate fact from fun.

In serving an audience, journalists can walk a fine line between stories that stress oddity as an interest element and those that contain actual impact. (See below for a full outline of audience-based interest elements.) If the story is boring, readers won't spend enough time on it to understand how it affects them. However, if the story is nothing but hot air and buzzwords, the readers find themselves consuming nothing but empty calories of news content. As you develop your skills as a journalist, you will need to know how to make a story engaging to the reader without resorting to infotainment.

FAKE NEWS

Con men, shysters and other peddlers of hoaxes are nothing new in this world. People swore they had seen the Loch Ness monster and Bigfoot. Others claimed they could sell you a medicine to cure your ills or a controlling stake in the Brooklyn Bridge. What makes today's cons more problematic for us is the volume of lies purporting to be truths and the speed at which they spread throughout society. Partisan bickering and digital aids have helped create a lucrative field of **fake news** that can give real journalists incredibly painful headaches.

Not every story that readers disagree with should fall into the category of fake news. Just because you don't like a political figure or a societal movement, it doesn't follow that positive stories about these things are fake. However, people are taking advantage of people who enjoy having their worldviews confirmed as they rake in cash based on click-driven advertising.

In 2017, Scott Pelley investigated the fake news phenomenon for "60 Minutes" and found a frightening world of news scams bent on pitting people against each other for sport and profit. One website garnered an audience of more than 150 million viewers publishing headlines like "Hillary Clinton Has Parkinson's Disease, Physician Confirms." (The story was based on the claims of a doctor who never met Clinton and was later denied by Clinton's own doctor and officials from the National Parkinson Foundation.) Some websites rely on computer "bots" at fake social media accounts to hyperinflate the number of retweets and likes a story gets in an attempt to make it seem legitimate or important.[6]

As a journalist, you need to find a way to break through this wall of fake news and illegitimate content if you want to reach your readers. Even more, you will need to find ways to convince these people that you aren't just one more carnival barker, crying out for attention with exaggerated claims and false promises.

INFO GLUT: CHOICES, CHOICES AND MORE CHOICES

Famed baseball slugger Reggie Jackson was once discussing Nolan Ryan, a man known for throwing fastballs that topped out at about 100 miles per hour, when he made this comment: "Every hitter likes fastballs just like everybody likes ice cream. But you don't like it when someone's stuffing it into you by the gallon." Media users today can understand that concept fairly well, as they deal with a glut of information from thousands of sources.

For generations, people who wanted to get the news were stuck with one or two newspapers, three TV channels, a few radio stations and a handful of news magazines. The lack of choices made for a homogenous understanding of what was going on in the world and a limited view as to how we define news. Although the number of dead-tree newspapers that can land on your doorstep today hasn't increased, the web has opened up a vast expanse of text-based news options for you. Cable TV provides you with hundreds upon hundreds of channels, many of them serving small-interest niches, including home repair and history. Satellite radio gives audiences access to not only a vast expanse of musical choices but also a number of talk radio stations and news outlets. Websites and social media outlets that aren't affiliated with traditional media also offer readers and viewers a wide array of perspectives on everything from "Star Wars" to knitting.

The sheer volume of choices can make it difficult for today's media users to make sense of the world around them. A 2013 study revealed that about half of the social media users surveyed reported that they had a constant fear that they were "missing out" on some important bit of information.[7] The global media agency Carat noted in a 2015 study that people feel overwhelmed by the number of information outlets and the volume of content they receive online. Thus, the study finds, about 44 percent of people rely on content their friends provide or recommend.

SHORTER ATTENTION SPANS

If you have ever seen a bird chasing a foil gum wrapper across the yard, you know how **"shiny-object syndrome"** works: Something bright and shiny grabs the bird's attention, and the bird goes after it. When something else shinier comes along, the bird becomes distracted by that thing, forsaking the original target. According to a 2015 study by Microsoft, people aren't much better than that bird when it comes to staying focused.

The research found that the human attention span now sits at eight seconds, or one second shorter than that of a goldfish.[8] The study goes on to say that we lose concentration in that tiny bit of time due in large part to the way our digital lifestyles have affected our brain.

This means that readers no longer will spend several minutes reading the overly long narrative lead you put on the city council meeting story. They also aren't going to sit still for a two-minute video of a person standing at a podium, droning on about parking regulations. The stimulus must be strong and steady over time, as you use concise writing or valuable video to grab the audience members' attention and keep it until you are finished.

AUDIENCE PARTICIPATION AND SPIRALING VIRAL COVERAGE

In January 2016, actor Alan Rickman died of cancer at the age of 69. He played a wide array of characters, from the Sheriff of Nottingham in "Robin Hood: Prince of Thieves" to stern Hogwarts professor Severus Snape. In a more traditional media era, Rickman's death would likely lead to a small bit of information in a television newscast and an in-depth **obituary** in many newspapers. In today's media world, however, not only were journalists writing about Rickman's death, but so were fans, colleagues and others, as their thoughts ping-ponged off of one another at a rapid pace.

James and Oliver Phelps, who played the Weasley twins in the "Harry Potter" franchise, tweeted their immediate reactions to the news about Rickman. Others, including Daniel Radcliffe and Emma Thompson, also offered their thoughts and emotions through various information outlets, which fans then shared repeatedly via social media. However, Emma Watson, who played Hermione Granger, created the largest viral spiral with her tribute to Rickman. She quoted Rickman, an unabashed feminist, who noted, "There is nothing wrong with a man being a feminist, I think it is to our mutual advantage." Twitter users immediately accused Watson of

This is a goldfish and it has a longer attention span than your readers do. That means, we have to work a lot harder and a lot smarter to get their attention and keep it.

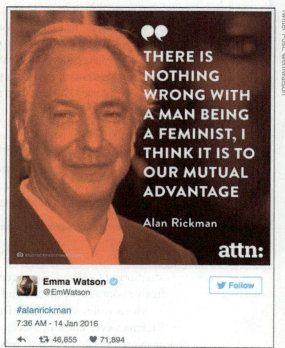

> THERE IS NOTHING WRONG WITH A MAN BEING A FEMINIST, I THINK IT IS TO OUR MUTUAL ADVANTAGE

Alan Rickman

attn:

Emma Watson
@EmWatson   Follow

#alanrickman
7:36 AM - 14 Jan 2016

46,655   71,894

In the wake of Alan Rickman's death, this tweet from "Harry Potter" co-star Emma Watson sparked backlash on social media.

CONSIDER THIS → A MEDIA DIET: AUDIENCE WANTS VERSUS AUDIENCE NEEDS

What we want from a media diet isn't always what's best for us. It is the job of good journalists to prepare a healthy blend of engaging content that will serve the readers and make them want to come back for more.

Just because you want something, it doesn't necessarily follow that the thing is good for you. Think about how a little kid comes home after trick-or-treating and rips into every chocolate bar and piece of taffy she gathered. It seems like a great idea at first, but then the stomach ache follows, and she realizes that gulping down 6 pounds of sugar in a single sitting wasn't a smart move.

Conversely, the things we know are good for us aren't always awe inspiring. Vegetables, like broccoli and cauliflower, often get left on a child's plate until the last minute of dinner. After a few lame attempts to spread them out on the plate or bargain with a parent regarding how much has to be eaten, the kid eventually gulps down a piece or two.

Just like this regular "diet" issue, a **media diet** often strikes a balance between what people want and what they need. The stories about a toddler who stole an ice cream truck in Australia or a water-skiing squirrel named Flippy are great fun, but they lack substance for most readers. Stories about legislatures passing bills or city councils trimming budgets hold the appeal of a Brussels sprout, but these stories can alert readers to life-changing outcomes.

Audience-centric journalism isn't about handing your readers a bucket of Halloween candy every day, but rather finding ways to provide information they need in an appealing way. As a journalist, you need to find ways to make readers pay attention to stories that should matter to them. You can do this through stronger reporting and clearer writing as you constantly find a way to answer the question, "Why should a reader care about this?"

An occasional story about a bear in a swimming pool or someone setting a world record for most eggs eaten in five minutes doesn't hurt, but it can't be the main course for a media diet. The overall goal of this book is to find ways to make those "vegetable stories" worth a second look as we give the readers something they need in a way in which they want. Consider this balance between wants and needs as you continue throughout the remaining chapters, and you will have a much easier time reaching your readers.

attempting to advance an agenda through Rickman's death. (Watson herself has often spoken freely about feminist issues and is a goodwill ambassador for the United Nations.)

Meanwhile, author J.K. Rowling tweeted back and forth with fans, who asked whether Rickman ever knew of a deep secret that Snape held back throughout the series. As Rowling answered these questions, other fans offered their thoughts on the issues associated with the character, the secret and what Rickman's work meant to them.

Through it all, media outlets ranging from fan blogs to news sites covered each aspect of Rickman's death and its reverberations. Rather than defining for the audience what is news, the media outlets tended to use what the audience felt mattered to help select content and convey it to other interested users. Most media outlets retained their sense of how best to structure and present the coverage, but audience participation and the sense that a story was "gaining ground" helped influence the amount and the focus of the coverage.

As a journalist entering the field at this time of viral content and heavy audience interest, you will find yourself pulled between traditional news values, such as conflict and impact, and audience interests that feel more like "junk food" information. You can no longer dictate to the readers what matters, as writers and editors could many years ago when the printing press ruled the news. However, you can use those news values to help you ascertain when an audience's interest has reached a critical mass that demands coverage. You can also use those values to your advantage as you repackage information and disseminate it to your readers.

DEFINING YOUR AUDIENCE

Far too often, journalists make incorrect assumptions about readers based on ill-conceived notions or outdated data. To make sure they don't fail their audience members, media organizations often solicit reader feedback to help them refocus their coverage. Here are a few ways you can get information about your audience:

READERSHIP SURVEYS

A readership survey allows a media organization to examine who is paying attention to its content, what content is most appealing to the readers and to what degree readers' wants and needs have changed over time. Association Media and Publishing lists several reasons for doing these surveys[9]:

- **It's been a while:** Media users' preferences change over time, based on various life factors and interest levels. Industry experts say that conducting a survey once every other year is considered a "best practice" within the field of media.

- **You're not sure where you stand:** The desire to "take the temperature" of your readers is natural if you want to know how best to keep readers happy. A survey can help you determine if the information you are providing is relevant and engaging to your readers.

- **You aren't sure if your approach is working:** News reporters occasionally assume that new ideas will be interesting to their readers because those ideas worked in other markets. These ideas could be anything from covering different types of stories to using various platforms to present information. A survey of readers will either confirm or reject those assumptions.

Most organizations have conducted surveys like these at some point, and it is important for reporters to look at them and see what the audiences really want.

HELPFUL HINTS ➡ DEMOGRAPHIC, PSYCHOGRAPHIC AND GEOGRAPHIC INFORMATION ON YOUR READERS

The various ways you can measure an audience can help you determine who is in your readership and what they want from you.

Identifying trends or interests within a large group of readers can seem daunting. The tools listed in this section will help you better understand who your readers are and if they enjoy what you created for them. Here are some ways to break your audience into some simple, useful chunks:

DEMOGRAPHIC INFORMATION

Demographics usually include things like age, gender, race, education and relationship status. These categories can then be broken into more useful segments, such as age brackets and specific educational levels. When coupled with those other "check-box items," demographics can help determine the types of people who use the content you create. Even more, you can refine your coverage approach based on what those demographics tell you. For example, if your readership is predominantly men and women ages 25 to 36 who have one or more children under the age of 10, you can tailor your coverage toward the interests most normally associated with that type of individual. This could be early marriage, young parenthood and early education.

PSYCHOGRAPHIC INFORMATION

Demographic information alone isn't enough to determine common ground among readers. **Psychographic information** allows you to examine an audience based on personality traits, values, interests and attitudes. This type of data includes things like strength of opinion on political issues and social ideologies.

For example, sporting traditions might dominate the social identities of some universities, while other universities have half-filled stadiums for every home game. Certain towns may profess a conservative sense of local politics, even though the people there treat the town like a "bedroom community" and rarely vote. Other towns may have a wide range of political views, but have a serious dedication to the local high school's events and to shops run by local merchants and vote in every town election.

GEOGRAPHIC INFORMATION

People care greatly about things happening near them, making **geographic information** a crucial element in understanding your audience. When someone robs a gas station in a small town, people want to know what happened and who is responsible. When a reader's school district considers a bond referendum, that person wants to know how much taxes will go up if the effort is successful.

Traditional newspapers know the circulation of their publications, including where distributors deliver the print copies. Webmasters can use analytics to determine where people are when they log in and engage with content. This is helpful for journalists who want to know if an event is too far outside of the audience's geographic interests or if readers in certain areas might have an interest in the publication reaching out farther into their territory.

WEBSITE ANALYTICS

It's not always who is reading the news that is the most interesting aspect of **analytics**, but instead what those people are reading. Either as part of website surveys or through the use of third-party web analytics, journalists can determine what brings people to a site. These analyses can examine which stories get the most clicks, the most screen time or the most comments. A survey of American Society of News Editors members found that nearly 97 percent of newsrooms monitor web metrics.[10] The five key metrics they said every journalist should know and value are:

- **Unique visitors:** These are measured based on the time frame under analysis. For example, if a reader visits a website at 9 a.m., noon, 7 p.m., and 11 p.m. during a single day, that reader would be counted as one unique viewer if the unit of measurement is "daily unique visitors." However, if the unit of measurement is "hourly unique visitors," that one person would count four times.

- **Pageviews:** This measures the loading of a single page as well as any reloading of that page. A single viewer could visit 10 pages on a single website for a total of 10 pageviews, or that viewer could continually refresh a single page 10 times for the same total.

- **Visits:** This is the single time that a viewer enters the website and navigates it until the viewer leaves. This information can be further parsed to determine where the person is coming from, what parts of the site accounted for the majority of the reader's visit and other similar bits of information.

- **Source:** Every visitor to a website has to come from somewhere. Source data can include things like the name of a search engine, a specific referring URL or if the visitor came directly to the site using a bookmark. Source data will help you determine what got your readers to show up, which can help you with marketing or promoting your information to them.

- **Session duration:** This measurement will allow you to see how long readers spent on a given site as well as how long they spent on any particular page. This will help you determine what content people used the most and what content saw minimal screen time.

Reporters can use these and other analytics to assess what stories drew the most people, held people's attention the longest and led to additional reading on the site. Just like any other tool, this can be misused or overanalyzed, but for the most part, reporters should look at these analytics to determine what mattered the most to the readers.

REAL PEOPLE

Surveys can give you a broad array of information from a large group of people, while web analytics can help you ascertain where people spend their time while on your site. However, neither of these can replace actually interacting with your audience members.

For years, reporters have relied on **official sources** to drive story selection and story angles. A number of logical reasons existed for this approach: Officials are easy to find, they carry a certain level of authority and their comments are "safer" for reporters than those that come from average citizens. (See Chapter 12 for more on the issues associated with absolute privilege and qualified privilege.) In addition, journalists often developed patterns with regard to what merited coverage and how best to cover it. As scholar Warren Breed noted while reflecting on his own time in a newsroom, older reporters passed down expectations and values to younger reporters, thus leading to a self-perpetuating cycle of repetitive content.[11]

© Erik Petersen

As a journalist with experience on both sides of the Atlantic Ocean, Erik Petersen understands a lot about how an audience can shape content for a publication and how digital media has made that even more important.

Petersen serves as the editor of Fort Lauderdale Magazine, the monthly publication for the city. Prior to returning stateside, Petersen spent 11 years at the Nottingham (U.K.) Post, where he worked primarily as a features writer and columnist. He has also served as a bureau reporter for The Kansas City Star.

Throughout that time, Petersen said he learned how audiences shaped the various publications at which he worked.

"In the U.S. we've got a de facto national media thanks to papers like the Times and the Post," he said. "In the UK, it's much more explicit. You've got London-based national papers like the Guardian, Daily Mail and Telegraph, and then you've got local papers. Because of the split, national newspapers cover all the national and international news, while local papers are what Americans would think of as one giant metro section."

These differences lead to different approaches to what made for content and what the audiences tended to expect in certain publications, he said.

"Local British papers tend to run stuff that U.S. city dailies wouldn't—real cat-up-a-tree stuff," Petersen said. "There are entire websites devoted to people in British local papers frowning and pointing at things—potholes, closed public restrooms and so forth. This habit of local papers running these stories in print has always been a sort of endearing running joke, and in the early days of online, papers took notice of how much it could drive traffic. Nonsense stories would go viral."

Even though the papers enjoyed the traffic spikes on the web, Petersen said he often worried about how the audience viewed the publication.

"People who are tweeting your story with 'LOL, it's all kicking off in Bath' are helping give you a massive spike on that story, but they're not building a community of readers who are committed to your publication," he said. "They're not from your area, and they're only reading your story because they're mocking it. It was a lesson that in my view took a while to learn because stories that create huge spikes are hard to peel away from, but British local papers now focus more on the more long-term process of building a community of local readers."

When he returned to the States, Petersen said he took that understanding of audience building as he approached his new challenge of reaching the Fort Lauderdale community, especially through the interactivity available on the web.

"Unlike daily papers, where the challenge has been how to compete in a world where daily news is now a much more open game, city monthlies now get to interact more regularly with our readers," he said. "In newspapers, it often felt like 'this is a threat we have to understand.' Here it feels more like an opportunity. Our readers are professionals who live in the city and have discretionary income. If a few times a week we can give them a product they find useful—say, something quick about a gallery opening or a new restaurant—it's a level of interaction we didn't have before."

In terms of moving forward in a digital world with an ever-evolving audience, Petersen said he worries less about the newest apps or devices and more about how best to reach his readers with quality content.

"I try not to get caught up in 'what works' as much as how we present it, because in most ways I think good journalism is still what works," he said. "For a while we heard a lot about how only shorter, quick-hit stuff would work in the new world. Well, I went to the University of Missouri with a guy named Wright Thompson who is one of the people proving that false. Just do good work, and then let the analytics side of things guide you in the particulars of how you present it."

ONE LAST THING

Q: If you could tell the students reading this book anything you think is important, what would it be?

A: "I think it's so important right now to be less top-down about building readerships and everything that comes with that, particularly in a big organization. Don't have one person with all the secret knowledge. Make sure every journalist—particularly the younger, junior ones—have ownership in what's happening. Likewise, journalists need to think like one-person media organizations. That's even down to the small things. It might not seem like the biggest thing in the world, but if I meet a journalist without a Twitter account, I wonder what they're doing. It's a simple tool for getting your work out there more—don't you want that?"

What no one really spent a lot of time thinking about in the newsroom, however, was the degree to which stories about robberies, city council meetings or formal speeches mattered to the audience members. In the days of limited media outlets, reporters didn't have to worry that they would lose readers to other publications. Even if there was competition, most journalists ascribed to a standard set of news values that would essentially guarantee that if a robbery occurred or a city council met, every media outlet would be there, dutifully covering it. Now, with a wider array of media options, understanding your readers becomes more important than ever.

To help you reach your readers and understand what **"real people"** want to see, consider both traditional and digital options. As you work on standard stories, such as meetings, speeches and news conferences, you might take time out to ask audience members what they like to read or what things they think matter. When you cover **lite-brite** stories, such as Fourth of July parades or the opening of a local library, you could spend more time talking to people about what they would like to know and why they read (or don't read) what your media outlet produces.

In a digital realm, you should read through reader comments at the end of your stories and other stories. Social media platforms, such as Facebook and Twitter, often have ways for you to keep track of a topic as well as the people most directly interested in it. This will allow you to strike up a conversation with these interested parties via email or Twitter and find out more about what matters to them. Always look for ways to find out from "real people" what they think matters and see if it merits additional attention from you and your media outlet.

Facebook

Trends for you · Change

Stephen Miller

#NationalColoringBookDay
@jendziura and @GetBullish are Tweeting about this

#WednesdayWisdom
2,891 Tweets

#CrazyExGirlfriend

#FWD2017 ▶
1,044 Tweets

James Baldwin
James Baldwin would have been 93 today

#nationalicecreamsandwichday

#RaiseAct
Trump backs proposal for 'merit-based' immigration system

Angelyne

Grant Show

This list of trending topics shows you how varied the overall levels of interest in a wide array of topics can be on any given day.

The "copy-taster" (left) selects material, while Editor Arthur Waters (seated, center, right) decides on the treatment of a story with a member of his staff, on a Saturday afternoon in the newsroom at the News of The World, April 1953. Journalists historically have put extra emphasis into the issue of being accurate and fair.

WHAT DO WE OWE OUR AUDIENCE?

With all of this in mind, the job of the journalist can seem a lot less fun and a lot more overwhelming than you might have originally thought. Although the discipline may seem more complicated than you originally thought, some basic elements of journalism remain crucial. As we noted earlier in the chapter, you don't have to pander to an audience to drive readership. Here are a few basic things news consumers need from you:

ACCURACY ABOVE ALL ELSE

No matter how fast you get information to someone or how incredible your mind-blowing visuals are, if your work lacks **accuracy**, nothing else matters. The first and foremost expectation audiences have of journalists is that we have put forth information that is factually correct.

This means you should go back through everything you write and make sure your facts are solid, your writing can't be misconstrued and your quotes are accurate. This might require one edit or it might take several, but spend whatever time you need to make sure you have everything correct. We will spend much more time on this throughout the book, but always remember this should be your prime directive.

CLARIFICATION OF VALUE

One of the bigger mistakes journalists make is to get into a rut when they report and write. This often emerges when city government reporters cover too many meetings or sports reporters rely on the "who beat whom" coverage to fill their story quotas. The idea of "we've always covered X" rears its ugly head when journalists forget that they're not covering meetings or games for the sake of covering meetings or games. They need to go back to the basic premise of this chapter: Write for the audience.

Journalists have often relied on who, what, when, where, why and how—the 5W's and 1H—when they write. When writing a story, it becomes imperative that we look at the idea of not only what happened but also why it matters to our readers. The lead will capture the core elements of who did what to whom, but the "why" element of the 5W's and 1H will drive home the value of the piece. Here's an example:

> Brown County firefighters responded to a fire at 123 E. Smith Drive late Wednesday night.

The core of this sentence picks up on four of the W's, but it lacks value because this essentially tells the readers that firefighters fought a fire. That's what they are supposed to do, and thus there's not a lot of value in that. The lack of an answer to "Why should I care?" leaves the readers without a sense of importance. A stronger lead can create improved value:

> A fire at 123 E. Smith Drive killed three people Wednesday and caused $280,000 in damage to Brown County's oldest historic home.

That shows value in terms of a sizable impact (death and damage) as well as an additional bit of insight regarding the importance of the house (oldest historic home in the county).

When you write for your readers, be sure you can clearly answer the question "Why should I care?" for them.

FAIRNESS AND OBJECTIVITY

Accuracy goes a long way to improving trust, but **fairness** and **objectivity** also contribute greatly to trustworthiness.

Journalists often hear that fairness means getting "both sides of the story," but in many cases, issues have more than two sides. A fair journalist gives stakeholders an opportunity to make their positions known. In some cases, those stakeholders may be less than genuine or may have their own agendas, which is why you need to be prepared with research and information when you speak to them. Fairness does not mean parroting your sources. Fairness means giving people the opportunity to put forth a viewpoint, which journalists have every right to question and challenge.

However, this leads to the idea of objectivity. Being objective is not akin to being blind to reality. In the wake of the 2016 election, the term "fake news" has taken over as a one-size-fits-all term for any news certain people dislike, leading to diminished approval ratings of the press and media credibility. However, objective journalists will examine statements presented as fact and push back against those that fail to pass muster. In one such incident, presidential adviser Kellyanne Conway defended President Donald Trump's proposed travel ban by referencing two Iraqis who masterminded "the Bowling Green massacre." Media outlets quickly researched the incident and found that no such terrorist attack occurred. Instead, they found that two men were arrested in Bowling Green, Kentucky, after attempting to send resources to al-Qaida. Conway eventually recanted, noting that she meant to say "Bowling Green terrorists."[12]

What objectivity requires of a journalist is to approach each topic and each source with an open mind. Even journalists who research a topic well might not be fully versed in it. You have to be able to put aside your personal views and biases when covering stories and give your sources the opportunity to provide you with information on the topic. You also have a duty to your audience to be as informed as possible so that sources don't pull the wool over your eyes and to push back against sources when they present falsehoods.

WHAT ATTRACTS AN AUDIENCE?

Don't be discouraged when you realize that audiences now determine what matters most to them. Instead, realize that you still have a lot of input when it comes to how you can meet their needs while still maintaining your own set of best practices. To do this, you need to understand what attracts an audience to your content and then use those items as starting points to drive your coverage.

The book "Dynamics of Media Writing" outlines a series of **interest elements** that can help you attract an audience.[13] To remember them, you can use the mnemonic **FOCII**, like the plural of focus, but with two I's. Here is a brief examination of those elements:

Oddity and conflict will draw readers to your publication. However, if the material fails to deliver more than shock value, they won't stick around for long.

FAME

This interest element relies on the idea that important people will draw the attention of readers. As noted in "Dynamics of Media Writing," it isn't always what someone does, but who is doing the deed that matters. According to the Centers for Disease Control and Prevention, the United States sees more than 800,000 marriages end each year with little fanfare. However, when actors Ben Affleck and Jennifer Garner split in 2015, it became news almost everywhere.

Fame falls into two main categories. The first category includes people who are famous for an extended period of time, like heads of state, actors and singers. The second category includes those people who are living out their "15 minutes" of fame, such as Powerball jackpot winners, internet sensations and news oddities.

ODDITY

People value rare things, which can be anything from the Hope Diamond to the kid in third grade who can belch the alphabet. Journalists often focus on oddities and present them to their readers as being different from the everyday elements of life.

News organizations occasionally highlight **oddity** with positive superlatives, such as the "largest ball of earwax in North America" or "the longest filibuster in state history." In other cases, oddity could come from negative outcomes, such as the 45-year-old Muncie, Indiana, woman who was arrested on suspicion of stabbing a fellow partygoer in the eye with a fork. The reason? The stabbing victim took the last barbecued rib.[14] In terms of the criminally weird, some publications, like the Toronto Sun, even have a "weird" news section on their websites.[15]

CONFLICT

If two or more people or groups seek incompatible goals, conflict will emerge. Whether it is two people who want the last barbecued rib at a party or two political parties seeking dominance in the House of Representatives, when mutually exclusive endgames present themselves, you will see conflict.

As we will discuss in Chapter 2, reporting on **conflict** requires more than getting side A of an issue and then assuming there is a side B that you need to even things up. When it comes to conflict, you can see various facets of conflict if you put in some effort to examining the issue. For example, any building project could have financial, societal and environmental ramifications for the area and your readers. You need to understand those various facets and explain how each outcome can be good or bad for your readers. No matter what happens, the outcome will matter to your readers.

IMMEDIACY

People don't like to feel out of the loop, and news journalists understand this. To best serve their readers, journalists do their best to get people the most important information as quickly as possible.

When journalists "break" news or get a "scoop" on the competition, they demonstrate the importance of **immediacy** as an interest element. Digital outlets like websites and social media outlets can provide journalists with 24/7 access to their readers, meaning that immediacy takes on a whole new level of importance. Prior to these ever-present platforms, journalists measured immediacy in increments of days or hours.

Newspapers published multiple editions each day, with the final edition bringing a close to their day of information dissemination. Journalists working for the publication then had to wait to see what competing papers and broadcasters got that they didn't. Television journalists had three nightly broadcasts, with the final version of the news coming out just before midnight, depending on the time zone. However, once those windows closed, the news went dark until the morning newscast.

Today, immediacy is measured in minutes and seconds, which leads to a hypercompetitive market in which speed dictates a lot of what we do. However, as immediacy becomes a primary issue in the field, we all have to make sure that speed doesn't trump accuracy. Fast is great, but fast and wrong is horrible.

IMPACT

As noted earlier in the chapter, people want to know "Why should I care?" Good journalists can answer that question when they focus on the **impact** of a story. In some cases, you can demonstrate impact with simple stories, such as pieces on tax-rate increases or business closings. In other cases, you need to go much deeper to show a longer range impact, such as how the "too big to fail" banking crisis of the mid-2000s came to a head or how changes in environmental laws will affect the quality of water in an area.

You can demonstrate the impact of a story in a quantitative or qualitative sense. Quantitative impact measures the range of the impact, such as how many people got the flu during a particular winter. Qualitative measurements show the severity of an impact, such as the death of one student at your school.

1 AUDIENCE-CENTRIC JOURNALISM

THE BIG THREE

Here are the three key things you should take away from this chapter:

1. **The audience matters most:** You aren't writing for yourself. You are writing for your readers, and they have specific wants and needs that you must address. The better you understand this, the more connected you will become with your audience members, and the better you will be able to serve them.

2. **Journalists owe the audience:** When it comes to your readers, focus on what you owe them each and every time you ply your trade. You have to be accurate. You need to show them value in what you write for them. You need to be fair and objective. If

you do these things, you will grow and retain a strong and loyal audience. If you don't, the readers can always go somewhere else for their information.

3. **Focus on the interest elements:** Fame, oddity, conflict, immediacy and impact serve as crucial interest elements for all media writers, but they are particularly valuable for news reporters. Each time you sit down to write a story, consider each of these elements and see which ones you think apply. This will help you focus your work and build strong and valuable content.

KEY TERMS

accuracy   12

analytics   9

audience centricity   2

conflict   14

demographics   8

demolisticles   3

fairness   13

fake news   4

fame   14

FOCII   13

geographic information   8

immediacy   15

impact   15

infotainment   3

interest elements   13

lite-brite   11

media diet   6

niche   2

obituary   5

objectivity   13

oddity   14

official source   9

pageview   9

platform   2

psychographic information   8

real people   11

session duration   9

shiny-object syndrome   5

silos   2

unique visitor   9

visit   9

DISCUSSION QUESTIONS

1. The first question this chapter asked is "Why do you want to be a journalist?" What is your best answer to that question? What makes this field worthy of study in your mind?

2. What is the source of most of the media you consume? Think about not just the platform (newspaper, magazine, TV, web, apps) but think about the sources

of media on those platforms. What makes that media valuable to you? How did you find the sources, and what made them a part of your consumption habits? What similar media did you reject or decide not to continue using? To what degree do you think the media provides you with audience-centric content?

3. Of the five interest elements listed in the chapter, which one drives you to consume media? Why do

you think this is? Which one matters the least to you? Why do you feel that way?

4. Of the information you consume on a daily basis, how much of it do you think would fall into the category of "infotainment"? What draws you to this material, and how much does that bother you now as a reporting student?

WRITE NOW!

1. Explore the demographic details of your school in terms of age, gender, race and the in-state/out-of-state gap. Look for specific details you think define your school. Then, select another institution within your state and examine the same elements. Use these findings to write a two-page essay that outlines the similarities and differences between these schools. Also, include your opinion regarding the degree to which those elements accurately reflect the similarities and differences between your two schools.

2. Select three articles that interest you from the media you consume. Look through them to identify the elements of interest outlined in this chapter. Write up a few paragraphs on each article, explaining why you found that these articles were of interest to you and which elements most and least factored into your interest.

3. Select an issue of your student newspaper (or online publication, depending on your campus) and compare it with the coverage of an issue of your local publication from that same day and time as well as an issue of a national publication from that same day and time. Write a short essay on each one of these publications to outline what audience(s) you think they serve and how well you think they are serving them. Use examples of stories that illustrate the points you are making regarding the quality (or lack thereof) of the coverage.

4. Conduct a short content analysis of one of your social media platforms (Twitter, Facebook, Instagram

etc.). Which of the people you chose to follow shows up most in your feed over the past 24 hours? What topics are "trending" in your feed, and how well do you feel those things represent your overall interests? To what degree would you say these items qualify as "news," and how do you think this reflects on you as a media consumer? Write a short paper that outlines your thoughts and findings.

5. Reflect on a time when you became an active participant in a social media phenomenon. It might have been your choice to tweet about an election or to post articles about a topic that you thought others should read. What drove you to do so, and how much thought did you put into your approach? Does this differ in any way from how you see yourself as an upcoming journalist, or is this part of a different way you see media usage?

6. Reflect on the issue of accuracy and how you feel it is or isn't present in the media today. As allegations of media bias, "fake" news and other similar issues come to the forefront, how do you see this overall field, and why do you perceive it this way? Write a short essay that clarifies this.

7. Select a news piece from a local publication and assess it for audience centricity. How does it do in addressing the 5W's and 1H, and how well does it tell you why it should matter to you? If you feel it has done well, explain what works. If you feel it hasn't, explain what doesn't work and how you would go about fixing it.

Visit edge.sagepub.com/filaknews to help you accomplish your coursework goals in an easy-to-use learning environment.

2 CRITICAL THINKING

LEARNING OBJECTIVES

After completing this chapter you should be able to:

- Understand the basic tenets of critical thinking and how they affect journalism.
- Assess the quality of your own thinking by applying the crucial aspects of critical thought.
- Enhance your reporting through stronger analysis of your approach to content gathering and news writing.
- Demonstrate proactive and reactive skills during the process of reporting.
- Use critical thought in analyzing content in terms of relevance and value to your audience.

THINKING AHEAD: HOW TO FULLY "GET" A STORY

As a reporter, you always need to get the story. However, the definition of "getting" the story differs from reporter to reporter. The central theme of this book is that getting the story means more than picking up facts and quotes as if they were items on a grocery list that you simply toss into your cart. Because you are the one "cooking the meal," so to speak, you need to understand how those items work to form the larger whole.

Getting the story means fully understanding your story and making sure that you can explain what is going on to your audience. It entails a lot of research beforehand, concentration during the entire reporting process and follow-up work once you begin writing. You need to understand how what you ask can lead to what your audience will know. You need to be able to balance the perspective of your readers and viewers with that of the sources you will seek. In the end, you need to be both self-aware and aware of others as you attempt to put together your work as a journalist.

Learning how to think critically will make you a better journalist and help you not only get the story but also understand the story as you pursue it. **Critical thinking** often gets lost amid the time pressure of a 24/7 news-on-demand world. Unfortunately, with the deluge of information that comes at you in rapid-fire fashion and from the endless sea of "publishers" on the internet, understanding how to think critically has never been more important.

Critical thinking is a skill you can develop over time. Some people are naturally curious and have an intuitive sense of exactly what questions they need to ask. Others need time to come to grips with what they learned and make it part of the bigger picture. If you are the latter, don't worry. It doesn't mean you aren't or will never be a critical thinker. What it does mean is that you will likely need to practice critical thinking skills a bit more in order to become better at it. The remainder of this chapter is geared toward helping you understand how to do that.

HOW DO WE THINK?

In their book "How Do Journalists Think," Holly Stocking and Paget Gross lay out a cognitive process by which journalists react to stimuli in their environment. The reporters then match those stimuli with previously understood categories they developed in their minds over time. In doing so, the journalists can use the old information stored in those categories to inform them about the new situation in front of them.

Perhaps this is a better way to look at it: Imagine your mind as a giant filing cabinet with millions of pieces of categorized information stored inside. When a term comes up, like "musician," you flip through your files quickly and see what you've categorized inside those files that fits that term. For

Bob Woodward (left) and Carl Bernstein, Washington Post staff writers who broke news on the Watergate case, at their desk in the Post. As the reporters followed this difficult story, they relied on critical thinking as they determined what they could accurately report and what needed more work.

some, it's country and western singers like Johnny Cash and Trisha Yearwood. For others, it's Drake and Ariana Grande. For still others, it's the Beatles or the Rolling Stones. You then pull all the information from that file and use it to assess the current person being dubbed a "musician." Was there ever a time when your parents told you, "That's not music. That's garbage" when you were listening to something they didn't like? Their rationale comes from their own sense of what music is and is not.

Stocking and Gross note that the way journalists think and categorize and report is "fraught with bias." They argue that journalists need to do more to understand the process of how they categorize information and what the implications are for those cognitive shortcuts their minds take.[1] One good way to do this is to engage in a critical thinking perspective. Because it's not possible to rewrite the way in which you think, instead this chapter will offer you suggestions on ways to think about how you think from a critical thinking perspective. While this chapter is all about critical thinking, it is not here alone that we will engage in this process. This approach to thinking will be woven into each chapter of the book.

DEFINING CRITICAL THINKING

The Foundation for Critical Thinking defines critical thinking as the art of analyzing and evaluating thought with a view to improving it. It is an ongoing process that provides individuals with the ability not only to examine a topic but also to reflect on how they are thinking about it. In other words, it is a process, not a goal, that will perpetually provide individuals with the opportunity to see what they are doing, question why they are doing it and grow through that process.

In his essay on critical thinking, scholar Richard Paul writes that critical thinkers seek to improve thinking by analyzing their approach to thought and then using that process to upgrade their thinking. Unfortunately, Paul says, students at most colleges and universities do not get the chance to learn this way in the classroom. He notes that 97 percent of faculty who responded to a nationwide survey as far back as 1972 agreed that critical thinking was an important part of education. However, Paul also notes that education is still provided primarily by a series of lectures that focus on the rote memorization of specific facts and the ability to regurgitate those facts when called upon.[2] While this is a bad thing for all education, it is particularly disturbing for those of us who teach in journalism, where thinking on the fly is crucial and the answers aren't on a Scantron sheet.

LEARNING HOW TO THINK

In his book "Thinking," Robert Boostrom outlines several cases in which students were accomplishing learning tasks but weren't thinking. One such case involved a conversation between Boostrom and his son, a middle school student. The boy was explaining that he needed to identify Thomas Jefferson in order to complete an assignment. When Boostrom suggested a few possibilities (signer of the Declaration of Independence, former president of the United States), his son explained that those answers were not correct. The boy then said that Jefferson was properly identified as the vice president under John Adams. When Boostrom asked how the boy came to this conclusion, his son explained that all he had to do was look through his textbook until he found Jefferson's name in bold and then copy down the phrase that followed.[3]

Don't try to snow your readers. The use of weak ideas and overblown jargon isn't helping anyone.

This example makes it clear that learning material is not the same as thinking, let alone engaging in critical thinking. Instead of examining why the "vice president" answer was the best answer, the boy simply knew that if he wanted to get credit for his homework, he needed to write it down. Many of the classroom experiences you have had to this point were likely similar in nature to what this boy experienced. You were told to memorize the states and their capitals. You were tested on whether you could remember the names or actions of characters in a play or novel. You had to complete timed tests based on applying specific mathematical formulas to a set of equations. While all of these activities give you knowledge, they don't make you think.

Memorization is not the enemy of thinking, but rather a complement to it in many ways. However, if you wish to succeed in doing good journalism, you need to go beyond memorization and learn how to think critically about what you are doing, how you will go about doing it and why you are doing it in the first place.

Linda Elder and Richard Paul of the Foundation for Critical Thinking argue that critical thinking is the ability to ensure that you are using the best possible thinking measures in any situation in which you find yourself.[4] You want to figure out "the lay of the land" or better understand the entire puzzle. To do this, you need as much information as possible as you reason out how to approach a problem, such as how to write on a given topic or how to tell a specific story.

Perhaps a better way of explaining this is to understand what makes certain people good at a game like chess. Great chess players understand the moves each piece can make and understand what strengths and weaknesses are inherent to those pieces. In addition, they can see the whole board, much like how a conductor sees a whole orchestra or how a quarterback sees the whole playing field. The great chess player not only can see what is happening, but understands what is likely to happen. Great players can see a few moves ahead and anticipate what they will see next.

Inferior players obsess about the pieces or become fixated on one portion of the board. They don't understand the entirety of the game well enough to make rational choices as to what to do several moves down the road and thus are stuck making simple decisions without looking ahead.

Good journalists are both proactive and reactive as they survey the chessboard that is their story. Rather than looking at the story as a single incident, good journalists look for patterns in behavior. They see what has happened before this moment in time and what ripples will continue to move outward in the future from this moment. To become good at critical thinking, you need to be prepared for what is likely to come next, adapt to changes that occur during the process and synthesize all of the incoming information into an overarching understanding of what is going on and why it matters.

To become good at critical thinking, you need to practice it on a daily basis.

THE REQUIREMENTS OF CRITICAL THOUGHT

In their volume on critical thinking, Joe Kinchloe and Danny Weil argue that critical thinkers possess "a radical humility" in which they are aware of the complex nature of life. They don't allow themselves to be limited by what they think they know. Instead, they approach each situation as if it is a "great wide open" of possibilities.[5] Journalists who are good at what they do often fit these parameters and thus far exceed their less complex colleagues.

The question then becomes, how does one engage in critical thought and see these larger ideas in more comprehensive ways? Elders and Paul argue that critical thought comes from reasoning. It is one thing to assert something, but it is quite another to be able to develop a logical framework from which one can make a clear and coherent point that can be defended against contradictory arguments. This approach to thinking comes from a well-trained mind, developed through practice and honed by challenge.

In other words, you learn how to do this through practice. Don't worry so much if you don't have a complete mastery of critical thinking right off the bat. Nothing you've ever done in life has come without some level of trial and error. For example, think all the way back to the first time you successfully tied your shoelaces. Whether you tried the "bunny ears" technique or the "loop, swoop and pull" method, you likely didn't get it right the first dozen times you tried. Then, finally, you found just enough loop and barely enough swoop that when you pulled, you got a partial knot that was hanging there by a thread. Still, you did it. The knots eventually improved until the point where tying your shoes became second nature. Chances are, you don't even remember the last time you did it or what you were thinking about at the time.

Critical thinking will eventually come to you as well, as long as you practice it.

HOW TO APPROACH A STORY AS A CRITICAL THINKER

Researchers Susan Fiske and Shelly Taylor once noted that humans are cognitive misers; we like to expend as little energy as possible when we are asked to think. To conserve that mental energy, we draw on previous experiences, break things down to the simplest way to look at them and find ways around hard thinking.[6] Even now, in your classes, it is likely that you're sitting back listening to a professor lecture. The professor is pouring information out and you are picking it up in dribs and drabs like a sponge. It is easy, it is simple and it is not what journalism is about.

A journalist takes notes as President Barack Obama speaks during a news conference in the East Room of the White House in Washington. What the core of the story is and how best to tell it will be part of the critical thinking process this reporter uses during the writing.

To become a good journalist, you need to be thinking all the time, and you need to be thinking more broadly about what it is that you are doing. If you are covering a contentious school board meeting, you can't just think, "Well, I got side A. Now I've got to go find someone from side B." What are the key arguments that A and B are making? What really separates them? Do they understand the strengths and weaknesses of the arguments they are making? Do you?

A deeper look at content and questioning what you are told are both trademarks of good critical thinkers. In addition, the critical thinker:

- Raises vital questions and problems by coming to grips with the topic.

- Gathers and assesses relevant information.

- Thinks open-mindedly within alternative systems of thought, recognizing and assessing as need be their assumptions, implications and practical consequences.

- Communicates effectively with others in figuring out solutions to complex problems.

Let's consider each of those items in turn.

RAISING VITAL QUESTIONS BY COMING TO GRIPS WITH THE TOPIC

Fully immersing yourself in a specific topic or area is one of the best ways to fully understand the stories on which you'll be asked to report. Some of the best bloggers are folks who focus on one issue: health care, politics or safety. Newspapers often have beat reporters who cover a specific topic or geographic location. Beats for public safety, education, city government, religion, finance and sports are common in newspapers. If you examine some newspapers' bylines closely, you will notice that specific individuals tend to cover the same types of stories.

Television stations, while often using the general assignment approach with their reporters, have reporters who cover specific time slots and specific parts of the coverage area. The media outlets do this because it gives the reporter a chance to develop relationships with sources through repeated contact.

Reporters can also learn how to find bigger-picture stories by seeing the individual stories that come out of a beat over time. For example, let's look at the case of a school district that wants to build a high school. To get the money needed to construct the school, the district must put a referendum on the ballot and ask the public to approve the borrowing of $20 million. The referendum has failed three times before, and the current school continues to fall into disrepair. Each time, the vote is approximately 60/40 against the project.

A solid reporter can look at the issue and note that it's been up three times before and failed all three times. It is a simple case of reviewing previous stories, talking to the school board members and interviewing district citizens about the plan. The story is important, but the author is failing to come to grips with the topic.

What makes the people vote the way they do? It might be worth some time to study similar school districts that have building projects under way to see what their schools cost. Is there a particular aspect of the plan that people think is not worth the cost? Is that Olympic-class swimming pool that adds $2 million to the price tag a real thorn in the side of people who voted it down? How about the $3 million sports complex for the football program? Are people dissatisfied with the costs of things they don't believe are tied to academics?

Who is voting against the plan? Are they people who have no children in the schools and don't want to spend for something they won't use? Is there distrust between the district and the board? Was there a time that the school board or school officials reneged on a promise or overspent wildly on something? Would they be more willing to approve the plan if a new board was in place or if some fail-safe measures were put in place?

Who is voting for the plan? What do they see as the benefits of the new school? Will it provide better overall education and improve the community, or will it give students something they can't get right now? Is it cheaper to build than to retool what they have?

All of these questions are valid, and they are vital to fully understand the whole story. By raising these questions, you not only become more informed yourself, but you have the chance to better inform your audience.

GATHERING AND ASSESSING RELEVANT INFORMATION

Usually, journalists are pretty good at gathering information. We go back through previous stories on a topic, read relevant documents on the topic, ask questions of sources and get as much information as we can about the upcoming event.

In his book "Newsthinking," Bob Baker notes that skilled reporters have a sense of what they will see when they attend a meeting, cover a fire or interview a politician. They have a sense about what makes the story newsworthy, and that sense helps them break down the story into simple pieces. They then develop a checklist of sorts, which helps them determine what information they have and what they need to make the story complete.[7]

However, gathering information is only half of the job. Assessing the information is the other half, and it matters more. In assessing the information, we allow ourselves to think about the story and what it is really going to tell people. Even more, it gives us a chance to see if what we have gathered makes sense.

Fairness and balance are two important aspects of journalism, but they should not prevent you from thinking critically about the story at hand. Getting to that heart of the story means thinking about what is really happening beneath the surface. Stories can use a series of simple quotes and facts, but those stories don't do much to help people understand the value of what you have written.

Let's say you're doing a story on a city council's decision to increase taxes to fund a public park. You've got a direct split on the issue, with five council members voting each way on it. When you

Gathering information requires you to research your topic and interview key sources. How you do this will determine the overall quality of your work.

start to question people about their position, chances are, most of them have a pretty polished answer as to why they support or don't support the tax increase. For those who support it, they might say, "Our children are our most precious resource. They need to be able to experience things that this park can provide." For those against the tax, they could tell you something along the lines of "This tax places an undue financial burden on the citizens of this city."

Good reporters know they need to get quotes from both groups on this. An even better reporter would talk to folks who aren't on the council about their feelings on these issues. However, a reporter who engages in critical thinking breaks out of the mold and questions the underlying assumptions in this story. What is an "undue burden" in the minds of those people? How much will this tax increase really cost citizens? How many kids will this park likely serve? Even if the cost is low, if no one uses it, does the park have value? What happened the last time a city built a park or raised a tax? Did the citizenry end up in the poorhouse?

There are dozens of other questions that could come up through this process of analysis, but the big thing to keep in mind is that you need to look beyond the simple aspects of the well-polished answers and get some bigger questions on the table. Sometimes, the end result is that the story is very simple: some people like the park, others don't. However, you won't know that until you start asking more complex questions.

THINKING OPEN-MINDEDLY

It is a good idea to come to a meeting, a speech or a news conference with some sort of idea as to what is likely to happen and what it will mean. That's what pre-reporting does for you. That said, you need to think for yourself and adapt to the situation. In "Newsthinking," Baker notes that good journalists tailor their approach to the circumstances surrounding the story. Journalists need to improvise and adapt to what is going on and then make it mean something to the audience.

If you attend a meeting and you plan to write a story on how the city council will approve a plan to build a skating rink, you obviously need to know all you can about that area, the plan, the cost, the council's feelings on the plan and so forth. However, you also can't get tunnel vision and

An editor at the Wisconsin State Journal first introduced me to this concept more than 20 years ago, and it might go back even further than that. The **Topeka test** is a way to examine your story to assess whether you've done your job educating your readers about the story they are reading and how it fits into a larger picture.

Imagine a salesman catching a flight from Topeka, Kansas, to a faraway city (New York, Los Angeles, London, etc.). He has a brief layover in your town, so he grabs a copy of your paper before he catches a connecting flight. The salesman then reads your article on the second leg of the flight. Is there enough background in the story that the salesman can fully understand your story? If not, you've failed the Topeka test, and you need to go back and take another pass at your story.

Let's take a look at a story that doesn't quite pass the test:

> New York Gov. Elliot Spitzer resigned Wednesday, amid allegations he had purchased the services of high-priced prostitutes and been subsequently caught by a federal probe into the call-girl service.
>
> "I cannot allow my private failings to disrupt the people's work," Spitzer said at a press conference held at his Midtown office.
>
> Spitzer's resignation will be effective Monday at noon and push Lt. Gov. David Paterson into the role of governor. The resignation takes place approximately 14 months after he took office.

While the story tells the 5W's and 1H to some degree, we don't really get a full picture of this incident. Is it rare for a governor to resign in this fashion? What makes Spitzer's case particularly shocking or different? Who is Spitzer? Who is Paterson? By answering more of these types of questions, you can have a much better feel for the value of the story, and you'll be closer to passing the Topeka test. Let's try this instead:

> New York Gov. Elliot Spitzer, who built a reputation as a fierce opponent of corruption and crime, resigned Wednesday after revelations that he patronized a high-priced prostitution service.
>
> "I cannot allow my private failings to disrupt the people's work," Spitzer said at a press conference held at his Midtown office less than 48 hours after his name came up in a federal probe into the call-girl ring.
>
> Spitzer's resignation will be effective Monday at noon and will make him the first New York governor to leave office amid scandal in nearly a century. His replacement, Lt. Gov. David Paterson, is a 22-year veteran of the state legislature.

While neither approach will win a Pulitzer, you'll notice how the second version offers more information with a few bits of context. We find out that Spitzer was an opponent of illegal activities, only to be caught in one himself. We figure out who Paterson is and why his new job will be significant. We find out how rare this event is and why it matters. In short, we get more information. All of this, mind you, is the product of critical thinking. By seeking broader layers of context, the reporter in the second case gave us a better sense of the importance of the story.

focus solely on that idea. If someone takes the podium and expresses disgust at the way in which a developer has polluted the city's rivers or if a council member resigns in protest over a proposal to ban smoking from local restaurants, you can't just stay focused on the skating rink. You've got to think fast and get on these other developments.

COMMUNICATING EFFECTIVELY WITH OTHERS

Are you writing for yourself, or are you writing for other people? Ask yourself that question each time you ply your craft. The journalists who report for themselves are thinking about filing a story, meeting a word count or just making a deadline. They want a solid lead, a decent set of quotes and a closing that in some way makes sense. However, journalists who write for their audiences are always looking for ways to tell the story so that it conveys value.

When you write, you must explain unfamiliar elements of the story to your audience. If you don't know what a tax-increment finance district is, do you really think your readers do? Don't pass the buck and force them to do the research you should have done.

You must provide enough context for your readers to firmly grasp not only this story, but the entire topic you are covering. If the audience missed previous stories on this topic, will they fully understand what is going on? Even daily stories on the incremental progress of the O.J. Simpson trial, the 2000 presidential election controversy and the 9/11 terrorist attacks provided readers with enough background to keep them up to speed. Stories that fail to give people enough information to fully understand them are of little use to the audience.

Use words you think your audience will understand. Don't be afraid to look things up and explain them to the audience. Give the audience members a sense as to how the story can affect their lives.

CRITICAL THOUGHT AND THE VALUE OF YOUR QUESTIONS

One of the things you'll note about the material above is that it involves a great many questions. While this sounds a little too obvious, questions are meant to elicit responses from a person who has information to better inform the questioner. It is not an obvious thing, however, as it pertains to journalism, because far too often, journalists ask questions for completely different reasons than the one stated above.

ASKING QUESTIONS TO GET QUOTES OR SOUNDBITES

One of the key aspects of the journalism business, whether print, broadcast or online, is the importance of having people issue their own thoughts in their own words. Whether it's the fire chief on TV explaining how the fire got started or the mayor in the newspaper laying out his budget, the story loses something if these people can't speak for themselves.

That said, quotes shouldn't be the main reason for asking a question. Instead, they should be a byproduct of good questions meant to help the journalist better understand

In this photo provided by the White House, U.S. President Barack Obama holds a health care speech that he is editing with Jon Favreau, head speechwriter in the Oval Office. Quotability of content is always a big concern for public officials. Although journalists ask questions to get quotes, it is important to make sure to dig deeper than the pre-planned glossy statements.

THOUGHTS FROM A PRO → JILL GEISLER, BILL PLANTE CHAIR OF LEADERSHIP AND MEDIA INTEGRITY, LOYOLA UNIVERSITY CHICAGO

© Loyola University Chicago

Jill Geisler understands the importance of merging journalistic endeavors and critical-thinking skills. Geisler holds the Bill Plante Chair in Leadership and Media Integrity at Loyola University Chicago and has written widely about leadership, management and critical thinking for the Poynter Institute.

Geisler said that journalists often know they need critical-thinking skills, but are often at odds in terms of exactly what those skills should include.

"My biggest concern (with professionals) was making sure that when editors and news directors said they wanted staffers to use 'critical thinking skills' that they really understood what that term meant," she said. "For some, it just meant the ability to read the boss's mind and see the potential story as they did."

To help her pupils better understand how critical thinking should work, Geisler developed exercises to help showcase what journalists traditionally do and how they can do it from a more thoughtful perspective.

"My simple example of critical thinking skills in a newsroom environment is this: A reporter, in checking out some activity that seems questionable (let's say, a tax break or a business practice, returns to the editor and says, 'I found out that it's perfectly legal. There's

no story.' Wait. There may be a terrific story. Why is it legal? Is it legal elsewhere? Who is responsible, if anyone, for the legal status? What stakeholders have we considered?"

Geisler said that one of the biggest issues regarding critical thinking is trying to break out of the mold in which only two sides of a story exist.

"I think the essential challenge of journalistic critical thinking can be heard whenever someone talks about getting 'both sides of a story,'" she said. "How many issues have only two sides? Journalists are often drawn to conflict—and that's not a bad thing on its surface. But when we reduce complex ideas and issues to two sides, we often edge to the extremes. We talk to absolutists . . . and we miss the many layers and nuance that could be explored."

Many great stories and better perspectives exist in those layers, Geisler said.

"Even when we understand the guiding principles of journalism: truth telling, independence, minimizing harm and transparency, we need to be vigilant about our own human frailty when it comes to decision-making," she said. "Not only will it help keep us on the right path in our reasoning, from framing of stories to use of language, it will increase our ability to identify logical holes and biases embedded in the issues, decisions, debates and people we cover. Just think of how that can improve our journalism!"

the subject's position on a given topic. Quite often, we view the best quotes as those that are glib and slick rather than informative and thought provoking. In this society of bumper-sticker slogans, we need to resist the urge to ask a question just to get that killer quote.

ASKING QUESTIONS TO CATCH UP

One bad example of this was an exchange between a firefighter and a television reporter. The firefighter was accused of several acts of insubordination and was in front of the Police and Fire Commission, which would decide whether to fire him. The story had been going on for more than six months, and the meeting that night was supposed to be a key one in deciding whether to terminate the firefighter. The reporter began her interview by asking the firefighter what had happened to this point and what he had done. The firefighter snapped at her, "You really don't know what's going on, do you?" She snapped right back, "My job isn't to understand the story. My job is to get the story."

As strange as it seems, these two people were irritated by the same basic problem: the reporter's failure to research before coming to the meeting. There is nothing wrong with knowing something about the topic. In fact, the more prepared you are, the better able you are to ask questions and write the story. However, you need to keep your eye on what is important here. Why are you asking this question? Is it really crucial to what you're doing, or are you just trying to show off? Is this helping my audience? The point of your doing this story is to help inform your readers or viewers. Is this question furthering that goal? There is a wide array of questions between asking a source what's going on and asking a source something about the 87th footnote on a position paper she wrote five years ago. You'll be better served to aim for that middle ground.

DON'T LET YOUR EGO GET IN THE WAY

This last point brings to bear one of the main things that can counter critical thinking: egocentrism. Richard Paul and Linda Elder of the Foundation for Critical Thinking noted that humans are the "self-deceived animal." They argue that people often think that their understanding of a situation is the one that matters, that their beliefs and desires are in some way superior to others. While we think about other people, we tend to think about how they relate to us and what we need to do about them. In short, it's all about us.

Journalism requires that we broaden our field of view. We should not be writing for us, but for those around us. While most news people deride advertising folks as slick-haired, sharp-tongued pitchmen, ad folks understand our job almost better than we do. They understand the importance of getting people to pay attention to their message. They know the message needs to be clear, simple and audience-centric. The reason, of course, is that advertisers rely on audience members who will purchase a product. For journalists, we are removed from that aspect of message conveyance, and thus we tend to forget about the people who are at home reading our stories or watching our newscasts. (To be fair, the ratings aspects of television news give TV journalists a little better understanding of this than their print colleagues.)

In many cases, egotism gets in the way. We tell the story the way we want to because we think it's important or, worse yet, because it's easier. Why bother doing a story on something important if your audience isn't going to get anything out of it? That's like preparing for weeks to give a speech to an arena filled with people and then delivering it without a microphone.

AVOID SELF-IMPORTANCE

In the age of self-publishing, everyone is an instant expert. People who get the most attention are those who say or do outlandish things. Or, as comedian George Carlin once noted about being a class clown, "That's the name of this game: dig me!" While having an opinion on a topic can be good, it can also get you into a lot of trouble. Former ESPN analyst Curt

If you take a look through newspapers today or turn on a TV news channel, you'll notice all sorts of "breaking news." Stories of people who have shot up a convenience store, celebrities who died of a drug overdose or whatever one of the Kardashians is doing this week just take over the airwaves and the news pages. In deference to the Kardashians' fan club, what do these stories really tell us? What do they really mean? How much critical thought went into finding them, examining them and telling them? Very little would probably be the most accurate answer.

Breaking news stories are cheap and easy to produce, they lend themselves to commentary from "experts" and they can grab readers and viewers quickly and hold them. Even those people who feign disgust with these types of news are still looking and reading. Much like those in the gapers' block, they can't look away.

It would be naive to assume that readers of this book have not stared open mouthed at a traffic accident. Even more, it is pretty likely that a student reporter or two in the class have been filled with excitement when they caught a story for the student paper about a student getting arrested for selling drugs or a professor being removed for having an inappropriate relationship with a student. Stories like this occur and shouldn't be ignored. However, sometimes in covering them, we get so fixated by each story, we miss the larger picture. How big of a problem are drugs on this campus? How many students haven't been caught yet? Why did a professor think he could have a relationship with a student like that and retain his job? How concrete are the rules that govern professor-student relationships?

To better formulate ways to think critically on topics like these and others, you need to resist the urge to focus on the cheap and easy and ask questions that dig a bit more. They need not be epic questions of man's existential dilemma. All they have to do is push the sources you'll be interviewing to give you more than the cheap and easy answer.

Schilling's social media posts regarding transgender people or Mount St. Mary's University President Simon Newman's statement that some freshmen are like bunnies and "you just have to drown the bunnies"[8] are just a few examples of people opening their mouths and rapidly inserting their feet.

Aside from those incidents, however, we've got a nation of self-important journalists who think what they think is important. It's egocentrism in its purest form, and it's not always good for journalism. The idea of doing quality journalism is that you are attempting to act as a conduit between the individuals making decisions and the people who are affected by those decisions. Your job is to gather pieces of information, make sense of them and present them to the audience in a way that allows your readers to make rational decisions about the material they've read.

Think about it this way: the journalist's job is to help display the information so that others can see it. Much like a frame does for a piece of artwork (as opposed to the media theory of framing), the journalist helps display stories. It makes little sense that the frame should overshadow the artwork. No one comes back from the Louvre and says, "Wow, was the frame on the 'Mona Lisa' beautiful!" If you do your job as a journalist, you'll be unnoticed, but your work will be appreciated and valued.

CRITICAL THINKING

THE BIG THREE

Here are the three key things you should take away from this chapter:

1. **Critical thinking starts with preparation:** The more research you do at the beginning of a story, the less likely you will be at the mercy of sources during your coverage of that story. This will help you find ways to ask critical questions of these individuals and obtain important information. It will also help you better adapt to your surroundings when things change and you need to shift your focus or come up with an entirely different story.

2. **Critical thinking helps you serve your readers:** As Jill Geisler says, the story is often in the layers and the nuance, and it can be found only through careful digging and sifting. If you find out exactly how a story affects your audience members, you can write a story that conveys those important details to them in a way they'll understand. This will give your readers a stronger sense of value, and they will thank you for it.

3. **Critical thinking takes time and practice:** Approaching journalism in this way takes extra effort and some deep thinking on your part. However, it will provide you with better opportunities to do good work that has value, which makes the effort worth your while. And remember, it's a skill that will take time to develop. However, just like any other skill, practice makes perfect.

KEY TERMS

critical thinking   19

Topeka test   26

DISCUSSION QUESTIONS

1. How critically do you feel you and your peers think when it comes to topics that interest you? To what degree do you think your approach to content is critical enough, and where do you feel you fall short?

2. In the age of social media and digital communication, do you feel critical thinking is undercut by this overwhelming abundance of media? How and why? Are some media more detrimental than others when it comes to this issue? Also, is there anything you think could help improve critical thinking in this day and age?

3. How difficult is it for you to think open-mindedly about a variety of topics? What makes it easier or harder for you to consider outside information and viewpoints that may contradict your own? Which topics are most and least likely to consider with an open mind? Why?

WRITE NOW!

1. Review the four trademarks of a critical thinker outlined in the chapter. Assess your own thinking process as it relates to news you read or topics upon which you wish to report by applying each of these four items. Then, write a short essay in which you analyze your thought process through the filter of these four items. How critically do you think when it comes to your news-processing and news-gathering efforts?

2. Find a news article on a topic of interest to you and analyze it for the four trademarks of critical thinking. Write an essay in which you apply each of the four trademarks to the content and determine the degree to which each applies. Also, outline the ways in which this piece could be improved with more critical thought.

3. Select a story on a topic about which you know very little and apply the Topeka test. Is there enough background in it to help you fully understand the story? What do you feel is missing? Do some research online to help you better understand the story. Then, rewrite the first three to six paragraphs in a way that will improve the overall understanding of the piece as well as incorporate the background you feel is missing. Finally, write a few paragraphs that explain what you did and why you think your version is an improvement.

Visit edge.sagepub.com/filaknews to help you accomplish your coursework goals in an easy-to-use learning environment.

YOU NEVER KNOW WHAT THE FUTURE HOLDS.

▶ Visit the author's blog at
dynamicsofwriting.com

Stay up to date on the latest in journalism

3 BASICS OF WRITING

LEARNING OBJECTIVES

After completing this chapter you should be able to:

- Apply audience centricity to your understanding of news and focus on what matters most to your readers.

- Write a lead for a news story based on the concept of the 5W's and 1H.

- Identify various approaches to lead writing and understand which lead formats work best in which situations.

- Identify and repair problematic leads, such as quote leads, question leads and "held a meeting" leads.

- Apply the basics of the inverted-pyramid writing format to your stories.

- Define and differentiate among the forms of quotes (direct, indirect/paraphrase and partial), and understand when to use each one.

- Understand the purpose of attributions, and apply them properly in terms of structure, verbiage and placement.

THINKING AHEAD: WRITING FOR A NEWSREADER

Basic news writing focuses on figuring out what is important and then giving that information to your readers. It sounds simple, and with a lot of practice, it can be. Problems tend to crop up when writers try to do too much, ignore some basic tenets of journalism and generally don't think about the audience before writing.

The purpose of this chapter is to help you understand the basic elements of good, straightforward news writing that clearly and effectively communicate crucial information to an interested and engaged audience. We also will get into the basics of how to mentally stimulate readers, use quoted material and effectively order your content.

As we mentioned in Chapter 1, the audience should be your focal point when you consider which stories you

want to tell. The more important the topic is to your readers, the more likely they will be to read what you have written. Beyond simply picking topics that matter, you have to tell your stories in a way that demonstrates value to your readers. With that in mind, you need to put your story together in a way that answers two simple questions for them:

What Matters Most? A big part of journalistic writing is figuring out what matters most and then telling that to the readers right up front. The format we will discuss below, called the **inverted pyramid**, will help you meet this need from a writing perspective. Before you can write in the proper order, however, you have to think in the proper fashion.

Examine each fact at your disposal, and determine what you think would matter most to your readers. Don't worry so much about what a source thinks is important, but instead worry more about what the audience members need to know. Here's an example that reflects a standard form of storytelling in a **press release**:

> Jacksonville firefighters responded to a fire Tuesday around 5 p.m., after a call came in to the 911 dispatch center.
>
> Ladder Truck 11, Pumper 32 and Chief's Car 2 arrived at 5:11 p.m. to find smoke coming from underneath the eaves of the three-bedroom, one-bath home at 411 S. Cherry St.
>
> Firefighters were able to contain the blaze to approximately half of the home, while the remainder sustained heat, smoke and water damage.
>
> Homeowner Jim Smith was seriously injured in the fire and was transported to a nearby medical facility, where he is listed in critical condition. His wife, Suzy, and his daughter Jane were unharmed.
>
> After the fire was extinguished, assessors stated the home received approximately $90,000 in damage. Investigative Service Agents determined the cause of the fire was a leaky gas stove that exploded when Mr. Smith lit a cigarette nearby.

From the perspective of the fire department, this makes sense. The firefighters are the star of the show, the event was detailed chronologically and all the information is in there for anyone who wants to find it. However, if you go home today and your roommate says, "Hey, your mom called. There was a fire at your house," would you really want to know first that the fire department responded to a fire? Probably not. The questions you might ask include:

> "Is everyone OK?"
>
> "How bad is it?"
>
> "What happened? What caused it?"

Notice that the answers to those questions are nowhere near the top, where they should be. Also consider how you would react if you asked those questions, and your roommate started with, "Well, Jacksonville firefighters responded to a fire Tuesday around 5 p.m., after a call came in to the 911 dispatch center. . . . " Just like you would probably scream, "Just tell me what happened!" your readers are feeling pretty much the same way when you don't focus on the important information first.

How Does This Affect Me as a Reader? The second question feeds off the first one in what you might think of as a selfish way: "What's in this for me?" Journalists often cover the big picture in broad strokes, but they would be better served focusing on the self-interest of the readership.

Journalists often fail to drive home the value of the story to their readers. In some cases, this is because the journalists lack a firm grasp on who is in the audience and what these people need to know. In other cases, the journalists themselves don't fully understand the story's impact and thus just parrot their sources. Even worse are the situations in which journalists are going for the "big story" and thus ignore the individual-level impacts.

Think about the individual reader of your story when you write it. A student doesn't want to know that tuition at the university will go up by a total of $12 million next year; the student wants to know how much will be tacked on to his or her tuition bill. Vacationers don't want to know about all the cases of "Death Flu" attributed to biting flies throughout the area; they want to know how to avoid the bugs and how to treat the illness if they get it. A worker doesn't want to hear that the company is decreasing the workforce by 2 percent; the person wants to know who is mostly likely to be fired and when.

HELPFUL HINTS ➡ BUILDING A LEAD FROM THE INSIDE OUT

The core of any good news story is in the **lead**, which is where you try to give people as much of the most important information as possible. A good place to start is the **5W's and 1H**: who, what, when, where, why and how. The goal of a lead is to create a single-sentence paragraph of about 25 to 35 words that captures these elements. You probably will not fit all of these elements into a single sentence, so you need to prioritize them. After the lead, you should include the remaining "W's" (and "H" if it doesn't make the lead) as soon as possible while you tell the story in descending order of importance.

FIG. 3.1 5W'S AND 1H

(Continued)

FIG. 3.2 CIRCLE DIAGRAM

When you build a lead, think about starting with a core and then adding layer after layer of information as you move outward. This will allow you to place the most important elements at the core and move to less important elements as you continue outward. This approach will help you create a stronger focus on what will matter to your readers.

You can start with a simple "noun-verb-object" structure that tells them "Who did what to whom/what?" that will give you a sense of what matters most:

> The Cleveland Cavaliers won the NBA Championship.

Then you can add in other elements that matter, such as "why" it matters.

> The Cleveland Cavaliers won the franchise's first NBA Championship, bringing the city its first major title in 52 years.

You can then add the "how" and the "when" to polish it up.

> Coming back from a 3-1 series deficit against the Golden State Warriors, the Cleveland Cavaliers won the franchise's first NBA Championship on Sunday, bringing the city its first major title in 52 years.

This lead, while not perfect, includes most of the W's and the H while emphasizing the things that make this particular championship important and rare. It meets the word count range, coming in at 33 words, and it gives you a lot of possibilities for what will come next in the story.

A QUICK LOOK AT TYPES OF LEADS

A **summary lead** like the one outlined in the earlier example is a fairly standard approach to capturing the 5W's and 1H as well as properly highlighting the interest elements discussed earlier in the book. Not every story will lend itself to that kind of lead, so it is important to pick a lead approach that will best emphasize the most important aspects of your story. Here is a brief review of several other common approaches to news leads:

NAME-RECOGNITION LEADS

Fame is a valuable interest element that will draw people's attention. The more important someone is or the more well known that person is, the more likely readers are to pay attention to the story.

During the 2016 Summer Olympics in Rio de Janeiro, four members of the U.S. contingent filed a false police report, claiming they had been robbed while enjoying some nightlife in the city. (The athletes later recanted the story after surveillance footage showed that they had vandalized a bathroom at a gas station and urinated around the building while intoxicated.) Although all four men were involved, the fame element came into play when various news outlets reported the incident:

> Ryan Lochte and three other U.S. swimmers were robbed early Sunday morning, according to the U.S. Olympic Committee.

Lochte was a 12-time Olympic medalist, making him the second-most decorated Olympic swimmer, behind teammate Michael Phelps. He was also previously named World Swimmer of the Year and American Swimmer of the Year. His three teammates, Jimmy Feigen, Gunnar Bentz and Jack Conger, were relatively unknown athletes and thus relegated to later in the story.

You should use a **name-recognition lead** when writing about someone you think people will know by name. If you aren't sure that your readers will know the person right away, consider using a different lead format.

INTERESTING-ACTION LEADS

Many news stories don't involve people who are well known but revolve around odd actions or strange occurrences. When the "what" matters more than the specific "who," consider using an **interesting-action lead**:

> A 27-year-old man told police he "never really meant to" blow up the Main Street Kwik-E-Mart when he used a lit cigarette to kill a spider near a running gas pump.

With a lead like that, your audience will read a few more paragraphs even if they don't know who the 27-year-old man is. When someone does something interesting, rare or downright weird, you can use an interesting-action lead to tell the story.

EVENT LEADS

An **event lead** works well for meetings, speeches and news conferences. This format will allow you to capture the theme of a speech, the key outcome of a meeting or the big news that emerges from a news conference.

The goal of using a lead like this is to focus on what happened, not that the event itself occurred. If you find yourself using the phrase "held a meeting" or "gave a speech," go back and rework your lead. Here are a couple examples of how this can work well or poorly:

MEETING

> **Bad:** The Johnsonville City Council held a meeting Tuesday to discuss increasing overnight parking rates.

> **Better:** Overnight parking rates in Johnsonville will double in the next year, the city council decided Tuesday.

Bad: Sen. Jane Gowan spoke at Big State University on Tuesday about the problems associated with student loan debt and what it will do to students throughout the country.

Better: Student loans will lead to a debt bomb that could dwarf the mortgage crisis unless the federal government steps in, Sen. Jane Gowan said Tuesday during a visit to Big State University.

SECOND-DAY LEADS

You will need to give your readers fresh information each time you cover a topic, which means finding the newest content and putting it at the top of your story. This is where a **second-day lead** can help you, as it allows you to tell people what happened now and tie it back to previous coverage on that topic.

These leads are helpful in situations in which news continues to unfold, such as a court case or a fundraiser. The term "second-day" is a bit of a misnomer because you might update a story several times a day or have an event that lasts weeks or months:

Nearly two years after the start of Toledo's "Valentine's Day" murder trial, a jury took 19 minutes on Tuesday to return a guilty verdict against suspect Sam Mank.

You can arrange the elements in your second-day lead in a variety of ways, but the overall goal is to keep the focus on the newest information.

IDENTIFYING PROBLEMATIC LEADS AND FINDING POTENTIAL FIXES

In an attempt to broaden appeal and reach beyond the basics, journalists often move past the 5W's and 1H to create leads that feel different or engaging. Unfortunately, in some cases the leads fail because they rely on clichés, overgeneralizations and other similar flaws. Here are some common problems associated with leads and some good ways to fix them:

Twitter Post @FrankLoMonte

Frank LoMonte @FrankLoMonte
45 mins ago

Ohio State's ban on signage in dorm windows raises First Amendment issues. insidehighered.com/news /2017/08/2...

3   6

A good tweet has all the key elements of a solid standard news lead or a great news headline. This tweet tells you everything you need to know about the topic and gives you a link to the full story.

"YOU" LEADS

Journalistic writing uses the third-person approach to create a feeling of neutrality for the readers. In an attempt to reach audience members on an interpersonal level, some writers rely on a **"you"** lead like this one:

> The Alpha Beta fraternity is sponsoring a blood drive Wednesday, and you should donate a pint for the cause.

This lead falls flat for a few reasons:

1. People don't like being told what to do and will often push back against this approach mentally. Given the general neutrality of traditional newswriting, a "you should" approach can feel off-putting to readers, even if they might otherwise be predisposed to take part in the event.

2. Numerous reasons exist that people can't donate blood, such as iron deficiency, fear of needles, body size, recent surgery, recent tattooing and health concerns. Telling people to do something they can't do isn't a great idea. Even if they can physically do it, they might know someone in another group that is hosting a blood drive that week and decide to donate there instead. Don't assume you know what people should do.

3. You are taking part in advocacy, which isn't really the job of news reporters. When you advocate for this group, you need to consider advocating for all groups, and that can put you in a tough spot. What happens when the next fraternity has an event and wants a similar bit of boosterism? What if you decide to stop covering events or if you don't have enough room to cover them all equally?

When you use a "you" lead, you set yourself up for a lot of headaches that could easily be solved with a simpler lead:

> The Alpha Beta fraternity is sponsoring a blood drive Wednesday, and students interested in donating should come to the union between 9 a.m. and 4 p.m.

This is neutral and still gets the same message across.

A question lead has a basic problem: You assume you know how your readers will answer the question.

QUESTION LEADS

A good journalist serves as a conduit of information between sources and audience members. The journalist should ask questions of the sources and provide the answers to the audience members. When you decide to use a **question lead**, you mix up the two pieces, and you can often create problems for your story:

> Who wouldn't want to live in a luxury residence hall in the heart of campus with free parking and a 24/7 food service? That's the question a local developer is asking of students at Northern University as he opens his Dream Dorms project this week.

A few things make this a problem:

1. The question is a straw-man approach. You know the answer before you give it to your readers, so it's not really a true question. That can be annoying to your readers. You're practically treating them like you treat a dog: "Who's a good boy? Who's a good puppy? Yes, you're a good dog!"

2. Maybe not every reader's answer will be the answer you expect. Returning students who live in their own homes probably wouldn't ditch their homestead to live in a dorm. Students who live at home to save money probably wouldn't think spending an exorbitant amount of money for a residence hall room makes sense. In short, you don't want to assume you have all the answers.

Go with something that simplifies the approach and lets the source do the hard work for you:

> Dream Dorms, a luxury residence hall in the heart of campus, opens this week and offers students at Northern University an alternative to the college's standard housing options, the project's developer said.

QUOTE LEADS

The words of world leaders, scholars and celebrities can inspire, provoke and entertain, but they fall flat as a lead in a news story. It isn't a crime to own a "quote-a-day" calendar, but it doesn't mean you should rely on it to fuel your writing. When reporters quote those famous people, it tends to sound ridiculous and hyperbolic:

> As Mahatma Gandhi once said, "An error does not become truth by reason of multiplied propagation."
>
> That's something the Smithville School District learned the hard way after having to correct 2,000 standardized tests by hand once the answer key was found to be wrong.

In the same vein, a quote from a source in the story won't be any better at bringing people into your story. When you start a piece with a **quote lead**, it is like being dropped into the middle of someone else's conversation:

> "I love to kill. When the situation arises, and someone says, they need me, I just grab a stick and go out there and kill it no matter what."

That could be a confession of a homicidal maniac or a defense-minded hockey player's thoughts on his penalty killing skills. It's a jarring lead, but it's also going to confuse your readers.

If this is going to be a news story, just tell the readers what happened and why it matters. If it is a feature story, consider using a longer narrative lead (see Chapter 4 for more on this) to move your readers into the piece more deliberately.

"MANY PEOPLE/SOME PEOPLE/ EVERYBODY/NOBODY" LEADS

Oddity is one of the interest elements noted earlier in the book, so focusing on how rare something is makes sense. However, when a writer becomes hyperbolic or overgeneralizes, the readers can feel cheated, and the leads can seem generic. Following is an example of a **"many people" lead**:

> Nobody thought Smithville State's football team would break a 56-game losing streak against the top-ranked Auburn Tigers, but the Honeybees eked out a 14-13 win at Jordan-Hare Stadium on Saturday.

Here are the problems with that lead:

1. It's clearly a **straw-man** lead, which we discussed above. You know the outcome of the game, so focusing on the improbability with an "us against the world" start like this doesn't make sense.

2. If you want to focus on the improbability in some way that makes sense, talk to the players, coaches and fans to find anecdotes that accurately reflect this.

> Before his football team took the field against the top-ranked Auburn Tigers, Smithville State coach Elmer St. Claire told his team that nobody thought the Honeybees had a chance to win.
>
> "I sat the guys down and told them, 'Fellas, it doesn't look too positive out there. Even my wife called a bookie and bet against us,'" St. Claire said.

3. Generalizations are a bad idea because you rely on vague information. How do you really know that "nobody" or "everybody" said, thought or felt something? Did you interview everyone, including the entire nation of Estonia, to make sure that nobody said that? Did you go back through the whole history of mankind to make sure that everybody did something you are presupposing in your lead? Probably not. Instead of doing this, use data and research to back up your statement and more accurately reflect the rarity of this event.

> In beating top-ranked Auburn 14-13 on Saturday, the Smithville State Honeybees earned their only win over a ranked team in the 114-year history of the school's football program.

THOUGHTS FROM A PRO ➡ JANELLE COGAN, ACTING ENTERPRISE EDITOR, SOUTH REGION OF THE ASSOCIATED PRESS

© Janelle Cogan

As the acting enterprise editor for the South Region of the Associated Press, Janelle Cogan sees a lot of quality news features, watchdog pieces and enterprise stories each day. Even with those longer stories and broader topics, she said that the basics of journalism remain at the core of her approach to content.

"Journalists need to ask and answer the basic questions," she said. "When you're writing and reporting a story, don't assume your audience knows the context or background of the subject matter—it's such a big part of your job to provide that. Give scope, give context."

Cogan held a number of positions at the AP, including desk editor, weekend supervisor and morning supervisor, before she took on the enterprise role. In this position, she works on stories that come from 13 states and Washington, D.C. Before joining the AP, she worked as a copy desk chief, an assistant city editor, a features editor and a designer. She said that in all of her time in media, the biggest changes have been to the volume of news that organizations have created as well as the speed at which it is delivered.

"No one is waiting for tomorrow's paper to see the results of the game, the election, the fire, the shooting," she said. "So the way we report and write that news has changed, too. We have to provide quick, understandable, digestible bites of news. When we have the latest numbers/report/development, we need to get it out there. So we write in a way that puts that info at the very top of the story. Especially as a story develops, we probably aren't writing in a terribly flowery or 'writerly' way. We are writing crisp, clear, basic sentences. We are authoritative. We are transparent."

To keep the writing focused, Cogan said that she pushes writers to "show, don't tell" a story, eliminate clichés and remove jargon. She said that she pushes her writers to cut superfluous words and to tell her the story in a clear and concise way.

"It's better to be straight with them—conversational, even," she said. "How would you tell me this story if we were chatting over coffee or a beer? That may just be the best way to start your story. A pet peeve of mine as an editor: When you pitched me this story, we were probably both excited about the idea—when you turn in a draft, if that excitement and that initial nugget is gone, you need to go back."

ONE LAST THING

Q: If you could tell the students reading this book anything you think is important, what would it be?

A: "Don't be afraid to take risks and get out of your comfort zone; you must try new things and expand your skills and horizon! In terms of being a journalist, this means: You aren't *just* a writer. You aren't *just* a photographer. You aren't *just* a VJ. You're a journalist. The format will change, and you should try all you can: write, take photos and video on your iPhone, create and post interesting tweets, produce an interactive, edit your colleagues' work. It's all important."

THE INVERTED PYRAMID: ORDERING INFORMATION AFTER THE LEAD

The inverted pyramid remains the standard of the field when it comes to journalistic writing. Although people often divert from this writing approach once they become more experienced, it remains one of the primary ways to effectively communicate important news content.

This writing approach forces you to make choices in the ordering of your facts based on descending order of importance. You have to figure out what would matter most to your readers and give them the information in that order.

Here are some things you need to do as you build your way to the bottom of your story:

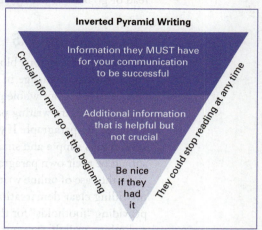

FIG. 3.3 VISUAL DIAGRAM OF INVERTED PYRAMID

Inverted Pyramid Writing

Information they MUST have for your communication to be successful

Additional information that is helpful but not crucial

Be nice if they had it

Crucial info must go at the beginning

They could stop reading at any time

DETERMINE THE VALUE OF YOUR INFORMATION

During your reporting process, you collected a series of facts, anecdotes, quotes and other information that will help you create your story. Some of these pieces of information will be more or less valuable to your readers, so you need to organize those items accordingly.

The inverted pyramid dictates that more important items should go higher in the story. Thus, the cost of an after-school program for disadvantaged children will likely go higher in the story than what one volunteer for the program thinks about it.

Some choices will be easy, while others will require you to nitpick at your notes for a while. Whatever choices you make, you should justify them to yourself and your editor. Even if your editor doesn't agree entirely with your order, that person will likely listen to you if you can justify your decisions.

SUPPORT THE LEAD

The lead should serve as a guide for you as you write the body of the story. Every sentence should contain a bit of information that in some way advances and supports that initial sentence. As you move deeper into the piece, look back at the lead to make sure it reflects what you wrote in the body. If you fail to do this, you can find yourself wandering off on a tangent and taking your readers to an unsupported conclusion.

Let's say you are writing about a city council meeting, and your lead deals with the creation of a historic district to protect older homes in the Third Ward. As you work through the story, you might use a quote from one city council member who objected to the plan. To help clarify the accuracy of that objection, you might use information from a second council member who explains that this person is just bitter because a similar plan in his ward failed last year. Then you decide to let the first council member defend himself, but that leads to an attack on a third city council member. Suddenly, you see your story moving from "the council created a historical district" to "council members engage in bitter sparring match."

You could decide that both of these issues matter to your readers, so this isn't to say that one has more merit than the other. However, you chose to lead with the historical district, so you can't abandon that issue in the middle of the story and detour into this fight. You can go back to the point where you veered into the argument and rewrite the body to better support the lead or go back to the lead and rework everything from the lead down to reflect the fight.

USE SMALL CHUNKS

When you write in long blocks of type, you can intimidate your readers and make it more difficult for them to engage in the material. To make it easier on them and give them a fighting chance to read your whole piece, you want to break up your paragraphs into small chunks.

When you are writing paraphrase, background or other similar chunks of text, stick to one sentence per paragraph. If you need two sentences in a paragraph, that can work too, but try to keep things simple and small. Direct quotes, which we will discuss a little later in the chapter, should be their own paragraphs and attributed to the sources.

In the case of online writing, the paragraphs usually have an extra return between them, thus providing clear demarcations for the chunks. In print publications, indents can be useful for providing "footholds" for the readers' eyes, somewhat similar to what the nubby protrusions of a climbing wall do for your feet and hands. The more of these little footholds you provide, the easier it is for the users in both cases.

KNOW WHEN TO STOP

You will gather far more information than you can use for many of the stories upon which you report. This means you will need to make choices as to what goes into your stories and what gets left behind. The better you get at making these decisions, the stronger your writing will be and the more succinct your stories will be.

Journalists occasionally become fixated on their own reporting to the detriment of the writing. The term for this problem is "notebook emptying," which denotes the idea of a journalist shaking every fact out of a notebook directly into a story. When you feel you are writing more but actually saying less, you should end your story and move on to your next piece.

QUOTES: LETTING YOUR SOURCES TELL THE STORY

The purpose of a quote is to give your readers the opportunity to hear directly from a source. You will almost always need to rely on sources and quotes to drive your stories, so you need to understand the various types of quotes and when you should use them. A good way to remember these elements is the mnemonic "DIP:" direct, indirect, partial.

DIRECT QUOTES

When people hear the word "quote," they tend to think of this approach to using source material. A **direct quote** is a word-for-word statement taken from a source and placed into your story. The goal is to accurately reflect the exact verbiage of that person and place it in between a set of quote marks. It is these marks that indicate the start and closing of a direct quote. (A discussion of fixing quotes is included later in the chapter.)

The Associated Press Stylebook serves as the "bible" (not Bible, per AP) for media-writing style. The goal in adhering to the stylebook is to create consistency both within a media outlet and among similar media outlets.

Trying to memorize this whole book can feel like catching sand in a pasta strainer: No matter how hard you try, you never catch it all. Even worse, AP tends to change style on some items from year to year, such as its recent decision to allow "they" in some cases as a gender-neutral singular pronoun. For a beginning journalist, the goal of learning AP style shouldn't be to memorize every change or item in the book, but rather to learn the kinds of things that are in the book so you know what to look up.

To help get students used to style, Fred Vultee, an associate professor at Wayne State University who spent more than 25 years as an editor for newspapers, offers his students some quick maxims that account for the majority of the style guide. Here is his "5-minute style guide," reprinted with permission:

THE FIVE-MINUTE STYLEBOOK

10 Percent of the Rules Cover 90 Percent of Style Questions

People

Capitalize formal titles when they appear before names (The message was sent to **President** Vladimir Putin).

Lowercase titles when they follow a name or stand alone (Bashar Assad, the Syrian **president**, fired his **foreign minister**).

Lowercase occupational or descriptive titles before or after a name (The article was written by **columnist** Joe Bob Briggs).

Refer to adults by given name and family name the first time they appear in a news story (**Michelle Obama**) and by family name only on later references (**Obama**).

Children 17 or younger are usually referred to by both names on first reference and *given name only* on later references. Children in "adult situations"—common examples are international sports and serious crimes in which they are charged as adults—are referred to by *family name only* on later references.

To avoid confusing two people with the same family name, such as husband and wife or mother and son, use both names on later references. A story mentioning Joe Biden and Jill Biden should usually refer to them as **Joe Biden** and **Jill Biden** even after they are introduced if there's any chance of confusion. Sometimes a title can be repeated to make the distinction (Joe Biden could be "Vice President Biden" or "the vice president" on later references; Jill Biden could be "Dr. Biden"). Only rarely, in some feature stories, will you want to refer to adults by given name on later references.

Do not use courtesy titles (Mr., Mrs., Ms.) in news reports except in direct quotes.

Abbreviate military and police titles before names according to a standard reference list such as the one in the AP Stylebook. Don't abbreviate titles when they stand alone or follow a name (**Gen.** Douglas MacArthur, the **general**). Exceptions are allowed for widely used initialisms (The fugitive **CEO** was captured at dawn).

Places

Most stylebooks will have a list of cities that are assumed to be understood without having the name of the state (**Boston**, **New York**, **Los Angeles**) or country (**New York**, **London**, **Cairo**) attached. Follow those guidelines with the usual exceptions for common sense if needed (Books that are popular in **London, Ontario**, might not be popular in **London, England**).

Do not abbreviate the names of U.S. states **except**:

(Continued)

(Continued)

1) In datelines, credit lines, or short forms of party ID: **Debbie Stabenow, D-Mich**.

2) In those cases, abbreviate state names of six or more letters only. (NOTE: the two noncontiguous states, Alaska and Hawaii, are never abbreviated.)

Do not abbreviate such designations as "street" when they stand alone. Only three of these are abbreviated—"street," "avenue" and "boulevard"—and they are only abbreviated when they appear with a numbered address. Do not abbreviate "south" or "north" indicating a part of a road unless it appears with an address (**South Eighth Street; 221 S. Eighth St.; 221 Abbey Road**).

Things

Capitalize proper nouns; lowercase common nouns.

Capitalize trademarks (I drank a **Pepsi**) or use a common noun as a substitute (I drank a **soft drink**).

Use abbreviations on first reference only if they are widely known (**CIA** agents helped overthrow the prime minister of Iran). Otherwise spell out the names of agencies on first reference (The U.S. Agency for International Development; **USAID**). If an abbreviation would be confusing, use a common-noun substitute (the State Law and Order Restoration Council; **the council** or **the junta**) on later references. When in doubt, err on the side of clarity. Abbreviations are not as familiar as you think they are.

Generally, don't abbreviate units of measure (pounds, miles, hours, etc.).

Capitalize **shortened versions of proper names**: the Michigan Department of Transportation, the Transportation Department, the Department of Transportation.

Time

Use only the day of the week for events within a week of publication (The summit ended **Saturday**. Negotiators will meet **Thursday**). Use "last" or "next" only if needed for clarity (The summit ended Friday, and the negotiators will meet again **next Friday**).

Never abbreviate days of the week. Use "today" to refer to the day of publication only. Do not use "yesterday" or "tomorrow" except in direct quotes.

Use month and day to refer to events happening a week or more before or after publication. Use cardinal numbers, not ordinal numbers, for dates (The summit began **July 11**. The seminar will be held **March 3**).

Don't use the year unless the event is more than a year before or after publication (He died **March 17, 2007**; the tax will take effect **Jan. 1, 2025**).

Do not abbreviate a month unless it's followed by a date (**January**; **Jan. 1**). Do not abbreviate months of less than six letters (**March**; **March 12, 1998**).

Use lowercase "a.m." and "p.m." to indicate morning, afternoon and night. Use "noon" and "midnight" rather than the unclear "12 a.m." or the redundant "12 noon." Always use figures for time, in this form: **8 a.m.**, **10:30 p.m.**, **1:45 a.m.**

Unless you need to emphasize one element over the others, generally follow time-date-place order: **Trials of collaborators will begin at 2 p.m. April 14 in New York**.

Numbers

The basic rule: Spell out numbers under 10. Use figures for 10 and above.

The main exceptions: Spell out any number, except a year, that begins a sentence (Twelve students attended. 1999 was an important year).

Use figures for **dates**, **weights**, **ages**, **times**, **addresses** and **percentages**.

For most numbers of a million or more, use this form, rounded off to no more than two decimal places: **1.45 million**, the **$18.1 billion budget**. If the exact number is important, write it out: He received **1,253,667** votes to **988,401** for his opponent.

Spell out numbers used as figures of speech (**Thanks a million**).

Spell out fractions when they stand alone (use **one-half** cup of flour). Otherwise write them as mixed fractions (**1½ cups** of flour) or decimals (**1.5 liters of water**).

Generally, use a 0 to precede a decimal smaller than zero (**0.75 kilograms**).

Convert metric measurements to English ones.

When to use a direct quote:

- **When a source gives you something beyond the facts:** In many cases, you will need to rely on sources for information you can't get elsewhere. A city council agenda can tell you what items will come up for vote, and a set of minutes can tell you who voted for or against a plan. A source, on the other hand, can tell you why he or she thinks the item was put on the agenda or how bad that particular plan will be for the city.

Jenna Duncan @jennafduncan
25 mins ago

'This is the dumbest thing I've ever done,' says man who rode out Harvey with wife, four dogs in a truck
dallasnews.com/news/weather/2... @dallasnews

↩   ⇄ ▾ 11   ♥ 17   ↪ ▾   ⋮

Sometimes a quote says everything you wanted to say and occasionally does so better than you could.

The information is often a personal opinion, so you want to let people know in that word-for-word style what the city council representative thought and why he or she felt that way:

> The Warrenville City Council voted 5-4 Tuesday in favor of an ordinance to sell naming rights for city parks, despite allegations of financial malfeasance.
>
> "If this plan goes as promised, it's a clear case of political pocket-lining," Fifth Ward Alderman Carl James said. "The only reason this thing should pass is if the council values its own finances over those of its constituents."

- **When a source says something in an interesting fashion:** Quotes in news stories work like spices in cooking: They add a dash of flavor to the main course. Colorful quotes, artful anecdotes and interesting insights can give your readers a sense of who a person is or how they view the world:

> Bill Jones, the owner of Big Oak Lodge, said several contractors have tried to buy his land over the past few years, but he has refused to sell to people who don't have an attachment to the natural beauty of the area.
>
> "This guy from the big city comes up here to try to buy me out," he said. "So, I ask him to look at the tree in front of the cabin and tell me what it was. He stutters and tells me, 'Uh . . . That's a tree made of wood, sir.' What an idiot."

INDIRECT QUOTES

In some cases, people say important things, but they don't say them particularly well. When that happens, you don't want to use a direct quote, but instead you want to rewrite their exact words into an **indirect quote**. This form of quoting, sometimes called **paraphrase**, allows you to capture the intended meaning of a source in a better way. Indirect quotes often improve a story when what a person said matters, but how they said it falls flat. Consider an exchange between an attorney and an uncooperative witness at a murder-for-hire trial:

Attorney: Mr. LaMack, are you an associate of the defendant, Johnny James?

LaMack: Yeah.

Attorney: Did he ask you to kill Jane Smith?

LaMack: Yeah.

Attorney: And did you kill her?

LaMack: Yeah.

Attorney: And why did you kill her, sir?

LaMack: Johnny asked. Said she would tell his wife they were sleeping together.

Attorney: What did you receive for doing this for Mr. James?

LaMack: Five grand cash and a pair of playoff tickets. I love the Knicks.

As important as that information is to a story, you won't get very far with a lot of direct "yeah" quotes. Thus, you want to condense the material into some indirect quotes and create a paragraph or two of paraphrase:

The life of Jane Smith was worth $5,000 and a pair of basketball tickets, her killer said Monday.

Convicted murderer Carl LaMack testified that he killed Smith at the request of his associate Johnny James, saying James had an affair with Smith and feared it would become public.

James stands accused of hatching a murder-for-hire plot with LaMack, who was found guilty of the murder last month.

In this case, you are able to write up what happened, relying on the core elements of the testimony and avoiding the problems associated with weak direct quotes. You can also use indirect quotes or paraphrase to sum up basic factual information, like you see in the final paragraph of the example.

PARTIAL QUOTES

When you have a few good words or a key phrase that can really provide a sense of value, a **partial quote** can give you the opportunity to present it to your readers. Consider this example:

The father of a sixth-grader who made a phony bomb threat to avoid taking a math test called his son's actions "harmless fun" and argued the boy should not be suspended.

In this case, you can get a sense of how the father feels about the boy's actions: He's not taking them seriously. The father might have said a longer sentence with more information, but pulling the words "harmless fun" out as a partial quote provides you with the ability to set up the words better and convey more meaning.

Use partial quotes sparingly, because too many of them can lead your readers to believe one of two bad things about your work:

1. My source is such a bad speaker that he can only utter two-word fragments of useful information before wandering off in his answers.

2. I'm such a bad reporter that I can only grab two or three words of what this person had to say for a direct quote.

However, when partial quotes have the ability to add flavor and punch to your piece, use them:

> Sen. Paul Peterson struck back at his opponent Wednesday, calling Jerry Jackson "a fat, brainless twerp" who wouldn't be fit for election to the position of "the village idiot's dumber cousin."

ATTRIBUTING YOUR INFORMATION

The ability to cite a source matters a great deal in all forms of writing. In your other courses, you likely wrote papers that required footnotes, endnotes or a bibliography. The purpose was to demonstrate where you got your ideas and thus allow the readers to determine the value they want to place on each statement. **Attributions** provide a similar value to journalistic writing, as they tell your readers who gave you the information in the story. The preferred verb of attribution in this type of writing is **"said."** It is easy to prove that someone said something, even if you can't truly determine what someone thinks, feels or believes. "Said" is also nonjudgmental, which helps you remain neutral in your reporting.

You can place the attribution at the front of a quote when someone important is speaking and you want to emphasize the "fame" information element:

> President Donald J. Trump said, "This country needs to do far more to increase employment here at home for our able-bodied men and women."

If the quote matters more than the person who said it, you can put the attribution at the end of the quote:

> "The superintendent of our school district is so stupid, he couldn't find his fanny with a Google map," district teacher Wilma Batterman said.

When you have a multiple-sentence quote, put the attribution after the first full sentence of the quote. This approach will give your readers a chance to figure out who said the quote and thus determine how much credence they want to give it before moving on:

> "Senator Smithers is a corrupt and evil politician," senate challenger Winston Featherstone said. "He never met a bribe or a kickback he didn't like."

As simple as they seem, attributions can lead to conflict between writers and editors. Word choices, placement and more can cause arguments as grammar rules run into issues of clarity and readability. Consider the following issues when you look at your attributions:

CONSIDER THIS → THE CASES FOR AND AGAINST FIXING QUOTES

Journalists often wrestle with the accuracy of direct quotes and the degree to which they should clean the quotes up. In the eyes of the purists, what sits between the quote marks is sacred and should be an untouched, word-for-word recounting of what the person said. For the pragmatists, cleaning quotes isn't a moral issue, but one of practicality: If you clean up the quote, you can make it easier for your readers to understand your source.

Your newsroom will likely have rules determining the degree to which you can tweak a quote, and those rules will determine what you do while you work there. That said, consider these issues when deciding if changing a quote makes sense:

Clarity: Your goal is to make a story clear and valuable to your audience. If you pick a quote that your readers could misinterpret, some journalists would argue that it makes sense to tweak the quote. Other journalists would say that you should find a different quote, even if it's not as good of a quote as the one you want to tweak. Either way, clarity should be on your mind when you review your quotes.

Fairness: With increased globalization of business, communications and sports, you may need to interview people for whom English is not their first language. In other cases, you will interview people who are victims of crimes and natural disasters, both of which can affect people across the educational and socioeconomic spectrum. If people in these types of situations speak poorly, your readers can place less value on what they have to say. Consider the issue of fairness and bias when you look at how direct quotes can lead to problems in your stories. You should also make sure you aren't drastically altering reality in your rewording within a quote.

Digital media: The presence of small, inexpensive recording devices, including digital audio recorders and apps for smartphones, has made it possible for everyone to easily capture quotes in a word-for-word format. Journalists can replay a quote a number of times to ensure quality and accuracy. However, journalists who write copy that changes quotes can face increased scrutiny when their quotes don't match up with the audio files posted by their competitors. If you clean up a mangled quote and another journalist decides to run the video or audio of that mangled quote, you can lose credibility in the eyes of your audience members.

Meaning: When you change a direct quote, you are playing God with the words and thoughts of a source. This means you substitute your best judgment for what the person actually said. This can be risky if you inadvertently change the intended meaning of the quote. Accuracy remains the foundation of journalism, so you need to make sure you get things right, especially if you start tweaking quotes.

VERBS

The preferred verb of attribution is "said," as noted earlier, because of its neutrality and simplicity. Some people would counter that the constant use of "said" is boring and repetitive. In a few key spots, certain words can replace "said" and keep both sides of this argument happy. Here are some examples:

- *Testified:* When a source offers statements during a trial or other legal proceeding, "testified" can work as a verb of attribution.

  James testified he couldn't see the face of the robber who attacked him.

- *Stated:* This works as a written version of "said." People say things, and documents state them.

  > The contract stated no one would be allowed to photograph or record the CEO's speech.

- *Announced:* Consider this an alternative to "said" for formal proclamations.

  > Sen. Rick Rothschild announced Tuesday he would not run for a fifth term.

- *Asked:* This works as an inquisitive version of "said." If someone is posing a question, "asked" is perfectly fine.

  > "Even though six people saw you aim a gun at Mr. Jones, you want this jury to believe you did not intend to kill him?" Attorney Willie Sharpe asked the defendant.

- *According to:* This one is a bit risky because it can denote a sense that the statement is doubtful. Even so, many news organizations allow it in small doses.

  > According to the latest CNN poll, Sen. Bill Jones trails challenger Arman Goode by 23 points.

If you go beyond these exceptions, you run a risk of inserting your own opinion into a piece. Attribution verbs like "yelled" or "laughed" can seem appropriate, but you are adding interpretation to those quotes when you do this. You don't want a source to come back to you and say, "I don't know why you think I was joking because I'm actually really disgusted by that situation."

Writers and editors often work together and apply the tenets of the publication's style guide to determine how far out on a limb they want to go with attributions other than "said."

STRUCTURE

In what usually amounts to a two-word sentence, the issue of word order doesn't seem like a big deal. However, grammarians would argue that preferred sentence structure dictates a noun-verb approach: "Smith said" or "he said."

Editors and writers often note that the flow and structure of a piece should determine the order of everything, including attributions, which makes verb-noun structure acceptable: "said Mick Fastback, who set a record in the 100-meter dash last year."

Each argument makes sense in certain circumstances. You wouldn't put verbs in front of nouns in most other sentences: "Walked I to the store." Or "Voted he did for Eisenhower." Doing this makes you sound like Yoda from "Star Wars." On the other hand, when flow and clarity dictate some grammatical rule bending, you shouldn't be tied to stuffy rules. Think about reporting on a fight at a bar. One participant might yell at the other, "Do you know who you're messing with?" It would be quite odd for that person to put aside rage for a moment and focus on grammar: "Do you know with whom you are messing?" Keep both angles in mind, although when possible, you should write in a way that reflects correct grammar.

REPETITION

When you write "said" in every paragraph, it can feel ridiculous and annoying. Some writers will argue that attributing every sentence in a story will limit the liability of the writer and clarify sources for the readers. Writers who don't like attributions will argue that readers can mentally "carry" an attribution forward a few paragraphs, as long as the source hasn't changed.

Neither side is absolutely right or wrong, so apply common sense and newsroom rules when you write. You should also consult with your editor before making a final decision on your approach to attributions.

BASICS OF WRITING

THE BIG THREE

Here are the three key things you should take away from this chapter:

1. **Use reader-centric structure:** When you are working on your stories, focus on what you need to do to get the readers the most important information first. You should include the core of everything that matters in the lead and write the remainder of the story in descending order of importance. Avoid chronological structure and instead build your piece based on the value of each fact you gathered.

2. **Rely on sources:** Find unique information and information that is uniquely said to use in direct quotes. When your sources give you important information that lacks the punch of direct quotes,

paraphrase that material. In both cases, you need to attribute this information to your sources. This gives you the ability to provide information while still remaining unbiased in your storytelling.

3. **Practice, practice, practice:** This form of storytelling isn't easy, because it moves away from the approach you are used to (chronological format) to something based on importance (the inverted pyramid). The only way you get better at this is to work in this format again and again until you feel comfortable in your approach to it.

KEY TERMS

DISCUSSION QUESTIONS

1. Of the five interest elements outlined in Chapter 1 (fame, oddity, conflict, impact, immediacy), which one do you feel is most compelling when you choose what you want to read? How about when you are writing for other people?

2. AP editor Janelle Cogan stated that good journalistic writing isn't flowery or fluffy but rather filled with "crisp, clear, basic sentences." To what degree do you agree or disagree with this as being the best approach for news stories? What types of writing draw you in

the most and how much do they match Cogan's view of what journalistic writing should be?

3. The chapter outlined several reasons to fix or not fix direct quotes. Do you think journalists have an obligation to clean up and fix quotes? Why or why not? Of the reasons listed in the chapter (clarity, fairness, digital media, meaning), which one do you feel most directly supports your position? Which one is least supportive?

WRITE NOW!

1. Select a poorly written news story from a local publication or area website and boil its lead down to a noun, a verb and an object. A sports story could be something like, "U.S. defeated Brazil," while a news story could be "Fire destroys store." Then, build a new lead from that core, incorporating the remaining W's and H as you see fit. After you rewrite the lead, write a short essay that explains what you thought was wrong with the previous lead and why you think your version is better.

2. Review how the chapter defines name-recognition leads and interesting-action leads. Then find two stories, one for each of these formats. Write a few paragraphs to explain if you think the approach the writer took was the correct one for each of the stories. Next, rewrite each of the leads in the other format. Finally, write a few paragraphs that explain under which circumstance you think your new lead would be appropriate. For example, a story in a local paper might use the mayor's full name in the lead for a story about his spending the entire city budget on lottery scratch-offs. This would make sense because the people in the town know him. However, a national paper, covering the oddity of the event, would likely focus on the action and withhold the mayor's name until the second or third paragraph.

3. Find a story that uses one of the problematic leads listed in the chapter ("you" leads, question leads, quote leads, "many people . . . " leads). Rewrite it to remove the problematic element and better emphasize the most valuable elements of the story. Then, write a few paragraphs that explain what was wrong with the original lead and why you think your lead improved upon it.

4. Find one of your favorite fairy tales or children's stories and write a standard news lead for it, incorporating the most important interest elements and relying on the 5W's and 1H. For example, "A 12-year-old girl returned to her Kansas home Sunday after vanquishing a witch, visiting a wizard and helping several residents of Oz gain personal benefits, including a brain and a heart."

5. Below is the information for a fire that was outlined in your text. Rewrite this into a four-paragraph brief, using the inverted pyramid as your guide. Remember to focus on putting the most important information (usually some or all of the 5W's and 1H) up high while ordering the other facts in descending order of importance.

> Jacksonville firefighters responded to a fire Tuesday around 5 p.m., after a call came in to the 911 dispatch center.
>
> Ladder Truck 11, Pumper 32 and Chief's Car 2 arrived at 5:11 p.m. to find smoke coming from underneath the eaves of the three-bedroom, one-bath home at 411 S. Cherry St.
>
> Firefighters were able to contain the blaze to approximately half of the home, while the remainder sustained heat, smoke and water damage.
>
> Homeowner Jim Smith was seriously injured in the fire and was transported to a nearby medical facility,

where he is listed in critical condition. His wife, Suzy, and his daughter Jane were unharmed.

After the fire was extinguished, assessors stated the home received approximately $90,000 in damage. Investigative Service Agents determined the cause of the fire was a leaky gas stove that exploded when Mr. Smith lit a cigarette nearby.

6. Find a press release online and rewrite it into a four-paragraph inverted-pyramid story for a local audience. Make sure you properly attribute the information in the release to either the company, the release or any individually identified spokesperson.

Visit edge.sagepub.com/filaknews to help you accomplish your coursework goals in an easy-to-use learning environment.

PRACTICE AND APPLY WHAT YOU'VE LEARNED

▶ edge.sagepub.com/filaknews

SAGE edge™

CHECK YOUR COMPREHENSION ON THE STUDY SITE WITH:

- **Practice quizzes** allow you to assess how much you've learned

- **Newswriting Assignments** allow you to broaden your reporting skills and practice writing

- **Test your knowledge** of AP Style with our AP Style Quizzes and Exercises

4 EXPANDED NEWS WRITING

LEARNING OBJECTIVES

After completing this chapter you should be able to:

- Understand how to structure stories in an expanded inverted-pyramid format as well as in other expansive writing approaches.

- Compare and contrast the elements of the inverted pyramid with those in narrative writing and nonlinear storytelling.

- Understand and be able to construct a narrative opening and a nut graph.

- Use secondary senses, like feel and smell, to augment your storytelling approach.

THINKING AHEAD: LEARNING TO BREAK THE RULES OF WRITING

Journalistic writing, especially the kind that makes for newspaper-style journalism, is a hard thing to get a handle on for many writers. It takes all of the rules we know about writing and changes them into a series of seemingly contradictory concepts regarding storytelling. Once you manage to dominate the basics, outlined in Chapter 3, things change even more, as some of the "rules" to which you grew accustomed get shifted, bent or otherwise reshaped.

These changes are reminiscent of learning to drive. In your first year or so as a new driver, the driver's education teacher likely had you putting your hands at the "10 o'clock and 2 o'clock" positions on the steering wheel. You learned how to look "left-right-left" before making a turn and how to check your various mirrors in a specific sequence before backing up. You kept a firm handle on your rate of speed at all times and used the "hand over hand" approach to make left and right turns.

Once you became a more experienced driver, you likely kept your hands in different areas based on your own sense of feel. You learned how to give a quick look into a mirror to judge the distance between you and a following car. You got better at finding the various switches around your dash. In short, you learned how to do the work more naturally, and you improved your overall flow. That said, if you broke too many rules or did things carelessly, you put yourself at risk for creating a disaster. Thus, you needed to know where those danger zones were and how best to keep yourself out of trouble.

This chapter will explain various formats of newspaper-style writing, many of which translate to other platforms, including magazines and digital media. The underlying aspects of these writing formats will help you better engage your readers and help them find value in your work. In the end, the goal of this chapter is to help you learn the basics of these writing formats and when it is best to use them so you can tell the best stories possible.

FIG. 4.1 EXPANDED INVERTED PYRAMID

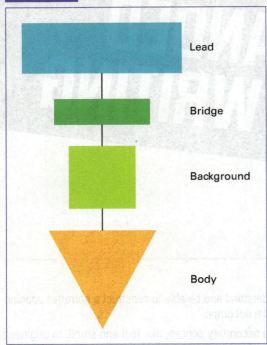

Lead

Bridge

Background

Body

EXPANDING THE INVERTED PYRAMID

The primary problem with a pure inverted-pyramid structure is that it can lack flow and cause a rough read. Thus, most writers who use this format will adapt it to fit the needs of their work while still adhering to the basic tenets of the structure. Here is kind of an "expanded" format of the inverted pyramid and how it works for news writing:

LEAD

The standard lead is discussed at length in Chapter 3, but it's worth a brief review here. Focus on the FOCII interest elements (fame, oddity, conflict, immediacy and impact) as you outline exactly what you think your readers want to know most. Include as many of the 5W's and 1H as you think will fit and will help your readers get a clear picture of the story to come.

BRIDGE: MOVING FROM A TO C

A **bridge** paragraph serves in the same way a physical bridge works in real life: It spans a gap and allows you to move seamlessly from one side of the gap to the other. Bridges in news stories usually come in a few forms:

- **Lead-cleanup bridge:** In the case of interesting-action leads, most bridges add a more specific "who" to the mix, naming the person who did the action. In the other three lead types, the bridge can be used to fill in any of the 5W's and 1H that didn't get covered in the lead.

- **Quote bridge:** When you cover a meeting, speech or news conference, a quote bridge often works well to engage the readers by using a source's own words to clarify the theme. In addition, a quote bridge can solidify the lead and reinforce the key aspects of it.

- **Advance-the-story bridge:** If you don't have a great quote or a key element that was missing from the lead, you can always follow the inverted-pyramid structure and use the second paragraph to get people deeper into the story. Whatever you think is the second most important thing can go here, and it will move readers from the lead into the body of the story.

BACKGROUND

Before you get too deep into the story, you want to make sure all of your readers have the same frame of reference. This is where a couple paragraphs of background will be helpful. After the bridge, you can add anywhere from one to four sentences of background to help fill in your readers. Usually, two sentences can nail it down for them, but if you have a particularly difficult or involved topic, you can use three or four sentences. Any more than that will end up turning your work into a history paper instead of a news story.

BASIC BODY ELEMENTS

You can build the remainder of your story's body with indirect quotes (paraphrases) and direct quotes from your sources. These items work best in matched pairs, with the paraphrase introducing the quote and the quote augmenting the material in the paraphrase.

One good way to think about how they work together is to think about a diamond engagement ring: The paraphrase is the setting, which provides the foundation for what is happening in the pairing. It isn't as shiny or pretty as the diamond, but without it, you wouldn't have much to show off. The direct quote is like the diamond: It's the glittering element that has vibrancy and draws the most attention. However, without the setting, you would have no way to show it to other people. By working together, paraphrases and quotes do the same thing as they create a valuable pairing that helps bring stability and vibrancy to your story.

News stories need shape and structure, in the same way that animated films need to be planned for, scene by scene, before the work can begin.

LOOKING TO END THE STORY

One of the worst experiences a reader can have is to reach the end of a story and feel that the story hasn't ended. To help your readers gain a sense of finality and closure, consider ending the story in one of these ways:

- **A closing quote:** Some quotes carry with them the sense of finality that signals to your readers that the story is done. If you wrote a story about a girl who was born with a heart defect and had just undergone risky surgery, you know you don't have the end of the story. However, a quote can help bring a sense of completion to the story:

> "We're glad she made it through," her mother said. "Everything from here on out is taking life day by day."

That kind of quote brings a sense that you have reached a junction point in the story that allows the reader to feel somewhat satisfied.

- **A wrap-up paragraph:** Not every story lends itself to passionate or compelling quotes. However, every story has to end, so you can look for a way to close off the story with a simple statement of fact. You don't want to have a paragraph where you summarize everything you just said or, worse yet, give your opinion on the issue. A story can end with a simple note:

> The city council will vote on the matter May 3.
>
> All money raised at the fair will benefit the "Save the Children" fund.
>
> The governor's next statewide listening session will be next month.

THOUGHTS FROM A **PRO** ➡ TONY REHAGEN, FREELANCE WRITER AND CONTRIBUTING EDITOR, ST. LOUIS MAGAZINE

© Tony Rehagen

Tony Rehagen is currently a freelance writer for magazines and online publications as well as serving as a contributing editor to St. Louis Magazine. He spent 10 years as a writer and an editor for city magazines, including Indianapolis Monthly and Atlanta. He was named a five-time finalist for the City Regional Magazine Association's Writer of the Year award, and his work has been included in the book "Next Wave: America's New Generation of Great Literary Journalists."

Even with all of these jobs and accolades, Rehagen said that some of his most valuable experiences came from his time as a reporter in a small Missouri town.

"It taught me how to get my hands dirty, to sift through public records, to not just take public officials (or anyone) at face value," he said. "On beats like that, you also learn how to cultivate relationships with sources, how to have off-the-record conversations that lead to key on-the-record information, and how to be mindful of people when you write about them."

As a narrative and literary journalist, Rehagen said he has to spend a lot of time with his subjects to really get a complete picture of them.

"I try to spend as much time as possible with the sources," he said. "And there are different types of time spent. First, there's the sit-down interview, which is important. Since I typically have months to do a story, I try to break that up over several interviews, if possible, catching people on different days. Then there's shadowing time—observing the subject doing something, hopefully something offering insight to their character or what they do. In those instances, you try to spend so much time that they forget you're there and then you get a candid glimpse."

A big part of crafting a strong narrative and a deep story is having "command of the character," so that he can tell how a source acts in any given situation and to what degree that behavior is in the nature of that source, he said.

Another aspect of writing like this is to understand that rules exist for the benefit of the writers, he said. Even though he knows he has more freedom as a writer, he said he doesn't believe in breaking rules for the sake of doing so.

"Well, first of all, you sort of have to earn the right to break a rule," he said. "If you want to lead with a quote, it had better be a damn good quote. If you want to bury the nut or (gasp) not have a nut graph at all, you had better have complete command of your story and have structured the hell out of it. That takes skill that even veterans don't possess on every piece."

At the core of each choice he makes, Rehagen said, is the way his choices influence and affect his readers.

"One thing I hate about this otherwise glorious renaissance of narrative writing is that somehow story length has become a goal," he said. "The word 'longform' is some sort of badge that justifies every piece being 6,000 or 10,000 words. Please. I'd argue that *most* stories can be told in 3,000 words or fewer. . . . If a reader is going to commit the time and attention to sit down with a long piece of journalism, don't waste their investment. Give each story only the scope that it deserves."

As long as you can bring a sense of finality to the story, your readers will feel content and be able to move on with life.

WRITING WITH A NARRATIVE FEEL

One of the biggest mistakes beginning writers make is to assume that **narrative writing** is easier than following the rigid rules of the inverted pyramid. This mistake is common, because the writers think they can slather on adjectives and describe scenes in more detail than a "Game of Thrones" novel. This doesn't work, because you still need the interest elements and core values of journalism at the center of the narrative writing. Perhaps a good way to understand this is to think about a birthday present: No matter how beautiful

A descriptive opening, like the one in the movie "Up" can help establish the overall tone and feel of your piece.

Photofest/Buena Vista Pictures

the wrapping is or how ornate the ribbons are, if there's nothing inside, it's going to be a disappointment. Once people get past the pretty outside elements, it's what is inside that counts.

Below are some basic elements of narrative writing that can both help you engage your readers and give them some value for their time:

USE A DESCRIPTIVE OPENING

A narrative approach requires you to find a way to put your readers into the middle of the story you are telling. In most cases, a descriptive opening can help you do this. One of the best forms of descriptive openings is a **scene setter**, where you establish what is happening in your story, what the environment looks like and how people should feel during your piece of writing. If you want people to feel like they are in a warm, safe environment or a dark, foreboding death trap, you can use a description to set the scene.

Think about this approach like the opening minute of a play: The curtain pulls back, the lights come on and then there is a moment or two before the actors begin their dialogue. The purpose of this is to allow you to soak in the environment, examine the set and see the characters before they begin their scene. You can use your first few paragraphs to do this kind of thing for your readers. Consider this example:

> Jimmie Williams sits in the passenger seat of the county-owned Ford pickup truck, craning his head out the window in search of his quarry. The wind pulls his graying mullet back and flaps at his cheeks, giving him the appearance of a golden retriever enjoying a summer car ride.
>
> As the driver pushes the beat-up F-250 along Highway 21 in Wabano County, Williams' head twitches in sharp, short turns like those of the hawks and owls that frequently hunt along this wooded stretch of road.
>
> Finally, his eyes lock on the target.
>
> "There!" he shouts over the road noise and the sounds of Johnny Cash tunes trickling from the truck's cassette player. "Right there, about 20 yards up on the right."
>
> Before the truck can even stop, Williams swings out of the cab with triumphant enthusiasm. He grabs a square, flat-head shovel out of the rack attached to the pickup's bed and hustles his beefy frame toward the mound of fur and flies on the side of the highway.
>
> "Sucker's about 15 pounds," he says as the shovel slides under the remains of a too-slow raccoon. "Big one for this time of year." Williams hoists his prize from the gravelly ground and heads back to the truck, where he flips it onto a growing pile of squirrels, possums and deer.
>
> He holsters the shovel into the rack and hops back inside, slamming the dented red door that reads "Wabano County Road Kill Patrol."

This opening puts you in a place and a mindset: An open stretch of county highway with two guys in a truck, looking for roadkill. If this opens a profile, you could follow up with a good explanation of who this guy is and why he's so into his job. If it is a story about diminishing county services, Williams could be a narrative thread to explain how things like clean roads could be in danger because of budget cuts. Regardless of the story, the opening can draw in your readers and place them within a specific environment.

WEAVE A NARRATIVE THREAD INTO YOUR PIECE

To keep readers connected to a story, you can find a person or an incident that allows you to individualize the bigger issues you are covering. Some people refer to this as a **"narrative thread"** or the **"kabob format."** Consider a story about a national spike in tuition costs and the problems the increases causes for college students. You could look at issues such as how the cost requires students to take out more loans, stay in school longer and work more hours to pay for tuition. Chances are, you know someone who has dealt with all three of those issues, so you should interview that person and use her to tie your whole story together.

Your descriptive open could start with your source at the beginning of a typical school day. From that point, you can follow her as she goes to school, talks about loans, reviews her graduation requirements and heads to a part-time job. At each of these stops, you can describe what this person is doing and how it affects her life. Once you do this, you can then leap from the thread into the broader strokes of the issue: statistics on how many people have these issues, the lifelong impacts of these choices and the diminishing quality of the educational experience these students face. The thread can give your readers a "real person" they can latch onto and thus see a human cost behind the big numbers.

TELL ME WHY I CARE: THE NUT GRAPH

Journalism requires more than good storytelling and engaging writing. It demands that you give people information that matters to them or that can affect their lives in some way. Poorly written narrative pieces miss this element and often leave readers wondering, "OK, so what was the point of that?"

To help your readers understand why a story has relevance and value, you should include a **nut graph** in your narrative pieces. The purpose of this paragraph is to tell your audience members, "This matters because of X, Y and Z, and here is how it fits into your life." A profile can shed light on someone people see every day but don't really know. A narrative story about people like the roadkill specialist described above can draw readers into more of a ground-level view of county services and budget cuts. No matter what you want to do with your story, you need to give people the most valuable interest elements, much like a lead would do in an inverted-pyramid story.

Here's an example of a nut graph for the roadkill story:

> Williams and his driver, a man who goes by the nickname Skrunch, are the only roadkill-removal team left in Wabano County, down from 10 crews just five years ago. Each day, they search the 287 miles of highways and 543 miles of gravel roads for dead animals, in the hope of keeping the roads cleaner for residents and tourists alike. However, repeated budget cuts now threaten to end the program altogether, leaving an annual average of 243,812 animal corpses to dot the county's landscape.

In this chunk of information, you can tell people what the story is about (loss of county services, especially road services) and why they should care (nearly a quarter million dead animals will be on display each year for their viewing displeasure because no one is there to pick them up) before they get into the rest of the story. A good nut graph can help set the stage for you to launch into the body of a narrative piece that has depth and value.

DRAW WORD PICTURES FOR THE READER

As you proceed into the body of your piece, you want to follow the ultimate advice of journalistic description: Show, don't tell. The best way to tell pictures to your readers is through a combination of strong reporting, keen observation and proper word selection.

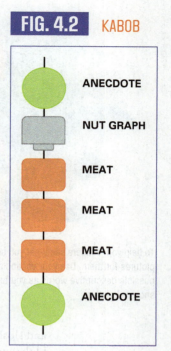

FIG. 4.2 KABOB

- ANECDOTE
- NUT GRAPH
- MEAT
- MEAT
- MEAT
- ANECDOTE

To help your readers see what you see, you need to draw word pictures for them. Use your vocabulary to select the best possible descriptive words as you tell them exactly what they should visualize.

To provide "**word pictures**," you need to have a strong mental picture of your scene and your sources. You also need a vibrant vocabulary that will allow you to properly capture key details of what you observed. Words that lack value in telling pictures are comparatives that fail to have a point of reference. For example, "tall" can mean a lot of things. A 5-foot-tall second-grader is tall compared with his classmates, but a 6-foot-tall professional basketball player is short compared with his teammates. You need to provide people with a much better sense of how they should visualize the person, either through an anecdote or by including a comparative element.

You should always go back through your word choices and see if the words will convey the precise feeling you want to communicate to your readers. You can pour the contents of a pitcher into a glass, but how does it move? Is it a fast and smooth pour, like milk, or is it a slow and labored pour, like glue or honey? Does the liquid maintain a constant speed, like water from a bucket, or does it splash and slosh, like gasoline pouring out of a container into a lawnmower? Or does it come out in blobs and globs, like pouring a dozen raw eggs out of a bowl into a blender? The more time you put into your choices, the more likely your readers will be able to visualize what you are seeing, and the more engaged they will become.

BUILD THE BODY

Long narrative stories often benefit from the use of subheadings or from a simple segmentation of the content, much like what you saw in the "kabob" approach. Very rarely will you have a long and detailed story that can smoothly move from point to point without having these breaks in the text. In addition, readers will often feel overwhelmed by the content if it seems to be one giant chunk. This is why most books use chapters and many others use subheadings: They give the reader a sense of completion while allowing the writer to set up another topic without having to force a transition.

During your reporting, you will find a few main themes emerging from your research and interviews. If you find three or four of these, you can create topical segments that you will want to discuss at length in the body of the piece. This will provide you with options for subheads and the ability to sort your content into those areas. For example, if you wrote a story on organic produce, you would interview a wide array of people, including farmers, scientists, consumers, health experts, grocery store officials and people involved in large agricultural companies. When you start writing, you might find a few basic storylines emerging:

Costs for Producers Versus Consumers

Health Benefits, Concerns, and Problems

Opportunities for Small and Large Farms

Standard news writing and reporting tend to rely on two primary senses: seeing and hearing. We see events as they unfold and we hear what people have to say about them. In most cases, that's as far as we go with our work, because those two senses have the ability to capture basic information.

However, as noted earlier, one of journalism's oldest adages is to show, not tell, which means it is important to give people the full sense of a place, a situation or a time. To do that, you will need to set a scene properly, and to do that, you will need to rely on secondary senses.

The sense of smell has been linked to memory and emotion,[1] so when you are writing feature pieces, take a big whiff of your environment. If you can find a way to explain what that smell is or give a good description of that odor, you can help your readers feel more attuned to the scene's setting. For example, a fire can smell pleasant if it's an open-pit campfire, with hickory and cedar logs crackling and glowing. However, a fire at a plastics factory or a tire plant can belch acrid black smoke into the air and make you want to shut off your lungs. Even pedestrian descriptions can take on new meaning if you can integrate the intensity of the smell to them. There's a difference between the light wisp of $400-an-ounce perfume emanating from a rich woman's wrist and the vapor trail left by a 14-year-old high school kid who put on his $1.99-a-gallon cologne with a paint sprayer.

If you can find ways to detect scents like baking bread, day-old cigarette smoke or fish-based fertilizer, you can place your reader in a specific environment.

The same thing is true when it comes to feeling and the ability to use touch and physical sampling to convey value. This obviously doesn't mean you should try to feel how sweaty an athlete is or pet a local politician's camelhair coat. However, as a feature writer, you can use a tactile examination to add value to your story.

How does the marble that lines the statehouse capitol building feel? Cold? Smooth? Solid? Or even better, can you describe what it's like trying to breathe in 115-degree heat? (One student described it as feeling like she was sucking exhaust directly from the tailpipe of an overheated bus.)

When you shake hands with a source, how does that person's hand feel? Soft, hard, gritty, smooth? How is the grip? Loose and damp or crushing and dry? (In shaking hands with an old-time baseball player, a journalist noted that the athlete had the grip of a trash compactor and a hand that felt like a baseball mitt lined with sandpaper.)

Think about the experiences you have had touching something foreign to you and how you can make those physical experiences clearer to other people. If you can use the sense of touch to help convey value to your readers, do so.

You can easily sort your source material into these topics and then build three body chunks out of them. If you have a narrative thread, you can use it to touch on these areas as you transition between them.

You could also break your body into temporal chunks, relying on a **chronological approach** to help tell your story in segments. A profile of an up-and-coming athlete who suffered a major injury and recovered fits this pattern nicely. You could do a chunk on life before the incident and one on the injury and its fallout. A final chunk could examine life after the injury and the player's return. Although this is a more chronologically based approach, it still has a few clear demarcations that lend themselves to segmentation.

NONLINEAR STORYTELLING

Traditional journalists tended to embrace the concept of linearity, in which they provide information in a predetermined fashion and it is consumed in exactly the same way. Whether it was organizing a story in an inverted pyramid or choosing which stories went on the front page, newspaper journalists saw their job as creating order for their readers. Broadcast journalists tended to do the same thing in their approach to video stories and stacking the newscast: They decide how to tell the story.

The democratization of information on the internet has altered this in a number of ways. Users have more choices than they did before as to which media outlets to use and what content to consume. In addition, they can choose how they consume content through actively interfacing with a website. The linear nature of how a journalist expects someone to proceed through a story is no longer a given.

Nonlinear storytelling is an approach to content delivery that understands that readers will not follow the path journalists set before them. The user can choose various elements to consume, ranging from blocks of texts and lists to video and interactive graphics.[2] This presents a challenge to journalists, in that they need to create content that will complement, not repeat, other elements of the story they want to tell. In addition, it means that writers can't assume readers will enter the story at a given point, that they will consume it in a preordained order or that they will go through every piece available.

VISUALIZING THE "STORY WEB"

To become a good nonlinear storyteller, you need to understand how users can control their own experiences and how those experiences can direct their interactions with your content. The best way to do that is to examine a visual "web" of information and see what you might provide and how readers might enter or exit your collection of content. Let's look at a basic story web on a topic that tends to be a big deal on most college campuses: parking.

At the core is the general idea of the story of parking on this one campus. From that core, you look at several basic elements of the story, such as financial aspects of parking, the general parking availability on the campus and the rules governing parking. From each of these areas, you can see how they grow outward into additional topics. The financial aspect can include things like charts for costs for specific parking passes and lots, the fines associated with tickets, the meter costs and more. You can also include things like the financial outline of the parking department, the costs associated with running the department and the year-by-year trend of parking fines. You might even add short videos featuring people talking about their worst parking fines or a list of people who have the largest number of unpaid tickets.

You can see how certain topics can link or couple across the web, such as costs across the peer institutions or how a parking map could be linked to an area of availability and an area associated with costs. All in all, these elements have the ability to expand and intersect throughout the entire project.

FIG. 4.3   PARKING STORY

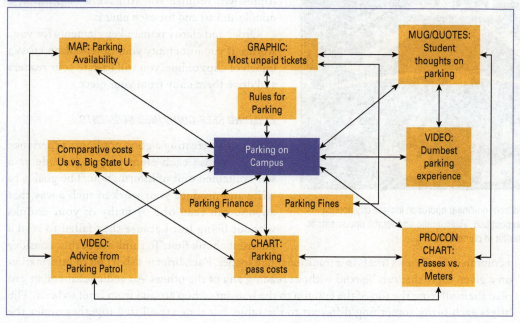

UNDERSTANDING USER-CONTROLLED NAVIGATION

You have no way of knowing where your readers will enter your content matrix or where they will go once they enter. In the parking story, a reader interested in the costs of your parking passes might hop in at that point, only to become interested in the costs of tickets and the weird ticket story videos. A second reader might enter at that same point, only to feel that the cost of parking on the campus is outrageous before heading over to the segment that compares your costs with those of peer institutions. A third person might come to the site because a friend said, "Hey! I did a video for the student newspaper about my weirdest ticket." That reader might watch all the videos and then leave.

You won't know everything readers will do upon finding your work online, but consider these thoughts as you build your work from a user-oriented perspective:

NONLINEAR VERSUS NONSENSICAL

Linear writing often feels restrictive to new writers, so the ability to use a nonlinear structure can feel exciting and freeing. The problem most of those writers face is that nonlinear writing still has an inherent structure, and certain elements of that writing remain linear in nature. Nonlinear does not mean nonsensical.

For example, using video segments as part of a nonlinear story will require the same basic structure as a standard broadcast story or chunk of raw video. A "how-to" element that you add into a nonlinear package will still have step-by-step instructions and require keen attention to

Stories that could benefit from nonlinear approach include city council meetings, where you can post text, video, audio and source documents to give your readers a full buffet of content options.

detail. Writing chunks of information about various topics will require you to have a beginning, a middle and an end for each chunk.

Order and clarity remain key elements for your stories. If you just empty your notebook and toss a bunch of clips online, you will irritate your readers and drive them away from your piece.

BUILDING SELF-CONTAINED SEGMENTS

The trick to creating a good nonlinear experience is to compose each element you include as a self-contained unit of information. The goal is to write and produce your work in such a way that anyone can read one or many of your chunks without being lost because they failed to read a different chunk first. To think about this, consider a column of local news briefs in a traditional newspaper. Each brief is a short bit of information on a given topic that can be read without reading any of the others. An audience member can read them all from the top of the column to the bottom or hop around from brief to brief. The briefs each bring something different to the table, but they are all tied together under the concept of "local news." If you take that idea and expand it to include additional media formats while simultaneously narrowing the topic to a single idea, like the parking piece earlier in the chapter, you have the right idea.

One of the easiest ways to write in news chunks in this format is to apply the basic elements of audience centricity and then build a mini-inverted-pyramid piece based on each of them. Consider each segment to be worthy of a lead sentence, such as "Parking Services issues an average of 114 tickets each week, most of which are for avoidable offenses." Then, build underneath that lead information about the variety of offenses: parking over the lines in the parking lot, failure to display a parking permit and parking in zones clearly marked "No Parking." You can then link that segment to other segments, such as "list of parking offenses and fines" and "rules for parking on campus." You could also link to some videos in which students explain their thoughts on parking, the "weirdest ticket" videos and other entertaining elements.

In each of these cases, you will get a self-contained segment that will allow your audience members to consume as much or as little content as they want without getting lost. Short, simple segments of information can motivate people to give your work a try and then maybe stick around for a while.

Writers who produce nonlinear stories often wonder what will happen to their work, because they cede control of navigation and consumption to the readers. Instead of fearing this idea, good nonlinear writers produce content that will draw readers deeper into the story than traditional media ever could.

In creating a nonlinear piece, you want to give your readers everything they could possibly need or want in the best possible format. You also want to avoid repeating information on multiple platforms for the sake of doing so. Think about your work the way you would look at a buffet restaurant. Good buffets have multiple stations, one for each phase of the meal: a salad station, a soup station, an appetizer station, a couple entrée stations and a dessert station. At each of those stations, you have various options that appeal to people with a wide array of tastes.

It wouldn't make sense to have a soup station with five choices that were all some kind of beef soup: "beef with barley and vegetables," "beef with vegetables," "beef with barley," "old-fashioned beef medley" and "Chef Jimmy's Famous Beef 'n' Stuff." The same thing applies here: Make sure that each piece adds value to the experience and that you aren't repeating content just for the sake of saying, "Look at all the content I have here!" If you give people a truly broad array of choices, they will immerse themselves in the experience and spend more time considering the options and avenues you afford to them.

In terms of interactivity, digital consumers tend to enjoy the ability to move freely and easily through a website, a story or a loosely constructed pile of content. Unlike newspapers or television broadcasts, a digital platform is meant

Consider how a buffet works when you consider how you want to provide content to your readers on the web: They have choices and you need to give them options.

to give the audience the ability to wander among various elements. The platform also inspires choice through that interactivity. Here, again, a buffet approach is a good one to model. Each food offering is self-contained and labeled so people know where to go to get what they want. They don't have to dig through a pile of beef brisket to get a piece of steamed trout. These entrées are set aside in specific serving trays, even as they are all grouped under a broader "entrées" serving station.

Furthermore, people can go from place to place and build a plate of whatever they like. They can follow the standard serving order of salad, soup, appetizer, entrée and dessert, or they can go right to the desserts. There isn't a bouncer named Turk at the dessert station, who is checking to see if you ate your three-bean salad first. People can grab as much of whatever they want whenever they want. It's personal choice and active consumption, just like in a nonlinear structure.

THE BIG THREE

Here are the three key things you should take away from this chapter:

1. **The story should dictate your approach:** When you get comfortable writing in a format or using video for your stories, you tend to gravitate toward those comfortable options. Instead of using the tool you like best, let the story itself determine for you the best way to write it. If you don't have a narrative thread, don't force it. If you have an important piece of news to share, don't bury it under a six-paragraph narrative introduction. Give your readers what they need in the best possible format.

2. **Take your time with description:** In narrative pieces, you need to give your readers the ability to see exactly what you see in their mind's eye. That

means going back through your word choices and making sure you have exactly the right descriptor. It also means slowing down to describe complicated concepts or intricate details. The clearer you are, the more engaged your readers will be.

3. **Give the story what it's worth:** As Tony Rehagen says, terms like "long-form journalism" and "narrative journalism" make people think that longer is better. That's not always true, nor is there a specific word count at which a lousy story becomes a great one. When you are telling your story, give the readers what they need to know in the format you think serves the story best. When that is done, you can stop writing.

KEY TERMS

DISCUSSION QUESTIONS

1. What is the purpose of a nut graph? What value does it provide to your readers, and how does it help you focus your story?

2. If you had a choice of standard inverted-pyramid stories or more involved narrative structures, which would you prefer and why?

3. Scientists say that smell is one of the strongest senses that links to memory and emotion. Is there a particular smell that brings you to a specific place and time in your life? What is it and how does it make you feel?

WRITE NOW!

1. Spend some time with a person you know, and create a "word picture" that describes that individual. Start with the person's appearance in terms of the basic elements of age, size, shape, hair color, clothing and so forth. Then integrate action-oriented elements such as movement, mannerisms and more. Use as much space as you need to capture this individual in a way that lets your instructor see him or her in the instructor's mind's eye. Pay special attention to your word choices as to most accurately describe this person.

2. Go to a public place and observe the activities around you. This could be a mall, a sporting event or anything in which people are tending to their business all around you. Take notes that will allow you to capture the overall vibe of the place, including the sound, feel, smell and energy of the environment. Once you are done, take your notes back and write a short scene-setting piece (1 to 2 pages).

3. Select a topic you think would matter to the people on your campus, and think about the various angles and aspects that would attach themselves to that topic. Then, assemble them into a story web, using lines to connect the pieces to one another in a nonlinear, yet logical and fluid, fashion. Write a short essay (2 to 2.5 pages) that explains your various nodes on the web and why you think these elements are germane to the overall topic at hand.

Visit edge.sagepub.com/filaknews to help you accomplish your coursework goals in an easy-to-use learning environment.

5 SOCIAL MEDIA

LEARNING OBJECTIVES

After completing this chapter you should be able to:

- Understand how best to reach your audience in a variety of ways through social media.
- Compare and contrast traditional media and social media with regard to usage, trust and value.
- Understand the basic benefits, drawbacks and usage strategies associated with social media.

- Become familiar with several social media tools that serve the various forms of communication, including text, photos and videos.
- Outline key elements of successful blogging.

THINKING AHEAD: RETHINKING HOW TO REACH READERS

The advent of **social media** forced journalists to rethink how they approach their jobs. The writing and reading now happen on both sides of the conversation, with readers and journalists often discussing issues through Twitter exchanges and Facebook **posts**. The explosion of low-cost digital technology has produced a rise in citizen journalists, who cover incidents on their own, as opposed to calling in tips to their traditional journalistic counterparts. Even more, many media outlets rely on the content these outsiders gather.

Media production is no longer a **one-to-many model** that is based on the credibility and presence of a standard media outlet. Instead, social media has resulted in a **many-to-many model** that gives anyone with access to the web or a mobile device the ability to build an audience and create content for it.

Social media has continued to grow as an important resource for users everywhere. A Pew Center research study on mobile messaging and social media found that from 2012 to 2015, the use of social media continued on an upward trajectory. Pinterest, a social sharing site akin to a series of old-fashioned bulletin boards, saw its users double from 15 percent of those Pew surveyed in 2012 to 31 percent in 2015. Instagram, a photo-sharing site, saw its usage double in that time span from 13 percent to 28 percent of survey participants.

In terms of specific tools, 36 percent of smartphone owners reported using messaging apps, such as iMessage, and 17 percent reported using tools like Snapchat, which we will discuss later in the chapter.[1] If these trends continue, social media will show continued growth and eventual domination on the information-sharing scene within a few short years.

As a reporter, you need to understand what makes social media valuable as a research tool and a publishing outlet. You also have to understand how the rules on these platforms may differ from those you follow as a journalist. This chapter will explain the basics of social media, including the positives and negatives of relying on it as a journalist. It will also outline the ways in which journalists can use it to further their work and engage their audiences.

THE CONVERSATION PRISM

Brought to you by
Brian Solis & JESS3

For more information
check out theconversationprism.com

Given the many tools and topics covered in social media, the entirety of the field can be daunting. Brian Solis, a digital media expert, has crafted what he calls The Conversation Prism, which helps to analyze the ways in which people use social media and the tools that meet specific needs.

WHAT IS SOCIAL MEDIA?

People who try to define social media often find themselves tripping over their words because social media's meaning varies from person to person. For some people, it's a way to reach out to friends. For others, it's a marketing tool. For even others, it's a more reliable way to get news on crucial topics of the day.

People often define social media as it relates to tools such as websites and apps. However, not all websites have the **Web 2.0** features that put the "social" in social media. In short, social media seems to be in the eye of the beholder, recalling Justice Potter Stewart's famous line about obscenity: "I know it when I see it."

For our purposes here, it might be best to think about social media the way that Daniel Nations, a trends expert, defines it: a digital tool that doesn't just provide information but also seeks to have you interact with it while you are getting that information. He makes the analogy that traditional media, like broadcast news and newspapers, are like one-way streets, while social media is a like a two-way street where readers get to join the discussion.[2]

Social media tools allow users to generate and share their own content in the form of text, photos, videos, graphics and more. The tools also allow people to build their own audiences based on congruent interests and conferred authority.

Perhaps the three most important things to understand for reporters in regard to social media are the following:

1. **The model has changed:** The mass media model in which one source transmitted to many people in the form of a newspaper or news broadcast isn't how this works. Social media allows anyone to become a source of information. This many-to-many model means that you are no longer a single voice of authority with a ready-made audience waiting to hear what you have to say. You are on the same playing field as anyone else who can send a tweet or share a photo. You can't assume you will gather a large audience simply because you always had one. You have to fight harder to grab people's attention.

If a tree falls in the woods and no one is there to hear it, does it make a sound? You could easily ask the same question about tweets and posts that lack an audience. In the days of traditional media, it was easy to rely on the brand name of the TV station or the newspaper to draw eyeballs. Circulation numbers and market share provided journalists with a sense of how many people paid attention to their work on a daily basis. Social media requires a lot more work on the part of the individual journalists to build, maintain and engage an audience. Here are some helpful hints based on the ideas of online marketing guru John Rampton[3]:

- **Identify goals and objectives:** One of the biggest mistakes people make in taking part in social media is to jump in without a sense of what they want to do or why people would look to them for information. Rampton suggests that you figure out who is in your audience, what those people want and what you want to accomplish in connecting with them.

- **Let them know you are human:** Rampton notes that connecting with audience members is crucial to growing a social media presence. He says that good social media professionals will post often, respond to posts from readers and connect with the audience on a personal level. He also states that you should engage with everyone who posts to your social media pages. If you let people know you will listen, they will want to stay connected with you. This will also help you reach back out to them and give them more of what they need and want.

- **Understand their needs:** If you know what people want to see, you can more easily deliver it to them. Rampton says that knowing and understanding an audience will allow you to interact with them on an intimate level.

- **Produce valuable content:** This is a standard throughout the field of journalism, but it bears repeating here in terms of social media. People who follow you quickly will be just as quick to dump you if you don't give them a reason to hang around. Rampton says that having the best content will continue to draw people to your work.

- **Consistently post at a comfortable rate:** Once people like what you have to say, they will want to see more and more of your content. Rampton says readers will get frustrated if people don't get new content each time they check in on social media. It is worth noting that readers can also feel overwhelmed if you dump a massive amount of content on them all at once. This often happens with traditional publications, like student weekly newspapers, that tweet out links to all the print stories on publication day and then go dark for six days. Meter your approach to providing information and you will cultivate readership habits.

2. **Authority matters:** With all of these additional information sources now available, people have more choices than ever for content. Their decisions regarding where to go and whom to trust are based on authority and trust. You have to prove yourself to be valuable and trustworthy in the eyes of your audience members. Journalists used to be trusted because they were the only ones out there, meaning that people heard only what the journalists wanted to say. Now, social media users can bestow authority on anyone they see fit. Even worse, from a journalist's standpoint, the people might be making bad choices regarding trust, so we need to make sure we can demonstrate our authority. Finally, authority is fleeting in this new model. If you fail to provide people what they need or you make one too many mistakes, social media users will stop paying attention to you and seek another information source.

3. **Not everyone follows the same rules:** In your journalism or communications program, you received strong ethical and legal training. Your instructors gave you reasons to make sure you were always fair, accurate and decent when you plied your trade. However, because everyone can use social media and because not everyone got that same training, you have to be careful as you use social media in your reporting. Aside from the trolls, who decide to make people's lives miserable just for sport, some social media users don't fact-check their content or worry about libeling someone. If you find something on social media and forward it, even if the content looks pretty safe, you are taking an unnecessary risk.

VALUE OF SOCIAL MEDIA

Social media outlets have value to reporters, as both tools to send information and tools to receive information. Social media allows you to reach out to people at the scene of an accident or a disaster. These tools give you the ability to capture and share information instantly to your audience. They also serve as a source of tips for stories, inside information and key sources for your stories. Consider these thoughts regarding the value of social media, from your readers' perspective:

EASY ACCESS ON ALL YOUR DEVICES

About 20 years ago, computers became a dominant tool in information gathering and dissemination. However, even at that time they remained bulky and mostly restricted to desktops. Even when laptops became more cost effective and portable, they remained shackled to landline internet connections.

In the subsequent two decades, technology has not only become faster, cheaper and better, but more ubiquitous. The advent of Wi-Fi and hotspots meant that users could grab information on the go with their laptops. The creation of tablet devices and smartphones meant that users could get access to the internet almost anywhere. Improved technology also allowed designers to build social media apps that were scalable and that met specific needs within the market. The cheap cost (in some cases, no cost) of the apps meant that people were more willing to try them, adapt them to their needs and use them to join social networks.

The 24/7 access to groups of trusted people who share information on a multitude of platforms gives social media a leg up in the world of Web 2.0. In addition, the way people can then use those apps to respond and become part of the discussion from anywhere engages people who want to be "in the know."

CHOOSE SOURCES YOU TRUST

In some cases, people are placed into a situation in which trust is inherent. Children tend to trust parents and teachers, until they are given ample reason not to. Spouses trust one another with various expectations in life until, again, one of them violates the trust of the other. For years, it was like this in media. With few sources, you had limited choices as to whom you would trust.

Today, the array of sources has grown exponentially, and readers can decide whom they trust and why they trust those individuals. Social media users provide everyone on a given platform the opportunity to earn their trust. If a user trusts you and you can demonstrate value to the user, you will remain a vital part of that user's network. If you fail in either of those areas, the user will stop paying attention to you, and you have no recourse.

THOUGHTS FROM A **PRO** ➡ MAC SLAVIN,
DIGITAL AND SOCIAL MEDIA SPECIALIST,
DETROIT TIGERS

© Mac Slavin

Mac Slavin attended a college media conference while he was a student at Wartburg College, where he saw someone speaking about some "new thing called Twitter."

"His session was so good, we all went back to our hotel rooms and created accounts," Slavin said years later.

Upon his return to campus, Slavin started using social media to reach the readers of the student newspaper. From there, he took on various internships and jobs that mixed his love of sports with his passion for social media.

Today, Slavin is the digital and social media specialist for the Detroit Tigers, where he manages all of the team's social media channels, helps with the team's paid social media advertising strategies and works with some of its mobile initiatives.

"During the season there's a ton of content collection," he said. "I'm always scrolling through our team photographer's photographs, on the field or concourse looking for photos or up in the press box tweeting about the game. There's plenty of time spent on content creation, graphics and events, but there's a lot of event and game coverage during the season."

"As you can imagine, the off-season focuses more on content creation. We don't have the players around or new highlights rolling in daily. We spend a lot of time planning what our content is going to be and creating fun and engaging pieces."

Slavin said it was the immediacy of social media that drew him to the field. He was able to break news on campus as a student and improve the reach of his sports coverage as a professional.

"We are able to get information right as it's happening," Slavin said. "We are able to get updates on everything from tragedies to the World Series in real time. I had friends in Paris during the attacks, and I was able to hear their version of the story as I was getting more in-depth updates on TV. On the other side, I had friends at the World Series last year, and I was able to experience it through their snapchat Stories like I was actually in the stands."

Immediacy, however, does have its risks, he added.

"Instead of fact checking, a reporter hits send," Slavin said. "During major events, it takes less than a minute to get thousands of retweets. Even if you submit a correction, your correction isn't going to have the same reach as your initial tweet. It's so easy to disseminate incorrect information it's ridiculous."

Even with the occasional bumps in the road, Slavin said he loves the way he interacts with his audience in real time through various social media platforms.

"One of the great things about social media is the instant reaction," he said. "You know if fans like your content, because they will share or engage with it. You know if they don't like it, because they'll tell you. There are definitely times when you want to ignore some of the engagement and avoid feeding the internet trolls, but there are a lot of

(Continued)

(Continued)

times you can use it for feedback. If you're more of a photographer or videographer, you'll start to build up a network of artists following you that will help critique your work. If you're a feature reporter, you'll undoubtedly get tweets with story ideas or types of stories fans want to hear. It's great."

"One of the other great things your audience can help you with is content creation," he added. "You have to be able to identify the authenticity pretty quickly, but from a brand standpoint, our fans are always sharing photos and memories with us. This helps create strong and extremely authentic content that is incredibly hard to duplicate."

ONE LAST THING

Q: If you could tell the students reading this book anything you think is important, what would it be?

A: "One of the biggest things people don't realize when they jump into a career in social media is that running a brand's social media channels is a HUGE difference than running their personal social media channels. Everyone uses social media differently. Some people use it to keep in touch with friends from high school, others use it to show off their photos of traveling or their newborn baby, and others use it to share funny cat videos they find when they are supposed to be doing work. Ultimately these are all centered around sharing, but the type of content is different, which is a topic that comes into play in the industry all of the time.

"There are people who love straight to the point, factual tweets, while others love sharing funny videos on Facebook. All of these users make up your community and you have to try and please them all as much as possible (or at least identify which fans are more important to your brand). There's definitely a bit of science and psychology involved in working in social media. There's a lot of experimenting and trial and error."

As a reporter, you can gain some credibility and trust because you are associated with a professional media outlet. Beyond that, however, it will be your job to demonstrate that you deserve the respect of your followers. On the other hand, reporters are also consumers of social media, which means you can extend trust to certain social media participants and consider them to be good sources for information. As you find people who post interesting and accurate information, you can add them to your list of worthy sources and quality tipsters.

READ, SHARE, REPEAT

In the days of traditional media, sharing was a physical act, in which you would clip out an article or save a magazine so you could give it to someone you think might be interested in a particular topic. This method was slow and limited to people you could reach either via direct contact or mail. Even more, by the time you thought enough of an article or a topic to cut something out, put it in a safe place and send it off, you probably figured this was not worth the effort.

The benefit of social media is that the interest and the sharing are almost instantaneous. If you find a news article that interests you, you can pin it on a Pinterest board, post it to your Facebook wall or tweet out a link. Even if you use "older" forms of digital media, like email, you can rely on the social media platforms to warehouse the content you want to share and then send off an email to someone with the direct link to the content. This approach happens rapidly, and you can share it with multiple people at the same time, regardless of where they are.

SOCIAL MEDIA TOOLS FOR YOUR TOOLBOX

One of the best things about social media is that it's always changing and adapting to the needs of users. The scalability for each platform gives the users options to reach more people as the platform continues to expand in usefulness and popularity.

For example, the earliest incarnation of Twitter was meant as a way to stay connected with people you knew through a **Short Message Service (SMS)** approach. To aid in that process, Twitter's initial prompt was "What are you doing?" Once the tool became more widespread and used for everything from breaking news to marketing clothing, the company decided in 2009 to change the prompt to "What's happening?" Other elements, such as the use of direct messaging, the creation of a **hashtag** element and the way the company allowed third-party applications to use the platform, all aided in its growth and development.

Here is an example of a collection of "pinned" items that someone has gathered on Pinterest. The board allows for people to save and share items of interest on a wide array of topics.

Even as the platforms, apps and other digital trinkets change from day to day in terms of presence and usefulness, several underlying values and typologies will likely persist. To that end, the next part of the book will divide social media options into different segments to show you the various tools available to you. That section will also discuss a few of the current items that best exemplify those segments and talk a bit about how they can be helpful to you as a journalist:

TEXT

The written word remains a dominant force in the field of journalism because of its pliability and simplicity. Social media has changed the way we use text in a variety of ways, including options to create long-form narratives and interactive elements without having to worry about the restrictions of traditional media. Blogging, long derided by professional journalists as a second-rate form of content, has blossomed as a valuable way to cover micro-niches of information. Bloggers often can reach specific audiences through text as they integrate hyperlinks, visuals and other elements that traditional platforms like print and broadcast cannot.

On the other hand, social media has forced us to shrink content to only a handful of words. **Microblogging** is a simple concept of sharing small bits of information with a wide array of people. In many cases, people who see what the users post can socially boost it, either by sending the content to other followers or by signifying its importance through some sort of "liking" process, akin to the one Facebook uses.

This approach to social media relies on making clear points in short bursts of text. The content in these forms of information dissemination can include a link to a larger story, with the short text message serving as an enticing headline. In other cases, they can launch a threaded discussion of short responses, akin to what readers might encounter on a website's message board or an article's comment section. Below are a few tools that rely heavily on text to reach interested audiences on a variety of devices:

If you are responsible for sending tweets that represent your organization, keep these helpful hints in mind:

Noun-verb-object (NVO): the core of a tweet: If you passed a beginning-level journalism or English class, you know that a sentence needs a noun and a verb, with a direct object (or other object) serving as a nice additional element. In most cases, the idea of "who did what to whom" serves as the core of good journalism writing in print and on the web. It becomes crucial for good tweets.

As we discussed in Chapter 3, consider using the NVO elements to create a tweet's "core" and then build outward from the core, with each concentric ring adding more value. This idea also allows you to more easily trim information when you need to.

Tweet to be read: When text-messaging services became available, most people did their tweeting and texting using a simple 12-digit keypad. This limitation made it more difficult to convey longer ideas or to write in complete thoughts. Since those early days, phones have incorporated full QWERTY keyboards, and tweeting can also come from desktops, laptops and tablets, making the typing and editing much easier.

With 280 characters, you can make your point without forcing your readers to reach for the Rosetta Stone to figure out your tweet. If you punch down your thoughts and they are too long to fit into a single tweet, look for ways to swap longer words for shorter ones. You can also rely on some of the old print headline rules, such as using numerals instead of spelling out numbers. However, keep simplicity at the front of your mind.

Spelling and grammar count: Not every tweet will be an award winner, but you can make sure you don't end up on a series of "Twitter fail" websites if you check your tweet over for spelling and grammar. In some cases, the spelling problems just make you look dumb, as is the case with the laundry list of "Twitter fails" that The Poke gathered. These

include people describing problems with their "selfstream" (self-esteem) or the concerns one user had about her grandmother's "die of beaties" (diabetes).[4]

However, in some cases, a typo can cause a major catastrophe. The makeup and beauty company Sephora made the mistake of failing to proofread a tweet that went out to thousands of users. The company used the tag #CountdownToBeauty as a way to promote the opening of its first store in Australia. However, the person who sent the tweet didn't realize that the "o" in "Countdown" was missing, thus leading to a vulgar message and an unrelenting amount of scorn from the Twitterverse.[5]

A longtime copy editor once noted that you can drown just as easily in a couple inches of water as you can in the Pacific Ocean. The point was that the small things can be just as dangerous as the big ones. When it comes to those 280 characters, check each and every one of them before hitting the send button.

Keep an audience-centric focus: Twitter allows you to pump out information quickly and from almost any venue. This gives you a great opportunity to reach your audience whenever you want. That said, you can't forget that people on the other end of your Twitter account only want content that relates to their lives.

People who follow you won't want to know about your personal problems or your thoughts on every single event of the day. They have lives to lead themselves, so unless you can show them why something matters to them, they will likely stop following you. You should keep an audience-centric focus when you take to Twitter as a purveyor of information. That means you should not only consider what you should or shouldn't tweet, but also when you should tweet and how often you should tweet. If you don't give people enough information when they need it, your readers can feel isolated and ignored. If you constantly pepper your audience with every nuanced moment of a speech or news conference, you can become as annoying as a toddler pulling on his mother's sleeve for attention. This can be a fine line to walk, but as you get used to using Twitter, meeting the needs of your audience will become second nature to you.

Be careful with the tweets of others: Good journalists vet information prior to reporting it as their own, and that traditional value should translate clearly to Twitter. Reporters wouldn't go on live TV with a rumor or publish secondhand information as fact in a newspaper without fully checking it out. However, so many people are more than willing to click the "retweet" button on things that come flying through their Twitter feeds without giving them a second glance.

As a reporter, you can consider Twitter to be a source for hints and tips, but before you share the information you get there, make sure it is right. The internet has a way of creating rumors or half-truths that people continue to pass along as facts. It also has a way of watching rock-solid facts get warped through misinterpretation and resharing. It doesn't take a lot of extra time for you to check out the facts of a tweet before you retweet it. If you take the time to make sure things are right, your readers will thank you.

TWITTER

Of all of the microblogging platforms that have emerged within a short period of time, Twitter has become the dominant force for both disseminating and receiving short bits of information. Each tweet is sent to a group of followers the user has established, and those followers can then modify, respond to or retweet the information. In November 2017, Twitter doubled the maximum size of a tweet, providing users with a 280-character limit. Reaction to the change was mixed, as many users argued more useful options would have been more appreciated. Even with this change, it is best to focus on short, tight tweets. The underlying aspects of tweeting listed in the "Helpful Hints" box are still valid, even if the larger character limit becomes the standard for Twitter.

Twitter helps you connect with your readers and helps your readers connect with you, all in real time.

Twitter is an outstanding platform for reaching readers of a given interest through hashtags and direct messages. In addition, it offers you the opportunity to provide up-to-the-minute content updates as a situation continues to unfold. For example, #CharlieHebdo and #JeSuisCharlie emerged in January 2015 in the wake of a violent assault at the offices of Charlie Hebdo, a satirical French publication that had drawn cartoons mocking the Prophet Muhammad. The first hashtag drew attention to the shooting, which was linked to Islamic extremists, and allowed readers worldwide to follow the developing story. The second hashtag was used as a solidarity movement to show sympathy and connection between people around the world and the slain journalists.

A reporter can use this platform to find sources on the ground near a developing news event or to find people with an interest in a general topic that the reporter is covering. Reporters can also use this tool to update readers as to developing situations, such as traffic crashes, important governmental meetings and even sports scores.

Reddit provides readers with an opportunity to voice their opinions on stories of interest in thousands of niche topics. The up and down votes determine the overall value of the content, as well as its placement, on the site.

REDDIT

This social media tool bills itself as "The Front Page of the Internet," based on its information aggregation and social interaction aspects. Users submit links to a variety of categories, including Education, Entertainment, Humor and Technology. Within each of these categories are **"subreddits"** that focus on specific areas of interest where readers can go deeper into narrower topics. For example, Education has a subreddit for News, which is then divided into dozens of other subtopics like world news, politics and business.

Readers of these posts can respond to them as part of an ongoing discussion. They can rate these posts by "voting up" or "voting down" each individual link. The most popular links rise to the top of the subreddit page and remain there until something more popular moves them down. The site includes search functions based not only on search terms of interest by the reader, but also through filter options that prevent dominant topics from overwhelming other content that might be of interest to readers. For example, a series of news "filters" listed in 2017 for the world news section included "Filter Trump," "Filter Syria/Iraq" and "Filter Israel/Palestine." You can subscribe to certain Reddit feeds and subreddits so you can receive alerts when new topics emerge or when particular topics are getting "hot." Many of the subreddits are monitored for quality or have specific rules to them to prevent things from getting out of hand.

Reporters can see a number of benefits from engaging with the Reddit site.

- First and foremost, they can see the trends in certain areas of interest, such as what stories are most popular in the wake of a big national or worldwide event. This can help reporters find stories of interest to track or follow as they look for ways to localize the topic or assess its impact on their audiences.

- Beyond that, many of the subreddits contain active posters on niche topics that could be helpful when a reporter needs a source on a given topic. For example, an entertainment reporter might be interested in what gamers think about the release of a new video game system or new title. The "Gaming" subreddit could be a good source for reporters to get a general sense of what serious gamers think of the new release.

- In addition, it is possible to contact sources of those posts with the hopes of establishing contact for an interview on the topic for a story. Having Reddit as a "clearinghouse" of sorts for a large array of people who are actively engaged on a variety of topics can be helpful for you as you work on stories where you have little initial insight or a limited number of sources. That said, as with any open source anonymous forum, you run the risk of dealing with people who don't conform to the same standards of fact checking and ethics you might. Don't assume the sources here are rock solid or that the people you interview always have the best of intentions. As stated throughout the book, make sure you are sure before you publish.

STORIFY

One of the things noted earlier in this book is that the giant array of content online tends to overwhelm readers. The purpose of Storify, according to its creators, is break through the noise and make sense of what people post on social media. People who use Storify practice many of the same strategies that traditional journalists use to tell stories. Users search a wide array of social media platforms, such as Facebook, Twitter, Flickr and others, and they gather content on particular topics of interest. The users then assemble those bits and bites of information to tell a coherent story to a larger audience.

This story can be in the form of a timeline, in which the user wants to recount how a developing event emerged in a chronological form. For example, in July 2012, James Holmes entered a movie theater in Aurora, Colorado, during the premier of "The Dark Knight Rises" and opened fire on the audience. Holmes killed 12 people and injured 70 others in the attack. In the wake of the shooting, The Denver Post used Storify to build a 4-day timeline primarily out of tweets from various witnesses, stakeholders and journalists. The story they told included links to Post photos and graphics as well as photos and tweets that other people published.[6]

Storify users can also develop more traditional stories through the use of the inverted-pyramid approach or by creating a series of informational "chunks" on various subtopics. About five months after the Aurora shooting, gunman Adam Lanza fatally shot 20 children and six adults at Sandy Hook Elementary School, drawing massive media attention to Newtown, Connecticut. Digital Media First compiled a Storify that was a collection of various links to blogs, detailed newspaper stories and other media reports on the shooting. The organization broke the coverage down into specific subtopics, such as information about the event, background on the shooter, the list of victims and information about the town.[7]

When you use Storify to help readers understand a given topic, you can arrange your content however you see fit, much in the way you can determine order within a traditional news story. The selections you make from other people's feeds and posts mimic the choices you make in selecting sources and quotes for inclusion in your piece. The crucial element here is that you have to gather as much information as you can find and then determine what best tells the story.

VISUALS

When you share photographs with your audience members on social media, you can take them to the scene of an exciting event, give them a sliver of time that will awe them or help them easily understand a concept that's difficult to describe via text. Visuals are like any other tool you have in your storytelling toolbox: Using them just to use them undermines their value and limits your effectiveness in getting your message to your readers. With that caveat in mind, here are a couple popular social media tools and some ways you can use them to reach your audience:

INSTAGRAM

This visually based social networking tool gives people the ability to shoot and share photos with their phones and other mobile devices. Instagram integrates some of the crucial aspects of other social media options, such as the ability to add text, Twitter handles and hashtags to augment coverage on a topic. In addition, users can share the images on platforms that reach people on Facebook and Twitter. Over the past few years, Instagram added a video feature, which allowed it to keep pace with potential competitors like Snapchat and Periscope.

Social media platforms, apps and sites have grown and developed over the past 10 years or so to help users share information through all sorts of communication formats. Throughout that time, most of the outlets discussed here have in some way crossed paths with Facebook.

Facebook serves as a hub through which almost 1.2 billion people travel on a monthly basis and that draws strength through its pairings with other social media options. For example, Twitter, Instagram, Flickr and other social media tools allow users to have the content they share simultaneously posted to their Facebook profiles. In addition, most websites now contain an option for readers to use their Facebook profile to log in as commenters and post content to a user's Facebook wall.

However, the question of Facebook's ability to create "social bubbles" for readers has led to concern among journalism practitioners and media scholars alike. Critics have charged that Facebook had a responsibility to eliminate false news, much of which was created purposefully by think tanks and internet trolls, as that content had real consequences.[8] A BuzzFeed analysis of Facebook news content leading up to the 2016 presidential election showed that fake news outperformed real news stories in terms of engagement.[9]

When it comes to figuring out what to believe and how to keep fake news from conning you, here are some simple suggestions:

- **"Who told you that?"** This is a common question many parents of young children ask when the kids hop in the car after school and tell a story that strains credulity. Parents always look at the source: a little kid. They also look at the primary source: "Who told you that?" Usually, it isn't a teacher or a principal or another trusted adult source, but instead, it's "that one kid" who has a really active imagination and loves

the attention. Apply the same rule to your media diet when you are reading content online: "Who told you that?" Legacy media, like the Washington Post and the New York Times, as well as major news networks (ABC, CBS, NBC) tend to have more credibility than "JimmyRulesTheUniverse.blogspot.com". It's not to say that bloggers are always wrong and major media outlets are always right, but always consider the source as part of your investigative process.

- **Strength in numbers:** This goes along with the first point, in that a blog can break major news, and if it turns out to be true, a lot of other journalists are likely to run similar stories quickly. Do an internet search for any other stories on the topic, using keywords. The more stories you find on a topic, the more likely that story is to have some merit.

- **The root of the rumor:** Just because a quick Google search yields a ton of stories on a topic, it doesn't always follow that you are going to be "fake free." Keep in mind, you need to read those other stories to make sure they aren't just citing the first story as their only source. Good stories will have multiple root sources, with various publications, websites and television broadcasts all using their own reporting with multiple, varied sources to confirm information. If you rely on stories with many, quality sources, it will help you separate the weak pieces from the stronger ones.

- **Click the links:** Much like citations in a research paper, links are supposed to provide clear evidence that supports the claims a journalist wants to make. However, just like students who are trying to fake their way through a last-minute research paper, some writers will cram their stories full of links that add no value with the idea of trying to fake people into believing the piece's main idea. When you see a link, click it to see if it really supports what the writer had to say. Also, see if it links to an outside source or if it's linking to another post or piece by that same author. Click around on the links within a story to see how strong the legs of the story actually are.

- **Be suspicious:** Humorist Jean Shepherd titled his 1966 novel "In God We Trust. All Others Must Pay Cash." Former President Ronald Reagan once noted of his dealing with Russia in nuclear disarmament that he would "trust, but verify." (The source of that is actually an old Russian proverb.) The core idea of both of these premises is simple: Be suspicious of what you are told until you can independently verify it through sources you trust. This is particularly true of things that merely reinforce your own worldview or stories that don't seem to match up well with reality. A good way to process "facts" that concern you is to presume everything you are told in a story is incorrect until you can prove to yourself that it isn't. You may seem paranoid or overly suspicious to some people, but at least you won't get duped.

Beyond the basics of sharing selfies and augmenting images with filters, Instagram has value for journalists in the field. This tool is great for people attempting to capture and share images from a breaking news situation or a visually engaging moment in time. In addition, the app allows users to geotag images, helping journalists better provide geographic reference points for their readers.

As a research tool, journalists can review Instagram feeds of other people to find out what happened at a major event prior to the arrival of the media or authorities. They can also use the tool to reach out to the shooters of those images to gain information from them, much in the same way a reporter would interview a witness at the scene of an accident or a crime.

Neil Shea is a long-form narrative writer who uses Instagram.

SNAPCHAT

This mobile app allows you to take photos and videos to send to friends and other contacts. Snapchat allows people to add filters, doodles and text to the photo or video prior to sending it. In addition, the receiver can "snapback" at the person who sent the original message, allowing the pair to engage in a back-and-forth conversation over the app. The app launched in 2011, and within three years users were sending more than 700 million snaps per day.[10]

What makes Snapchat different from other social media apps is that the content is preprogrammed to self-destruct within 10 seconds of the receiver viewing the message. However, options within the app allow you to create stories through a collection of videos and photos that

Snapchat gives you a chance to tap into a variety of interest areas with visuals and text.

you can package and broadcast to followers, specific friends or the entire world. The app also has options for re-viewing previous snaps and even saving snaps you send or receive.

In 2015, Snapchat launched its Discover feature, which gives users the ability to follow various professional media outlets that use Snapchat to send out bits and bites of information to app users. Much in the way that Twitter can reach mobile users with short blasts of breaking news or information about a developing story, the Snapchat Discover feature provides journalists with a similar option just with a different app and more visual options. Journalists and media outlets noted that this form of social media will be helpful in engaging potential news consumers and drawing them into longer form content as well.[11]

VIDEO

The line between social media tools that provide still images and those that convey content via video is a muddy one at best. Even though the apps and many current cameras allow you to capture both photographs and video at the same time, as discussed in Chapter 10, there are some crucial reasons to use video. Rather than rehash those here, below are a couple of video-related social media tools that can be helpful as you gather and share information with your audience:

YOUTUBE

This site serves as the standard bearer for video uploads and sharing. According to a 2014 analysis, the site received approximately 300 hours of new videos every minute.[12] The site allows users to upload videos of varying lengths and quality for anyone with access to the site via the web or a YouTube mobile app. The site offers long-term storage of the videos as well as standard video playback features. Like other forms of social media, YouTube allows users to rate and share content as well as follow and subscribe to the feeds of various users. The site contains a wide array of content, including music videos, television show clips, movie trailers and original films.

In terms of journalistic opportunities, the site allows the creation of user-specific "channels" where users can upload and store content for viewers to watch at any time. The site also offers video blogging options, advertising capabilities and an expansive reach for content. Perhaps even more important, this social media channel allows citizen journalists to aid the mainstream media in telling stories and also to tell their own stories without the proverbial middleman. According to the Pew Research Center study mentioned earlier, 39 percent of all videos news organizations use comes from raw footage shot by nonprofessionals.

In addition, YouTube provides a home base for videos that have gone **viral**, thus exponentially expanding the videos' reach. For example, in 2015, a number of protests on the campus of the University of Missouri drew national attention. Protestors called for the resignation of UM President Timothy Wolfe and University Chancellor R. Bowen Loftin after a series of racial and workplace related issues raised concerns regarding leadership quality throughout the educational system.

After both men resigned, journalists attempted to capture the resulting actions of protestors, who had taken over Carnahan Quad on the Mizzou campus. Those on the quad clashed with photographer Tim Tai regarding the journalist's right to be present at the event. Student Mark Schierbecker captured the exchange between Tai and several protestors on video. Near the end of that confrontation, assistant professor Melissa Click confronted Schierbecker and called for "some muscle" to remove him from the quad.[13] Schierbecker's video went viral on YouTube, with more than 2.8 million views. A second longer version, which included his run-in with Click, garnered another 355,000. Other users subsequently uploaded versions of his video, the news coverage of it as well as "memed" versions of the video.

YouTube provides you with the opportunity to provide video content to your audience as well as share the video of others to help inform the people you serve.

PERISCOPE AND FACEBOOK LIVE

These services allow users to create live streaming video and broadcast it to anyone else using this platform. It combines the video-sharing approach of YouTube, the immediacy of Twitter and the underlying concepts of Skype. Megan Pruitt of Social Media Week equated Periscope to having "your own live TV station."[14] One advantage it has over its competition is that you can make your broadcast available for replay for people who missed it live. Periscope, which is owned by Twitter, drew more than 1 million users within less than two weeks of its launch. Facebook later followed with its Facebook Live platform, which has many of the same benefits as Periscope. Given its dominance of the social media field, it is possible that Facebook will surpass Periscope in market share by the time this book hits the shelves.

Many local bands and DJs use these social media tools to showcase their skills and draw followers as well. Businesses have used the video service to conduct live product demonstrations or to take viewers behind the scenes of their operation.[15] As on Twitter, you can follow specific "scopers," and as on Facebook, you can show your support for users. (In this case, it's through giving the broadcasters "hearts" for their efforts.) The app also integrates "push" notifications, so when a broadcast occurs in one of your preset areas of interest, Periscope will alert you to the new "scope."

Journalists can use this tool to get in front of breaking news stories. Anna Jasinski at PR Newswire for Journalists called Periscope "a game changer," noting that early users in March 2015 covered an explosion in New York City with live footage before the traditional media outlets even arrived.[16] The app works with hashtags in the same way Twitter does, so you can title a broadcast with a tweetable headline to garner viewers. In addition, you can allow people watching your video to weigh in with comments and thoughts, thus increasing your interaction with your audience.

Aside from breaking news situations, Jasinski notes that journalists can use short live videos to promote upcoming pieces on other platforms or to seek sources for stories that need help. It is also possible, she says, to conduct a Q&A with your audience.

LIONEL BONAVENTURE/Getty Images

Blogs serve a variety of purposes for journalists, including as sources of information, sites filled with sharable content and as a way to reach readers with content beyond traditional media.

BLOGGING

The term **"blog"** came from a shortened version of "web log" and was one of the earliest forms of mass communication opportunities for many people who wanted to write online content. The writings tended to take a diary-style approach, with the most recent content showing up first on the site and older posts being pushed deeper down the page. This gave dedicated readers the opportunity to easily find the most recent missives of their favorite writers and new audience members the ability to easily dig through the history of the blog.

Sites like Blogger and LiveJournal launched in the late 1990s and gave the general public an opportunity to create online diary-style pages of content. Unlike traditional media, the blog posts were done in a variety of styles and sizes, giving authors the ability to format their work as they saw fit. The size of the posts varied from author to author, and the use of language varied as well, a clear departure from space-driven, style-monitored professional journalism. As blogging became even easier and more popular, many mainstream media outlets and professional journalists tried their hand at the approach, with varying levels of success. Consider these suggestions as to how best to approach this form of journalism:

FOCUS ON AUDIENCE INTERESTS

Blogs often serve niche interests, and as such, your readers will have specific desires when they click on your site. To retain as much of your audience as you can, you should establish the purpose of the blog and then adjust it based on the interests and needs of the readers. For example, if you decide to publish a blog that explores the issues sixth-graders face in private schools, you may find an active and engaged readership. The more you learn about the people who are surfing your site, the more you will know if you should focus on boys, girls or both. You will also learn whether your blog is more popular with students than with their parents, which will require you to adjust your topics and the way you address your audience. You might also determine which types of topics will draw more readers or push readers away.

ESTABLISH A TONE

Traditional news journalism has long relied on the use of facts and quotes to create a clear, objective approach to conveying information. Agencies like the Associated Press (AP) and United Press International served to guide the style and structure of the content, while organizations like the Society of Professional Journalists provided ethical standards for practitioners. This sense of "tone" helped provide consistency across the field.

In the world of blogging, you can set your own tone based on how many of those tenets you want to embrace and how many of them just cramp your style. As you adjust your language and

HELPFUL HINTS ➡ HOW BEST TO USE SOCIAL MEDIA FOR YOUR AUDIENCE

The number of social media tools you can use to share information has the potential to overwhelm people. When you decide to use social media as a journalist, it is important to keep a few things in mind so you can provide the best overall experience for your audience members:

- **Content is king:** The one rule above all else in journalism is that if the content is good, people will want to see it. All of the gizmos, gadgets and grandstanding can't replace strong, clear reporting on valuable topics. If you don't have anything important to say, don't waste your audience members' time shoving it at them via 237 social media platforms. All you are doing is annoying them.

- **Right tool for the right job:** Each of the tools outlined above, and the hundreds of others that will continue to develop in the next few years, has a specific purpose. You need to make sure that you figure out what benefits and drawbacks are associated with each of them before you use them. Then, you can use the tool effectively for your audience members. A Periscope video of a student government meeting is likely going to be as boring as watching paint dry. Live-tweeting a football game after every play will be as annoying as a pestering 3-year-old in a candy store. Figure out what your audience will want and how each tool can get it to them. Then ply your trade with their needs in mind.

Social media allows you to link to audience members in a wide and viral pattern. Taking advantage of social media will allow you to spread your message far and wide.

- **Less is more:** Social media tools continue to emerge at a rapid pace, giving citizens and journalists a vast pool of options when it comes to getting information out to an interested audience. However, as discussed earlier in the book, the desire to be first on every platform and with every tool can lead to "shiny-object syndrome." Instead of chasing after every app and trend that social media throws at you, become well versed in one or two dominant tools per communication method. For example, don't have 29 video apps and sites that you pump random content out to. Instead, pick one or two video tools or platforms and grow a quality audience for each of them. This will help you showcase your skills as a professional and keep you focused on the crucial element of journalism: storytelling.

approach to content, you will want to consider your readers' needs and the expectations they have regarding your work.

For example, ESPN.com and Deadspin.com both use their websites to cover sports on a national level. However, ESPN relies more heavily on a traditional tone, including the use of third-person writing for most news stories, a stronger sense of the inverted pyramid and the AP's approach to word choices. Deadspin has no problem using profanity in its work or having its writers infuse themselves and their thoughts into the content. (A headline like "So, the Warriors Got Their Asses Kicked" is among the more PG-rated examples.) The tone for each website works well because the audience members know what to expect. When you build your own blog, make sure you know your readers well enough to understand which tone will work best for you and them.

OFFER QUICK READS

Just because the internet allows you to write an infinite number of words with impunity, it doesn't follow that your readers will read all of them. As noted elsewhere in the book, the average human has an 8-second attention span, so you need to get to your readers quickly and give them what they need in a hurry. Look for ways that you can provide simple bits and bites of information with links to larger stories. In the case of posts that delve into analysis, you might want to hit the highlights up top before going deeper into your own "take" on the topic. Regardless of your approach, consider this basic blogging adage: If you wouldn't take the time to read it, don't take the time to write it.

BE TIMELY

Traditional news publications had deadlines that attached themselves to the physical creation of a product. Newspapers needed to be printed and delivered, so writers, photographers, designers and editors adhered to strict time restrictions as they completed their work. News broadcasts went live at 5, 6 and 10 p.m., thus forcing reporters, editors, producers and anchors to be ready by that time with all the stories for that newscast. Digital media has both a 24/7 news cycle and a total lack of deadline, leading to both positive and negative outcomes.

If traditional journalists missed a deadline, the news outlet didn't carry their stories, photos or videos. The reporters would have to wait until the next day or the next deadline to publish their work. Digital journalists, on the other hand, can produce content immediately upon learning something newsworthy. This gives them an advantage over their traditional counterparts. However, without a true "deadline" to keep their feet to the fire, digital journalists don't have the same pressure to get something done as traditional journalists. With that in mind, digital journalists need to force themselves to be timely in everything they do.

When you get information you believe to be factually accurate, post it right away. As you find additional nuggets of news, post those as well, keeping your readers up to date on the topic at hand. Your goal in producing a blog is to both be timely in terms of getting content posted and keeping people engaged with ongoing news.

5 SOCIAL MEDIA

THE BIG THREE

Here are the three key things you should take away from this chapter:

1. **Content is still king:** Regardless of what approach you take to social media, you need to realize that the old adage "garbage in, garbage out" still applies. Social media users expect value each time you reach out to them, so don't waste their time with worthless content. Your ability to use the latest app won't impress them, but your ability to give them useful information will.

2. **Right tool for the right job:** Don't use every social media tool on Earth just to prove the point that you're good at using social media. If you spread yourself too thin or you become repetitive across channels, your work will suffer and your audience will disappear. Think about how each of the tools

discussed in the book, such as video, photos and text, provide specific values to your audience members. Then, play to the strength of each tool when you decide how to convey your content to your readers and viewers.

3. **Be careful:** Social media can be deadly to you and your users. An ill-advised tweet or a shared Facebook post that you failed to fact-check can undo years of accumulated credibility. Before you click on the retweet button or share some information, stop and think about what you are sharing and how it could come back to hurt you. Only after you confirm the facts or verify the information should you pass it along to your audience.

KEY TERMS

blog 90	one-to-many model 75	subreddit 84
hashtag 81	post 75	viral 88
many-to-many model 75	Short Message Service 81	Web 2.0 76
microblogging 81	social media 75	

DISCUSSION QUESTIONS

1. What social media platforms do you use? Whom do you follow on those platforms? Do you tend to follow the same people or different people across platforms? What made you choose these platforms and these sources for information on them?

2. People who use social media tend to opt in to networks of like-minded individuals. What do you

see as the benefits and drawbacks to picking out a few trusted media outlets and ignoring the rest?

3. How do you view social media in comparison with more traditional media, such as newspaper outlets and broadcast news operations? What makes these social media options better than these traditional organizations? What makes social media worse?

WRITE NOW!

1. Select one of the dominant social media platforms you use frequently (Twitter, Facebook, Snapchat, Instagram etc.) and analyze your social networks. Categorize the people (or groups) you "follow" on this platform by dividing them into areas that best explain who they are, such as "family," "high school friend," "sports star" and "media outlet." Do the same for the list of people and groups that follow you. Which groups have the most members? Which people or organizations do you attend to the most? Do these groups differ between the folks you follow and those who follow you? Write a short essay that encapsulates your findings.

2. Select a social media tool that you think has value as a storytelling option. Research the tool and provide a biography for the tool, including who created it, how long it has been around and any other relevant issues associated with it. Then, outline how you think you can best tell stories with this tool. What are some of the positives associated with the tool and what are some of the drawbacks? Write a short essay on your findings. Include examples of how you have seen the tool used well and poorly.

3. Below are several sets of facts that could be used to create a news story. Use each set to create a tweet of no more than 250 characters (saving 30 characters for links to the article and retweet possibilities). Focus on the noun-verb-object construction, and avoid "text speak" ("U" instead of "you" etc.) in your tweets.

   a. State Highway Patrol officers responded to a call of a disruption to traffic on Interstate 21 early Tuesday morning. Upon arriving, police found that a 2010 Nissan Xterra had struck a 1997 Toyota minivan. The Xterra's driver lost control of his vehicle and slammed into the minivan, crushing it into the concrete guardrail on the left side of the freeway. The driver of the minivan, Jayne Johansen, 34 years old, was pronounced dead at the scene. The other two passengers, Jack Johansen, 8 years old, and Carl Johansen, 5 years old, were taken to a local hospital, where they later died. The driver of the Xterra, whose name has not been released, was arrested on suspicion of vehicular homicide. The officers say alcohol was a contributing factor to the crash.

   b. The Monroe City Council met Monday night to discuss several issues, including the fate of Windborne Lake. The city owns the artificial lake and land around it, but recently developers have asked about acquiring the property. Davis Group petitioned the council last month, asking to purchase the land for $3 million. The council held a vote Monday as to if that offer should be accepted. The council voted 7-2 in favor of the offer.

   c. Coach Jerry Gibb of the Homestate University Stallions football team called a press conference Thursday afternoon. He noted that he had recently been made aware of several incidents of teamwide hazing. He acknowledged that hazing is against university policy and state law. He investigated the complaints and found that three members of the team had engaged in hazing. Starting running back James Jackson, third-string wide receiver Billy Combs and backup punter Chester Charles did haze freshmen teammates. As a result, Gibb said he had suspended the players for Saturday's game. The Stallions play the division-rival Cougars of Jonesburg College.

YOU NEVER KNOW WHAT THE FUTURE HOLDS.

▶ Visit the author's blog at
dynamicsofwriting.com

Stay up to date on the latest in journalism

DYNAMICS OF WRITING

Remembering that first journalism class: "I was scared out of my mind."

I was recently on a panel that discussed student media and self-censorship. Most, if not all, of the people on the panel were former journalists and several people in the audience had made the transition to the field to the classroom. One theme that came up repeatedly was the way in which students "these days" didn't have SOMETHING about them. It might be drive, it might be curiosity or it might be a skill. In any case, many of the people who spoke recalled that when THEY were students at THAT age, THEY had whatever it was that the students today seemed to lack in their estimation.

Search ...

Categories

Select Category

Shredded Tweets

Tweets by
@DoctorOfPaper

Vincent Filak
@DoctorOfPaper

In the most over-the-top way possible? twitter.com/Poynter
/status...

6 INTERVIEWING

LEARNING OBJECTIVES

After completing this chapter you should be able to:

- Prepare for an interview by creating open-ended and closed-ended questions that are based on the research you conducted.

- Compare and contrast the various types of interviewing opportunities and understand the similarities and differences germane to them.

- Be able to approach a source for an interview and then conduct it in a way that creates a smooth flow of ideas between the source and you.

- Identify problematic questions and be able to restructure them to improve the interaction with your source.

- Conceptualize the value of a source and the information you need to get from the source, and critically think about how best to approach and interview the individual.

THINKING AHEAD: AVOIDING THE AWKWARDNESS WHILE SPEAKING TO OTHERS

The ability to speak with other people and gain information is a basic element of everyday life. From asking a server what the restaurant's special is all the way through to finding out how your best friend's day went, life is a series of questions and answers. You ask questions, you get answers and you gain knowledge. At its very core, this is the premise behind interviewing.

Beginning journalists often note that interviewing is a stressful and awkward aspect of the job. They fear asking stupid questions, getting rude reactions and finding

themselves lacking the information necessary to write a good story. Even veteran journalists note a pang of anxiety when they have to approach a new source or conduct a difficult interview.

The purpose of this chapter is to examine what makes for a great interview. We will recap the basics you know and then look at some more complicated issues associated with specific sources and situations. This chapter should leave you with a better overall sense of what should happen before, during and after a good interview.

Steve Debenport/iStock.com

Whether you interview someone one on one or as a member of a journalism pack, it is important to understand who this person is and why she matters to your story.

CRITICALLY THINKING ABOUT INTERVIEWING'S PURPOSE

Before we dive in to the nuts and bolts of interviewing, you need to think about the big picture of interviewing. Although you can memorize the basics of interviewing, you will conduct better interviews if you use some critical-thinking skills. People who use rote actions during interviews fail to understand what they want to accomplish and thus undercut the overall value of speaking with the source. When you begin a story, you often rely on the 5W's and 1H to help you see the most important aspects of your piece. Let's take a look at a few of those basic items in a different way to see how interviewing and critical thinking can intersect and benefit you:

WHO IS THIS PERSON?

This question seems almost too basic, but it is an important one to ask before you approach your subject. As we discussed earlier in the book, you can break your readers down through demographic and psychographic analysis to better understand who they are and what they need. You can use the same approach as you analyze your source before you conduct the interview.

Consider how you might approach interviews about your area's school system in the wake of budget cuts. If you interview the superintendent, you might start with something like, "How are these cuts affecting the classrooms of your district in terms of overcrowding and access to educational materials?" If you wanted a frontline look at how the budget cuts affect the children, you might interview a second-grader with questions like, "How many friends are there in your class?" or "Do you have to share your book, or do you get your own?" Sure, you'll get fewer quotes from the child, but you can follow up with more "how" and "why" questions after you establish your rapport with him or her.

Think about how often this person works with the media. People with a long history of media relations will likely answer questions differently than people who have never worked with a journalist before. If you understand this person's level of experience, you can tailor your questions and your approach to improve the quality of that person's answers. Professional media operatives know how to bob and weave as they dodge questions, so you might need to be more aggressive. First-time interviewees could feel nervous about answering any questions, so you should handle them with a softer touch.

WHAT VALUE DOES THIS SOURCE HAVE TO THE STORY?

A grizzled journalism veteran used to remark that the goal of any media endeavor was to add something to the sum of human knowledge. If you keep that idea in mind when approaching a source, you will better understand the value of that source. Many beginning journalists have the goal of getting a certain number of sources into a story, without determining the degree to which those sources matter to the story. This is particularly true when you look at localization stories and personality profiles.

In the case of localizations, reporters look for people to react to a recent news item in the hope of providing a local flavor for a national or international story. In theory, localizations have the ability to show a "hometown impact" for a broader topic. In practice, reporters often end up asking people at the mall what they think about a complex national policy that they don't understand. This is where understanding value comes into play.

If you have to conduct localization interviews, look for people who can contribute value to your story based on their experiences or their education on a given topic. Instead of asking shoppers what they think about international trade deficits, talk to a local professor of international economics or a business owner who operates in the import/export field. The latter types of people will have a better grip on what has just occurred and a stronger sense of why it matters.

Democratic Senate Candidate Bruce Braley talks with reporters after he escorted his 85-year-old mother Marcia Braley to the polling station Nov. 4, 2014 in his hometown of Brooklyn, Iowa. The value of a source will often determine the amount of effort you put into getting an interview with him or her. Some people are singularly important to a story while others can be easily replaced.

The same concerns regarding value arise in **news features** and **personality profiles**. When you look for an individual you want to profile, you will want some outside sources to discuss that person. That said, you can't make up for lack of quality sources through interviews done in bulk. You need to determine what level of insight a source can provide based on the story you are trying to tell. If you are doing a profile of a professor who just won a major award in the field of nuclear physics, interviewing a dozen students who took her Physics 101 class isn't going to do much for your story. Instead, you should interview the people who presented the award, nationally recognized physicists who can speak on her work and even departmental colleagues.

HOW BADLY DO I NEED THIS SOURCE?

Value often intersects with rarity. The T206 Honus Wagner baseball card, for example, has commanded upward of $2.8 million, in large part because only 50 to 200 copies were ever known to exist. Conversely, millions of copies of today's baseball cards are produced, often making even stars worth only a few pennies each. In a similar vein, when you examine your approach to an interview, you should consider both the rarity and the necessity of a source as it relates to your story. The more places from which you can gather information, the less valuable any one source will be. However, if only one or two people can give you the answers you seek, you might be put in a precarious position.

Think about a story like a county fair. If you are there to do a light news feature on how much fun people are having at the fair, you have a wide array of sources from which to choose. If you approach one family that is playing games at the midway, and no one wants to talk, you can move on to another group of people. However, if you need to find out if the fair broke an attendance record, and only the executive director has that information, you know you have to find her and get that answer.

CONSIDER THIS ➜ EMAIL INTERVIEWS

The acceptability of email interviews varies from situation to situation and from organization to organization. Some journalists see them as an easy way to gain quick access to a source, while others view them as a copout that provides less valuable information compared with a traditional interview. Here are some of the positives and negatives associated with this approach:

Email interviews can be beneficial in some ways and harmful to your work in others. Before you cue up a message and submit questions to a source, think about the pros and cons of this approach.

- **You get quick access for simple answers:** The people you want to reach might be busy at work or trapped in a meeting, but thanks to mobile devices and a quick click of the "reply" button, they can give you what you need right away. If you need a simple answer such as "PAP stands for Pittsville Action Party, right?" or "How old did you say your son was?" a quick email response will do the job quite efficiently.

- **They produce ready-made interview transcripts:** One of the common refrains from people who don't like something written about them is, "I never said that." The best part about email is the ability to capture the exact words your source chose to use and put them into your story verbatim. If a source doesn't like how people reacted to the story and tries the "I never said that" defense, you can publish the email and show that you are right. It's like a security blanket for your reporting.

- **Sources tend to like it:** Rather than spending 20 minutes on the phone or looking for a block of time in the day's schedule, the source can time-shift the interview to the first open moment he or she has and respond quickly at that point. Sources also feel more in control, as they can compose themselves before answering questions and get a stronger sense of how exactly to communicate their feelings in a coherent fashion. Email is ubiquitous, so most sources understand how to use the tool and feel comfortable using it to interact with people.

- **You end up with weaker reporting opportunities:** Email interviews don't allow you the opportunity to follow up on crucial issues right away. With an in-person interview, when a source introduces a topic or offers an opinion, a good reporter can jump in right away and ask for clarification or push back on a misperception. An email interview doesn't allow that. It also doesn't allow you to see how a source will react to a question. If you ask your chancellor, "Is there any truth to the rumor that you are taking a job as chancellor of Southeastern Central College?" his reaction might be worth more than the quote he provides. If he turns red, quickly throws a file from his desk into a drawer and says, "No, why? Where did you hear that?" you know you have something. If you asked that question via email, the chancellor can curse up a blue streak in his office and scream, "WHO TOLD THAT REPORTER ABOUT MY JOB INTERVIEW?" Then, he can calmly sit down at the computer and write, "I have no immediate intention to change jobs, as I love it here at Northwestern Central University."

- **You don't bond with your sources:** The best way to get to know someone is to spend time with that person. Face-to-face interviews and frequent phone calls that include a little small talk can go a long way to create bonds between you and your sources. This can be incredibly valuable when you have big stories or you need an inside tip. If the only thing your sources know about you is your email address, you will never develop those kinds of connections that can lead to exclusive stories.

Before you do an email interview, check with your editor to see what rules exist about them. Also, consider the type of information you need and the type of story you are writing as you determine the viability of an email interview. If email is the right tool for the job and your company allows it, give it a shot. If not, don't be lazy or scared; set up a more traditional interview with your source.

In some breaking-news stories, information is routed through a single public-relations agent, which makes that person crucial to your story. The same concern is true when only one or two people know what happened in a closed-door meeting. If you understand the rarity of a source, you can determine the degree to which you are willing to acquiesce to that person's requests. An important source could demand that you guarantee him anonymity or that you do not release certain details of an event. If you cannot get that information unless you agree to those demands, you and your editor will have to seriously consider these requests. On the other hand, if a family at the county fair demands anonymity before telling you how much they enjoyed the corndogs (laugh if you want to, but this does happen), you can politely decline and move on.

UNDERSTANDING THE INTERVIEWING BASICS

The basic elements of interviewing remain constant, whether you are doing interviews for news, public relations, advertising or any other form of media. Here is a quick walkthrough on those basics:

PREPARING FOR THE INTERVIEW

Before you set out to interview someone, you need to feel fully prepared for that interaction. You need to know enough about the person you will interview and what that person can add to your story before you ask that person to spend time with you. This will help you understand why this person

Getting the interview is one of the most important aspects of your job as a reporter. Where you meet, how long it will be and why you need to speak with the source are all key points that should be fleshed out up front.

matters to you and also how to get the most out of the time you spend with the source. Find out as much about this person as you can by reading previous articles, any information on promotional websites and any trade press (media outlets that cover the person's specific field of interest) to come up with a well-rounded understanding of this person.

GETTING THE INTERVIEW

When you want an interview, you should contact the person via phone or email. This initial contact should establish who you are, what you need and why you think this person has value to your story. You should also explain if the interview needs to be done by a certain point in time and how much of the person's time you will need to conduct the interview. This will establish a set of expectations for your source and help ready him or her for the upcoming interaction.

INTERACTING WITH YOUR SOURCE

When possible, it's best to meet a source face to face. This will establish a stronger bond between you and the source. It will also allow you to observe that person and his or her environment, which is crucial for longer pieces and personality profiles. You should ask to meet your sources on their own turf, be it an office, a home or another place the source frequents. Sources tend to be more relaxed in their natural environment and thus will be more at ease when answering questions. You want to be professional and polite up front, easing into a more laid-back vibe only if the source asks you to ("Don't call me Mr. Smith. You can call me John."). When in doubt about how best to act, mimic your source's behavior and lean toward being slightly more conservative than the source.

WORKING WITH YOUR QUESTIONS

You should come to an interview with a set of prepared questions, many of which are based on things you learned during your investigation of your source. Four or five basic questions will give you a good starting point for standard news pieces, but investigative stories and personality profiles will require more and deeper questions. The goal is to have at least a rough sketch of the big items you want to cover in the interview so that you don't forget to ask something and thus create a gaping hole in your story.

Once you get your questions roughed out, go back over them to make sure you are clear and coherent in what you are asking. In some cases, the questions can make sense in your head, but lose something between your brain and your notepad. You also should ask someone else to review the questions if you aren't sure you are getting your point across. These questions don't need to be the end-all and be-all of your interview, but they should provide a strong foundation for it.

INTERVIEW FLOW

A good story isn't just a series of statements and quotes about a given topic. The piece must have smooth transitions and logical movement within it that will create **flow**. An interview works the same way if you do it well, so you need to have a sense of how your interview will go before you sit down with your source. If you create interlocking questions that will seamlessly move from one topic to another, you can create flow. This will make the

The 5W's and 1H are crucial to telling your story, but most interviews will require you to go a lot deeper than just these simple queries.

The great thing about having someone else look over your questions with you or for you is that sometimes what you mean isn't what you're asking. Here are a few question types that can lead to painful interviews:

Inaccurately based questions: You've likely heard the phrase, "Ask a stupid question, get a stupid answer." Failing to research can lead to questions that aren't factually sound, and therefore land you in exactly that situation. A question like "So, has your company changed a lot since it was purchased by the Japanese?" assumes some critical points. It assumes the company changed in some way (you're asking if it's a lot or a little, not whether it changed). It also assumes the company was purchased by the Japanese. When you find out it was actually purchased by the company's closest rival in the United States, you look ill informed.

Imprecise questions: Comedian George Carlin once quipped that when people asked if he'd always wanted to be a comedian, he responded, "Well, not in the womb, but after that, yes." While it's a bit glib, it brings to light the point of what happens when you don't ask the most precise question. Had these people asked, "At what point in your life did you know that you wanted to be a comedian?" they might have gotten a much better answer.

Loaded questions: It's easy to allow assumptions to wander into your questions. If you ask an athletic director, "Is so-and-so still your football coach?" you imply that reasons exist for that person to be removed. If you ask, "What is the reason you've yet to fire Coach so-and-so?" you imply that this issue is on the table and that the director either has thought about it or should be thinking about it.

Loaded questions create problems because your sources will find themselves answering from a defensive position. In some cases, no good answer exists for these questions. The most famous example of this is the question, "Senator, have you stopped beating your wife yet?" If the senator answers "yes," this implies that he has finally stopped beating his wife. If the senator answers "no," it implies the beatings are still ongoing. A pure answer to that question will not allow the senator to assert his innocence when it comes to the allegations that he is beating his wife.

Running through your questions with someone can help you figure out if the questions are loaded or if they're just hard questions that deserve honest answers. Just because a question could anger a source doesn't mean the question is loaded.

"It made sense when I wrote it" questions: An awful lot goes on between the brain and the pen when it comes to writing down your questions. Sometimes, questions seem brilliant and clear in your mind, so you reach for your notepad to capture your clarity. Unfortunately, when the questions land on the paper, they come across with all the grace of someone falling down a flight of stairs. However, you can't see the problem with a question like this prior to asking it, because it's still clear in your mind. You notice the problem only after you get that awkward look from your source, and then it's too late.

Ask someone to look over your questions and make sure you are making sense. It's a lot better to have a friend or colleague say "I don't get it" than to have a mayor or a senator or even a professor utter that line. When your proofreading friend runs into trouble, try to explain what you meant to him or her. In talking through the problem, you can rework the phraseology to improve the question.

interview feel more like a conversation than a series of random questions. If the interview has this conversational feel, the source will feel more relaxed and thus provide more complete answers. In addition, flow tends to spark secondary questions on important topics, which allows you to dig a bit deeper in those areas.

A reporter makes notes during a news conference with U.S. President George W. Bush. Bush spent nearly an hour fielding questions during his last news conference as president of the United States before President-elect Barack Obama was sworn in on Jan. 20, 2009.

TAKING GOOD NOTES

Make sure you take good notes throughout the interview so you can use the material later when you start writing your story. In addition to taking notes, you should invest in a good digital recorder or a quality app for your smartphone that records conversations. However, don't assume a recorder will save you from having to write things down. Apps fail, batteries run out of juice and digital files get corrupted. Also, some sources will not allow you to use a recorder, or you might not be able to get close enough to a source to make a recording device effective. You should learn to write without looking at your notepad, and you should develop your own form of shorthand to maximize your note-taking ability so you don't miss anything when a source is speaking quickly.

THE END OF THE INTERVIEW

At the end of an interview, you should offer your source an opportunity to speak on a topic that you might have missed. A simple closing question of, "Is there anything else you think I should know?" can give a source the sense you are interested in other topics that matter to him or her. The end of the interview is also a good time to gather information on other potential sources: "You mentioned that (NAME) would be a good source for this story. Could you give me her contact information?" These "cleanup items" can give the source the sense of finality and help you pick up a few extra bits of important information before you leave.

FOLLOWING UP

In the case of a breaking or developing story, you should keep in contact with your sources to make sure your readers have the freshest information possible. If a suspect in a homicide is on the loose, you want to let your audience know the minute that person is caught. If a tight election or bond referendum is coming down to the wire, you will want to tell your readers what the result is and what it will mean to them going forward.

For news features or personality profiles, you should gather multiple "cleanup questions" for your source before sending an email or making a call to that person. Repeated calls to verify name spellings or perform fact checks can annoy the source and undercut your credibility. That said, you should never feel bad about checking back with a source when you aren't sure about something you want to put in your story. It is always better to be slightly annoying than to be wrong.

TYPES OF INTERVIEWS

Below are various types of interviews and some ways you can conduct them. The list, while not exhaustive, reveals a core set of situations you will face as a journalist and how best to prepare for them. (We will talk more about these interviewing approaches in the next few chapters as well.)

Of all the terms associated with interviewing, "**off the record**" is perhaps the most misunderstood. Professional journalists even struggle with exactly what this term means and how they are allowed to use the material an off-the-record source gave them. The underlying assumption of this approach is that a source is trying to present information in a way that cannot be traced back to that person. An off-the-record interview is therefore an agreement between a reporter and a source. Consider these issues before engaging in an off-the-record interview:

Former White House Communications Director Anthony Scaramucci resigned 10 days after he began his job with the Trump campaign after a profanity-laced interview he gave went viral. Scaramucci said he thought the interview was off the record, but the journalist said no such agreement had been negotiated.

- **Did you both agree to go off the record?** An off-the-record conversation requires both parties to consent to the stipulation that this content won't be attributed to the source. A source cannot decide to unilaterally go off the record. If a source attempts this by saying, "Well, off the record, I think . . .," you should stop that source by saying, "No, I don't agree to this, and whatever you say next will be attributed to you." However, once you both agree to go off the record, you should abide by the terms of the arrangement.

- **How will the information be used?** Before you begin the interview and allow the source to go off the record, you need to have a mutual understanding as to how this content will be used. In some cases, the reporter and the source will agree that the content is "not for direct attribution," which means the reporter can use the information, but will not use the source's name. Attributions like "According to a senior White House official" or "A source close to the mayor said" fit this definition. In other cases,

the material is "not for attribution," which means the material can't be attributed to the source, but can be used. A third version of off-the-record material is "deep background," which means the source will reveal the information, but it can't be used without additional independent reporting. This is more of a news tip than a true interview.

- **Is it worth it?** When you go off the record, you need to have a good reason to do so. If you can get the information only from this source, and the information is crucial to your readers, you should give serious consideration to conducting an off-the-record interview. If the source just wants to use your story to throw mud at other people or the source is just being difficult, it's probably not worth risking your reputation.

BREAKING NEWS

Young reporters often find themselves covering a lot of breaking news, which can range from car crashes and fires to hostage situations and tornadoes. Most newsrooms have a police scanner (or multiple police scanners), and when something comes across the airwaves that piques your editor's interest, it's time to grab a notepad, consult a map and get on the road.

Robert Nickelsberg/Getty Images

A journalist covers Washington, D.C. policemen keeping back protesters after the inauguration ceremony confirming Donald Trump as the 45th president of the United States.

Broadcast journalists also spend a good bit of their time at breaking news events, with good reason. The immediacy of the event plays well to the "live" element television offers to its viewers. Quite often, the first indication that something is going on at a scene comes from television reporters and their video cameras. On-scene interviews are important for all media, but broadcast has a special need to make sure it can get an interview with someone during the event.

When you arrive, you might find that the event is still ongoing, as in the case of a 12-hour standoff between an armed man and police. Sometimes you will get there after the event is done and the officials have moved from taking care of a threat to cleaning up after the incident. In either case, your first responsibility is not to your news outlet, your readers or your editor, but to yourself. Always make sure that you are prepared for anything and that you do not put yourself in harm's way to get an interview. You also need to avoid becoming an impediment to the people who are dealing with the crisis.

Your goal at the scene is to make sense of this situation as quickly as possible, so the 5W's and 1H will drive the questions you will ask. Who was involved in the shooting? Why did the man attack the woman? How did the fire start? What are you doing to find suspects? When did you first hear about this accident? Where did the riot begin? Those types of questions are likely to produce a solid opening news story for any medium. In some cases, you'll have multiple questions that emphasize a specific W, such as "Whom do you suspect of stealing from the bank?" and "Who first noticed that all the money was missing?"

The one thing you won't have at your disposal is a lot of background information. You hear about a fire at Main Street and Fifth Avenue, and that is all you know before you head to the scene. You probably don't know if there was a fire there before or if the building has significance. All you know is that you need to get over there and find out what happened. In the case of breaking news, it is permissible to not be fully informed prior to conducting an interview. You can ask a police chief or a firefighter some basic questions without that source looking at you as if you are an ill-prepared fool. That said, certain questions are dumb no matter the circumstances. If you run into the family that just lost all its possessions in the fire, the question "So how do you feel about that?" will only raise the ire of the family in a tense situation and make you look like an insensitive clod.

NEWS CONFERENCE

News conferences give a person or an organization an opportunity to disseminate a single message to multiple media outlets at once. A news conference is a great thing for these folks, because it prevents them from having to release information in drips and drops. It also keeps them from answering the same five questions on the phone or via email all day. It's good for television, because it provides a ready-made event for reporters to cover and videographers to shoot. However, if you are looking for a good interview that yields some specific information, it's one of the worst places to be.

Journalism through these **"pseudo-events"** (a term coined by Daniel Boorstin in his 1961 book "The Image") changes the dynamic of the interview. While the journalist traditionally controls an interview, a news conference allows the source to dictate the content and purpose of the event. The source starts out with a specific message and sets the agenda and the tone for the event. That message is polished and probably prepared with the help of multiple people. Reporters don't get the opportunity to follow up on key issues very often, and the source has the right to walk away from the throng of reporters at any point in the process. What can make a news conference even worse is that you might have a great question on an important topic. If you ask it at a press conference, dozens of reporters, circling like vultures, are ready to take down the answer and report on what should have been your exclusive story.

Lt. J. Paul Vance of the Connecticut Police addresses media by his car before departing a press conference the morning after a mass shooting at Sandy Hook Elementary School.

To find your way around these problems, you want to sit back at most press conferences. Let the other people ask questions first and see what you can pick up. A press conference can be full of journalists who aren't engaging in critical thinking and are more than happy to ask questions in an attempt to show how much they know about the topic. Figure out what other people know and then take notes not only of what the source said, but also some follow-up questions you want the source to answer later.

You also want to talk to people after the news conference and ask a few follow-up questions. If you can catch a source after the big event, you have a chance to get a few good answers that will distinguish your story from that of your reporting colleagues. You can also take that opportunity to poke back at a source who might have said one thing to the smiling faces of the gathering crowd, but had told you something else at a different point in time.

PERSON ON THE STREET

A **person-on-the-street interview** can add flavor to a feature story or add perspective to a news event. While the head of a company, the sponsor of the state fair or the promoter of the event might paint one picture, the front-line worker, the fairgoer or the participant in an event might paint quite another.

While public figures are beholden to the public, private citizens who have done nothing wrong have every right to decline to be interviewed, and you need to respect that. Therefore, you need to approach the person-on-the-street interview differently than you would most other interviews outlined in the chapter. A mayor or an executive who engaged in some newsworthy activity is fair game for media attention, but the "real people," as they are sometimes called, have no duty or obligation to answer a reporter's questions.

Some people are thrilled that their names will be in the paper or that they will be on TV later that night. Other people view your request for an interview as though they've been selected for additional screening while trying to make it through security at the airport. In either case, be polite and explain what you're doing. If you've got video equipment, try approaching slowly and without having the camera aimed at them as you approach.

Jorge Ramos, a news anchor at Univision, is escorted out of a news conference. Ramos later returned to the news conference and argued with President Donald Trump about his immigration policy for nearly 5 minutes.

HOSTILE

When a controversial story breaks, some sources can be rude, intimidating and threatening. They can do their best to try to get you to back off and leave them alone. Regardless of how much bluster someone foists in your direction, you have every right to ask questions of someone who did something that has wronged the public.

You aren't asking questions for your benefit, but for the benefit of the readers you serve. The public has the right to know if the mayor stole from the town reserve or if the gym coach was arrested for assaulting a student. Your duty to be fair and balanced requires that you call people and ask them to justify their actions or explain themselves to your audience. You might feel awkward or scared in this situation.

You need to steel yourself against what is sure to be an unpleasant exchange with the source and focus on the issue at hand, making sure that you are even-handed in your approach to the subject. The mayor might not have stolen, but instead might be the victim of a political hatchet job. The coach might not have assaulted a player, but the student made the accusation because the coach cut him from the basketball team. Regardless of how weird you feel in these situations, you must offer the key players in your story the opportunity to speak.

Prior to making that phone call or seeking that hostile source, you need to figure out exactly what you need to know up front and be ready with the hard questions. While other interviews require you to throw a few softball questions to loosen the subject up, a guaranteed hostile interview requires you to be direct. You need not be caustic in your approach, but you have to get to the heart of the issue quickly, as your first question might be your last.

If you get information from the source, you need to make sure that you check that information with other sources. In the case of a contentious situation, such as a crime or a firing, people will have specific agendas that they will attempt to push. Your goal is to sift through the information and get the best set of facts available to you. If you call a recently fired city worker and ask why he was let go, he might tell you that he retired or resigned because the job wasn't fun anymore or because he wanted to spend time with his family. Those appear to be legitimate reasons for leaving a job, but check with his supervisor and see if that information holds water. The supervisor might say the person was fired for stealing city property or for drinking on the job. With that information in hand, make sure you get in touch with the worker again and lay out the information you just received and ask for a reaction. Never feel bad about going back to a source to ask more questions in the light of new information.

If the subject becomes more hostile or more threatening, as in "I'm going to sue you," you need to continue to be more polite and more persistent. Getting in a shouting match with a source does very little good. You need to keep the source talking and try to keep the source on point. Keep taking notes as the source speaks, even if she keeps telling you, "I'm not talking about this." As long as you have identified yourself as a reporter and stated your purpose, the source understands what you are there to do, even if she doesn't like you or your purpose. Still, the source has the right to hang up the phone or walk away at any time. If the source continues to talk, what she says is fair game.

Kelly Furnas knew his staff had only one chance to get this right.

And the nation was watching.

Virginia Tech student Seung-Hui Cho had engaged in a shooting spree on the morning of April 16, 2007, killing 32 people and sending the Virginia Tech campus into upheaval. The event also sent the staff of the Virginia Tech Collegiate Times into action as the reporters, editors, photographers and designers scrambled to cover the worst outbreak of campus violence in United States history.

Furnas, then the editorial adviser of the Virginia Tech Collegiate Times, had helped his understaffed crew break the news, deal with the requests from national media and produce journalism across multiple platforms for hour after hour in the first few days following the shooting. Now he had a more difficult task: teaching students, already tired and weary from the constant pressure of covering this epic event, how to conduct interviews for the 32 obituaries that would commemorate the lives of the victims.

After handing out packets of information regarding each of the victims to his staff members, he gave them about a 30-minute briefing on how to handle interviewing for an obituary.

"The students I talked to were terrified of the fact that they would need to call these families and I said, 'You don't assume that these families don't want to talk,'" Furnas said, recalling that day at a college media conference a few months after the shooting. "That's a very important thing to these families to tell the story of their son's or daughter's lives. That's a *very* important thing. A lot of people not only want to do it, but expect to do it."

Media outlets vary on how they tend to cover obituaries. On television, it's less common to see new interviews with friends or family on the first day of the story. A simple recap of the person's life read by the anchor over some file footage often suffices for the broadcast audience. In many cases, it's up to the newspaper to handle these type of stories, as the newspaper serves the dual purpose of both informing the public and serving as a record of life (births) and death (obituaries) for a particular area.

How a publication handles obituaries often depends on its size, its circulation area and its sense of what its readers expect. In some cases, the obituaries are all paid for through funeral homes or various internment services and are written by the families in memory of the person who died. Some news outlets assign staff reporters to create obituaries for every person who dies within the readership area, drawing from basic demographic information provided by the funeral home and interviews with family and friends.

If you interview a family member or a friend of someone who died as part of that person's obituary coverage, you could find yourself conducting an unpleasant interview. Some family and friends will be happy to share their memories and recollections, as it is cathartic for them to talk about the person who died. Others, reacting out of grief, will angrily rebuke you and wonder aloud what kind of monster would bother them in this time of sorrow.

In either situation, your ability to remain polite and almost apologetic will be your greatest tool in getting through the interview.

You need to explain that you are sorry to intrude on their grief, but that you wanted to help your readers know a bit more about their friend or family member.

(Continued)

(Continued)

You need to remain calm if you get the backlash and, unlike a hostile interview, you need to know when to simply let the interview end.

In the case of a hostile interview, the subject brought the problem upon himself or herself. As a reporter, you have every right to be firm and insistent.

In the case of an obituary interview, you need to be more willing to leave the subject alone when the interview becomes untenable.

"When you make that call and someone says, 'I can't believe you're calling me,' you say 'I'm sorry, thank you for your time' and you don't call them again. That's it," Furnas said. "But if they want to talk, or they think they might want to talk, or they can't talk now but might talk later, talk to them. You're a human being. They're a human being."

This also is one of the few times where you need not be concerned with controlling the interview. If the source is telling long stories or giving you a lot of anecdotes, feel free to let that person continue to elaborate, even if it's not exactly on point. When the source stops, you can always redirect the interview toward the point you need clarified or the specific question you need answered. As this is probably a traumatic time for the source, you want to make sure you are being as sensitive as possible.

"You talk more about the life. That's my lesson in writing obituaries," Furnas says. "It's not, 'Tell me about how they died.' No. You don't ask that. You ask, 'Tell me about his life. What were his interests? What did he like to do? What was he like growing up?' Those are the stories people love telling. That's better journalism."

PROFILE

When working on a profile, you need to give yourself plenty of time to prepare for and conduct the interview, because you need to gather more than the 5W's and 1H. You need to gather feeling, emotion and understanding, so you should spend more than one interview session with your subject.

The first go-around you can do after gathering the basic types of information you'll need to make sense of the subject. Read old stories on the person, dig through websites and seek other resources to help you accomplish this. While you'll need to have a series of questions for that source, don't fling them at your source in a rapid-fire manner. Engage the source with broader questions and observations to prod the source into longer answers and better anecdotes.

After completing the interview, you will want to talk to as many people as possible who know the source. Talk to them about not only the person but also the things you've noticed and the stories you've heard from the source. See how well those stories jibe with what the source told you and also see if you're really on target with what you think to be important.

Once you complete those interviews, go back and set up another interview with your subject. This time, you'll have additional items from other sources to share with your subject. If there are incongruities, you can iron those out at this point. If the sources brought up stories the subject had failed to mention,

Celebrities and even regular people can make for fascinating subjects when it comes to personality profiles.

you can ask about those here. In the end, you should have more information than you know what to do with when you leave. If you find that you need more, don't be afraid to go back.

OTHER PURPOSES FOR INTERVIEWS

Aside from the general information you will want to glean from the interviews and the chance to observe your sources in their natural environments, you will also have the opportunity to do a few other things in interviews. You need to take advantage of these opportunities to really fine-tune your story, add some flavor to your writing and perhaps even get your sources to reveal more than they might want to. Here's how:

You always want to use multiple sources to confirm information before you present it to your readers as fact.

CONFIRMING INFORMATION

You might have done an amazing job of researching the merger of Company A and Company B, and you might feel like you have a great handle on what happened and why. That said, if you are interviewing the new president of Company AB, you have a golden opportunity to make sure you got it right.

Spend some time with that source reviewing the facts you gathered. Ask if your figures are correct or if the timeline you assembled is right. Have the source work with you to make sure that you got things clearly outlined regarding how a merger works its way through various corporate and government channels. Just because you think you have all the answers doesn't make it so. When you have the expert with you, take advantage of that expert.

For the most part, you will use closed-ended questions to work through this process. Closed-ended questions are questions that are meant to have simple answers and don't demand a great deal of extrapolation. "Is this correct?" is probably one of the more basic confirmatory questions, and it will get you a pretty simple answer. Anything that can be answered with one or two words is likely a closed-ended question.

Getting "Yes" or "No" or "Mmm-hmmm" as an answer to a question doesn't do much to really liven up your story. However, the answers to these questions help you make sure you got things spelled right or correctly ordered. As a word of caution, however, don't allow the source to snow you under and move you away from certain areas because you aren't sure of yourself. For example, you might ask the source, "I understand you got a $6 million bonus for this merger, is that correct?" The source, not wanting to look like a corporate fat cat, might come up with seven reasons why that's "not technically accurate." You can allow the source to outline why he believes that, but you should talk about the bonus with other people involved in the merger.

FISHING FOR QUOTES

Quotes are the spice of any story, as they allow your sources to speak directly to the audience in their own words. You capture the flavor of a source based on word choice, phrases they use or just the information they give you. To that end, you want to ask a few questions that will garner some decent quotes.

Even though it has been more than 30 years since he became a sportswriter, Pat Borzi still remembers what it felt like to be a rookie reporter covering a professional sport.

"My first few times in a major-league locker room, I was absolutely petrified," he said. "I stammered. My hands shook. A couple of times, while I waited for a player, nearby teammates taunted me, and I got flustered and embarrassed. They were testing me, seeing how I'd react."

Since those early years, Borzi has covered a wide array of sports for a variety of publications. He spent eight years as a sports staff writer at the Miami Herald and another 8 at the Portland Press Herald. During his six years at the Newark Star-Ledger, he covered the Yankees, the Mets and the Olympics. He currently works as a Minnesota-based freelance writer, contributing to the New York Times, USA Today, espnW.com, MinnPost.com and other publications.

Borzi said although he has gained a great deal of experience over those years, he still feels a twinge of nerves on occasion when asking for an interview.

"Even now, I'm still a little anxious approaching people I've never met in a clubhouse setting," he said. "It's awkward. They don't know you. You don't know them. But experience teaches you how to handle the awkwardness, put the person you're interviewing at ease, and deal with anything unexpected."

Whether an interview is a quick question after a game or a longer set of items as part of a deeper piece, Borzi said certain rules apply to his approach.

"Malcolm Moran, the former New York Times and USA Today college basketball writer, was one of my mentors, and I follow his lead on this: Never say, 'Talk about such-and-such . . .,'" he said. "First, it's not a question. Second, it's lazy. You watched the game, presumably you did your homework, and you can't take 10 seconds to think up an actual question? That's obnoxious. Most importantly, you're not giving the person you're interviewing any idea what you're looking for."

Borzi also said stronger and clearer questions will almost always lead to better and more engaging answers.

"Ask a specific question, the more specific the better," he said. "'What pitch were you looking for in that spot?' 'What did you see that convinced you the touchdown play could succeed?' Things like that. Short and specific are always better than long and rambling. And avoid offering multiple-choice: Was it this, or was it this? Generally the athlete will pick one or the other instead of giving a more insightful response." Some of the things Borzi said he learned covering sports can be specific to athletics ("Never stand next to the laundry bin. You don't want a filthy, sweaty towel landing on your head."), but the most important things apply to all interviews.

ONE LAST THING

Q: If you could tell the students reading this book anything you think is important, what would it be?

A: "One big thing is LISTEN," he said. "Tape everything to be sure you quote people accurately. But even so, make eye contact with your subject (especially in a group setting) and listen to what's being said and asked. Don't stick the tape recorder in their face and absent-mindedly look around the room. People notice stuff like that. It's rude. Worse, you may miss an answer that's worth following up, leading to a better story."

You need to ask some **open-ended questions**. These questions end up evoking longer answers because the source needs to elaborate on a thought, a topic or a feeling. Questions about how something works or what a person feels about something are usually open-ended questions. If a source is a good interview subject, sometimes he or she will turn a **closed-ended question** into an open-ended answer.

For example, if you asked a boxer who was the toughest opponent he ever fought, you have posed a closed-ended question that won't be good for much in terms of producing quotable material. However, the source might feel inclined to expand upon the topic and give you some decent information and some worthwhile quotes.

You can always mix both closed-ended and open-ended quotes to produce quotes. The question of "How come?" or "Why do you say that?" can always follow a question like "Who was the toughest person you ever fought?" and thus allow you to troll for some quotes.

PROVOKING A REACTION

Sometimes, you will feel a need to poke at a sore spot, a touchy area or pick at a wound in order to get a response from a source. Many times, you need to pose a tough question to an unwilling source. You have a job to do and you need to get important information from sources. However, there are some key points to remember before you jab at a source and evoke his or her wrath:

DOES THIS MATTER TO MY STORY?

Sometimes, people want to know something because they just want to know it. An infamous interviewing moment occurred during the 1992 presidential campaign as part of an MTV-sponsored forum when a young woman asked then-Gov. Bill Clinton "Boxers or briefs?"

This is an example of someone asking an embarrassing question just for grins. As a journalist, you hold yourself to a different standard, so figure out if the potentially painful question is being asked because it is germane to the story. If the question has value, don't be afraid to ask it.

AM I ASKING THE QUESTION AT THE RIGHT TIME?

An interview is more of a chess match than it is a barroom brawl. Take your time and plot your moves intelligently. If you set the hard question up with a few softer questions, you will not only have gained some knowledge from the source, but your rapport might get you a good answer to the tough question.

AM I ASKING THE QUESTION IN THE BEST POSSIBLE WAY?

Just as a stupid question will elicit a stupid answer, a blunt question will elicit a blunt answer. If you ask a man on trial for murder, "You killed your wife, right?" you'll likely get an answer full of colorful language that we can't print in this book. That said, if you ask it a bit better, you might get a little information out of your source: "The district attorney has charged you with first-degree murder, which means he thinks you not only killed your wife, but planned it with cool deliberation. To what degree is any of that true and what would you like to say on your behalf?" Neither question is likely to get you an admission of guilt, but the second version will likely keep the interview rolling and give you a chance to hear this man's side of the story. Just because you have to ask a hard question doesn't mean you need to ask it in a cruel or tactless way.

6 INTERVIEWING

THE BIG THREE

Here are the three key things you should take away from the chapter:

1. **Be prepared:** Most of the anxiety reporters feel and many of the bad questions they ask come from a lack of preparation. You should approach an interview the way you approach a final exam on which you need a great grade: Study the background material until you feel comfortable, practice your approach to the material a few times and then go for it.

2. **Understand your purpose:** The type of interview, the value of a specific source and the time you have to cover your story will all play a big role in how you

approach your source and conduct your interview. Although certain aspects of interviewing are universal, knowing how to modify your approach based on your needs and the situation can be crucial to your success.

3. **Listen:** As Pat Borzi says, you can't throw out a series of questions, stick a microphone in a source's face and call it good. You need to listen to the source so you can ask important follow-up questions. Listening also demonstrates a sense of professionalism that will leave your source with a much better impression of you.

KEY TERMS

closed-ended question   113
flow   102
loaded question   103
news conferences   106

news feature   99
off the record   105
open-ended question   113
personality profile   99

person-on-the-street
interview   107
pseudo-event   107

DISCUSSION QUESTIONS

1. What are some of the benefits and drawbacks of open-ended and closed-ended questions? When are each helpful and when are each problematic? How do you think you would best use each of these in an interview?

2. Many beginning journalists say interviewing is one of the biggest fears and weakest skills. Do you feel that way? Why or why not? What do you look forward to in conducting an interview? What worries you about interviewing someone?

3. Of the various purposes outlined for interviewing in the chapter (confirming information, fishing for quotes, provoking reactions), which one do you think is the most important for good journalism? Which is the least important? Why?

4. If you had to interview the head of your university one hour from now for a profile you want to write on him or her, what kind of background research would you conduct? Where would you go for this information, and how would you prioritize the things you wanted to find?

WRITE NOW!

1. Select a prominent person on your campus or in the surrounding area and research this person as if you were going to conduct an interview with him or her. Consider both news-based sites like newspapers and television station websites as well as promotional sites, such as a company's webpage or professional sites like LinkedIn. Once you feel you have enough information about this person, write up a list of five to seven questions that you would ask this person during an interview. Then, write a short paper that explains what you learned about this person and why you think these questions would lead to information that matters to you and your campus or community audience.

2. Conduct an interview with a person of interest in your area on a topic that matters to you and this person. It could be as simple as interviewing your roommate as to why the apartment is always a mess or as big as interviewing the governor of your state regarding funding for higher education. Prepare for the interview properly, and create a list of questions that get to the core of your purpose. Then, write a 1- to 1.5-page news story based on this interview, using a lead of some sort to introduce the topic and then using direct and indirect quotes for the remainder of the body. (If you forgot the basics pertaining to quotes, go back to Chapter 3 for a refresher.) Once you are done, analyze your story to determine if your interview yielded enough quality paraphrases and quotes. If so, what do you think made you successful? If not, what went wrong? Write a 1- to 1.5-page reflection paper on your experience.

3. Find a link to a video or audio interview between a journalist and someone of interest to you. This could be an athlete, a politician, an actor or anyone else you think would matter to you. Analyze the interview and the questions the person asks. Does the interviewer ask questions that provide revealing or engaging answers? How forthcoming is the subject of the interview? Are the questions tough or weak? Does the interview have a strong theme or does it wander a lot? Write an essay (2-3 pages) that analyzes this interview and explains how you would have done things differently, if at all.

Visit edge.sagepub.com/filaknews to help you accomplish your coursework goals in an easy-to-use learning environment.

7

BASIC REPORTING: NEWS THAT FINDS YOU

LEARNING OBJECTIVES

After completing this chapter you should be able to:

- Define and differentiate among various types of events you could cover, including meetings, speeches and news conferences.

- Explain how to analyze an event for important news content and how best to share that information with your readers.

- Conduct research and locate human sources crucial to your reporting effort.

- Understand how to report for non-event-based stories, such as localizations, crime and natural disasters.

THINKING AHEAD: GETTING READY TO HIT THE FIELD

At the risk of oversimplifying the field, you can divide journalism into two basic types of stories: those you find as a reporter and those that find you. We will discuss the first type of stories in the next chapter, as stories you find are often more complex and require additional effort on the part of the reporter. The stories that find you crop up in everyday reporting and include planned events and natural disasters.

This doesn't mean the second type of story is easy or not worth your time. Meeting, speech and news conference stories provide the bread-and-butter coverage for reporters who want to keep readers abreast of things happening in their area. Game coverage of area sports will draw readers who want to know which teams won or lost. Business owners and taxpayers need reporters who will localize broader topics and help explain what new national laws mean in their neck of the woods. Event stories will give your readers a lot of important information.

In this chapter, we will review the types of basic stories that need reporting. In addition, we will examine the things that make events beneficial or problematic from the point of view of a reporter. Finally, we will talk about coverage beyond events and discuss how to cover those stories. Once you feel comfortable enough with the various reporting techniques you learn here, you can pair them with the lead writing and storytelling techniques you learned in Chapters 3 and 4.

REPORTING BASICS

The core of your writing will come from your reporting. If you do a lousy job of preparing for an event or gather weak material at an event, you will have a hard time writing a story about that event. As a journalist covering something of importance to your readers, you need to have a solid plan in place as to how to approach the task at hand. The information listed below will help guide you through any reporting effort:

RESEARCH THE TOPIC

If you don't feel well versed in a topic upon which you are reporting, you will be incapable of doing a good job as a writer. Think about it like taking a test: The more you study and the better you study, the more confident you will feel heading into the test. You want to understand what is going to happen at an event before it happens, and you want to know what questions you should ask of your sources. Here are some tools you can use to feel ready for action:

Few stories you write will be something without prior coverage. Before you start calling sources, make sure you read previous stories on the topic.

PREVIOUS STORIES

News rarely occurs in a vacuum, which means you won't report on something that has never happened before. A county board meeting where commissioners will vote on an automobile tax is the result of several other meetings at which the commissioners discussed the topic. A controversial person speaking on your campus likely garnered coverage during previous speeches on other campuses. A political figure announcing her retirement at a news conference has likely received coverage of some kind from your publication at some time in the past.

Before you start working on your story, look at what other people wrote on your topic. You can find interesting angles that haven't been covered, uncover more detailed background information for your story and get a better sense of the entire narrative. Previous stories will also help you look beyond your individual story to determine what will happen after this single event. It's like the cliché about seeing the forest through the trees: You want to see the whole picture before you attempt to contribute to it.

SOURCE DOCUMENTS

You want to get your hands on original documents so you can compare what people say versus what has been done. For example, a story you find on a local political figure might note that a campaign volunteer filed a formal ethics complaint, charging the politician with voter fraud. The story might cite the complaint or even quote part of it, but you want to see the entire complaint before you consider including a mention of it in your work. The original journalist might have confused certain aspects of the complaint or could have an axe to grind with the politician. If you examine the source document, you can determine for yourself the degree to which you should take it seriously. In addition, you would want to see if other documents explained what happened to that complaint. Is it under review? Was it thrown out? Did the person recant? In short, until you know what happened, you want to play it safe.

Groups and organizations you cover generate a lot of source documents that can benefit you in your reporting, including meeting **agendas**, meeting **minutes**, official correspondence, formal emails and more. Ask for copies of these items as part of your reporting prep work so you can get a handle on the most accurate version of reality.

OFFICIAL WEBSITES

Public institutions like universities and governmental bodies maintain websites that list everything from official biographies on their leaders to official charters and bylaws. These sites can give you a glimpse into people who might become valuable sources. The sites can also help you verify crucial information, such as budget figures and the outcomes of prior votes.

Private institutions and individuals also maintain websites that contain important information for you. Corporate websites can give you the educational background on an organization's CEO or the history of the organization. Sites like these can help you craft questions as you prepare to interview a speaker from that company at a news conference. The sites can also help you as you try to get a sense of what an organization that is petitioning the city council actually does and how its proposal could affect the readers in your area.

Even "nonofficial" websites can be insightful if you need to compile some information quickly on a quirky topic. Some niche sites will give you answers to questions like "Who was the last Major League Baseball player to win 30 games in one season?" to "How many more touchdowns did the players in the National Football Conference score than those in the American Football Conference?" Other sites can help you clarify concepts like "What does 'footprint' mean as an architectural and development term?" You never know what you will need to know for a given story, so don't be afraid to research it before you attempt to report on it. As always, however, make sure you trust the website before you publish information you find on it, and double-check the information with your human sources.

SEEK SOURCES AND PLAN INTERVIEWS

Your research should help you determine which people will matter to your story and who will provide what angle on it. Many of the events you will cover as a beginning reporter will have those sources available to you without too much trouble. In most cases, those sources will be offering information to you and anyone else in the room as part of the meeting, speech or news conference you are covering. This makes life a little easier on you, presuming that you know each source's identity, because you can grab information and quotes while that person takes part in the event. (If you don't know who people are, this chapter includes an easy way to collect quotes from them anyway. See the box later in the chapter on quoting people you don't know.)

The research aspect should help you figure out who the main players are at a meeting or who is likely to favor or oppose an issue. If you cover sporting events, your research should give you a sense of which players are stars and which ones are unlikely to contribute to the final score. You then know which people you need to find or to whom you should pay attention.

Prior to the event, make contact with the sources to let them know you will be there and you might like some one-on-one time with them. If a group brings in a speaker, contact the head of that organization to see if the speaker has time before or after the event for a few questions. Before you attend a news conference, check with the PR practitioners running the event to see if the main players will be open for extra interview time at some point. When you are covering a meeting, find out who put forth the proposals that most interest you, and reach out to those people before and after the event. The more time you put into the front-end reporting, the better your story will be when you are working against a deadline.

MAKE SURE YOU ARE SURE

Accuracy remains the core value of all journalism. If you fail to give your readers accurate information, they will distrust you and eventually stop reading your work altogether. In most cases, we don't attempt to mislead our readers with our errors, but instead we just screw up. Here is a list of ways to fix avoidable errors before they make it to your audience:

CHECK SPELLING

Nothing can undercut your credibility faster than misspellings in your work. Fortunately, we live in a period of time when computers can autocorrect your work and word processing software includes spell-check options. Even with these technological blessings, you shouldn't rely entirely on them to keep you out of trouble. As anyone who has texted a friend knows, the corrections your devices make aren't always the right ones, and if you don't look carefully before you publish your content, you can find yourself in a heap of trouble.

Go back through your work and read word by word to make sure you typed the right word or that a spell check didn't make things worse. This will keep you from praising a "pubic speaker," offering to "asses a situation" or something worse.

REVIEW PROPER NOUNS

Spell check can save you in some cases, but not in the case of how proper nouns are spelled. You need to go over each instance of names, places, events and more to make sure you spelled these words right. Errors often emerge in one of two ways when we fail to carefully examine proper nouns:

1. We assume that if every instance of a proper noun is spelled identically, all of them must be spelled right.

Whether you use a word-processing program or a pen-and-paper approach, you need to carefully edit your work to avoid spelling errors.

CONSIDER THIS ➡ IS OBJECTIVITY DEAD?

In the early part of the 20th century, writers like Walter Lippmann noted the need for the media to become an objective, fact-based force that provides information to the general public. During that era, many publications had used scandalized content and what some referred to as "yellow journalism" to drive sales and galvanize public opinion.

In the following decades, journalists learned the values associated with objectivity, applying it to their writing and reporting. Journalists were told to avoid letting personal biases influence news coverage. Stories centered on conflict required a source from Side A and a source from Side B. Facts, not opinion, were central to good journalism. Many of those tenets remain part of journalism education, and many news outlets still aspire to the idea of providing facts to the audience members without interjecting any sense of bias.

Journalistic advocacy and opinion, however, have found their way into the media from the days of Lippmann until now. Edward R. Murrow famously sparred with Wisconsin Sen. Joe McCarthy during the days of the "Red Scare" in the 1950s. Walter Cronkite stated in a 1968 editorial that the Vietnam War was unwinnable. "Alternative" press outlets emerged in the 1970s that rejected objectivity in place of advocacy journalism, in the hope of bringing attention to important issues. Scholars also note that even when journalists had espoused the idea of objectivity, they could not fully detach themselves from the stories they told, and thus personal biases and ideologies crept into the content.

In more recent times, the line between fact and opinion has become further blurred. Partisan media outlets offer readers and viewers information that merely confirms their worldviews. Anyone can start a website, blog or social media presence and blast out content that fails to meet the rigor and the standards of what journalism students are taught to embrace. The idea of "facts" as indisputable has become a point of debate, with some noting that we now live in a "post-fact" society. In April 2017, Time magazine asked a question on its cover that hit at the heart of this issue: "Is Truth Dead?"

Given these concerns, journalists now must deal with the issue of how to proceed with their approach to content. It can be easy to forsake the idea of objectivity under the guise of "fighting fire with fire." On the other hand, journalists can decide to stick with the facts and only the facts, seeking balance even as other media outlets "don't fight fair." Neither approach offers a perfect answer, but in the current climate, how we deal with objectivity will define the profession and our relationship with our audiences for years to come.

2. We examine one or two instances of a proper noun and find that we spelled it right. Thus, we stop looking for other cases where we might have spelled the noun differently.

Go back to your source material and give each instance of a proper noun a proper examination before you publish. Even if you write something flattering, the subject of your work will be displeased if you get a name wrong.

LOOK INTO THE NUMBERS

Journalists often portray themselves as math-phobics who entered the field to avoid playing with numbers. Even if that describes you perfectly, you will still have to deal with numbers in journalism, so get used to checking your math in your stories. Sometimes, the math is as simple as realizing that the numbers don't add up:

Running back Chester Charles rushed for 178 yards in the game, gaining exactly 84 yards in each half.

Children's book author Emma Mae Fleeger died, Sunday, Oct. 25, 2016, at the age of 87. Fleeger was born in 1929 on Christmas Eve to Karl and Becca Sue Fleeger in Hope, Oregon.

State Superintendent James Francis argued that a 3 percent reduction in his $5.3 million budget would be easily handled by drawing down school reserves by $150,000.

In each case, you can clearly see that the math doesn't add up:

If you multiply 84 by 2, you get 168, not 178.

Fleeger's December birthday would make her age 86, not 87.

A $5.3 million budget with a 3 percent cut leaves a $159,000 hole, not a $150,000 one.

In some cases, the math is more complicated, as you need to check figures against a detailed budget or you need to calculate interest over a protracted period of time. If you aren't sure that the math works, ask an expert to help you. If you still aren't sure, don't publish the material until you feel confident in your arithmetic.

Overall, the best bit of advice to which you can adhere is this: Be suspicious. Each time you see a fact, consider a way in which that statement might be wrong. Then, use credible sources to verify the fact. If you approach every element of your work with the idea that it's probably wrong until you can prove it right, you will create clean copy with fewer chances for errors.

EVENT COVERAGE

Rookie reporters often cover preplanned events that will provide some basic information to their readers. The goal of covering these events is to tell people something valuable, interesting and engaging about what occurred during the event. As a reporter, you serve as both a conduit of information that helps connect the readers to the event and a sieve that sifts out all the minor elements of the event and shows the readers only the most important things that happened.

Below is a list of potential events you might cover as well as the benefits and drawbacks of each:

SPEECHES

A speech is an opportunity for someone to talk to a group of people for a specific period of time on a topic of interest. Speeches often become one-sided affairs, as you have one person discussing a subject without any pushback from another source. For example, if you have the head of the state's Democratic Party speaking about the many benefits of voting for Democrats, you don't hear about the potential problems with voting Democrat or the benefits of voting for another party.

Even with those drawbacks, a speech is often the easiest type of event to cover for beginning journalists. The person at the front of the room is presenting information that he or she has tailored to a specific audience. You will likely have enough advance notice to research the speaker and the topic, so you will have a lot of background available for your story. The people who sponsored the event will have additional information for you, and you have an audience full of people who can tell you what they thought about the speech.

As a reporter, your goal is to contact the people in charge of the speech (or the speaker) to get some individual time with the person before or after the speech. You want to get information from the group that sponsored the speech, so you can better explain why this person matters and why the speech occurred at this point in time. During the event, you want to find the core message of the speech so you can convey that to your readers in your lead. You also want to keep an ear out for valuable and interesting quotes that will support your lead. After the speech, you should interview people in the audience to get reaction quotes that will give you a sense of

On Saturday, Jan. 14, 2017, in Washington, D.C., 12-year-old Ryan Battle, NAN Youth Rep, addresses the crowd at the We Shall Not Be Moved march, organized by Rev. Al Sharpton's organization, National Action Network (NAN). Speech stories are some of the most common reporting assignments for journalists.

how the listeners felt about the event. As always, keep an eye out for things that happen outside the lines or when the speaker goes off script and says something particularly newsworthy.

For example, in September 2016, Milwaukee Bucks President Peter Feigin was speaking to the Rotary Club of Madison about the basketball team's mission statement, prospects for the season and the excitement surrounding its new arena. During that speech, Feigin spoke out about Milwaukee itself and its history of race relations, noting, "Very bluntly, Milwaukee is the most segregated, racist place I've ever experienced in my life. It just is a place that is antiquated. It is in desperate need of repair and has happened for a long, long time."[1]

The quote was buried deep in the original story, but it became a hot topic for other publications and sports journalists who spoke out on each side of the issue. Later that day, Feigin issued a statement praising the city and his love of that part of the state,[2] but the issue continued to be a point of discussion in the following days.

MEETINGS

Groups, organizations and governmental bodies use meetings to create rules, decide on actions and move society ahead a little bit at a time. As a conduit to an interested public, you should look into various meetings and see what might matter to your readers. Much like a speech story, the goal of a good meeting story is to find out what happened at the event, not to report that the event happened. In addition, you don't want to report on every aspect of the meeting but rather the few items you see as critically important.

You need to get a copy of the meeting's agenda prior to the event. Most states and governmental organizations have a rule requiring public bodies to post an agenda in advance of any meeting. The rules that govern the posting of the agenda vary from state to state, with some requiring only 24-hour advance notice while others require that the agenda be posted several days in advance. Once you obtain a copy of the agenda, look for any items that seem interesting to you or that would affect your readers. If the agenda states the group will enact policy, spend money or fire someone, you probably want to keep an eye on those items. If you aren't sure what the agenda is telling you, call a source or two prior to the meeting to get a better understanding of what is likely to happen.

Portland Mayor Ethan Strimling speaks during a meeting in the Portland City Council chambers about rent control proposals to members on Wednesday, Aug. 24, 2016. Journalists cover meetings to inform their readers about important decisions officials make.

At the meeting itself, you need to gather information on those key items, including if the measures passed or failed and who voted on each side. If you know who voted which way, you can ask each person for their rationale after the meeting finishes. For example, in 2011, Illinois' then-Gov. Rod Blagojevich was in the process of being convicted of abusing his power as the state's leading governmental official. The most eye-catching charge was that he tried to sell the state's U.S. Senate seat that Barack Obama vacated upon becoming president in 2008. The state's lawmakers set about an attempt to impeach Blagojevich, and the measure passed the Illinois House of Representatives by a 114–1 margin.[3]

As noted earlier in the book, "oddity" is an element of interest, and this singular dissenting vote clearly fits that category. If you covered this story at that time, you could easily find a "pro-impeachment" source from the House, but the most interesting source would have been the one "no." That vote belonged to Milton Patterson, a Chicago-based Democrat, who noted that he would need more information to vote on the measure. He also argued that he didn't feel it was his job to impeach Blagojevich.[4]

As the people speak during the meeting, write down bits of information you think will be helpful in telling your story as well as any good quotes that people provide during the meeting. After the meeting, you can interview your sources to clarify the points they made during the event or to seek elaboration on the things they said. You can also double-check basic facts like name spellings and contact information before you pack up and head back to the newsroom.

NEWS CONFERENCES

When people or organizations understand that a given topic will interest a lot of journalists, they usually call a **news conference** to meet the needs of the media. The goal of a news conference is to create a singular, well-polished message that the host can deliver once. This will prevent the source from answering the same question over and over throughout the day as various reporters catch on to the story. This approach gives a specific set of information at one point in time and allows reporters to all ask whatever they need to all at once.

As a reporter, this kind of event can seem easy to cover. The host will provide all the material you need in a usable format, the sources you need are present and everyone seems interested in meeting your reportorial needs. The event is essentially built for your benefit.

That said, you need to consider potential problems associated with a news conference:

- **Everyone gets the same story:** In some cases, this isn't a big concern, because everyone wants the same story. For example, after an important basketball game, most of the reporters want to hear from the coach, the team captain and an important player. When all three of them show up at a set of microphones, answer all the basic questions and move on, this is much easier than having to track each of them down and ask questions they have likely answered for other reporters. However, when it comes to more nuanced stories, like a company

One of the more difficult things you face as a rookie reporter is quoting people you see at public events before you can learn their names. In meetings, for example, you have people sitting around a table, talking about crucial issues and putting out great information. The quotes might be perfect, but if you can't attribute them to a named source, your editor won't let you use them. If you wait until after the meeting to get names and then interview the people, you will miss out on what these people are saying when it counts the most.

Here is a simple way to gather quotes and information from your sources before you know who they are.

Take a look at this image of a simple meeting:

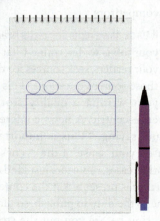

FIG. 7.1 TABLE SKETCH 1

You have four people in the frame, and you don't know any of their names. To make life easier on you, draw a quick sketch of the table and position the people around it based on what you see.

Then, try to pick out a defining characteristic of each person. For example, you might notice that the woman speaking has blonde hair or is wearing a red shirt.

FIG. 7.2 TABLE SKETCH 2

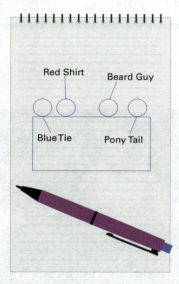

Whatever characteristic you most associate with her, use that to label her on your diagram. Pick out similar characteristics of the other people and fill in the other spots at the table.

Then, use those characteristics to label your quotes like this:

Red Shirt: We can't continue to fund the program at this level.

Beard Guy: I understand the need to save money, but we need these services for people who can't afford health care without the county's assistance.

(Continued)

(Continued)

When officials want to get information to a group of journalists all at once, they often rely on a news conference. These events can have positives and negatives of which you should be aware.

announcing that it will lay off a few hundred workers, you might want to ask questions based on some intimate knowledge you received from an inside source. If you ask those questions at the news conference, you lose your chance at an exclusive story. When it comes to writing a story from a news conference, it will take extra effort to find an angle that distinguishes your work from that of your competitors.

- **It turns news reporting on its head:** As a journalist, your job is to determine what matters most to your readers, seek sources for that topic and ask those sources questions. This process leads to your writing a quality story that is audience-centric. A news conference inverts this process because a source is calling you and saying, "This is important. You should come here and write about it." In some cases, your sense of the event's value and your source's sense of it are similar. However, in other cases, reporters just kind of go along with the source's way of thinking and cover whatever is presented at the conference as important news. The duty to report is not the same as the duty to publish, so make sure you feel what you learned at the event is worth writing before you put the story out for your audience.

- **It can be a snow job:** Just because an organization or a person hosts a news conference to announce something, it doesn't necessarily follow that the information is accurate. In the early 2000s, energy giant Enron collapsed into bankruptcy as corporate scandals engulfed the company. A three-year Department of Justice investigation found that the company often lied about its holdings, used fraudulent measures to prop up its stock value and engaged in other unsavory activities to increase profits. At the center of this was the company's CEO, Ken Lay, who was charged in 2004 with 11 counts of conspiracy and fraud. After his arraignment on these charges, Lay and his defense team held a news conference near the courthouse and categorically denied that Lay did anything wrong.[5] In 2006, Lay was found guilty and faced a possible 45 years in prison,[6] although he died of a heart attack before his sentencing. If you go back through what Lay said at his news conference and compare that with what the court determined, you can clearly see that Lay's media event was nothing but a snow job.

Not every news conference will be filled with tall tales and outlandish lies, but you should always be aware of the goal of a news conference: to tell one side of a story. Your goal as a journalist is to make sure you are telling all sides of a story, which means you need to find sources who could offer you another way to look at the issues raised in the news conference. If you have a hard time coming up with anyone who might disagree with the people hosting the news conference, consider asking those people for potential sources.

SPORTING EVENTS

The field of sports journalism is far too vast to outline all of the various intricacies associated with it in this book. Much of what you have learned in this book, from how to write strong leads to how to do quality interviews, will apply in sports as well. That said, one key event not covered above applies to sports journalism: the game story.

Sports reporters often find themselves in the middle of the action, covering celebrations and heartbreak.

Gamers require you to attend an event that has an unknown outcome and determine what matters most so you can communicate it to your readers. However, each sport has a series of rules that can make it difficult for you to capture the essence of the event. Some things seem simple: In American football, the players catch and run with the ball in their hands, while in soccer, the rules forbid players to use their hands. Other things are more complicated: In basketball, only the player who passes the ball to the person who immediately scores gets credit for an assist. In hockey, two players involved in helping a teammate score will each get an assist.

Authors Scott Reinardy and Wayne Wanta[7] list the following items as essentials for any game story:

- **The score:** Game outcomes are important, so who won and who lost (or if a tie occurred) will matter to your readers. Reinardy and Wanta note that although some authors get leeway to try various forms of storytelling, the score should appear in game stories no later than the third paragraph.

- **The atmosphere:** The feel of the crowd can vary from place to place and sport to sport. You could witness Game 7 of the World Series with a packed stadium full of crazed fans or observe that a few folks were sleeping in the stands while two last-place teams battled it out in the middle of the year. The overall feeling of the event can play a major role in telling your story to your readers.

- **Records:** If two undefeated teams are facing off for the right to claim a championship, that can be a major part of your story. Conversely, if two teams are battling for futility, as neither has won a game this year and you are watching the last game of the season, this can lead to some drama as well.

- **History:** Rivalries are a major part of sports and can turn a midseason game between two .500 teams into an epic battle. It can be something as simple as a conference game between two high schools or as complex as the New York Yankees and Boston Red Sox rivalry. Before you attend a game, find out if any historical significance is attached to the two teams fighting it out. If you miss that, you could miss the whole point of the story.

- **Statistics:** Sports stories are often buried in numbers when writers don't know which statistics matter most. The goal in covering a game is to gather accurate statistics that help explain how it was that one team got the better of the other team. The value of statistics will vary from sport to sport, as will the amount of value you should place on specific statistics. Also keep in mind that you should look for statistical anomalies, including record-breaking performances or novel outcomes.

For example, an August 2013 Boston Red Sox/Houston Astros game had a number of potentially memorable moments: The Sox won 15-10, making it a high-scoring game. Steven Wright made his first major-league start and didn't make it past the first inning. The win helped keep Boston at the top of the Eastern Division, pushing its lead over second-place Toronto to 1.5 games. However, it was Red Sox catcher Ryan Lavarnway's efforts that became part of the record books when he allowed four passed balls in one inning. Wright's knuckleball, a pitch that is often erratic and difficult to catch, eluded Lavarnway enough times to help him tie a record set by Ray Katt of the New York Giants in 1954 and equaled by Geno Petralli of the Texas Rangers in 1987.[8]

Twitter post @annahigginsuva

Anna Higgins @annahigginsuva · Aug 13
VSP positioned on 7th St while law enforcement is also positioned atop the Town Transit Station.

Cavalier Daily staff member Anna Higgins live tweeted the chaotic events that happened on and around the University of Virginia campus in Charlottesville, Virginia, as part of the "Unite the Right" white supremacists gathering in August 2017.

- **Injuries:** Any time someone is hurt, be it a serious or minor injury, readers will want to know. In some cases, it can be a devastating injury that leads to the end of a career, such as New York Jet Dennis Byrd, who was paralyzed on Nov. 29, 1992, when he slammed head first into a teammate during a game against the Kansas City Chiefs.[9] In other cases, it can be something almost far-fetched, such as what happened to Kansas City Royal George Brett, who missed part of a 1980 World Series game because of hemorrhoids.[10]

As with other events you cover, you should check to make sure you got things right.

Interviews with players, coaches and fans should help you fact-check your information as well as gather some crucial quotes.

BASIC TIPS FOR ALL EVENT STORIES

As noted earlier, all events have pros and cons. Regardless of which topic you cover or which event you attend, here are some basics to help you navigate event coverage as a beginning reporter:

UNDERSTAND YOUR PURPOSE

If someone else assigned you to cover the event, meet with that person and find out why this event merits coverage. Editors often have a strong sense of what makes for audience-centric content, given that they likely started as reporters. For example, your editor might know that a specific item on a meeting's agenda deserves special attention. If you don't know that going in, you might be looking at something else entirely when it comes to the core of your story. This will lead to an awkward situation when you come back with Story A and your editor is expecting Story B.

IMPROVISE AND ADAPT

Although preparing is crucial, the ability to adapt to a changing event can help you salvage your story when things change. You might head to the city council, fully prepared to write a story about how the city will use $6 million to fund a road-repaving project. You met with city council members in advance to get good quotes before the vote and spoke with contractors who are expected to get the contract. Then, without any warning, someone on the city council gets upset about another topic and the mayor decides to table the repaving vote so the council members can dig into the new topic. This means you now have to adjust to a new topic, new information and a whole new story.

Speakers can change their minds and decide to talk on a different topic than the one you have planned. Events can get changed or moved. Meetings can take all sorts of twists and turns. A good journalist can adjust on the fly to these changes and look for the core of the story, even if that story isn't the one that was expected. When these things happen, go back to what makes for the core of a good story:

- What is going on?
- Why does it matter?
- How does this affect my readership?

Once you focus on these items, look for the people who can tell you the most important information and the sources who can provide you with the best background on the topic.

LOOK OUTSIDE OF THE EVENT

An event story isn't always what was planned, nor is it always what's happening on the agenda or at the podium.

In May 2016, Univision anchor Maria Elena Salinas spoke at California State University, Fullerton as part of the school's graduation ceremonies and ended up becoming national news.

Salinas delivered part of her speech to the College of Communications in Spanish, and she also called out presidential hopeful Donald Trump. Audience members shouted for her to "get off the stage" and some called her "trash." When she noted that she would like to "say a few words in Spanish," someone shouted back "No!" Whatever she had planned to say was lost along the way, and the issue of her back-and-forth with the hecklers became the bigger story.[11]

A 2008 Kirkwood, Missouri, city council meeting turned deadly when Charles Lee "Cookie" Thornton arrived and began shooting at people in City Hall. Thornton had a long-standing grudge against the city after his demolition business had received several citations and Thornton himself had been ticketed for disorderly conduct. Six people, including Thornton, died as a result of the shooting.[12]

A Big 10 college football game between 11th-ranked Wisconsin and 7th-ranked Nebraska in 2016 went into overtime, with the Badgers upsetting the previously undefeated Huskers 23–17. However, the bigger story that emerged nationally was the action of several people who showed up for the Halloween-weekend game dressed as political candidates. A person wearing a Donald Trump costume was photographed using a noose to "lynch" a person in a President Barack Obama mask and prison-striped clothing. The photo went viral on Twitter, forcing the university's police and administration to respond to the image.[13]

Not every story from an event comes as an agenda item or a key play in a game. You need to keep your head on a swivel and look for all sorts of items that might make for important and newsworthy content.

STORIES BEYOND STANDARD EVENTS

Somewhere between covering your first speech and conducting a massive investigative project will be a series of stories that will require you to do some additional work. Two types of stories tend to fall into the middle of that spectrum: localizations and disaster coverage.

Visions of America/Getty Images

Media crews and forest service personnel meet with locals during Ventura County's Day Fire of 2006. When an international, national or statewide event affects your readers, consider doing a localization story.

LOCALIZATIONS

The most basic question readers want answered when they read news is, "How does this matter to me?" Instead of bemoaning the nature of self-interest, journalists should use it to their advantage. For example, if you read a story about state budget cuts and how much money is being allocated to which projects, you might get bored quickly and put it down. However, if the lead on the story discussed how budget cuts were leading to a 50 percent increase in tuition at your school, that story would probably hold your attention from the first word through the last.

When it comes to broader topics on state, national or international levels, people will often pass those stories by with the attitude of, "This doesn't affect me at all." However, journalists can draw readers in through the use of **localization**

THOUGHTS FROM A **PRO** ➡ RYAN WOOD, GREEN BAY PACKERS BEAT REPORTER, USA TODAY NETWORK-WISCONSIN

© Ryan Wood

When a famous athlete speaks from his or her locker, a throng of microphones, notepads and recorders encircle that person, hoping to capture a few important bits of news to share with a passionate and unyielding fan base. These reporters follow teams from city to city and state to state, asking questions about everything from specific plays in games to allegations of criminal activity and "friction" between teammates.

Ryan Wood, a Green Bay Packers beat reporter for the USA TODAY NETWORK-Wisconsin, is often behind one of those pads or recorders, as he dispatches content about this football team from the National Football League's smallest city.

"I've seen good—potentially great—reporters peel out of the business because there are other jobs that provide better lifestyles," he said. "Why haven't I? Because I honestly can't imagine myself doing anything else. If it weren't for that, I'd probably be doing something else."

Wood began his career as a sports reporter and an editor at his college newspaper before he transitioned to his professional career. He worked the sports beat at the DeKalb (Illinois) Daily Chronicle, where he covered Northern Illinois University athletics. He also covered the athletic programs at the University of South Carolina and Auburn University before taking on his current job covering the Packers.

As a reporter in a demanding field, Wood said he relies heavily on the basics when he's digging into his stories.

"Accuracy is unequivocally the highest priority," he said. "While I've been covering the Packers for less than two years, my readership grew up consuming everything they could about the team. If I misspell a player's name from 50 years ago, someone is going to notice. Knowing that creates a healthy amount of paranoia; I cannot get facts wrong, no matter how seemingly insignificant."

Wood said he learned a great deal about how to report in each of his previous jobs, especially how important it is to work well with sources.

"Probably the No. 1 lesson I didn't understand in college was the importance of reputation with the people you work with, especially sources," he said. "This business is based on relationships. There is a constant give and take. In college, I had a hard time seeing the gray in situations. It was either black, or white. No middle ground. So I ended up dying on a lot of hills that weren't my hill to die on."

As a Packers beat reporter, he said going into an interview with specific reporting goals has helped him write the most complete stories possible.

"As I interview, I'm primarily doing two things," Wood said. "The first is paying attention to any holes in an answer and coming up with probing follow-ups to fill in the missing information. I'm also thinking about how the information being presented fits into a story."

Wood also said that he not only prepares based on the interview topic, but he also does a lot of prep work based on the person he is interviewing.

"It's a real trick to get answers from people who would truly prefer to say nothing at all," he said. "Reporters have to be creative in their approach to interviews, and also smart. While some questions simply have to be asked, the goal of

(Continued)

(Continued)

an interview is to get the best answers possible. Too many reporters fall in love with their own questions, and the interview becomes more about what's asked than what's answered. There is more than one way to ask a question. When I'm interviewing a player, I know there are trigger words that need to be avoided because they'll raise red flags, and you'll wind up getting nothing more than clichés."

In this line of work, 40-hour weeks are a myth and the salaries can be less than ideal, but Wood said even with all the chaos associated with his field, he loves the job.

"You'll probably have to move a lot, always willing to go where the job is," he said. "You have to be at least open to the idea of living away from family. You have to be willing to work nights, weekends, holidays. I'll probably never have a normal Christmas while I cover the Packers. . . . If you accept the profession's less glamorous aspects, it can be an awesome job. Obviously, it's a lot of fun covering the NFL. Sure beats working for a living. But the best part of this job is the chance to wake up every day and tell a story."

ONE LAST THING

Q: If you could tell the students reading this book anything you think is important, what would it be?

A: "The most important thing for anyone entering the field is to horde as much experience as you possibly can. Get involved in student journalism. When I was in college, I lived in the newsroom. Ate there. Slept there. Pulled all-nighters doing homework there. Made my friends there. Met my wife there. The newsroom was my home. I've gotten emails from folks with English degrees and zero student journalism experience who wanted to know how to enter the business, just because they wanted to write. I never have anything positive to tell them. They can't, at least not in a full-time basis. If you want to give yourself the best chance to succeed, learn the tools of the trade. Nothing prepares you for life as a professional journalist like being a student journalist."

stories that take those wide-reaching concepts and bring them home for the readers. Here are a few stories that might seem pointless to you as a reader of a school or local publication:

- An explosion demolishes an oil refinery 1,000 miles away from your town.
- A Chinese firm has received permission to build an engine that was previously constructed only in U.S. cities.
- The Environmental Protection Agency passed new guidelines about chemical runoff concentrations in the wake of several groundwater contamination outbreaks.

As a reporter, you could look at these issues quickly and dismiss them, or you could look at them critically and think about how each could affect your audience. For example, the explosion at the oil refinery means that a company has one fewer facility that is creating usable petroleum products. That could mean higher gas prices for people in your area if there is less fuel in circulation. It could also mean other products refined there might be in shorter supply, thus producing either scarcity or price hikes for consumers.

In the case of the Chinese factory building engines, that story might matter to your readers if your city housed one of the factories that previously had a monopoly on construction. This could mean job losses or wage cuts. On the other hand, if a company nearby is responsible for supplying parts used in the construction of the engine, it might be a financial boon for people in your readership area. The same pro and con are possible in the EPA story: Local farmers might be upset about the guidelines and how they affect their ability to fertilize their fields. Conversely, if your area had chemical problems, it might be a great day for your readers, who will now see improved water.

Not every story will have a local impact, but you should dig around on everything from the latest cooking craze to the international deployment of troops from your country, just to be sure. Look at stories that happen elsewhere and see if they matter to your readers. If you have a good local angle, use it to drive your story.

CRIME AND DISASTERS

Reporting on things like hurricanes, car crashes and other mayhem doesn't lend itself to a lot of hard and fast rules. Some people become passionate about covering **breaking news**,

NBC Television newscaster, Lester Holt, left, interviews Kieran Burke, right, an FDNY fire marshal and resident of Breezy Point whose home was burned Nov., 1, 2012 after Superstorm Sandy left millions without power or water in the Queens borough of New York. Disaster coverage can be dangerous and scary, so be careful and be calm if you need to report on these topics.

including murders and robberies, while others will do their best to avoid ever seeing blood on the job. How you react during each of these incidents will be an entirely individual thing.

That said, here are three universal truths to this kind of reporting:

STAY CALM

When you arrive on the scene of a fire, you may come face to face with a group of firefighters desperately trying to revive a heavily burned victim. If you go to a traffic accident, you could see mangled cars and blood strewn across an entire city block. At these or any other unsavory disaster scenes, you might be fighting the urge to throw up. Whatever you feel at that point, you need to keep your head in the game. Take a deep breath and collect your thoughts. You need to do the job you were sent to do: Talk to people, gather information and be prepared to tell a story. A panicking reporter is a useless reporter.

STAY SAFE

Rescue professionals like firefighters and police officers are trying to do their jobs at the scene of an accident or during a standoff with an armed individual. You are also trying to do your job at that point in time, which means asking questions and gathering facts. In some of these cases, regardless of how important you feel about yourself, their job needs trump yours. If the officials put up special crime-scene tape or tell you what you can't touch, you should listen to them. If you don't, you could get arrested or injured. Worse yet, you might mess up a crime scene and make it impossible for them to find out what happened.

Even when there aren't people telling you what to do or what to avoid, use common sense in determining your best course of action. Don't drive into a flooded area and expect the police to rescue you. Don't enter a wildfire zone to get some video and assume everything will be fine. A dead or wounded reporter is about as useless as a panicking one.

As is the case with sports reporting, you have a few crucial elements to gather at the scene of a crime or a disaster. Here are some things you should consider getting when you go after a breaking news story:

- **Any death or severity of injury:** We talked earlier in the book about impact as one of the interest elements, and you will rarely see a more severe impact than death or serious injury. If someone sustains an injury severe enough that loss of life is possible, you will want to find out who can keep you updated on that person's condition.

- **Damage amounts:** You can also measure an impact in terms of property damage or loss. In the case of a fire, everyone in the home might have escaped safely, but the house burns to the ground. In the case of a rainstorm, poor drainage might lead to massive amounts of damage in people's basements. Experts, such as insurance investigators and fire marshals, can give you a dollar amount associated with these kinds of losses, thus helping you show the magnitude of the impact.

- **Identities of people involved in the incident:** Fame is another area of interest that will matter to your readers, so you should do your best to figure out who was involved in this situation. In some cases, a person involved in a crime or disaster can have broad-reaching fame. For example, in October 2016, two men burst into a luxury apartment in France, tied up the resident at gunpoint and stole nearly $9 million worth of jewelry. Although the dollar amount alone would have drawn attention locally, the event became an international story when the name of the victim was released: reality TV star Kim Kardashian West.[14]

  Even if the person involved in the incident isn't famous in the broadest sense of the word, the identities of people involved in accidents, fires, robberies, shootings and more matter to your readers. It could be a small town's mayor, the head librarian at a local school or even just someone everyone seemed to know. People in your audience will likely know someone involved in these incidents. Get that information out there for your readers to help them connect to your story.

- **What happened:** Actions matter a great deal when it comes to a disaster story. You need to figure out for your readers what happened. The officials at the scene of a crime or who are helping abate a disaster will be able to fill you in on the nuts and bolts of the situation. You need information from them to help walk you through how the incident started, what made it continue and what will happen next. Their insight is crucial for you to help explain the situation to your readers.

BASIC REPORTING:
NEWS THAT FINDS YOU

THE BIG THREE

Here are the three key things you should take away from this chapter:

1. **Be prepared:** You will never feel worse as a reporter if you go to an event and you have not prepared for it. If you don't study the topic, understand the intricacies of the event or know what to expect, you will have a difficult time gathering information and an even harder time writing a good story. Do enough prep work to feel grounded in the topic and ready to gather information with confidence.

2. **Find the story:** The point of covering events isn't to note that the event happened, but rather what happened at the event. Not every element of one of these gatherings is worth your attention, so figure out what will matter most to your readers and focus on it. This is particularly true of news conferences and meetings. A lot of things will happen during the course of these types of events, but you need to boil down the event to its most crucial elements for your audience.

3. **Be safe:** In terms of covering disasters, you need to take care of yourself and stay out of harm's way. In every other story, you need to be safe in terms of keeping errors away from your copy. Always double-check everything you do as a reporter and a writer before you decide to move on to the next thing.

KEY TERMS

agenda 119	gamer 127	minutes 119
breaking news 133	localization 130	news conferences 124

DISCUSSION QUESTIONS

1. What are the pros and cons associated with speeches and news conferences? In each case you have a person of importance speaking on a given topic. Which do you think is easier to cover? Why? Which do you think is likely to generate content that is valuable for your audience? Why?

2. When you see interviews with people on television, what makes them good and what makes them awful, in your opinion? How would you go about improving the overall value of these interviews?

3. Of all of the story types we discussed in the chapter, which one sounds most appealing to you? Why? Which one sounds least appealing to you? Why?

WRITE NOW!

1. Analyze a meeting story in your local paper. What elements of the story were valuable and helpful to you? What aspects of the story did the writer touch on that you think didn't work out very well? Explain what could have made this better.

2. Analyze a game story from a local publication, examining it for the elements listed in the book as critical for all game stories. Did it meet the expectations for these key story components? Did it use these elements in the proper spots and effectively? What is your overall sense of the quality of this game story?

Visit edge.sagepub.com/filaknews to help you accomplish your coursework goals in an easy-to-use learning environment.

PRACTICE AND APPLY WHAT YOU'VE LEARNED

▶ edge.sagepub.com/filaknews

⑤SAGE edge™

CHECK YOUR COMPREHENSION ON THE STUDY SITE WITH:

- **Practice quizzes** allow you to assess how much you've learned

- **Newswriting Assignments** allow you to broaden your reporting skills and practice writing

- **Test your knowledge** of AP Style with our AP Style Quizzes and Exercises

BEYOND BASIC REPORTING: NEWS YOU HAVE TO FIND

Chip Somodevilla/Getty Images

LEARNING OBJECTIVES

After completing this chapter you should be able to:

- Find news features by opening up the aperture of your mind and learning to see elements of everyday life as potential story ideas.

- Understand the basic elements of beat reporting as well as the types of beats you could cover as a journalist.

- Engage in the basics of beat reporting through proper research, source development and continual follow-up work.

- Understand the value of personality profiles as well as some best practices for profile reporting.

- Apply the three interviewing phases of personality profiles.

- Understand the role of the watchdog as part of bigger investigative pieces.

THINKING AHEAD: HOW TO FIND BIGGER STORIES THAT MATTER

In the previous chapter, we talked about the news that finds you: meetings, speeches, news conferences, disasters, sporting events and so forth. These stories matter a lot to your readers and provide a good sense of what is happening in your coverage area. However, reporting is about more than notifying readers that events occurred. You have to find important stories and seek deeper pieces. If you want to think about it in a simple way, the basic reporting pieces tend to be about the who, what, when and where. When it comes to advanced reporting, you will dig more deeply into the how and why.

To help you get past the basics, we will talk about some of the deeper stories you can cover and ways in which you can find them. We will also discuss some of the tried-and-true reporting practices that yield better overall journalism as you go beyond the simple daily grind of reporting. This chapter will also outline how beat reporting works and the ways you can use open-record laws to find fantastic stories. Through these four story types, you can delve deeper into the world of reporting and create stories that will engage and impress your readers.

A journalist runs out of the Supreme Court carrying a copy of the decision in *Burwell* v. *Hobby Lobby Stores* June 30, 2014 in Washington, D.C. The high court ruled 5–4 that requiring family-owned corporations to pay for insurance coverage for contraception under the Affordable Care Act violated a federal law protecting religious freedom.

THE NEWS FEATURE: HOW TO FIND STORIES IN EVERYDAY LIFE

In Chapter 2, we discussed the importance of critical thinking and how it can improve your overall approach to journalism. When it comes to finding stories that matter to people, critical thinking becomes essential as you determine what you need to do and how best to do it.

A great bit of advice in finding story ideas comes from author Jenna Glatzer, who notes that coming up with broader story ideas happens when you learn to think that everything you experience could become a feature story. "Once your brain has opened up to this kind of idea generating, you'll be amazed by how much more perceptive you'll become in general,"[1] she writes in her book, "Make a Real Living as a Freelance Writer."

For example, let's say you are a courts reporter and you head to the courthouse for your daily dose of pleadings, convictions and outcomes. This day could be like any other day if you let it. However, if you follow Glatzer's advice and open up your mind to story ideas, you'll be amazed at some things you will be able to locate as potential story ideas.

Start with entering the courthouse, where you need to pass through a metal detector as a part of the security system. As they wait their turn to enter the building, people in line are grumbling about how the courthouse used to have more detectors and let people use different entrances. Stop and think about that as a story idea: When did the courthouse stop using the other entrances and why? Is it a security issue or a staffing issue? Did budget cuts lead to this, or are officials having trouble finding qualified security personnel?

During the scans, a young man entering the courthouse gets stopped for carrying a small pocketknife. He has a choice: Leave and return without the knife or leave the knife at the security station. He says he's late for his appearance and doesn't want to wait in line, so he'll just leave the knife there. "Don't forget to pick it up before you leave," the officer says, handing him a claim ticket.

Again, story idea: What is and what isn't allowed inside the courthouse? How many people get stopped each year? What is the weirdest thing someone tried to bring in? Also, how much stuff gets left behind each year? What is it? Where do officials store this stuff? What happens to it after six months or a year?

If you are having trouble figuring out how to get started finding off-the-beaten-path stories, here are some tips to get you going:

- **Stop tuning out:** As much as technology allows us to access more places and things than ever before, it has also isolated us and helped us create our own mental bubbles. Headphones that pump in music only we can hear, smartphones that allow us to text constantly and social media platforms that cater to our specific interests build a little cocoon of self-interest for us. As a reporter, you have to understand that the stories aren't in those places, but rather all around us in the world at large. The only way to find those stories is to stop tuning out. You might overhear a conversation at a café that sparks your interest in a new trend in your area. You could notice a plaque or a marker that commemorates a person or event that might intrigue you. You might feel awkward as you step out of your comfort zone, but this is what reporting requires of you.

- **Look for simple things:** Too often, we try to find a story that will win a Pulitzer, cure cancer and secure the future of Western civilization. That's counterproductive in two ways:

  1. You probably won't find that kind of "big story" every time you go looking for it, so it's going to be a fruitless endeavor.

  2. Looking for that story will make every smaller story seem worthless by comparison and thus cheat you out of a number of good story ideas.

Instead of looking for the giant story, look at the simple things and see what you can figure out about them. Writer Malcolm Gladwell took a simple approach when he dug into the complex world of ketchup. He started with a simple premise: There are dozens of types of mustard out there, but why does one type of ketchup tend to dominate the market? His piece, "The Ketchup Conundrum," used more than 5,000 words and at least a half dozen experts to explain why ketchup is ketchup.[2]

Think about simple things, like "Why do blue jeans have a small pocket with rivets on it?" or "Where do used bowling pins go when they're too beat up to use anymore?" If you go after some of the small stuff, you'll have a lot of options for interesting stories.

- **Follow up properly:** Reporters who spend a lot of time on event stories are used to **hit-and-run journalism**. They go to an event, they cover the event and then they move on to the next event. However, when it comes to finding bigger or better stories, you need to be able to look at things beyond the day one coverage and seek out other angles for your pieces. Follow-up stories will provide you with an opportunity to continue the coverage of an event or look at an event in a more complex way.

For example, if you go cover a famous poet who speaks on your campus, you can obviously nail down the basics of the speech in a single story. However, chances are pretty good that this isn't the only speaker who will show up on your campus that year. If the poet was part of a "speaker series," it would make sense to figure out who else is speaking and when, as part of a larger preview. That would give you a solid, simple day two story.

Instead of stopping there, think more critically about the series on the whole. Who gets to decide who speaks on campus? What are the requirements for speakers, and who has spoken here over the years who might merit special attention? You also might look into how much this person got paid for his speech and compare that with the rates of pay for the other speakers on your campus.

- **Wonder more:** Little kids are great for a variety of reasons, not the least of which is their sense of wonder. A 4-year-old's favorite question is "Why?" Kids want to know how stuff works, why it happens and the answers to all sorts of other important questions, like the one comedian Dana Carvey's son once asked: "Does God have feet?"[3] At some point, we stop incessantly asking "Why?" because we fear looking stupid or because we stop caring about how things work. We stop engaging with the world around us and we no longer enjoy the wonderment we once experienced as little kids.

That's a shame, because wondering more will lead to some incredible stories. When you notice things happening around you, stop and wonder for a minute or two. Open up your mind to that moment where you start more sentences with "I wonder . . . ," and you will have more story ideas than you can shake a stick at. (I wonder who came up with that euphemism or what it meant . . .)

Throughout the day, you continue to cover court cases and pick up stories on the outcome of each. The only things that remain constant are the court's bailiff and the court reporter. More potential stories: You can dig into the way in which bailiffs and court reporters work. Where did the bailiff go to learn how to perform the duties of the job? How does that little typewriter-like thing (often called a stenotype machine) work? How did the court reporter learn how to type like that? Is there a movement away from this technology, in the age of digital capture?

This example could go on for pages, but the point is that once you learn how to see stories in every corner of your coverage area, you can become a more robust journalist.

UPI reporter Helen Thomas interviews President-elect John Kennedy at Georgetown University Hospital, during Kennedy's visit to his wife Jacqueline. Thomas covered 10 presidents while serving as a beat reporter and columnist as part of the White House press corps.

BEAT REPORTING

Reporting in a consistent area allows you to know topics, sources and issues better than if you switched from area to area every day. This approach to news coverage is called **beat reporting**, and it allows journalists to become experts on areas of reader interest as they mine for deeper and stronger stories.

Readers seek certain beat reporters' bylines because they know those reporters can provide crucial information in key coverage areas. Beat reporters cultivate sources through repeated contact with them on a variety of stories. They also frequent the "hub" of activity for the beat, such as city hall for local government reporters or the courthouse for criminal justice reporters. Here is a quick look at some traditional beats and how journalists do good beat work:

TYPES OF BEATS

Beats usually fall into one of three categories:

1. **Thematic beats:** These are based on topics of interest to readers and usually involve an intimate knowledge in a specialized area. A publication with a modicum of reporters can assign one reporter to cover sports, another to cover education and yet another to cover local government. A larger publication might subdivide those areas so that one reporter covers boys' sports at the local high school and another covers girls' sports. If more reporters exist in the sports section, the publication might divide those beats even more finely, with certain reporters covering specific sports. Education could be cut into K-12 and higher education, if a college or university is within that publication's coverage area. Government could divide into city, county and state coverage, with one or more reporters in each area.

2. **Geographic beats:** In some cases, a reporter covers not so much a specific topic, but a physical area. Reporters can define their beats geographically, such as a rural reporter, who

Bettmann/Getty Images

is responsible for covering farms and agriculture in a specific part of a county, or a neighborhood journalist, who might blog about everything happening within a several-block area. Instead of becoming experts on specific topics, geographic beat reporters become well versed in everything that happens around them in a physical area. Many reporters who work in small newsrooms take on this kind of approach so that a reporter or two can become a central junction point for important content in that area.

3. **Conceptual beats:** Some topics don't really fit into either of the previous types of beats and carry with them a more nebulous sense of the content they provide. These are beats that journalists tend to conceptualize for themselves or that use specific types of tools to mine for content. Things such as a multicultural beat or data journalism can fall into these conceptual beats, as reporters rely more on the ideas and tools than a specific place or topic. These reporters can go across coverage areas and work with journalists in traditional beat areas. For example, a data examination of political donors might come from a government beat, but it is the data journalists who dig into the story. Granted, the data itself isn't the story, but it often reveals the story and many beat reporters are often unable to dig into this the way trained data journalists are. Issues such as race relations or gender gaps can take place in any field, but deeper pieces on these issues might require one person or journalistic team that can see the forest through the trees.

GETTING STARTED: HOW TO BECOME IMMERSED IN YOUR NEW AREA

Trying to find stories in a new area can scare a reporter to death. You don't know what matters and what doesn't or which sources are great and which ones are weasels. You need to figure out how to churn out quality pieces that go beyond "held a meeting" stories, and you probably don't know where to start. Here are some basic pointers to get you moving in the right direction:

INTERVIEW YOUR PREDECESSOR

In most cases you won't start a never-done-before beat. You will take over from someone who got moved to another beat, plans to retire or will be leaving the publication for another job. Take advantage of

Editor Glenn Wallace talks with reporter Crystal Anderson about story ideas and coverage in the newsroom at the Golden Transcript in Golden, Colorado, on Dec. 29, 2015. Conversations between reporters and editors are important in conceptualizing how best to find and cover stories.

Seth McConnell/The Denver Post/Getty Images

this opportunity to pump your predecessor for information to get a running start on your new beat. Here are some specific questions to ask:

- What big stories are coming down the road on this beat?
- What stories need extra work or should be followed up?
- Do you have any "I wish I had gotten to that" topics you think are really valuable?
- What were some of the most problematic parts of the beat?

- Which people were really helpful sources? Which ones made you wish you never took this job?
- Where should I spend most of my time, both physically and in terms of coverage?

Don't take everything your predecessor says as gospel, but use these starting points to find your footing.

READ YOUR PUBLICATION

Before you can figure out what you should do or shouldn't do, you need to see what has been done and what hasn't. If you look through a good chunk of your publication's recent archives, you can get a feel for the overall tone of journalism done there as well as which stories matter most to editors and readers. You might have a great idea for a news feature on the beat, only to find out it's been done a half dozen times already. You might assume your beat includes certain parts of a topic, only to find that another reporter on a different beat usually covers those areas. The goal is to get a lay of the land so you can best determine your first couple of steps. In other words, preparation is the staple of all good journalism, and it's going to help you get ready to cover a beat.

TALK TO YOUR BOSS

Each boss will expect different things from you on a beat. Some bosses will demand a heavy load of event coverage, with a sprinkling of profiles and deeper pieces. Other bosses want you to minimize your coverage of meetings and spend more time doing investigative pieces and personality profiles. Depending on your news outlet, social media may be more or less important to your approach to coverage. To fully understand what the expectations are, you should have a good discussion with your editor to figure out what approach you agree is best for your beat. This will help you avoid getting off on the wrong foot on the beat or feeling lost on the job.

Cecilie_Arcurs/iStock.com

Building a beat requires you to get out of your comfort zone and meet new people. Take time to introduce yourself to people you don't know on your beat and show that you have an interest in their stories.

BUILDING YOUR BEAT: HOW TO MAKE FRIENDS AND INFLUENCE PEOPLE

Once you feel confident about the general parameters of your coverage area, you want to establish yourself as the key contact for people interested in your beat. You can find a wide array of stories if you know where to look and to whom you should speak. Here are a few big ways to make yourself indispensable on the beat:

GET OUT OF THE OFFICE

One of the biggest mistakes beginning reporters make is to send off a series of introductory emails or make a bunch of random calls to ask sources, "So, what's going on by you?" The sources you reach are busy people and probably aren't going to say, "Thank goodness you called! I have so many story ideas I want to give you!" If you want to call the people or email them as an opportunity to set up in-person meetings, that's fine, but the phone can't be your main connection to the beat.

Get out of your newsroom and go to where the news happens on your beat. In the case of a beat like education, you could visit schools and the administration office to get a lay of the land. City Hall is going to matter a lot to you if you cover local government and it never hurts to know the desk workers at the police station or courthouse if you get the crime beat. When you are physically around, you have a much better chance of finding out what people are doing as well as seeing things that might make for nice news features.

BUILD SOURCES

The more time you spend talking to people on your beat, the more information you will get from them and the more trust you can build with them. When sources learn to trust you, they will be more willing to work with you on stories and even feed you news tips. The sources can help you figure out what is and isn't a big deal in the area, ranging from the annual school board elections to the annual sturgeon-spearing season.

Talking to sources is a lot like developing any other type of relationship. It will take time to get a sense of each other, learn what you can say or do and how you should expect to treat one another. If you are one of a dozen reporters this source must handle each day, you can get lost in the shuffle, so don't be discouraged if you don't bond instantly. Slow and steady wins the race.

GATHER DOCUMENTS

As mentioned earlier in the preparation phase, you should read everything you can get your hands on so you have a firm grasp of your beat. This applies as well when you start digging into your beat at the ground level. You want to get copies of all the important documents related to your beat and determine how they can help you make sense of your coverage area. Basic documents you want to get include things like meeting schedules, budgets and lists of important committees.

You want to have copies of the governing documents of the organizations associated with your beat, such as the constitution, charter and bylaws for boards of directors or governance groups. It will be helpful for you to determine what a group can and can't do at any point in time. You can also gather the minutes from the previous meetings to determine what the group did and when. These will also help you determine who voted for or against certain items, thus allowing you to get a better picture of board participation.

Get copies of any financial documents that will help you see where money enters specific organizations on your beat and how it is spent. In some cases, these documents are available online and require very little work to acquire. In other cases, you might need to rely on an open-records request or two. In either case, it is a good idea to have these on hand, as money tends to be of significant interest to readers of all kinds.

1. **Don't dis the desk jockeys:** The biggest mistake new beat reporters make is mistreating secretaries, program assistants, desk sergeants and other people who ride a desk. These reporters also tend to ignore the custodial staff, building supervisors and other maintenance people. This is a huge mistake. Custodians know when people are fired before most of the upper-level managers do. Secretaries process all the paperwork that makes something happen. Assistants know when a boss is doing or not doing something. When it comes right down to it, you're better off getting to know these people and treating them well. Simple chatter while you wait, offering a "happy holidays" to them or even just stopping by to see them can lead to a much better beat experience.

2. **Get close, but don't get too close:** This can be extremely hard, but when people spend a lot of time together, they tend to develop a sense of friendship. Relationships like this with sources can be great in some cases: They'll share more with you. They'll trust you more. They'll give you info that you alone will get. The relationships can also be horrible: They'll ask you to cover their "pet" projects. They'll beg you not to write about their kid's drunken-driving arrest. They'll try to manipulate you. You need to establish a professional, courteous relationship with your sources on the beat. You can be friendly, but in the end, you aren't friends. Keeping a firm line between you and your sources can keep you out of some awkward situations.

3. **When you start to burn out, let someone know:** Coverage can suffer if you spend too much time on a particular beat. When you find that you're running out of ways to make the city council interesting or you can't think of another way to profile a school teacher, talk to your boss and see if there's something that can be done. You might be stuck there, but a boss can offer you a few ideas on how to go after coverage in a new or interesting fashion. In other cases, it might be time to shake up the beat system. It's a lot like the old "rotational farming" system: When your soil has been sapped of nutrients because you grew the same crops too often, sometimes, you need to get something new planted in there.

CONTINUING COVERAGE: SIMPLE WAYS TO REFRESH BEAT REPORTING

Even reporters who are bursting with energy and ideas when they enter a beat can find themselves falling into a coverage rut of meetings, speeches and news conferences. Keeping a beat fresh requires journalists to remain active and look for new or different things to do each day. Here are a few tips to make that happen:

KEEP IN CONTACT WITH SOURCES

Each time you work on a piece, you want to keep in contact with the story's key sources. These people are vital to your storytelling and your ability to keep your readers up to date on the topic at hand. Once you finish your story, look for reasons to reach out to these people and see if they have anything else of interest to tell you. If you keep a list of people with whom you spoke for important beat stories, you can find a reason to check in with them frequently.

The type of beat you cover will likely determine how often you should contact certain sources. A big-city reporter on a police beat will want to check back with record keepers and public information officers at least once or twice per day. A small-town education reporter might check in with certain teachers once every two weeks or so. Establish a reasonable schedule for follow-up calls and stick to it. This will get you in the habit of checking back with people of interest. It will also get those people in the habit of talking to you, which will keep them on the lookout for interesting stories. It might also inspire them to reach out to you when they have something important to say.

REVIEW OLDER STORIES

Once you do a big story, the question remains: Did this have an impact? In most cases, people who find themselves being questioned as a result of a bigger story will promise change or vow to "look into" whatever it is the story is covering. For example, investigative journalists in Milwaukee researched the worst landlords in the city, outlining horrible living conditions, shady business practices and outstanding debt.[4] In one story, the Journal Sentinel found that former University of Wisconsin basketball star and former NBA player Devin Harris was behind a company that had nearly $200,000 worth of building code violations.[5] The paper checked back on this story several months later to find that Harris' company had paid off what it owed and was continuing to rehabilitate its properties around the city.[6]

Portland Press Herald/Getty Images

Residents Noorhussein Ibrahim, right, and Jibril Koshin, left, showed a reporter a plywood door that they were asked to use as an emergency exit by landlord Gregory Nisbet at 188 Dartmouth Street, on Monday, Dec. 15, 2014. This reporter is updating a story about the living conditions at this home, which experienced a fire more than a month earlier.

Clearly, the paper's reporting had an impact: The taxes and fines were more than four years old at the time of the first story but had been paid less than four months after the story broke. This was one of the many follow-up pieces done in the wake of the "Landlord Games" series, with many of the stories noting people or companies paying up or fighting the city. The goal of these follow-up pieces was to provide additional information on a topic of interest to readers in hopes of keeping them current once the original reporting had piqued their interest.

The goal with follow-up stories is to see if things people said initially are coming to fruition. A city council member might be embarrassed by a report that he missed five of the city's 12 meetings in a year and thus promised to do better this year. It's worth a follow-up examination to see if the representative lived up to that promise. The same thing is true of stories based on deadlines, such as a goal to hire a superintendent of schools by a certain date or the unveiling of a five-year plan to create a more diverse police force. It is important to write about those big plans, but without follow-up stories, no one will ever know if those big promises came true.

CONNECT THE DOTS

The benefit of spending a good amount of time on a beat is that you can see things more broadly than general-assignment reporters, who see an area only once in a while. The day-in, day-out coverage can yield good, small stories, but when you have the opportunity to connect the dots, you can show people the bigger picture. For example, you might notice in your education coverage that a series of retirements over several years has left the school district with a large number of teachers under the age of 26 and with less than three years of experience. If you track that over several years, you might notice that this trend seems to be continuing, with few teachers staying past their fourth or fifth year before leaving. Is this a trend of burnout, or is it a problem with the administration?

The same thing is true for covering a broader city beat, such as entertainment or government, where noticing trends over time can lead to an interesting analysis piece. Perhaps there is a building on the main thoroughfare of your small town with a good overall history of maintenance, ample parking and agreeable property tax rates. However, every business that moves into it ends up leaving within a year of signing a lease. Is it a case of businesses that can't meet a need for that town, or is the landlord someone who is being unreasonable with rent and upkeep demands? Why don't people go there enough to help a business make a viable run in that spot? Once you notice the situation, you can connect the dots and tell your readers about the bigger story.

Katie Couric interviews Senator Marco Rubio at the Versailles Restaurant in Little Havana on Jan. 10, 2015 in Miami, Florida. Profile stories require you to spend quality time with your subject.

PERSONALITY PROFILES

People enjoy reading about the lives and experiences of other people, which is why personality profiles draw heavy readership. Every person has a story, and when you can tell that story in an interesting and compelling fashion, you give your audience a treat. Whether you find an interesting person as part of your beat coverage or you wonder about the daily efforts of someone like the roadkill specialist used as an example in Chapter 4, profiles start with people who intrigue you. These people can be famous public figures or the people who toil in obscurity, but something about who they are or what they do makes you want to learn more.

We briefly discussed this kind of story when we discussed narrative writing, but to write one of these stories well, you need to combine strong interviewing along with keen observation. Let's take a look at the reporting approach you must have to get a great profile off the ground:

INTERVIEWING FOR THE PROFILE

The profile interview will take several stages and will involve multiple sources. The truth is, most people don't really have a strong sense of how they represent themselves to the outside world. People who think they are funny might come across as insulting. People who feel shy might actually be seen as quiet and confident. The trick is to meld the internal musings of a source with the outside observation you and others conduct to best tell this story.

THOUGHTS FROM A PRO ➡ JAIMI DOWDELL, SENIOR TRAINING DIRECTOR, INVESTIGATIVE REPORTERS AND EDITORS

© Jaimi Dowdell

As a college student, Jaimi Dowdell found her calling after a particularly frustrating first experience with reporting.

"When I was an undergrad in college I took a reporting class," she said. "It was at Mizzou where we worked for the (Columbia) Missourian (newspaper). It was one of my toughest semesters because I felt like my editor didn't see any potential in my work. I left the semester feeling like reporting might not be my career after all. I knew I couldn't take the advanced reporting class and have another semester of failure. A friend told me that he'd taken the computer-assisted reporting class and he thought I'd like it. Turns out it was a great option for me."

After learning how to engage in deep digging and statistical analysis, Dowdell found her passion for investigative stories and data-driven journalism. Today, she is the senior training director for Investigative Reporters and Editors, a nonprofit organization dedicated to improving investigative reporting. She was also honored as the 2016 Spotlight Fellow, which has her working with the Boston Globe. Previously, she did computer-assisted reporting at the St. Louis Post-Dispatch.

"At IRE, we believe that all journalism should be investigative reporting," Dowdell said. "Journalists need to be verifying facts, asking better questions and getting documents to back it all up; it's simply good reporting. **Data journalism** is part of that."

Good reporting also requires journalists to avoid taking things at face value and making sure to check their facts, she said.

"Get away from anecdotes. Verify information," Dowdell said. "Stop relying on what people say. If the police chief says crime has decreased, get the data and prove it yourself. If the mayor says your community took a financial hit because of lost tax revenue, get the revenue data to see if that is true. By verifying facts and not relying on anecdotes we can inform issues in the community."

When it comes to bigger investigations, Dowdell said the amount of time it takes to dig deep can be frustrating, but inevitably worth it.

"When working with data it seems like it always takes a bit longer than you anticipated," she said. "With the demands on daily journalists this can be a bit daunting. The best advice I can give reporters who want to do this kind of work is to set aside a little bit of time each day to focus on moving some sort of project forward, even if it means coming into work 20 minutes earlier or spending a little less time on social media or chatting with co-workers. By making yourself work on something every day you'll chip away at a project and before you know it you'll be ready to publish."

ONE LAST THING

Q: If you could tell students reading this book anything about journalism or anything you think would have value to them, what would it be?

A: "Investigative reporting is important and chances are good that if you don't do this work no one else will. We have potential to make a real impact on our society."

Let's look at a few basic elements of interviewing your source and what you can get out of those interviews:

As you build a profile story, you will likely have questions that come up about information you gathered earlier in the process. Be sure to check back with your sources when you have concerns.

FIRST INTERVIEW

To create a well-rounded view of your source, you will need to commit to several interviews with that person. The first interview will give you a rough sketch of this person and who he or she is. Research you conducted prior to the interview should help guide you into some general topics, such as the person's educational background, life experience and general interests. This interview does the heavy lifting in establishing those basic elements and confirming information you plan to include in the profile.

Broad, open-ended questions work well in this situation, as they allow the source to reveal information in a more fluid, less constrained way. Take special note of specific things the source discusses as important or noteworthy so you can ask the source to develop those ideas. For example, a wealthy businesswoman might make mention of her first job as a waitress in a small-town diner and how important that job was. A good follow-up question would be, "What was it about that job that made such a difference in your life?" It might also be interesting to find out if that diner still exists. If it's nearby, you could visit it and see if anyone there remembers her. Another interesting thing might be to go out to eat with this businesswoman and see how she treats the waiters and waitresses. She might tip really well, even if the service isn't great, because she remembers how hard the job was, or she might be very demanding because she knows the job can be done much better.

You want to listen to your subject for small moments that reveal potentially interesting life experiences. A teacher might mention an interest in high school theater productions, which could reveal a long-held interest in the arts. A priest might have a faded military tattoo on his forearm, giving you a chance to ask about his life before the seminary. When a source opens a door just a crack for you, don't be afraid to peek in and see what's behind it.

It is also important to take note of people your subject mentions during the first interview. If the chancellor of your university says that Mrs. McGreevey, his freshman English teacher from high school, was the first person to really understand his passion for education, you need to find out as much as you can about her. You also want to contact her, if possible, for an interview so you can figure out how she viewed the chancellor as a 14-year-old boy. The same thing is true if a source mentions a best friend from college, a football coach who helped the source become a better player or a colleague at a previous job. These people are ready-made secondary sources for you and will helpfully reveal other aspects of this person.

These **secondary sources** will be vital to your overall profile because each person can provide a different view of your source. When it comes to selecting your secondary sources, worry less about the number of people you want to interview, but rather the way the sources connect to your profile subject. If you were to profile a professor at your school, selecting 10 students from his introductory writing course would give you only one angle on his life. If you interviewed his wife, his mother, his best friend from high school, his first boss and one student, you would have a more complete picture of this person. Keep that in mind when you look for secondary sources.

SECOND INTERVIEW

Once you interview most of the secondary sources you wanted to reach, get back together with your profile subject for a second interview. This interview gives you the opportunity to fill in some holes and clear up some discrepancies. The source might have mentioned that Mrs. McGreevey was his freshman English teacher, but she remembers having him as a junior and has the records to prove it. That kind of thing can be distracting for readers if you don't clear that up before writing your profile.

Another benefit of the second interview is that you now have questions that came from your interviews with the secondary sources. Most profile subjects will remember certain stories or provide specific anecdotes about their interactions with friends, family or colleagues because those things mattered to them. However, the outside sources will likely have different stories and anecdotes they remember about the source. This is a great chance to ask about the story the subject's mom told you about the time the source made mud balls in the backyard and threw them at the house. It might also be interesting to find out if the source remembers the time she told her sister that the closet was haunted, just so she didn't have to share clothing space with a sibling.

THIRD INTERVIEW

The last interview is a luxury you might not have, so you might end up doing a lot of this work during the second interview. If you can meet a third time, this is the chance to do some serious observation to add color and feel to the piece. By this point in time, the source is used to your being around. The source probably feels comfortable enough to be "normal" around you. You also probably have all the major questions about this person answered, so you can spend more time catching the details and descriptors that will allow you to paint a great word picture for your readers.

You want your readers to be able to see your subject in their mind's eye, so gather some basic information about what this person looks like. You

Profile stories rely on description, both in terms of the source and the setting. Be sure to look around you during your interviews to capture the essence of the source and the ambience of the room.

can start with the basics, such as height, weight, hair color, eye color and so forth. Then, move into things like the way the person dresses and presents himself. Does the source wear a three-piece suit or a T-shirt and jeans? Is this person fashion conscious and can tell you what designer made every piece of their clothing? When the person stands or sits, is posture a big deal? Does the source slouch or stand ramrod straight? How does the source speak? Is it loud and boisterous or quiet and reserved? How does the source laugh or yell?

You then can move into other aspects of that person's surroundings, such as what the person values. Some people surround themselves with walls full of awards and honors while others fill bookshelves with toys and knickknacks. Some offices are crammed and messy while others are meticulously maintained. Some people fawn over houseplants or muscle cars while others love travel or musical instruments. What that person values will help you let your readers see the person.

Look for chances to see how the person interacts with others. If the person is the boss, does she treat subordinates well or poorly? If the person is a politician, does he pretend to know or love people, only to tell you on the side he has no idea who these people are? A profile subject who is cold and distant at work but is amazingly loving at home provides you with one type of picture. A subject who never wants to go home but loves work provides you with a different picture. By the time this third interview is over, you should be ready to write a killer profile filled with depth and richness.

WORKING AS A WATCHDOG

Good journalists are inherently nosy. They desperately want to dig into a story and figure out what is really going on behind the veneer of bright lights and big smiles. They also want to hold people in power to account for their actions. All of these elements often converge in what people in this field tend to call "**watchdog journalism**." The media serve as the "watchdog" for the public, barking loudly to alert readers to areas of concern and steadfastly guarding the public's best interests. They shine a light on areas of public interest and demand accountability from public officials and private companies.

Stories in this vein can emerge from a variety of sources and in an array of formats. Beat-based journalists build trust with sources over time, which can lead to one of them providing a tip on a shady deal or a curious situation that's currently flying under the radar. For example, a good city government reporter might find out from a city council representative that a major land deal the council is ready to vote on will financially benefit the mayor's brother-in-law. A sports writer on the baseball beat might get a note from a team source about an injury a star player suffered or a head's up that a malcontent pitcher is about to be traded.

Investigative journalists often serve as watchdogs as they dig into piles of data and documents. Reporters who do this often rely on the **Freedom of Information Act**, or FOIA, which is a law used to provide open access to the actions and records of federal agencies. States have similar laws called "**sunshine laws**" or "open-meetings/records laws" that provide the public with access to documents and official meetings state agencies create or hold. These agencies must disclose any information and allow the review of any documents that a citizen requests as long as the material doesn't fall under one of several exemption areas, such as personal privacy and national security. (To learn more about how this law works and how to file an open-records request, turn to Appendix C.)

Many of the biggest stories of the century involved watchdog journalism. Bob Woodward and Carl Bernstein brought the Watergate scandal to light with dogged reporting at the Washington Post. This led to the resignation of President Richard Nixon in 1974. Staff members at the Associated Press dug into the issue of labor abuses and seafood in 2016. Their collection of work led to reforms in the industry, the freeing of 2,000 slaves and a Pulitzer Prize for Public Service.

CONSIDER THIS ➡ IS THE BIG STORY WORTH IT?

Many journalists fear bigger stories, such as those related to data analysis or open-records requests, because they involve more time than they can seem to spare. Others fall in love with their ideas and have a hard time deciding when the story isn't really there. As Jaimi Dowdell notes, investigative reporting has a lot of value, and it is often where journalists tend to have the greatest impact. With budget cuts, staff shortages and a general sense that breaking news is easier, administrators often have difficulty approving a large outpouring of personnel and financial resources for a story that might not pan out.

Dowdell offers some things to think about when you need to figure out if a deeper story is worth the extra time and effort:

- **Does this story answer a question?** The best investigations and data stories answer a question. Stay away from noun stories. Don't do a story on "crime" or "salaries," because it just won't be that good. Seek to answer a question or explain a phenomenon, and you'll be in better shape.

- **Does the story break new ground?** Look and see what has been done on the topic. Just because a story

was done in the past doesn't mean it can't be done again, but how can you move it forward? What is different? Why is this important now or to your community?

- **Does the story have potential for impact?** We want people to care about your work. Why should they care about this? Is there room for change?

- **Are there victims or does this affect people?** Again, you want people to care about your work, and this helps.

- **Does this have a point to it?** Keep making yourself write down a sentence or two explaining the story. What is the story? What is the news? If you can't do it in a couple of sentences, you need to go back to work. Keep asking yourself, "Is this a story?" Get feedback from other people. Be honest with yourself because your time is limited.

At the end of the day, you need to have a passion for the story and a desire to stick with it. Otherwise, no matter how good the story or how deep the pool of resources you have, the story will fail.

At the core of these and many other stories is the desire to find out why something works or doesn't work and a dogged determination to get answers from people who probably don't want to give them.

8 BEYOND BASIC REPORTING:
NEWS YOU HAVE TO FIND

THE BIG THREE

Here are the three key things you should take away from this chapter:

1. **Anything can lead you to a story:** If you open your mind's eye and stop tuning out, the world around you is nothing but a giant bin of story ideas waiting for you to dig in. The more you view the world around you with wonder and ask "why" about things that you see, the more likely you will be to find interesting answers and fun stories.

2. **Focus on people:** Profile stories are fantastic stories because they give your readers an inside look at people of interest. However, focusing on people goes beyond basic profile stories. If you see what scares people or what excites people, you can find some fantastic stories right in front of you. Also, it never hurts to be nice to people when you are on a beat or other reporting assignment. Never overlook people, regardless of their social status or employment role.

3. **Don't be afraid to dig:** Deep stories will take more time than traditional event stories and in some cases might not seem like they are yielding much value. Don't worry if your first open-records request is rejected or a few people initially don't want to talk to you about your story. If you remain persistent in your work, you will eventually get the things you need to tell the story you want to tell.

KEY TERMS

beat reporting 142	Freedom of Information Act 152	sunshine laws 152
conceptual beats 143	hit-and-run journalism 141	thematic beats 142
data journalism 149	secondary sources 150	watchdog journalism 152

DISCUSSION QUESTIONS

1. What makes for a good personality profile in your opinion? Is it all about the person, or do the writing and reporting help you care about the subject? Think about the last time you read a profile. What worked and what didn't when it came to helping you see the person in your mind's eye and understand who that person is?

2. Think of a simple thing in your everyday life. What would make you care enough about it to write a story of some kind? Are you interested in how something is made or why something works? Do you wonder who a person is or how that person ended up where he or she is in life? Did you see a business or a house that always intrigued you when you drove by but you

never bothered to stop? What made that small thing worthy of your attention and how could you turn it into a story for a broader readership?

3. What stories do you most enjoy reading on a daily or weekly basis? (Chances are, they aren't meeting or speech stories.) What makes these stories worth reading? When you think of writing a story, how often do you use stories like these as a guidepost for your approach to story selection and story writing?

WRITE NOW!

1. Read through a newspaper or website that covers your campus or city to find a story that might be worth a follow-up story of some kind. Write a short paper (1 page, typed, double-spaced) that explains the story and how you would propose to advance it. Include potential sources for that story. After discussing this idea with your instructor to help sharpen your approach, do some additional research and interviewing on this topic. Gather enough information to write a story that advances the topic. Incorporate at least two human sources. The story should be 2 to 2.5 pages typed, double-spaced.

2. Review two weeks' worth of content from a local publication. Note the bylines (names of the writers) on the stories and see if they appear on stories in specific beats. Does it look like your publication operates on a beat system? How many beats could you identify, and what were they? Approximately how many stories does a reporter on a beat produce over two weeks, and what kinds of stories are they (profiles, events, breaking news etc.)? Write up your findings.

3. Read your campus news outlet (paper, website etc.) and your local publication as well for stories that would merit a good follow-up or news feature. It could be a story that looks at the big picture of a topic, such as what happened to a building project that was promised several months ago. It could be a broader news feature on groups that bring speakers to campus or that books theater and musical acts for the area's arena. Research the topic, interview the sources you think would help you understand the issue and write a multiple-source story on the topic.

Visit edge.sagepub.com/filaknews to help you accomplish your coursework goals in an easy-to-use learning environment.

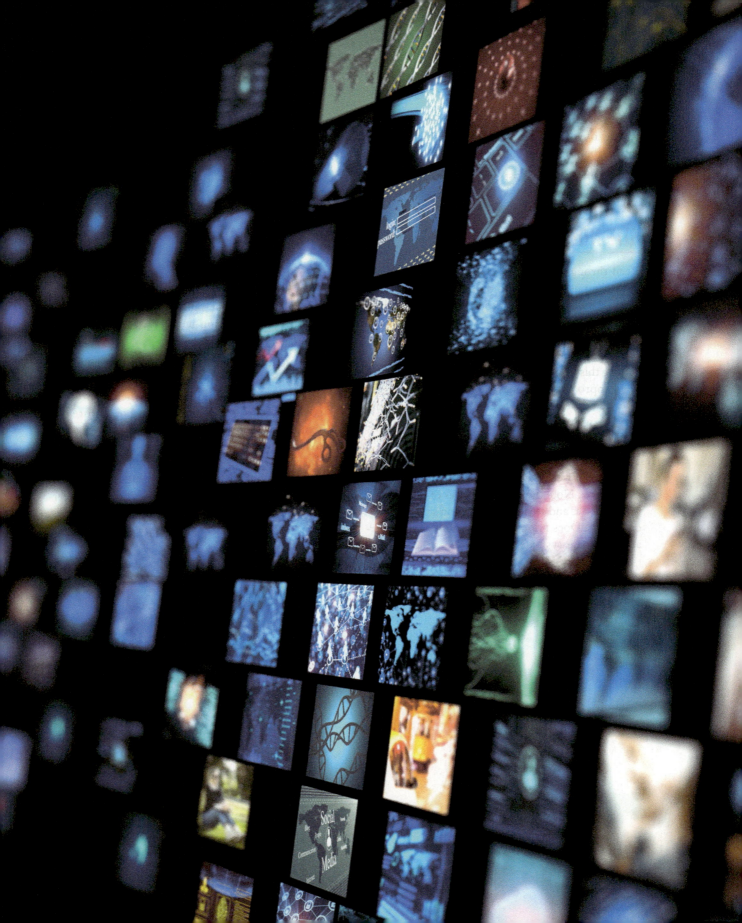

9 BROADCAST-STYLE WRITING AND VOICING

LEARNING OBJECTIVES

After completing this chapter you should be able to:

- Construct a standard broadcast story, keeping in mind the impact of audio and video on your storytelling.
- Define and differentiate among the types of broadcast stories and explain how and when to use them.
- Apply strategies of writing for the ear instead of writing for the eye.
- Understand the differences between print and broadcast writing in terms of script style, formatting and story structure.
- Apply concepts of pace and flow to sentence construction and story structure.

THINKING AHEAD: WRITING SCRIPTS AND BUILDING STORIES

Throughout the 20th century, broadcast journalism evolved to meet the advances in technology and the needs of an ever-changing audience. As the devices became less magical and more ubiquitous, users began to use broadcast content as a companion for their daily lives. No longer did they actively attend to the machine, but instead let the news, sports and entertainment information of the day fill the background as they worked on other things. That trend has continued, as distracted audiences balance daily life with a variety of media devices and a constant stream of content. This means that broadcast writing will vary from the standard inverted pyramid you see in newspapers and on many websites.

Broadcasters work like print reporters in terms of filing content for traditional media platforms as well as posting content on the web and using social media to reach potential viewers. Regardless of the platform on which you place your video work, you will need to write in a broadcast style to help augment your video, tell your story effectively and reach your audience with quality content. At the core of broadcast writing is the standard set of principles that guide all journalists: factual accuracy, ethical behavior, fairness and audience centricity.

This chapter will outline the ways in which broadcast writing is similar to and yet different from the types of writing you have done to this point. This examination will include an analysis of the various types of audio and video stories broadcast journalists use to tell stories. We will also look at the best ways to improve your scripts and serve your audiences. The next few chapters will build on this basic skill by adding video and audio gathering as well as techniques to edit all of this together to create a complete digital experience for your viewers.

Broadcast style takes into account how the messages are sent and received. While text-based journalists write for people who read the content, broadcasters must think about how their work sounds when it is spoken and when it is heard.

BROADCAST STYLE: DIFFERENT, YET THE SAME

Journalists who use video and audio have different needs from those of text-based reporters, thus making their job easier in some cases and more difficult in others. The use of video, for example, can make it easier for a broadcast journalist to set a scene for an audience. Conversely, a distracted audience and time restrictions can force broadcast journalists to do a lot more storytelling with a lot fewer words.

Because of these differences, broadcast journalists often get a bad rap for oversimplifying the news or using less formal verbiage to tell their stories. This is unfair, as the broadcast journalists are simply using the tools available to them in the best way possible to serve the audience. Their approach isn't better or worse, just different from text-based journalism.

Broadcast journalists still focus on the interest elements noted earlier in the book, but they place a premium on immediacy. The use of video and the "live" nature of broadcast journalism allows them to accentuate the "now" element of journalism. That can make the content seem fresher to the viewers, and it can help the viewers feel more up to date on important topics.

The style of writing also provides an interpersonal feel to the content. Unlike print-style reporters, broadcast journalists appear in their own work, both through video clips known as standups and through the use of interpersonal language. While both forms of media attempt to remain objective in news coverage, broadcasters can use second-person writing to reach the viewers and also take part in the journalism, through investigative pieces and participatory stories.

Broadcast also relies on the use of the spoken word and the video image to tell stories. Pairing these elements can be a challenge, as some stories are crucial but lack compelling visuals and other pieces are too complex to wedge into a minute or two of TV time. However, the more practiced you become at writing and video work (see Chapters 10 and 11 for more on this), the better prepared you will be in working through these issues.

THOUGHTS FROM A PRO ➡ LAUREN LEAMANCZYK, INVESTIGATIVE REPORTER, KARE-11

If a broadcast story isn't visually appealing and packaged interestingly, it will fail, veteran TV reporter Lauren Leamanczyk says.

"This is the most vital part of television news," she says. "It is important for the reporter to think about the visual elements from the moment a story is conceived."

Leamanczyk is a member of the I-TEAM at KARE-11 in Minneapolis. Prior to arriving in Minnesota, she served as an investigative reporter and fill-in anchor at WBZ-TV, the CBS affiliate in Boston. She also worked at various stations throughout the Midwest.

Leamanczyk says she spends most of her time on a story thinking about how best to reach her audience in a meaningful way.

"In morning and afternoon meetings, there is a lot of discussion about what a viewer will find interesting, why it's important to them and the big 'who cares' factor," she says. "Our entire existence relies on viewers. If we don't give them content they find necessary, informative and appealing, they'll find another news outlet."

As she works on a story, Leamanczyk says she always tries to "bring the viewers" to the scene and help them feel something, through character development, strong visuals and natural sound. She also focuses on pairing the visual with the script, because that approach can make the difference between a good package and a great one.

"I work with professional photographers and editors and we talk about the visuals right away," Leamanczyk says.

"I make sure to set up the b-roll opportunities when I set up the interviews. When I write a script, I keep the video and audio in mind. Do not write a line of track without knowing how your video editor will cover it."

Throughout the scriptwriting process, Leamanczyk says she focuses on storytelling both in terms of the words she uses and how she voices the script.

"It is tempting to affect an 'anchor voice' to track a package," she says. "Avoid this! Take a deep breath and speak with authority, but also as you would tell a story to someone who is in the room with you."

Even on tough deadlines and with complex pieces, Leamanczyk says she starts by asking herself "What's the point?" of the story before diving into her writing.

"It can be tempting to get bogged down in the minutiae of a story but that can easily be lost on TV," she says. "Know you're writing what you want the audience to take from the piece."

ONE LAST THING

Q: If you could tell students anything about media writing or anything you have seen in your time in the field, what would it be?

A: "Rid yourselves of the notion that TV news is somehow glamorous. It is hard, requires standing for hours in a bone chilling cold to get one shot or soundbite and forces you to miss time with your family. It doesn't pay very well until you get to the large markets and no one will do your hair or makeup. You will find yourself in situations that are uncomfortable and people will often not be happy to see you. Trying hard is no guarantee of success.

(Continued)

> It is also exhilarating, at times gives you a front row seat to history and allows you to stretch your creative muscles. You will get paid to experience people and places that you would never come across in your daily life, and on occasion it affords you the opportunity to affect real change.
>
> I love the adrenaline. I love the wacky culture of newsrooms. I get a rush out of the people I meet and the stories they entrust me to tell. I feel like sometimes I've been able to make a difference by doing that. That's why it's all worth it to me. You have to decide if it's worth it to you."

Good broadcasters invest time in creating quality scripts that help them tell stories effectively.

SCRIPT WRITING 101

Given these strengths and weaknesses, you can understand now why broadcasters need to make some adjustments to their writing. Consider these suggestions when you write your **script**:

WRITE SHORT

Writers in various text-based formats often talk about avoiding "flabby" writing and trimming unneeded words to make the writing "leaner." If print and web writing are lean, broadcast writing has to be skinny. You need to write short so that your audience members can get what they need without getting lost. This means starting with the noun and the verb and adding only what is crucial as you construct your sentence. This means finding the perfect adjective or adverb instead of using three passable ones. This means you should use common vernacular in a straightforward way. Keep your writing short and tight.

USE ACTIVE VOICE

Broadcasters who want to keep their copy tight will rely on the noun-verb-object structure discussed throughout the book. This form of writing, often called **active voice**, creates a strong "who did what to whom" approach that gives your viewers a clear picture of what happened. In contrast to **passive voice**, the structure allows for concrete nouns and vigorous verbs, both of which help audience members get crucial information easily. It also uses a sentence structure that best reflects how we would normally speak. Consider the following sentences:

Active: I left my car unlocked, and someone stole my wallet from the glove box.

Passive: Because the car was left unlocked by me, my wallet was able to be stolen from the glove box.

The first sentence sounds like something you might actually say, while the second sentence sounds like a word jumble. In addition, the first sentence has 14 words, and the second one has 19.

WRITE FOR THE EAR

One major difference between text-based content and broadcast content is how the audience members interact with the content. Print publications and websites provide text that people consume with their eyes. Broadcast journalism has journalists speaking the content and people hearing it. With that in mind, you need to write less for the eyes and more for the ears of your audience.

Aside from keeping sentences short, you need to use common words and keep word usage to common meanings. Don't use anything that would have your audience reaching for a dictionary unless it is absolutely necessary.

> **Standard print approach:** The Graves Elevator company has issued a full recall on its most recent line of cars after engineers discovered that the flywheels in the governors were not properly slowing the cars' descent.
>
> **Standard broadcast approach:** The Graves Elevator company says it is recalling its newest elevators after engineers discovered the cars were going down too fast.

You also need to use words that take advantage of sound and senses. Certain words have sounds built right into them, like "hum" and "click" and "slap." Other words have specific feelings that go with them as well and appeal to the senses. There is a difference between a "fragrant fruity wisp" of a smell and "an overpowering stench." The same is true when it comes to touch: "moist" is different from "wet," which is different from "soaked." Make sure your word choices convey the most accurate meaning while still catering to the ears of your audience members.

Journalist Dan Rather sits on the set of CBS News June 10, 1999 in New York City. Rather's speaking pace and rich vocal tone made him a favorite broadcaster among many U.S. viewers.

CONSIDER PACE AND FLOW

In broadcast journalism, your writing can't just be "good on paper." Sentences that meet structural standards and abide by rules of grammar might work in a newspaper or on the web, but if the sentences don't sound good when read aloud, they won't work on TV or radio. This is where issues of pace and flow come into play.

- **Pace:** This is how quickly or slowly you can read through a piece. Tighter sentences can quicken the **pace**, while longer sentences can slow the story down. This is also true of the word choices you make and the amount of superfluous information you have in your writing. This isn't to say that all stories should race by and that all copy should be stripped of details. However, you need to let the pace match the story's overall feel. If you write a story about a

During her "Thoughts From a Pro" interview, Lauren Leamanczyk used a few terms that might be confusing to you, such as "track" and "b-roll." Here is a list of terms used in broadcast that will help you become conversant in discussing scripts and video. Keep this handy as you move through the next few chapters.

- **Soundbite:** Some people call this an actuality or a bite. The purpose of this element is to allow the source to speak to the audience in his or her own words on camera. This is the videography version of a direct quote in a text story.

- **Tracking or voicing:** This process involves the reporter recording the script for use as part of the package. Depending on the software, reporters can "track" the story into an empty file and place it into the package, or they can play the video once it is assembled and read the script on top of the video.

- **B-roll:** Video captured that will provide the images that showcase what the reporter is saying in the script.

- **Frame:** This is an action that places the subject of the shot into the viewfinder of the camera. It can also refer to the material that you selected in the viewfinder for capturing. If you frame your shot well, the subject will look natural in the image. If you don't, the source can look tiny or squished in the shot.

- **Look room:** The space in a framed shot that prevents the subject from staring directly into the outside edge of the shot. The look room should be present in the direction that the subject is looking or moving.

- **Cut:** A sharp transition from one shot to the next shot in video.

- **Pan:** When a videographer moves a camera from side to side while recording.

- **Zoom:** A camera technique that closes in on the subject of the shot to make that person or thing appear increasingly larger.

- **Package:** A full story that includes bites from interviews, voice-over work by the reporter and b-roll.

- **Wallpaper:** A derogatory term for video that doesn't enhance the storytelling of a story. Good b-roll will match the shots to the text of the script. Wallpaper is video that only provides visual elements for the sake of having video. For example, a story on a city budget might include wallpaper video of buildings or signs that feature the city's name.

- **180-degree rule:** An approach to capturing and editing video that keeps all action on one side of a 180-degree axis to avoid "jump cuts" and disorienting video.

lazy summer day on a quiet lake, you want that story to have more of a methodical and purposeful pace to it. If you write about a rapid-fire exchange between angry school board members or a fast-moving football game, you want the pace to reflect that as well. Word choices, sentence length and story length all contribute to the speed of a piece.

- **Flow:** This is how smoothly a script moves from point to point in a story. Shorter sentences may quicken the pace, but using them inappropriately can create problems with flow and rhythm. Longer sentences may improve flow in some cases but can also make your reader feel lost.

Think of your punctuation like traffic signals: Commas are like "Yield" signs, and periods are like "Stop" signs. When you use too many commas, you can slow and speed and slow and speed to the point of giving your readers motion sickness. If you use too many periods, it can feel like you're stuck in rush-hour traffic on a freeway, jerking along in stuttering movement.

To improve the flow, you need to find ways to limit your use of punctuation within your sentences. Then, you need to find ways to smoothly transition between sentences through word repetition and matched ideas, much in the same way you would in essay writing. If you find that your story lacks flow, go back and see where it hit some bumps and smooth them out.

KEEP IT CONVERSATIONAL

As Lauren Leamanczyk mentioned earlier, you might feel the urge to use your authoritative "anchor voice" when you read your script. The instinct to do this comes from a desire to make yourself and your work sound important. However, when you take on that persona, you often sound arrogant or goofy, leading to a disconnect between you and your audience.

Broadcast expert Robert Papper has noted that the writing isn't entirely conversational, primarily because of the number of grammar and structure problems that arise in casual conversations. Instead, the form of writing is more along the lines of how we wish we would speak if we collected our thoughts before we spoke.[1] With that in mind, stick to words and thoughts you would normally use during conversations and avoid using your "anchor voice" when you voice your script.

THE BASIC ELEMENTS OF BROADCAST STRUCTURE

Unlike other forms of news writing, broadcast journalism follows more of a chronological approach to storytelling. Web and print tend to follow the inverted pyramid, but broadcast presents information in more of a "circular" approach, with the reporters telling their stories in a simple beginning-middle-end approach. That said, this does not mean broadcast doesn't focus on the interest elements we discussed earlier in the book or that broadcasters ignore the conventions of news. Let's break down a simple story to show some of the similarities and differences between broadcast and other forms of writing.

THE LEAD

Broadcast reporters have to find a way to grab the viewers' attention before moving into the meat of the story. Viewers are often distracted or busy while the news is on, so the reporter has to use the lead like print and web journalists use a headline. This will help draw the viewers into the story.

Here's a standard print story lead:

> A 25-year-old Melville police officer accused of robbing drug dealers and giving the money to local charities should not be seen as a hero, prosecuting attorney Vance Dunbar told a jury Wednesday afternoon in his closing statement.

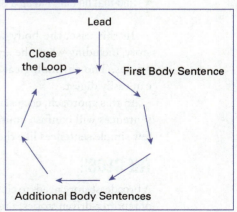

FIG. 9.1

This inverted-pyramid approach gives the readers everything they need in one short, tight sentence. In broadcast, however, a sentence like this might not grab the viewers fast enough, and thus they will miss a lot of what is going on. A **broadcast lead** provides some information of importance to alert viewers as to the main theme of the story before moving into the meat of the news.

> This Melville cop is no Robin Hood. That's what a prosecutor says jury members should remember during their deliberations today.

The broadcast lead alerts the listeners who should care (people in Melville) without getting into the specifics (who the officer is, what exactly he is accused of doing). The broadcast lead helps audience members orient themselves to the topic at hand quickly so they can avoid missing important information.

THE BODY

A broadcast story follows a "loop" approach more than an inverted pyramid; it introduces the most important thing in the story before moving in a chronological or topical direction before circling back to "close the loop" on the topic. The initial one or two body sentences will act like the lead of an inverted-pyramid story, filling in key details and giving the audience members a sense of what matters most.

> After three days of testimony, the jury will decide the fate of police officer James Wiglet. He is charged with robbing drug dealers and donating the money to charity.

What comes next will be the various elements of the story that help tell a story in a chronological format.

> Wiglet was arrested in December after he robbed an undercover F-B-I agent who was running a drug sting.
>
> After his arrest, several drug dealers came forward and said Wiglet had robbed them as well.
>
> Prosecutors then charged Wiglet with eleven counts of armed robbery.
>
> During the trial, Wiglet testified that he only took the money to benefit the poor of Melville and that he didn't keep a dime.

In this case, the body walks the audience members through the various stages of the story, including when the arrest occurred, what the charges were, and the rationale behind the crimes. The chronological approach puts the story into a format that listeners and viewers can easily digest.

In this approach, each sentence has a single point of information in it. Long or complicated sentences will confuse your viewers, so stick to one idea per sentence. The body should be a few simple sentences like these, especially if video is not involved.

THE CLOSE

A broadcast story needs to close the loop to help the journalists bring closure to the piece. In the case of reporter-driven stories, a reporter can use a **sign-off** approach that helps end the piece simply:

When journalists write for broadcast, they need to consider not only how the audience will hear the information but also how easy the script will be to read. Reporters for text-based publications don't need to worry about how sentences sound out loud, but broadcasters don't want to sound like they have a mouth full of marbles when they deliver the news. Here are a few things to think about when you write your script:

FORMATTING

To aid in the readability of the scripts, reporters will double- or triple-space the content. Radio scripts tend to be structured so the text runs across the whole page, but television and web-video scripts will keep text on the right-hand side of the page. The left side usually will contain information about video elements, the insertion of soundbites and camera directions.

TENSE

When you write for broadcast, you want to emphasize the sense that things are happening now. To make this more evident, broadcasters write in the present tense instead of the past tense. This means you will use "says" instead of "said" for attributions and refer to other actions, even those recorded earlier, with an emphasis on the present.

PRONUNCIATION

As mentioned earlier, broadcast journalism caters to the ear, not the eye. This forces reporters to focus on how things sound and take precautions to avoid words that can cause stumbles and stutters on air. For times you can't avoid those hard-to-say words, you will include phonetic explanations for them called **pronouncers**.

These tend to help with names that don't look like they sound, such as Hall of Fame quarterback Brett Favre, and

cities with complex names, like Weyauwega. The pronouncer breaks the word down into syllables and shows where to put the emphasis on the word. It should not replace the word, but rather follow it in parentheses. This will allow people who know how to say the word to avoid confusion while still helping out people who need the pronunciation assistance. Thus, you can tell your viewers that Brett Favre (FARV) attended an event in Weyauwega (wy-uh-WEE-ga) last week.

ABBREVIATIONS

When you use these, you can confuse people who might not understand that Dr. means Doctor instead of Drive or St. means Saint instead of Street. Some abbreviations are acceptable because we see them more than we see the actual word, such as Mrs. instead of missus.

Acronyms and **abbreviations** need special attention in your script. When you condense a series of words like the North Atlantic Treaty Organization to a single word, you produce an acronym that needs to be pronounced as such (NATO). However, when you just create a series of letters that need to be spoken individually, you need to use hyphens to avoid confusion. A broadcast script should call the Internal Revenue Service "the I-R-S" as opposed to "the erse."

NUMBERS AND SYMBOLS

You want to use fewer numbers and less complex ones in your broadcast scripts to help your viewers better understand and retain information. Complicated numbers can confuse people ("The state fined the university $101, 238.43 for code violations"), so it's better to round the numbers to more easily understood amounts ("The state fined the university more than one hundred thousand dollars for code violations").

(Continued)

(Continued)

Spell out symbols that have multiple meanings or that are placed out of order in terms of readability. The example above moved the "dollars" after the amount so that the words came in the exact order you would say them, as opposed to "dollars, one hundred thousand," which is how the print sentence orders the items. Symbols like # have multiple meanings, so use the words to help out the reporters: "Call us on your smartphone by dialing pound sign three-five-nine, or join the conversation on Twitter, using hashtag TriviaGame."

For W-P-D-Q, I'm Millie Sistrunk.

This closing lets the viewers know the reporter is done reporting, and it's time to go on to the next story.

Other approaches include a look-ahead if the story has the potential to lead to additional news:

The jury is expected to render a verdict within the next two days.

You could also provide people with an option to use one of your other media platforms, such as a website, to continue examining the issue. In these cases, the reporter or anchor usually uses a graphic to reinforce this point:

Should Wiglet go to prison for his actions? Go to W-P-D-Q-dot-com and participate in our reader poll.

National Public Radio's Carl Kasell organizes news stories before delivering one of his last newscasts for the Morning Edition program at NPR Dec. 30, 2009 in Washington, D.C. A newscast includes stories written in a variety of formats.

STORY TYPES AND FORMATS

Each story you write will have to deal with the strengths and weaknesses outlined earlier in the chapter. That said, not every broadcast story is the same, and understanding the various story formats and how they work is crucial to storytelling on this platform. In addition, various media outlets will use different forms of page structure, formatting and other elements on their scripts. Let's walk through the formats and outline how to write for each of them:

READER

This is the simplest and oldest form of television and radio-style storytelling. A **reader** script has the anchor or the reporter simply reading a story to the audience members with no audio or video augmentation. When you see an anchor look into the camera and tell you about an armed robbery or a speech, this is likely a reader. To help visually "tag" the story, a small over-the-shoulder graphic may appear behind the anchor, such as a set of handcuffs or a badge for the armed robbery story or a stage and a microphone for the speech story.

Readers traditionally run between 10 and 20 seconds and are about four or five sentences long. Because they have no video, you need to select clear and descriptive words to make your point. In other forms of broadcast writing, your goal is to match your words to the video that is running while you voice your script. In the case of readers, you are looking to replace the video with your word choices, so you need to rely on clear nouns and descriptive modifiers. A good reader story will allow the audience members to see the story in their mind's eye.

VOICE-OVER

This story form pairs video and a script in the simplest way possible. A **voice-over** (or VO) has a reporter or anchor begin on camera as he or she reads the story. After the initial shot of the journalist, video images begin to roll with the voice track continuing "over" the video. The video doesn't usually include any additional audio, although some natural sound associated with the story might be present. For example, a story on an animal shelter could include video of dogs barking and that barking could be audible as the anchor continues to read the script. The script will either end when the video ends or will contain one additional line after the end of the video, thus allowing the journalist to appear back on screen as he or she finishes the story. These stories tend to run 20 to 30 seconds and require about five to eight sentences to tell the story.

This is the first type of storytelling that challenges you as a writer to find ways to match what the audience is seeing with what you are saying. As you build your video package, which we discuss in Chapter 11, you will need to review the shots you have and then write content that mirrors your visuals. If you fail to do this, your story will confuse your audience members. Research has indicated that people learn when they hear and see information, but only if those elements are telling the same story. Thus, if you have a script talking about a giant crowd and you have video showing a sparse gathering, this will impair your audience's ability to understand the story.

You will need to consider the exact length of your script in terms of time and then see what video shots come into play at what points in the script. This will involve some practice runs as well, with you reading your script as you roll your video so you can see what parts of the script need to grow or shrink. You also need to consider either reordering your shots or reconstructing your script depending on what you see during your practice runs.

VO/SOT

This term fits both audio and video packages and takes the voice-over approach one step further. **VO/SOT** stands for voice-over/sound on tape, even though tape recording is becoming a thing of the past. The story integrates one or two soundbites but still relies on the anchor reading the content around those soundbites, much like a VO. The anchor starts reading the script while on screen, and after a few seconds, the video starts. The script will note where the anchor should

FIG. 9.2   AN EXAMPLE OF A VOICE-OVER SCRIPT

{REPORTER On Camera}

STUDENTS AT WEST DOYLE ELEMENTARY SCHOOL GO BALD FOR A GOOD CAUSE.

{Take VO: Images of school, students getting heads shaved}

{Super: "West Doyle Elementary"}

KIDS IN GRADES ONE THROUGH FIVE SHAVED THEIR HEADS TODAY TO HONOR THEIR SCHOOLMATE, JASPER NOLL.

THE FIFTH-GRADER HAS A RARE FORM OF CANCER AND LOST HIS HAIR DUE TO HIS TREATMENTS.

STUDENTS SAID THEY DID NOT WANT JASPER TO FEEL BAD BECAUSE HE IS BALD SO THEY LOST THEIR LOCKS AS WELL.

TWENTY LOCAL BARBERS DONATED THEIR SERVICES TO BUZZ THE NEARLY 200 STUDENTS AT WEST DOYLE.

{End VO }

{REPORTER On Cam}

FOR ADDITIONAL IMAGES OF THE EVENT, PLEASE VISIT OUR WEBSITE AT W-H-L-E-DOT-COM.

FIG. 9.3   A SPLIT-PAGE VO/SOT THAT DETAILS A CRIME STORY

Video	Audio
	(ANCHOR)
ON CAM	A U-W-Q student was suspended tonight after being charged with animal cruelty.
TAKE VO	
SHOTS OF CAMPUS	
SUPER: University of Wrigleyville-Quad City Campus	
PICTURE OF JESTER	Police say Carley Jester threw her roommate's cat out of a third-floor window during an argument Wednesday.
PICTURE OF CAT WHILE ALIVE	A neighbor called police after the cat landed on his porch. Jester was arrested and subsequently suspended by U-W-Q.
	The cat suffered broken bones and internal injuries and died shortly after.
SOT [WASHBURN BITE]	Amanda Washburn says she cannot understand why Jester killed her cat.
SUPER: Amanda Washburn, Carley Jester's roommate	
	(SOT: AMANDA WASHBURN)
	JUST BECAUSE SHE DIDN'T WANT TO WATCH THE BACHELOR TONIGHT IS NO REASON TO GET SO UPSET. THAT WAS JUST SICKENING.
ON CAM	(ANCHOR)
	Jester is in jail on a ten-thousand-dollar bond.

Notice the way in which the text the anchor reads, on the right side of the script, runs parallel to the visuals outlined on the left side of the script.

Broadcast journalism has traditionally been viewed as an interpersonal medium, in which reporters and anchors attempt to establish a rapport with the audience through language and approach. One of the simplest ways is through the use of second-person language that directly addresses the viewers.

In traditional print style, third-person writing is preferred, with an emphasis on objectivity. Writers wanted to keep the readers at arm's length to avoid a sense of bias or impropriety. It also conveyed a sense of authority without seeming overbearing. However, as niche media continued to develop and writing styles became more lax, many other forms of media have adopted the "you" approach to writing.

The degree to which you feel this works will depend in large part upon the type of media outlet for which you are writing and its tone. In some cases, "you" can seem pushy or arrogant, while in other cases, it can feel connective. Some more traditional publications will hold the line on first and second person in the writing, while others see an opportunity to reach out in a way that only broadcasters could before.

Consider this option and determine how much value it brings to your writing. Also, work with others at your media outlet to come up with a policy on using non-third-person writing. Weigh potential benefits against drawbacks and move forward accordingly.

pause to allow the soundbite to air as well as when the soundbite will end so the anchor can continue reading the script.

As is the case with the VO, the video and the script must match visuals and text properly to avoid confusing the audience. In addition, the anchor has to work on his or her timing to make sure that the script stops at an appropriate point to let the soundbite play. If the anchor reads too quickly, the viewers will have no audio until the soundbite plays. If the anchor doesn't read quickly enough, the soundbite will interrupt the script reading. Most VO/SOTs run for about 35 to 40 seconds.

PACKAGE

These stories are what most people think of when they imagine a broadcast news story. The content is edited and voiced in advance so the producer can plug the entire thing into the newscast at a specific point and just let it run. The term "package" conveys the idea that this is all packed up and ready to go, requiring no live work from the reporter. The anchor will do a brief lead-in to the content, and then the producer will play the package. Stories like this will have the reporter voicing the story throughout the piece. The reporter will also integrate several soundbites from multiple sources as well as a standup shot. The standup is the opportunity for the reporter to appear on screen and explain something important that hasn't been covered in the script or the bites. In some cases, the reporter will use the standup to transition between key aspects of the story, while in other cases, the reporter can use the stand up to conclude the story and sign off. Packages usually run between 1:30 and 2 minutes.

New Year's Eve College

Air Date: 1/1 10 p.m.

Run Time: 1:35

Video	Audio
ON CAM- ANCHOR	(ANCHOR LEAD IN) NEW YEAR'S EVE CAN LEAD TO HEAVY DRINKING AND RISKY BEHAVIOR.
B-ROLL SHOTS OF STUDENTS DANCING SHOTS OF STUDENTS DRINKING FROM CUPS	TO COMBAT THIS PROBLEM, STUDENTS AT KUENN COLLEGE CREATED AN ALCOHOL-FREE NIGHT OF FUN. NEWS NINE'S LORI GOLD WAS WITH THE STUDENTS AS THEY PARTIED THE NIGHT AWAY (VO- LORI) THIS NEW YEAR'S CELEBRATION HAD EVERYTHING YOU WOULD EXPECT FROM DANCING . . .
SOT [SPARKS] SUPER: Sue Sparks, Event Coordinator	TO THOSE RED PLASTIC CUPS . . . HOWEVER ONE BIG THING MISSING WAS ALCOHOL AND THAT'S JUST WHAT STUDENTS AT KUENN COLLEGE WANTED.
B-ROLL SPARKS PLAYING TWISTER, STUDENTS PLAYING GAMES	(SOT: SUE SPARKS) "We wanted a fun night without having to worry about people getting hurt. Alcohol can really mess up a good night."
SOT [SPARKS]	SPARKS SAYS A FRIEND OF HERS WAS HURT AT A DRINKING PARTY LAST NEW YEAR'S EVE. SHE DIDN'T WANT THAT TO HAPPEN TO OTHERS, SO SHE SAYS SHE TALKED TO THE ADMINISTRATION ABOUT A NO-BOOZE FESTIVAL. (SOT: SUE SPARKS) "Everyone at Kuenn was super supportive and thought this would be great fun for everyone on campus."
B-ROLL STUDENTS DANCING B-ROLL CAMPUS POLICE LAUGHING, ADMINISTRATORS DANCING	STUDENT GOVERNMENT OFFICIALS GAVE SPARKS ONE-THOUSAND-DOLLARS TO BUY SNACKS AND SODAS FOR THE EVENT.
SOT [ROCKWELL VID] SUPER: Richard Rockwell, President of Kuenn University	KUENN PRESIDENT RICHARD ROCKWELL GAVE SPARKS FREE USE OF THE UNION AND PAID FOR CAMPUS POLICE TO PROVIDE SECURITY. ROCKWELL SAYS THIS IS MONEY WELL SPENT.

SOT [LORI STAND UP]	(SOT: RICHARD ROCKWELL)
SUPER: Lori Gold, News Nine at Night	"We want our kids to have fun and be safe so this was a no-brainer. Everyone up and down my administration was on-board for this one because we all know that alcohol can lead to some really bad outcomes. That's clearly not how we want our students' year to begin."
	(SOT: LORI)
END PACKAGE	"This year's event drew more than a thousand students, faculty and staff, which Rockwell says makes it a huge success.
	Even though Sparks plans to graduate this spring, she says other students are already talking about doing this again next year.
	For News Nine at Night, I'm Lori Gold"

Just like other forms of journalistic writing, the key to a good package script is to have a clear sense of what the story is trying to tell the audience. Much like the lead in an inverted-pyramid story or a main idea in an essay, the package has to have a core element around which the rest of the piece is built. Beyond that, broadcast script writing requires you to see what visuals you have that can help you tell that story. If a story is about overcrowding at an animal shelter, you need to have video of the animals all crowded into a small space. If the story is about a victorious sports team, you need video of team and fan celebrations. If you don't have these things, it means you have to make a choice: Rework the script approach to fit the video, or go get video that fits your script. As with all journalism, the truth should trump convenience, so don't change the story just because it's easier to do so.

Once you see what kind of video you have, you should go through your interviews and select your soundbites. Bites can run from 8 to 15 seconds, depending on their value. If they run shorter than 8 seconds, they can feel abrupt, and if they go beyond 15 seconds, they can feel interminable. If you feel you have a compelling reason to break these guidelines, feel free to do so, but make sure the soundbite is worth it. Listen to the audio for nice, tight, self-contained bites that make their point without the need for a lot of explanation before or after they air. You don't want to have to set up the bite with several lines of script or spend a lot of time translating what the source meant after the bite finishes up.

If you want to think about building a package like building a house, the soundbites are like bricks: They are solid and unalterable and tend to set the foundation of the piece. The script text and b-roll are more like the mortar: They fill in the spaces between the bricks, and they are much more pliable. With this in mind, you want to figure out where your bites should go in the package and how you want the script to lead into and out of them. If you need 20 seconds worth of script time to properly lead into the first source's initial soundbite, you can write the script to fit that need and edit the b-roll accordingly. If the source needs to almost immediately enter the story, you can rework the script text to help that happen as well. The goal is to build the package in such a way that the script and soundbites work in tandem to give the viewers a complete and clear sense of the story.

9

BROADCAST-STYLE WRITING:
AND VOICING

THE BIG THREE

Here are the three key things you should take away from this chapter:

1. **Write for the ear:** Broadcast is spoken on one end and heard on the other, so you need to figure out how your script will sound coming out of your mouth and if it will translate well to the ears of your viewers. This means you need to work on the word choice and sentence structure that best fits the aural nature of broadcast journalism.

2. **Purposefully tighten your writing:** You want to keep your writing tight and short, but only to the point that it doesn't damage your story's overall flow and pace. The goal is to have a strong and clear script that communicates important information in a conversation and smooth fashion.

3. **Match your script to your story:** You have audio and video elements at your disposal, so you want to keep them in mind when you write your script. Make sure you can pair your video to the words you choose. Keep the overall feel of the story in mind when you build pace into your script. Look for ways to use words with auditory quality, like "popped" and "zipped" instead of "fell apart" or "moved quickly."

KEY TERMS

180-degree rule 162	look room 162	sign-off 164
abbreviation 165	pace 161	soundbite 162
acronym 165	package 162	tracking 162
active voice 160	pan 162	voice-over 167
broadcast lead 164	passive voice 160	voicing 162
b-roll 162	pronouncer 165	VO/SOT 167
cut 162	reader 167	wallpaper 162
frame 162	script 160	zoom 162

DISCUSSION QUESTIONS

1. What do you think are the positive and negative aspects of writing for broadcast? What makes it easier to accomplish than other forms of writing and what makes it more difficult?

2. Do you think the conversational tone of broadcast journalism is more or less helpful when it comes to effectively communicating with an audience? Consider issues such as credibility and clarity equally as you discuss this topic.

3. Given the dominance of social media and other on-demand, nonlinear content, how important do you think broadcast journalism is?

WRITE NOW!

1. Find a print story and rewrite the lead in broadcast style. Remember to keep in mind sentence length, writing for the ear, verb tense and conversational writing.

2. Below is the information you used in Chapter 3 to write an inverted-pyramid story about a fire. Use this same information to write a 20-second reader for a radio news program or a nightly TV newscast. Keep in mind the differences between inverted-pyramid and broadcast structures as well as the importance of using shorter sentences and descriptive words.

   Jacksonville firefighters responded to a fire Tuesday around 5 p.m., after a call came in to the 911 dispatch center.

   Ladder Truck 11, Pumper 32 and Chief's Car 2 arrived at 5:11 p.m. to find smoke coming from underneath the eaves of the three-bedroom, one-bath home at 411 S. Cherry St.

   Firefighters were able to contain the blaze to approximately half of the home, while the remainder sustained heat, smoke and water damage.

   Homeowner Jim Smith was seriously injured in the fire and was transported to a nearby medical facility, where he is listed in critical condition. His wife, Suzy, and his daughter Jane were unharmed.

   After the fire was extinguished, assessors stated the home received approximately $90,000 in damage. Investigative Service Agents determined the cause of the fire was a leaky gas stove that exploded when Mr. Smith lit a cigarette nearby.

3. Watch the first 10 minutes of a local news broadcast and identify examples of the types of stories outlined in the chapter (reader, VO, VO/SOT, package). (Not every newscast will use all four of these.) Write a short essay in which you identify each of the story types that was present as well as a brief synopsis of the story that used each format. Then, explain if you think each format was properly applied to the story or not. If not, which format would you have used and why? For example, you might argue that a story on a budget should have been a reader instead of a package because the video consisted of nothing more than images of buildings and paperwork.

4. Watch a video story posted to a TV news website. As you listen to the person, assess how tight the writing is. Does the person communicate effectively and clearly, or does the person waste a lot of words? Identify places you think the person did well and other places you think the person used flabby writing. Write a short essay that encapsulates your analysis.

5. Use a smartphone and capture a 20-second bit of video. Then write a series of broadcast-style sentences that would augment this video. Consider descriptive words, pace, style and flow in your writing.

10

COLLECTING AUDIO AND VISUALS IN THE FIELD

LEARNING OBJECTIVES

After completing this chapter you should be able to:

- Identify the tools you can use for audio and video collection.

- Compare and contrast the forms of audio and video equipment, focusing on benefits and drawbacks of each.

- Understand how to tell stories with audio and video equipment.

- Outline the way in which collected material can be used to tell stories.

THINKING AHEAD: HOW TO GET ENOUGH MATERIAL TO BUILD A GOOD STORY

When technology made audio and video cheaper to capture and easier to publish, many journalists gravitated to this form of storytelling. What was once the dominion of broadcasters with large budgets quickly became something everyone could do with nothing more than a mobile phone and a YouTube account. What resulted could charitably be described as a landfill of weak and pointless content.

Audio and video journalism requires access to specific tools, but saying it is all about the gear is like saying writing is all about the ability to type. Access and understanding make

it possible to gather the content, but it is the journalistic skill and technological acumen that make for good stories.

The purpose of this chapter is twofold. First, the chapter will outline the various types of tools available to you as an audio and video journalist, as well as their benefits and drawbacks. Then, we will examine the ways in which you can use these tools to gather quality content within the field. The basics outlined here will dovetail nicely with the script-writing aspects of Chapter 9 and the audiovisual editing elements of Chapter 11.

TOOLS OF THE TRADE

To collect audio and video well, you need to understand the tools of the trade and which ones will help you the most. A crucial mistake most new journalists make is to invest heavily in high-end gear, assuming that higher prices will yield better content. However, as most good journalists will tell you, the quality of the journalist matters more than the prices of the equipment.

You want to understand what each type of tool brings to the table for you and which ones make the most sense for you. Below is a list of tools for audio and video collection. The better you understand their benefits and drawbacks, the more informed you will be when you buy your gear.

MICROPHONES

The obvious purpose of a microphone is to collect sound so you can use it as part of your storytelling. However, not every microphone is created equal, and not every microphone has the same purpose. Here are some of the basic microphone styles and what they accomplish for you as a reporter:

Devices like mini-recorders have built-in microphones to help you capture sound. The quality of these microphones tends to be much weaker than other forms of sound-gathering equipment.

A traditional stick microphone is great for interviewing subjects, voicing a podcast or doing a standup. It allows you to collect quality audio when you can position it close to the source of the sound.

A lavalier microphone allows you to record sound from an interview subject without having a stick mic intrude on the shot. The unobtrusive nature of these devices make them great for that purpose.

- **Built-in microphone:** Most audio and video devices have a built-in microphone to collect sound. The benefit to these is that if you remember the device, you won't forget your microphone. The downside to these types of microphones is that they are usually the worst in terms of quality, and they have the smallest range. In addition, they tend to be omnidirectional, and thus they pick up everything around you, not just the content you want to record.

- **Stick microphone:** These microphones are what most people think of when they hear the word "microphone." These cylindrical tubes traditionally have a caged ball on the end and can be held in the hand of the reporter or the source. These microphones are great to gather directional sound, as is the case when you want to interview a person or voice your reporter's track. However, they are large and bulky and visually unappealing.

- **Lavalier microphone:** These microphones can be wired or wireless, depending on the type you prefer, and are unobtrusive. They clip easily on the tie or lapel of a source and record sound well. The downside is that they are easier to break than stick mics, and they capture all the sounds and movements of the source, such the ruffling of clothing or the jostling of the mic.

- **Boom microphone:** Occasionally called a "shotgun mic," this form of directional microphone allows you to gather sound from a distance by extending the boom pole over the top of the source and pointing the mic toward him or her. However, it is important to keep checking to see if the mic is capturing the sound, as any time a source moves, the mic might be out of range or turned the wrong way.

Boom microphones allow you to get closer to the action and record it in a crowd.

luminis/iStock.com

AUDIO RECORDERS

As technology has improved, these have gone from being about the size of a lunch box and recording on cassette tapes to being about the size of a pack of gum and recording on digital media. The quality of these devices varies widely, with some of the older models still involving the use of micro-cassette tapes. Those older models had extremely limited recording times (based on the capacity of each cassette) and produced far inferior sound.

Modern recorders are usually powered with a small battery and can capture hundreds of hours of audio with clear digital quality. In addition, the content is automatically converted to a web-friendly audio file and can be easily uploaded. Costs range from $30 to several hundred dollars, depending on the quality of the microphone, the capacity of the recorder and additional special features.

VIDEO CAMERAS

The wide array of equipment available to you can be intimidating if you don't understand what each of the options does for you. Even more, the cost of the equipment can scare you away from buying something, for fear of making the wrong choices. A simple Handicam-style machine that is preset to grab content might be just what you want, or you might need something that allows you to manually focus, white balance and alter the exposure.

Broadcast expert Michael Hernandez noted a few key things to consider when purchasing video equipment.[1]

WHAT IS YOUR GOAL?

If you want the full experience of managing specific settings on the camera and keeping the focal length under your control, you might want a more professional camera, like those you would see at TV stations. If you just want to capture simple interviews for posting online and have no technological acumen when it comes to video, consider a smaller, simpler camera. You should also consider if you plan to shoot both video and stills with this camera or if you want this to be a video-only piece of equipment.

WHAT RECORDING FORMAT DO YOU WANT?

Hernandez recommends avoiding the old-fashioned tape-based cameras, but some TV stations still use this type of equipment. Some cameras have internal hard drives, while others operate on

You can outfit higher-end cameras with a wide array of accessories that make it easier to shoot in a variety of conditions.

removable media, like SD cards. Consider that removing the media will allow you to get the camera back out into the field more quickly than having to download everything from a hard drive. Also, if the memory chip goes bad on a removable-media camera, you can get a new SD card. If the hard drive goes on the fritz, your camera won't do you much good.

WHAT ARE YOUR SOUND OPTIONS?

Built-in microphones on cameras are just as limiting as those discussed above in the audio device section. The ability to plug in an external mic should be a serious consideration if you plan to do any packages. Some cameras have **XLR inputs**, which are the professional standard, while others have only a **mini-jack port**, which is similar to the plug on the end of your headphones. Hernandez notes that XLR is the preferred format, although at the very least, you want to have some option for an external mic.

WHAT ACCESSORIES MATTER?

Consider that accessories can make a camera much more expensive, but they can also make the camera a much better piece of equipment. A camera that doesn't have an external battery option is limited to a single charge of the camera. However, cameras that allow you to exchange batteries will give you much more shooting time. A mounting spot for a light, an additional mic or other elements might be important to you if you are going for a more professional feel. You also want to make sure you can mount the camera to a tripod. Other options, such as lens filters, can also be important if you know what you are doing with them.

If this all seems overwhelming, consider starting with a small, simple camera, and get used to what it can do. Once you feel comfortable, you can either upgrade that model or look for a camera that will better meet your needs.

STILL CAMERAS

A still camera simply captures the light that bounces off objects and records it on a form of media. The way it captures that light or how it preserves the resulting images will make the difference between a simple "pinhole camera" and a high-end digital model. As is the case with most of the other pieces of equipment we outlined in this chapter, the complexities of the camera can be best discussed at length in a dedicated textbook. That said, understanding what the various forms of camera do and how they do it will help you pick the best tool for your photo job.

Photography professor Tim Gleason has outlined a few basic cameras as well as their benefits and drawbacks.[2] Consider these photographic options:

CONSIDER THIS ➤ THE SMARTPHONE—THE AMPHICAR OF JOURNALISM

In the early 1960s, a West German auto manufacturer marketed a vehicle to people in the United States who wanted a boat and a car but could not afford both. The **Amphicar** emerged as a dual-purpose vehicle that allowed people to enjoy the road and the water without breaking the bank. However, as users soon discovered, the Amphicar was a lousy car because it also had to be a boat, and it was a bad boat because it also had to be a car. By 1965, the company had stopped marketing the vehicle in the United States, and by the late 1960s, it was gone altogether.

Today's smartphones serve journalism in much the same way that Amphicars served vehicle buyers back then. The phones can send texts, search the web, take photos, shoot video, capture interviews, record phone calls and more. However, as is the case when an item attempts to do a lot of things, the quality of any one thing will suffer.

Photographers often argue that the best camera is the one you have with you. This means that if all you have with you is a smartphone, and you need to shoot a breaking news event, the phone is fine. However, photojournalists know that the **smartphone** is not a substitute for a high-end DSLR system with multiple lenses.

The same thing is true for videographers, who would prefer a full set of video gear to an iPhone's video app. The lighting options and recording settings on that more complex device are much better. That said, if it's the difference between no video and using a phone to grab some grainy shots of a big event, using the phone makes sense.

Yoichi Okamoto/LBJ Presidential Library via Wikimedia Commons

President Lyndon Johnson drives his Amphicar near his Texas home in 1965.

When it comes to recording interviews or phone calls, an app might work well, or it might fail you. Some apps stop recording if you receive a phone call or a text message, so this might not be a great option for you. Then again, if the phone is what you have, and you trust it, use it.

The larger point is that doing quality journalism will take more than your phone and every 99-cent app you can find. Although smartphones give you a lot of options in a small package, they are the worst option compared with professional equipment.

When you know where you are going and what you need to accomplish, consider packing a pro set of gear for that specific purpose and relying on your phone as a backup device or to do secondary work. This approach will improve the odds that the most important elements of your work will get the best overall treatment. It also means you will have your digital Amphicar to make sure you don't miss anything.

The DSLR is a professional-quality camera that allows you to change lenses, add stabilizing equipment and attach flashes for shooting in low-light conditions.

MOBILE PHONE CAMERA

This is the simplest digital camera. It is easy to use and it's ubiquitous, so it is a popular photo option. However, in some cases, the camera has only a digital zoom function, meaning that the more you zoom in, the more distorted the image will be. In addition, the sensors in the camera are much weaker compared with dedicated photography devices.

COMPACT CAMERA

This is the camera grandma would always break out for birthday parties and family reunions. Gleason notes that the compact market is dying, because of the advances in mobile-phone technology. However, compact cameras often have stronger flashes as well as improved lens and zoom options. These are a step above the current phone cameras, but they don't compare with professional cameras.

MIRRORLESS AND DIGITAL SINGLE-LENS REFLEX (DSLR) CAMERAS

These camera systems often consist of a single body with interchangeable lenses. They also have much larger sensors, capture higher quality images and contain quicker systems that allow faster shooting. An initial investment of a body and lens can be relatively inexpensive, but a full kit can run a few thousand dollars, depending on the options.

When it comes to still cameras, what makes for a good system is directly related to what you are shooting. For simple mug shots or a lot of still shots, a mobile phone camera will do the trick. However, if you want to shoot athletic events, you will need to invest in the **digital single-lens reflex** equipment. If you want to buy a video camera with a still-shot option, consider what you are getting and what you are giving up to have that option.

TYPES OF MATERIAL YOU GATHER

To build a decent video package, you will need to gather a variety of elements that can work in concert to tell a story. Some of these elements are obvious, while others are obvious only when they are missing. Here are a few things you will want to grab when you are out collecting audio and video content:

AMBIENT SOUND

Sound can be just as effective as images when you want to bring your audience members to a scene. The sound of a babbling brook or the noise of a construction crane can provide viewers with a sense of place and feeling. What some people think of as background noise, good journalists see as **ambient sound**, or **natural sound**.

When you enter a scene, you should consider gathering some natural sound from the area. This can be as simple as the sounds of cows eating and mooing on a farm or of traffic speeding by on a busy highway. Some journalists will even record several minutes of an empty room to gather a clean background track for their work later. Radio expert Randall Davidson explains that not every room sounds the same, as fluorescent lighting, ceiling height and building material can all create different echoes and tonality. Thus, he says he often gathers about five minutes of "silence" to lay under his voice track so that the background sound in his voice track can match the interviews he does later in that same room. This helps the package sound cleaner and stronger when he is done.[3]

B-roll allows you to cover your audio track with images that help tell your story. Arranging your shots so they make sense and augment your audio is crucial in broadcast journalism.

B-ROLL VIDEO

If you are assembling a video package that includes a voice track, you need to gather additional video that will help you tell the story. This video is often called b-roll and serves as a way to show the viewers information as the reporter talks about it. The goal of b-roll is to have it match the reporter's words, so they can tell the story in tandem. For example, if a reporter covers a Fourth of July parade, the voice track might say, "With their flags flying and banners waving, residents of Springfield cheered on a Fourth of July parade on a beautifully sunny day." The b-roll needs to reflect this, with images of flags, banners, a parade and a beautifully sunny day. If instead it shows a few people marching in the rain or no flag-waving citizens, the audience can become confused.

When you collect b-roll, you should have a pretty good idea of what you want to say in your script. If you are part of a reporting team, make sure you and your partner are on the same page when it comes to how you want to approach the story and what kinds of shots you want to gather. Then make sure you record enough of that video, using multiple types of shots and various angles.

INTERVIEWS

As with all other forms of journalism, the interview is crucial to your ability to tell a good story. We discussed the basics of interviewing as a skill in Chapter 6, so we won't be repeating those items here. What matters at this point is how you capture quality of the video and audio. Here are some crucial tips on how to do that:

- **Seek silence:** Even with a great microphone, you don't want anything impeding your audience's chance to hear what your source has to say. With that in mind, you want to find quiet places that will lack distractions, such as a private office or an out-of-the-way hall. Many cameras with external microphone options will have sound gauges that allow you to see how loud the background volume is and if you are capturing your interview well enough. If you don't think the audio quality will be good enough for your audience, find another place to do the interview.

  If you can capture a person in his or her natural environment, that's great, as long as it doesn't interfere with the quality of the audio. For example, if you want to speak with a zookeeper who works in the "big cat" house, you can grab an interview in front of a lion's den. Any ambient sound of a growling or roaring feline could add value to the piece. However, if you want to interview the head of a construction project, you probably don't want to do that interview in front of the site where all the backhoes and bulldozers are knocking down an aging structure.

You will need to capture three types of shots when you shoot video in the field. Here is a brief discussion of each type of shot. We will dig more into how they are best used in your stories in the next chapter:

Use a long shot when you want to show a lot of content in a single frame and to establish the scene for your viewers.

Use a medium shot for interviews and simple actions. The medium shot is the most commonly used shot and is a reliable element of video storytelling.

Use close-up shots when you want to show tiny details like these water droplets on this blueberry.

Long shot: This shot, also called a wide shot, is used to show a lot of action within the frame to provide the viewer with a sense of "the big picture." This shot is often used to establish a scene. You can take a shot of a crowd of high school students who are cheering for their football team. You can take a **wide shot** of a crowded street or an empty church. This shot is almost always at the front of a package to place the viewer at the scene of the story.

Medium shot: This shot frames the action of one or more individuals or provides a small slice of a larger event. The medium shot is effective for soundbites as well, because it allows you to frame the person from the torso up, capturing both facial expressions and any meaningful hand gestures. The medium shot is perhaps the most useful of all the shots, in that it is how most people view the world. When we talk to other people, we are almost always viewing them the way we would in a medium shot. A small family dinner, a person typing in a computer lab, a mechanic working on an engine and hundreds of other real-life situations are best viewed as medium shots.

Close-up shot: This is also known as a detail shot. It is meant to provide your viewers with a tight shot of a small piece of action. Close-ups follow from medium shots, the same way a medium shot follows from a long shot. The key to a close up is that it must be easily identified and provide value within the shot sequence. Not all sequences need a close-up shot.

- **Mic proximity:** The proximity of the microphone to the source is crucial in capturing the soundbites you want, so you need to get it as close as you can to your subject. Lavalier microphones that clip nicely onto the source's clothing work well to capture sound while remaining unobtrusive. If you have to use a stick microphone, you need the microphone close to the source and angled toward the source's mouth. However, you want to keep the mic out of the shot in most cases. To do this, either hold the mic low when interviewing the source to keep it out of the frame, or have the source hold the mic so the top of it is no higher than the middle of his or her torso.

Interviews in broadcast require you to work with your source as well as your videographer to create an informational and visually pleasing experience.

- **Clean background:** When you interview a source for a video, you want the audience to stay focused on that source and what he or she is saying. One of the more distracting things to an audience during an interview is a disruptive background. Distractions vary from a local fool jumping around behind the source to a giant sign or painting in the background. Beyond that, if you have the background set up poorly, your sources might seem to have a flagpole or a tree growing out of their heads. Look for a simple background in places where you can minimize distractions.

CAPTURING VIVID VISUALS

To become a good photojournalist, you will need to practice in various situations, settings and conditions. Any good photography book will help you better understand the issues regarding camera settings, lighting setups and more. Instead of reinventing the wheel here when it comes to the technical aspects of the job, we will provide a few key bits of broader advice. Here are some basic thoughts on photography from a reporting perspective:

TELL A STORY

When you shoot, focus on telling a story. Just like a lead of a story should tell people what has happened and why it matters, each individual frame you use should convey value and meaning for your audience. Images need to tell a story, whether they stand alone or if you use them as part of a slideshow.

When you pick among various shots, first consider all the technical aspects discussed in this chapter, such as focus and the rule of thirds. If the image is technically clean, then consider if this piece actually tells your readers something that should matter to them. The best photos will convey value, evoke emotion and engage readers.

In the case of slideshows or galleries, don't dump your entire memory card onto the web and call it a photo story. You should look through your photos and determine the value of each shot, as we noted above. After you make that first cut, you should figure out if you have images that repeat one another, such as a medium photo of two people talking and then another medium

One of the most overlooked elements of photography is the text under the photo, often called **captions** or **cutlines**. These few sentences of copy can make the difference between a great photo experience and a confusing one. The purpose of the caption is to add value to the image and help the audience members have a better appreciation of the image.

A standard photo caption is usually two sentences. The first sentence should explain what's going on in the photo without being patently obvious. Look at the photo of the man on the phone and then compare these two captions:

Smithville Company President Bill Smith talks on the phone while colleague Jane Jones looks on.

Smithville Company President Bill Smith finalizes a deal to merge the company with a Thailand investment group while merger committee member Jane Jones points out crucial details of the project.

In both cases, the caption discusses what's happening, but the second one gives the readers more information and helps make better sense of what's going on in the image.

A second sentence should tell people why the photo matters and provide context and value that enhances the image.

Smithville was the third largest manufacturer of widgets in the United States before this merger, which will make it the most powerful global widget company.

To create quality captions, you will need to ask your subjects a series of questions, including who they are and what they are doing in the shot. You will also need to make sure you include the names of anyone you can identify in a shot. This will improve the storytelling and show your readers you care.

photo of those same people laughing. Pick one or the other, based on what you think best tells the story. Then, you need to order your images in a way that will tell the story as you see it. This could be a chronological telling of a story, such as a day in the life of a daycare worker. It could also be a series of categorical chunks, such as the work, faith and hobbies of a local religious figure.

This organizational approach is just as important for images that tell a story as it is for text-based stories. A random series of perfectly written paragraphs isn't much of a story, and neither is a mishmash of various images. Keep the idea of storytelling at the front of your mind when you work with images and you'll be in good shape.

GRAB ACTIONS AND REACTIONS

The goal of professional photographers is to capture a perfect sliver of time. In most cases, spontaneous moments that inspire actions and reactions qualify as great opportunities for shooters to do this. Images that fail to include actions and reactions are often called **dead art**, as they are lifeless pieces of photography. A few examples of dead art include:

- **Building photos:** "Where" qualifies as a crucial element of any good story, but if all you do is show people the exterior (or interior) of a building, you aren't telling a story. Few things will bore a reader more than a photo of a building where an event previously occurred. A photo like this one of a bank with a caption that says, "This bank was robbed last week" doesn't help tell a story. If you are desperate for art and you want to create a sense of placement for your readers, consider creating a simple map to show the bank's location.

- **Group art:** "Say cheese!" is something your parents forced you to do when you were at a childhood birthday party, but it's not good for photojournalism. Look at this photo of a woman and two children. This could be an interesting story if we captured something besides people posing for the shot. Instead of getting these people to gather and pose for you, get shots of them doing something associated with the story. If you can do this surreptitiously, you can avoid awkward moments and prevent them from staring into the camera.

- **Posed/poser art:** When people are told to "act naturally," nothing they do will seem natural. You can have the standard "person with arms folded in front of them shot" that makes the person look completely unnatural. Even worse, the "thumbs up" or "peace sign" posers think they look cool when they actually look ridiculous. Try to capture things as they naturally occur.

- **Mug shots:** These photos can have value when no other visuals are available. For example, if you run a story about a crime and you want to include a photo of the person arrested on suspicion of that crime, the jailhouse mug shot is likely to be your only chance at art. However, if you can get a photo that is more telling, you should aspire to do so. In the case of a profile story, you will want to spend time with the profile subject in his or her natural environment in hopes of using photos to augment the text. For example, if you write about a local man who grows vegetables to feed the homeless, you will want to photograph the man working in his garden or gathering vegetables. A mug shot won't do.

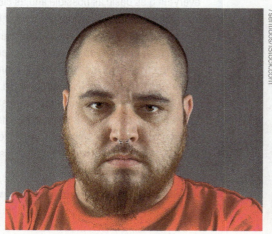

THOUGHTS FROM A PRO → BRIAN URBANEK,
VIDEOGRAPHER, WDJT CBS 58

© Brian Urbanek

Brian Urbanek has spent much of his professional life on the back end of a camera. He has covered the NCAA Men's Final Four, the NFC Championship Game and Super Bowl 50 as a videographer. He has also produced live full-game broadcasts of high school basketball and football games, as well as college hockey and minor league baseball. He also has worked as a documentarian, with his short documentary "Homeless in Chicago" receiving screenings at multiple film festivals. A radio version of this piece took home the bronze at the New York International Radio Festival. Currently, Urbanek is a videographer for WDJT CBS 58 in Milwaukee, where he says he loves his ability to shoot, edit, produce and write for his audience.

Urbanek says his biggest challenge when he started shooting news stories was to make sure he nailed down the basics.

"When I first started my goal was to first just keep everything as basic as possible and as clean as possible while I figured out the whole process of gathering content for news," he said. "I had multiple years of shooting experience, just not for TV news. So there was a slight learning curve involved with that. But once I started to understand that and all my shots were clean and airable, then it was eventually time that I started thinking about how I can be a little bit creative and do more than just the basics. Then I pushed myself to become even more and more creative. It was baby steps. I knew I couldn't run before I crawled."

As a videographer, Urbanek says the biggest challenge is to tell a story with images before the story is written as a script. He says working with his reporter to come to a common understanding of the piece helps him as he collects video.

"I always encourage my reporter to do the interview first, before I start shooting my b-roll," he said. "Then, as I'm shooting my b-roll, I'll just chat with my reporter and ask, 'So, how might you see this story unfolding in your script?' Hopefully it matches us to how I see it unfolding visually in my head. If so, we're all good. If not, I'll re-adjust or I might make a suggestion based on what shots I have and a potentially creative way of telling the story I may have been thinking of."

The use of video to tell a story matters to both the journalists and the audience, Urbanek says. He says that each story varies in its focus and tone and that the videography should reflect those differences. When it comes to certain shots or certain approaches, he says the most important thing is to have a reason behind his approach to shooting.

"I don't believe in rules when it comes to videography and photography, only guidelines," Urbanek said. "However, if you aren't able to back up something that you did and why you did it, there's no good reason to break one of these guidelines. Sometimes an inexperienced videographer might have too much headroom and make the shot just look silly. It's one of those intuitive things that some people can just tell when a shot looks bad, others can't. But 'bad' is relative and if you can argue why you shot the shot that way to advance the story, who is anyone to tell you that it's 'bad' or 'wrong'? Videography and photography is an art and is subjective."

Perhaps the biggest thing he has learned as a video journalist is to balance the time he takes as a shooter with the time he will need to help create the overall package.

"One of the biggest challenges that we face in TV news is 'how can we tell as compelling and creative of a story as possible in the amount of time that we have?'" Urbanek said. "And when it comes to TV news, time is not something that we often have a lot of. A lot of times as you're shooting a story, you don't have time to stop and think to be creative. You need to be thinking creatively *while* you're working. If you stop to think, you could miss a very special moment that you'll never be able to get back."

ONE LAST THING

Q: If you could tell the students reading this book anything you think is important, what would it be?

A: "The advice I'd like to share comes from one of my favorite filmmakers, Casey Neistat. He's a YouTuber and has produced commercials for companies such as Mercedes and Nike, and a TV series for HBO.

Basically, he says imagine a straight line. On the left end of the line is where you currently are. Then imagine the right end of the line is 'everything you've ever wanted to do in life.' Then what goes in the middle? What goes on the line in between those two things? In one of his daily vlogs Casey said, 'The only thing in life that stands between you and everything you have ever wanted to do, is doing it.'

Basically, if you want to be a filmmaker, just pick up a camera and start shooting things and telling a story—even if it's with your iPhone. Now you're a filmmaker. If you want to be a writer, start a blog on a topic that you're interested in. Now you're a writer. If you want to be a graphic designer, start creating logos for your uncle's small business. Now you're a graphic designer. Instead of thinking about and talking about what you want to become, just become it. There's no better time to start than now. If you just start doing it, then you are it—whatever that 'it' is."

ABIDE BY THE RULE OF THIRDS

As counterintuitive as this might seem, you want to avoid centering your shot perfectly. People read from left to right, and their eye tends to go to a spot about two-thirds up and about one-third from the left when they consume content. This reading ideal applies to photography and video, and is called the **rule of thirds**.

To help you understand this better, you want to think about having a tic-tac-toe board overlaid on top of your photo. The power points of the frame will be at the intersection of those lines, so you want your dominant element positioned at one of the four intersections.

Not every shot will have great action on all four points of the frame, but if you don't have anything happening along any of those points, you have a lousy shot. If you see a lack of action

As you can see with this photo, the dominant elements are touching the majority of the power points of the frame where the lines intersect. This makes the shot more pleasing to the eyes.

on these points, consider cropping the shot to reposition your dominant element. If you have two subjects sharing the frame and there is a vast empty space between them, use a different shot, if possible.

MAKING YOUR VIDEO VALUABLE

A basic difference between a computer and a television is how individuals interact with these devices. Television is a **passive medium**, meaning that viewers engaging the device will expect to consume the content as it washes over them. Computers are **active-media** devices, meaning that users expect to interact with them as they consume the content. This difference makes it difficult on reporters who gather video for the web. While TV viewers might sit still for a while and watch a video, web users are likely to become bored quickly and click elsewhere before the piece is finished.

To improve the overall content of your work and the likelihood that people will watch it all the way through, here are some suggestions you can consider as you capture your video. (You can review editing tactics that can be helpful in Chapter 11.)

If you are working with a videographer, it is crucial that you both understand what you want to gather at your shoot and how you want to cover the news.

PLAN YOUR SHOOT

In all the other chapters on reporting, we discussed the importance of research and preparation. When it comes to doing video work, the same basic rules apply. Most good journalists can mentally plan their stories. They know what the lead should be on a story as well as how to get each source into the story. They can see certain quotes as being good bridge paragraphs or solid closing elements. Use these same ideas and approaches to mentally plan your video shoot.

You know you want to capture establishing shots, interviews, solid close-up shots and more. If you research the event and plan the shoot, you can go there with a mental "grocery list" that will help you gather those elements. The planned-shoot approach will also help you avoid forgetting necessary items, such as cutaway shots.

Once you get good enough at this, you can move your planning into the next phase, where you shoot for the edit. This approach to videography will allow you to gather shots with the idea of how they will become part of the package. Thus, you can take a long shot and assume you will need a medium shot of some kind next that centers on the same topic. You can then capture the medium shot and look for the next moment that would logically continue the storytelling in the package. If you shoot for the edit, you will save a lot of time when you build your package.

PROPERLY FRAME AND COMPOSE YOUR SHOTS

As we noted in the photo section, you want to follow the rule of thirds when you frame your video. Make sure your subjects have look room, which means they aren't looking directly out of the frame or squished into the edge of the shot.

When you shoot video, you want each frame to be able to stand on its own as if it were a picture or a painting. Today's high-end cameras will allow you to capture stills from video, so this concept is more than an artistic ideal. You might want to grab a frame of video and make it a dominant photographic image or part of a gallery, and this approach will help you.

However, video involves motion, and you need to consider that as you size up your shots. Someone who is completely still at one point and well framed might decide to scoot his chair forward or start walking around, thus ruining a shot.

Even smartphones have devices that can improve their stability and allow you to capture video that doesn't feel like you were shooting during an earthquake.

STICK WITH STABLE SHOTS

Stability is one of the most difficult aspects of shooting because you are capturing moving images while attempting to stay still. When a camera wiggles, even a little bit, the resulting video can look like it was filmed during an earthquake. When you follow a subject or constantly shift the position of the camera, you can create a feeling of additional motion that is likely to disorient your viewers and make them focus more on the shot than the content of it.

To improve your shots, use some sort of stabilizing device. Standard video cameras often come with mounting option that will allow you to attach them to a tripod. Even multimedia devices like smartphones now have "gear packs" that will allow you to turn them into a tiny version of a broadcast-quality camera.

Photographers who shoot sports or need to move frequently rely on monopods. These options are also available for some video cameras and multimedia devices.

If all else fails, here are some other ways to remain stable while shooting:

- Look for a solid surface like a table or a desk, and put the camera on it.

- Lean against a solid object like a tree or a wall to help steady yourself.

- Squat or kneel to lower your center of gravity and increase your stability.

- Put your free arm across your chest and tuck it under your shooting arm or use both hands to hold the camera.

KEEP FOCUSED

If your images are blurry or of weak quality, you aren't helping your viewers. The main idea behind video is to give people a sense of what has happened as a series of actions unfolded. If they can't see what's going on or the image is out of focus, you aren't doing that. Exceptions are obvious, as in the case of video shot on the scene of a disaster, but if you have the opportunity to reshoot blurry shots, you should take it.

When you use cameras with a zoom, you want to zoom in as tightly as you can on the focal point of the image and manually adjust the focus. Then, as you back out of that zoom to a point where you are satisfied with the framing, you will still have everything in focus. Also, don't rely on autofocus to do the work for you. The camera might not focus on your dominant visual element. In addition, if you leave the camera in autofocus mode, it can continually readjust itself throughout an interview or a shot, thus adding distracting focal shifts in the frame.

GET MORE THAN YOU THINK YOU NEED

A common phrase often overheard on a college campus is "You can always retake a test. You can never relive a party." Although it's not the best way to make the most of your tuition dollars, it is a good reminder that certain events occur only once, and you need to make the most of them. As far as videographers are concerned, this is a good way to remember that you should get a lot more video than you think you will need.

Video journalists once had the unenviable task of attempting to preserve both battery life and tape space while shooting. This meant that they often had to figure out how much of each they had left and what was worth shooting. Today, digital technology allows you to have much longer battery life and much more recording space via tiny digital storage units. It is easier to gather a few more shots of an event when you are there than it would be to go back later and hope you can scrape together an extra shot you just realized you want. It is better to have something and not need it than it is to need something and not have it.

TAKE MULTIPLE SHOTS OF THE SAME THING

Along the same lines of the "gather more than you need" advice, you want to grab multiple shots of the same thing. Various shots give you options when you edit and can convey different aspects of a subject. The editing process, which we will examine in Chapter 11, will force you to use long, medium and close-up shots to create sequences of action.

Take shots from various sides of your axis so that you can show multiple vantage points of an ongoing event. Look for ways to capture action from a long shot as well as a close up to create a sense of continuity and flow in your package. If you don't end up using all of your shots, you can delete them. However, if you didn't get them in the first place, you will be out of luck, and the quality of your story will suffer.

LEARN TO RELAX

Some of the biggest problems with shooting don't come from the camera or the event, but from the shooter. Novice videographers want to get in and get out as fast as possible, grabbing a few quick shots and moving on. If unpacking all sorts of gear or capturing people on video makes you feel uncomfortable, you are going to focus more on how fast you can finish the job as opposed to the quality of the job.

Don't set up your gear 200 feet from an event and then see how close a zoom can get you to the action. Get up close and personal with the scene and spend time getting those detail shots you can't see from far away. Work the scene for additional shots and learn to talk to people before, during and after you film them. If people get tense with you around, feel free to explain what you are doing and why it matters. People will generally understand that you have a job to do and as long as you aren't causing harm, they will let you work.

The more times you shoot video, the more natural the process will become. If you feel awkward, the people you are filming will feel awkward as well. The more confident you are in your approach, the more natural your shooting will become.

COLLECTING AUDIO AND VISUALS IN THE FIELD

THE BIG THREE

Here are the three key things you should take away from this chapter:

1. **Equipment matters, but so does storytelling:** The quality of your equipment will help you improve your end products and your ability to gather material. However, if you don't have a story in mind before you press the record button, you are going to end up with weak content. You need to understand the purpose of your package before you hit the field.

2. **Get as much of everything as you can:** Gather more than you think you'll need, just to be on the safe side. This means taking multiple shots of the same subject, using various types of shots and looking for additional interviews. You can always cut shots or get rid of interviews later, but if you don't get them when they are available, you might not get another chance to grab them.

3. **Relax:** If you don't feel natural with the camera, your subjects will sense it and react poorly to you. Even more, if you spend half the time thinking about how long you need to be shooting before you can pack up, you won't take enough time to gather enough good content. Get used to the idea that you are toting around a camera and that you will need to spend some quality time up close and personal with your subjects. Don't panic. Just relax and enjoy the shoot.

KEY TERMS

active media   188

ambient sound   180

Amphicar   179

boom microphone   177

built-in microphone   176

caption   184

close-up shot   182

cutline   184

dead art   184

digital single-lens reflex   180

lavalier microphone   176

long shot   182

medium shot   182

mini-jack port   178

mug shot   185

natural sound   180

passive medium   188

rule of thirds   187

smartphone   179

stick microphone   176

wide shot   182

XLR input   178

DISCUSSION QUESTIONS

1. How often do you watch videos online? What makes the video compelling and what about the best videos keeps your attention? What makes you turn away from videos online? About how long are the videos you most often watch? What is the length of those you avoid?

2. What makes for a compelling slideshow? How many images will you sit through? What makes you give up before the end of a slideshow?

3. The chapter calls the smartphone the "Amphicar of journalism," arguing that it doesn't do video or photos as well as more professional devices. What do you think of the smartphone as a journalistic tool? What do you see as its benefits and drawbacks?

WRITE NOW!

1. Watch a newscast on TV or on a television station's website. Select two stories that vary in tone: one a serious news story and the other more of a news feature or lite-brite story. Outline the basic point of each story. Then, compare and contrast the packages in terms of length, soundbites, shot selection and tone. How are these similar? How do they differ? Is each package effective in telling its story?

2. Record at least five minutes of video in which you alter your shot selection (long, medium, close-up) and the subjects you are shooting at least every 15 seconds. Apply the techniques for shooting in an attempt to avoid video problems discussed in the chapter (poor focus, unstable video, weak audio etc.). Review your video after the shoot, and analyze the degree to which you were successful with your approach to this shoot. What do you think you did well? What could have worked better? Which problems did you most frequently encounter?

3. Select a topic you think would make for a good slideshow photo story. Collect enough photos to complete a slideshow of at least 20 images, and include at least two long, medium and close-up shots. Remember, variety is important in image collection, as is the ability to create a beginning, a middle and an end of the story. Write two-sentence captions for each of the images, and put the images in what you perceive to be the best order using a slideshow software program of your choosing.

Visit edge.sagepub.com/filaknews to help you accomplish your coursework goals in an easy-to-use learning environment.

YOU NEVER KNOW WHAT THE FUTURE HOLDS.

▶ Visit the author's blog at
dynamicsofwriting.com

Stay up to date on the latest in journalism

DYNAMICS OF WRITING

Remembering that first journalism class: "I was scared out of my mind."

I was recently on a panel that discussed student media and self-censorship. Most, if not all, of the people on the panel were former journalists and several people in the audience had made the transition to the field to the classroom. One theme that came up repeatedly was the way in which students "these days" didn't have SOMETHING about them. It might be drive, it might be curiosity or it might be a skill. In any case, many of the people who spoke recalled that when THEY were students at THAT age, THEY had whatever it was that the students today seemed to lack in their estimation.

Search ...

Categories

Select Category

Shredded Tweets

Tweets by @DoctorOfPaper

Vincent Filak
@DoctorOfPaper

In the most over-the-top way possible? twitter.com/Poynter /status...

11 EDITING AUDIO AND VIDEO

LEARNING OBJECTIVES

After completing this chapter you should be able to:

- Understand the importance of using audio and video bites to augment your text-based storytelling.

- Assess the quality, value and importance of soundbites for audio and video storytelling.

- Know the various forms of video shots you can use while building a package as well as the benefits and drawbacks of each shot type.

- Identify problems associated with video and understand why these problems detract from your storytelling.

- Understand how to assemble a quality video package for presentation on the web.

THINKING AHEAD: EDITING YOUR RAW MATERIAL INTO A POLISHED GEM

Collecting quality raw material is crucial to the overall editing process. As the saying goes, "Garbage in, garbage out." However, you can start with well-collected material and essentially turn it into a messy pile of trash through poor cuts, bad selections and an overall lack of editing savvy.

Editing is about choosing the best possible elements of the raw material and presenting them to your audience. You can choose to do this as a series of stand-alone elements,

such as short soundbites or simple selections of **raw video**, or you can build broadcast-style packages that tell bigger and broader stories.

The purpose of this chapter is to go through how to separate the wheat from the chaff as you work through your digital material and how to create compelling audio and video messages. This chapter will also provide a step-by-step walkthrough of how best to create a solid story that has value to your audience members.

Broadcast journalists need to integrate audio, video and quality writing into their work to tell the best possible stories.

AUDIO BITES ONLINE

As recorders became simpler and cheaper, most journalists saw the benefit of recording interviews so that they could reassure themselves that what they heard was right. Today, most journalists rely on some sort of audio recorder to cover meetings, capture interviews and gather various other audio elements.

One of the underused aspects of this desire to capture content straight from the source's mouth is the creation of audio soundbites for inclusion on the web. In many cases, sources will tell short stories or give simple anecdotes that are too long for quotes or that require a sense of sound for them to come across well. Reporters should look for ways to cut audio bites out of the raw interview and post them online.

An audio bite is like any other tool you have in your storytelling toolbox: It will be beneficial only if it is used properly. In many cases, the value of the bites comes down to the quality of the audio and the level of importance each bite brings to your story. Consider these issues when you select stand-alone soundbites:

CHECK FOR CLARITY

The quality of the audio is always crucial in deciding if you want to go through the trouble of cutting an audio bite out of a larger interview. A large amount of background noise, microphone jostling or other similar audio problems can limit the effectiveness of the bites. In addition, if you have bad audio quality, you can annoy your audience members and detract from their overall experience with your work. If you feel the sound quality is strong enough to make for good bites, you can then hunt for a few audio chunks that will aid your reporting.

TELL A STORY

Audio adds value in specific ways that text cannot. It can give your audience members a sense of emotion that a few quick print quotes just won't. Audio bites that tell a story will help you enrich your work and give the people consuming your work a better sense of who your sources are.

For example, if you are sent to cover an auction where a prominent local farmer's land is being sold through foreclosure, you can get a wide array of quotes from various sources, including the farmer. However, a few one- or two-sentence quotes won't have the same impact as an audio recording of those interviews. The sadness in the voice of the farmer's daughter as she talks about how she always imagined taking over the farm can come through in an audio bite. The farmer, stopping to choke back sobs as he tells how he inherited the farm from his father and his father's father before him, will provide a sense of emotional turmoil that can't be captured on a printed page or a computer screen.

Audio has the ability to grab the voice of an excited child who just got candy during a parade, a proud soldier returning from overseas or the anger of a protester outside a city council meeting. When you can capture those elements in an auditory fashion, you are giving your audience a much better experience.

The chapter on shooting video should help you understand how to collect high-quality, well-structured video. That said, sometimes you aren't the one shooting the video, or circumstances will conspire against your efforts to create clear, clean visuals. When assessing your video, consider some of the following issues to determine if the video will pass muster. Remember, nobody has absolutely perfect video, and there isn't a rubric of some kind that will give you a passing score to determine if the video is usable or not. The items below should give you guidance as you examine your work and make choices.

UNSTABLE IMAGES

The quality of the video you shoot will usually start with the stability of the images on the screen. Depending on the quality of the camera and the environment of the shoot, a simple jostle or minor wiggle can either slightly disorient viewers or induce a heavy bout of motion sickness. As noted in the videography chapter, shooters who use a tripod or seek ways to stabilize themselves during the shoot should be able to keep the movement to a minimum. However, if you find that the "camera wiggle" compromises the value of the video, avoid those shots.

AWKWARD FRAMING

The human eye has its own version of framing that allows you to see things in a harmonious and pleasant way. The best-framed shots are those that mimic the eye's natural framing approach. The well-framed shots eliminate empty or distracting background elements without getting too close to the action in a way that repels the viewers.

If you feel that a visual element in a shot is too tiny or too far away, some video programs allow you to tighten your **crop**

vm/iStock.com

Blurry video is a distraction and limits your audience's ability to understand your story.

and bring those elements closer. However, if you do this, you will likely trade size for quality, so make sure you don't swap a clear and distant image for a close and fuzzy one. In other cases, if you find that a visual element is overwhelming your shot, such as when a source's face is all you can see in a frame, you might want to skip that shot and find a different video clip.

POOR FOCUS

Blurry video feels cheap and amateurish, which means you sacrifice your credibility as a professional journalist in the hopes of augmenting your story. Most cameras have an "**autofocus**" option that will help you avoid massively blurry video, but this has problems as well. The autofocus will often continue to focus and refocus throughout the recording, making for an odd viewing experience of constant adjustments. Even more, the camera doesn't always agree with you as to what should be in focus. Thus, your mayor might be blurry throughout his whole soundbite on the importance of fiscal responsibility while the tree behind him is perfectly clear.

Good shooters know how to use a **manual focus** to keep the video sharp and make the most important visual element in the shot the clearest. However, if you or another journalist fails to keep the shots sharp, you want to reconsider using any clips from that raw material.

WEIGH SIZE VERSUS VALUE

The benefit of audio bites is they can do more work than a typical text-based quote because they often run longer and have more "meat" to them. This can be a problem, however, if the audio runs too long or fails to add important information to your story. Good journalists will balance the size of any element against the value that element brings to a story. Writers will trim back quotes when longer versions might bore their readers. Designers will shrink or enlarge photos as to make efficient use of space. Photographers will crop images to home in on the action of the frame and eliminate useless or distracting elements. The same basic premise applies to audio editing.

Some people can tell a story in a 60-second clip and keep you riveted to the story from start to finish. Others can make a 6-second soundbite seem like an eternity. The point is that not all stories will lend themselves to audio bites, and not every story can make the grade. You need to look at how long the audio bite will run, how engaging that bite is and whether the size and value are congruent. If they are, grab that chunk of audio and make it part of your overall story. If not, don't waste your time or the time of your audience.

VIDEO BITES ONLINE

The audio quality issues noted above remain a concern in video-bite selection, but you also need to consider the quality of the video itself. Poorly lit video, poorly framed shots or otherwise problematic video (see the box "Identifying Problematic Video" in this chapter) will create even bigger problems for your viewers. Make sure that the visuals themselves are as appealing as the story the source is telling when you decide to use the video with your story.

Occasionally, the importance of the event will override the issue of video quality. For example, citizens often capture breaking news events with the video recorders on their smartphones. The video can be grainy or wobbly, but when that video is the only live recording of an explosion, a shooting or otherwise breaking event, you should weigh the importance of the material against the quality of the visuals.

PAIRING SCRIPT AND VIDEO

Video, audio and a reporter's script must match. If you are responsible for packaging these elements, you need to find ways to maintain symmetry among them. If you have a reporter talking about how much fun the kids from Ryerson Elementary are having at the museum, you need to have a video clip or two of kids having fun at the museum. If the reporter is talking about how much fun they are having and you have a shot of two kids crying, you need to rethink your approach.

The same thing applies to **sequencing** shots within a package. If a reporter notes that many parents are opposed to a school board referendum, you want to have a soundbite from a parent who is opposed to the measure. A bite from a proponent or from a school board member, though potentially valuable, is incongruent with your reporter's approach.

Some stories are difficult to tell visually. Stories on things like school violence offer few video options, outside of your standard interviews. If you use video that shows random schoolchildren, you imply that they are either the victims of violence or the perpetrators of it. When editors lack

CONSIDER THIS ➡ USING RAW VIDEO

An alternative to cutting bites or building packages is to simply post the raw video footage you gathered and let your viewers see what has happened. For example, in July 2014, New York police officers attempted to arrest Eric Garner on suspicion of selling loose cigarettes. During this arrest, Garner repeated "I can't breathe" 11 times as police pulled him to the ground, where he lost consciousness. He later died at an area hospital. A bystander used his mobile phone to capture this confrontation, and news stations posted the entire exchange on their websites. In cases like this one, the less involved the reporter is, the better the audience members are served.

However, not every mayoral announcement or every postgame interview will merit an extended, uncut video. Unfortunately, some reporters tend to become lazy and prefer to dump giant videos online just so they can say, "Hey, we have video on our site!" When you look at the issue of running raw video online, consider the following questions:

Will someone watch this? Sticking with the audience-centricity principle of the book, you should first consider if this is something someone will want to see. In some cases, the answer is obvious, as rare things mesmerize people. If you have tornado footage, video of a vice presidential candidate falling off a stage or a crow that can say "Grandma," you're probably running that footage. However, if you scan YouTube, you can find dozens of community meetings or local events that have fewer than 100 views. If you think your viewers won't watch it, don't post it.

Is it boring? This is an offshoot of the first question, because people will usually watch something of any length if it is exciting and engaging. The film "Gone With the Wind" won the Oscar for best picture and is still regarded as an incredibly important film, even though it spans more than 238 minutes. However, commercials that come before YouTube videos can seem interminable, even though they usually last only 15 to 30 seconds. If the raw footage that accompanies a story has value or if the footage is short enough to give the viewers something important quickly, post it. If the video could put people to sleep more quickly than a shot of NyQuil, skip it.

Does it tell a story? Journalism is about storytelling, which is why journalists need to practice ways of putting content together in a coherent fashion. A story has a beginning, a middle and an end. It also gives people a sense of what happened and why it mattered. When it comes to raw video, if you are lucky enough to have a story that unfolds perfectly in real time, get out of the way and let the video do the work for you. When a video chunk can give people a simple story arc and make them feel like they learned something, it merits inclusion. If you find that you need to do too much to prop up the raw video with a long backstory or other intrusions, just take the broadcast approach and start building a package.

quality video for a story like this, they often wallpaper over the reporter's script with some benign video of bulletin boards or school bags. The most common shot is one in which the videographer sets the camera on the floor of a hallway and captures images of students' feet as they walk past.

Although television needs video to make a story work, you can avoid the use of video on an online story and rely on the printed word instead. If the video is good and can match up nicely with the essence of the story, use it to help tell the story in a more complete manner.

Digital editing software allows you to edit broadcast stories much more easily than previous generations of journalists, who relied on tape-to-tape machines or grease pencils and razorblades to select and slice film.

BUILDING A STORY FROM START TO FINISH

To tell a story in a longer and more involved way, web-based reporters can draw from the experiences of their broadcast counterparts in creating packages. The previous video and broadcast chapters have given you some insights as to how to gather material, write scripts and use specific formats for storytelling. These previous chapters have given you a macro-level view of working with video, which is crucial to understanding its value and applicability. However, this chapter will provide you with more of a micro-level approach to building a video package for the web. The programs available for video editing vary in terms of how to attach audio to video or where to click to find certain editing tools. Avid, Final Cut and Adobe Premier are three of the most common programs in the field, and a step-by-step guide for each one is included in Appendix D. Between those program-specific walkthroughs and the information below, you should have a pretty good overall understanding of this process from start to finish.

IMPORT YOUR VIDEO

Although you can edit video in many new digital cameras or on smartphones, these platforms offer fewer options for properly assembling the footage. If you have the option of editing on a laptop or a larger computer, you should consider it, as you can better view the quality of images and you can do more detail-oriented work. Pull your footage from your camera, phone or memory device into the program so you can see what you have at your disposal. The new footage will be added to your library of raw material so you can pick the shots you want to use.

REVIEW YOUR FOOTAGE

One of the best things about digital editing programs is that you can easily see the chunks of video. Unlike old tape-based systems, you can see how many shots you took, get a general sense of what material is present in each video chunk and take quick looks at various segments of those video shots. The old system is akin to having to look at a room through a keyhole, while the digital system is like being able to teleport to any point in that room at any time.

Take advantage of this opportunity to scan through your work. This will give you a sense of how many types of shots you have, what interviews will play a large role in your story and if you need to go back and do additional shooting. You can also start to either physically or mentally sketch out how you think this story will evolve. When you know what the raw material looks like, you can better plan out what you want to do with it.

WORK WITH YOUR AUDIO TRACK

As we discussed in Chapter 9, you will be an active participant in telling the story in a broadcast-style package. Before you go out to a shoot, you should have an idea of what the story will tell people. When you return from the shoot and review your footage, you can fine-tune this idea and flesh out your script.

If you will want to lay down your **reporter's track**, voicing the audio for the package, you can do so once you start building your package. If you prefer to do this as a separate audio file, you can record your voice on your phone, a mini-recorder or any other program that can create digital audio files. You can then import this like you did the video. If you run into a problem voicing your audio track, you can either delete the track and start over, or simply reread the content within the same take and edit out the problems later. As you continue editing, you can trim your audio track to better fit within the overall package or revoice a chunk of audio for a specific use or based on a change in your script.

Review your video to see which shots tell the best stories and which audio helps convey your messages properly.

The most important thing is to determine how you want to assemble your package. Some people feel more comfortable writing to the video portion of the story, using specific words and sentences to attach to the video they shot. Others feel better writing a script and then collecting video to match up with their idea of what the story should say.

SELECT SHOTS AND FORM SEQUENCES

Good video journalists pick through their shots like grocery shoppers picking through produce, finding specific things that will aid them in meeting their overall goal and then carefully choosing only the best version of that item. Just as a shopper might spend a few minutes carefully examining a tomato or a melon, a reporter must take equal care in going through the various shots and making the best overall selections.

Each shot has value in telling a story, but your work in assembling them into a single package also has a large impact on your overall storytelling approach. (See the box on shots for a more detailed examination of this topic.) You can move from a long shot to another long shot to another long shot in an attempt to provide broad overviews of multiple housing developments. You can rely heavily on medium shots, which would allow you to tell the story in a very plain and yet easily consumable way. You can use a series of close-up shots to give people a strong sense of detail if you are telling a story about a local embroidery club and you want the detail of the needle and thread piercing the cloth.

In most cases, you will mix the shot types to create sequences that provide a variety of views on a given topic. Moving from shot type to shot type will require clear cohesion of ideas within the sequence. For example, look at your lecture hall or computer lab. You could start a video about what's going on in there right now with a long shot that shows multiple people taking notes or working on computers. You could then move to a medium shot of an individual student writing or typing. A close-up could then follow that shows the pen writing on the paper or the fingers on the keyboard. The logical progression provides your viewers with an easy sense of what is happening: People are working in a classroom. However, if you started with the close-up, moved to the long shot and then jumped back to the medium shot, you would likely confuse your viewers.

HELPFUL HINTS WHEN TO USE EACH SHOT IN YOUR STORY

The previous chapter introduced you to the various types of shots. Here is a closer look at when these shot types work well and when they don't:

A long shot can establish a scene, such as a large forest, a crowded fair or a majestic mountain range.

A medium shot mimics what your eye traditionally sees and can give your audience a connection to the people in the frame.

A close up allows you to see details like no other shot.

LONG SHOT

Use it when you want to:

- Establish the scene
- Show the massive size of something (crowds, desolation, devastation)
- Move from one setting to another
- Provide respite from too many close-up and medium shots

Avoid it when:

- Details are important
- It leaves too much wasted space within the frame
- You have a primary speaker within a frame

MEDIUM SHOT

Use it when you want to:

- Get an interview with a subject that will be used for soundbites later
- Focus on an action-reaction sequence between people or within a small group of people
- Provide the viewers with a small piece of action within an event
- Move from a long shot to a more intimate shot

Avoid it when:

- The scene lacks value
- The participants can't be adequately framed in this fashion
- It fails to provide the impact that a different shot would provide
- You have used too many of these in a row without breaking for a close-up or a long shot

CLOSE-UP SHOT

Use it when you want to:

- Focus on a detail that would otherwise be overlooked
- Provide the viewers with an intimate look at something
- Capture a small action

Avoid it when:

- You can't tell what is happening in the frame
- The close-up shot doesn't follow logically in a sequence from the long shot to the medium shot to the close-up
- It jars the viewer because the action doesn't translate at that level

When you move between shot types, you should consider them on a long shot–medium shot–close-up shot continuum; you can't jump from one end to the other without moving through the midpoint on that line. So, you can go from long to long to medium to close-up to medium to medium to long without too much problem. However, if you go from long to close-up to long to close-up, you will end up disorienting your viewers.

During the selection process, you also need to determine how long each shot will be in the sequence. In most cases, shots of b-roll can range from 4 to 6 seconds without too much trouble. If you go shorter, the pace of the piece will speed up, and in some cases, it will feel rushed. If the shots go longer, the piece will move more slowly, and you run the risk of boring people. Soundbites tend to run between 8 and 12 seconds in most standard broadcast pieces, although circumstances can dictate that they be shorter or longer.

The idea with most of these "rules" is that you can break them if you have a good reason to do so. However, if you break them because you don't know any better, you can create a painful viewing experience for your audience members.

AVOID GIMMICKY TRANSITIONS

Early work in broadcast required editors to physically chop apart the tape with a pair of scissors or a razor blade, thus leading the primary form of editing to be known as a "cut." Digital technology allows you to do a lot of the more "Hollywood-style" transitions now, ranging from **wipes** and **fades** to explosions and spirals, but these new options won't turn you into the news version of Steven Spielberg.

When you use transitions other than the cut, you draw attention to the editing process and thus distract the viewers from the content itself. The purpose of your editing is to tell a story, not amuse people with gimmicks. If you stick with the standard-cut approach, you will have a much cleaner package and a more focused audience.

ADD GRAPHICS AND OTHER ELEMENTS

The inclusion of graphic elements in a video package can help your viewers better understand the content and free you from adding bulky information to your script. For example, if you use a graphic of superimposed text (often called a "**super**") with your soundbite, you can identify your speaker and that person's attachment to the story (Sue Smith, County Fair Participant). This prevents you from having to incorporate her name and value into your script.

Other great uses of a graphic include displaying **pie charts** during an election story, showcasing a mini-biography for a new police chief and providing the website for a group you featured in your story. Digital tools make these elements easy to add and can help your audience members better consume specific content elements.

As with every other tool outlined in this book, you should consider the value of graphics before you add them. Some graphics, such as supers, will almost always add to a story, while others seem out of place because they are too complex for their brief appearance on the screen. Before you build a graphic, you need to determine if it will add value to the story and if you can use the graphic in a natural, nonjarring way as part of your package.

© WAOW-TV

Brandon Kinnard's passion for sports journalism and his love of audio/video storytelling landed him an amazing gig in his home state: sports director at WAOW-TV in Wausau, Wisconsin. He started at the station as a weekend sports anchor, having already spent two summers as a media relations director for the Green Bay Bullfrogs baseball club and having worked for his college TV station.

Kinnard said that the key to doing well with video-based storytelling is tied to the video itself.

"Rule number one is to write to your video," he said. "Video tells the story in television. I started out doing a lot of radio in college, so it took me longer than I'd like to admit to really learn that. Video and audio are gifts to those of us who work in TV. They give us a distinct and very valuable tool that our friends who work in print don't have."

During his earlier years in broadcast, Kinnard said, he often forgot how important the visual was to his stories.

"My main suggestion to people starting out in this would be to let the video speak for you," Kinnard said. "In sports, we do quite a bit of highlights on a daily basis. Seeing as I started out in radio, I at first felt the need to 'over talk' during those. Now, I prefer a much slower-paced style, and I let the video speak for itself, while providing a few comments along the way."

On top of these changes to his style, Kinnard said, he needed to adapt his broadcast approach to help tell stories differently on the web.

"We post all of our stories to the Web and we always re-write them into more of a print style," he said. "Sometimes, this requires a drastic overhaul, and the script ends up looking much different than it did as a broadcast story. The story arc and main points are always the same, but sometimes you have to tell it in a very different way than you did in the broadcast story."

Regardless of the platform or the approach to his content, Kinnard said that he keeps the audience he serves at the forefront of everything he does.

"In television, we cater a great deal to our target audience," he said. "That can be tough for those of us who work in sports—because much of the time, our audience isn't necessarily sports fans, the way it would be if we were working at ESPN. They're casual sports fans at best, and that's fine . . . .We just need to make sure we keep that in mind when reporting . . . .Our station reminds us of the target audience all the time."

ONE LAST THING

Q: If you could tell the students reading this book anything you think is important, what would it be?

A: "The best piece of advice I can give is just to be wary of your surroundings. News, especially in TV, is all about being observant—noticing things your audience might not and telling them about it/why it's important. Pride yourself on being observant. Take the extra time and go the extra mile to make your story better, don't just go through the motions."

REVIEW THE PACKAGE FOR ANY ERRORS

The process of creating a package can lead to errors similar to those of any other journalistic endeavor. You can mix up the names of your sources or misspell them. You can forget to introduce a concept before you begin explaining it. You can forget a crucial aspect of the story, thus undercutting the whole purpose of your piece. In video work, other errors can also occur, including things like **jump cuts**, truncated soundbites and poor sequencing. No matter the cause or the error, before you put the final product out for public consumption, you should do your best to polish the package and remove the problems.

In most cases, video packages are only a minute or two long, so you can review them multiple times. On your first pass, you could assess your speech quality and your pace in the voiceover. When you review it a second time, you could pay particular attention to how well the video matches the audio. A third examination could look for visual errors, such as bad video sequences and the use of graphics. At a certain point, you have to be passably satisfied with your work, and you need to publish it. Once you do, keep an eye on the way your audience reacts to it, including online comments and social media shares. If someone points out an error, you can always examine the story and determine if you need to rework the package or issue a correction. If the story becomes popular for positive reasons, you can plan a quality follow-up to that story.

When you want to tell stories that involve complex numbers or complicated processes, consider using a graphic as part of your package.

11

EDITING AUDIO AND VIDEO

THE BIG THREE

Here are the three key things you should take away from this chapter:

1. **The edit matters:** Good video editors can do a lot of things with so-so video. Bad video editors can wreck incredible footage. You need to know how best to use video and audio, what approach to take in which situations and how to give your audience members a valuable experience when they watch your content.

2. **Video tells the story:** As Brandon Kinnard said, video and audio are gifts, and we should treat them as such. Use the sounds and images you have available to their maximum potential, and get out of their way.

The less often you inject yourself into the mix, the better you are.

3. **Cater to your audience:** When it comes to selecting video or audio content, creating packages or posting raw video, keep the audience needs at the forefront of your mind. An audience should get material that is relevant and engaging, so make sure you are thinking about what will matter to viewers and how to engage them. This will help you figure out what will work and what won't when it comes to video.

KEY TERMS

autofocus   197

crop   197

fade   203

jump cut   205

manual focus   197

pie chart   203

raw video   195

reporter's track   201

sequencing   198

super   203

wipe   203

DISCUSSION QUESTIONS

1. What are the benefits and drawbacks of the three types of basic video shots outlined in your book? When should you use each of them?

2. Brandon Kinnard noted that he felt that journalists should "let the video speak for itself." Do you agree or disagree with him on this issue? Based on your experiences with broadcast journalism and internet

video packages, how well do you feel professionals follow his advice?

3. How much "raw video" do you find yourself watching online? What makes it worth watching, or what makes you avoid it? Do you think the people who post it think more about their own interests or those of the audience members who will be watching it?

WRITE NOW!

1. Use an audio recorder while conducting an interview with a source. After the interview, use a simple audio editor to select and save two soundbites that range between 15 and 25 seconds each. Write a short essay (1 to 1.5 pages) that explains who this source is, the topic of the soundbites and why you feel these are valuable stand-alone soundbites.

2. Use an audio recorder while conducting an interview with a source on a topic. After the interview, select two soundbites that range between 10 and 15 seconds each. Write a 1-minute-long script that incorporates those bites. Voice the script and integrate the soundbites into your piece and save it as a simple radio-style package.

3. Review a broadcast news package you find either on television or online. Analyze the overall quality of the video in terms of the possible problems your book describes (poor focus, awkward framing, unstable images). Assess the degree to which b-roll, soundbites and a stand-up are used effectively. How well did this reporter do in creating a clear and engaging news package? Write a short essay (2 to 2.5 pages) that discusses your findings.

4. Use video from the video bank available to you online to create a simple package. Write a brief script on the topic and voice it. Then, insert the soundbites where you placed them in the story and top it off with effective b-roll. Make sure to match your video to your script and properly write in and out of your bites.

Visit edge.sagepub.com/filaknews to help you accomplish your coursework goals in an easy-to-use learning environment.

12

LAW AND THE MEDIA

LEARNING OBJECTIVES

After completing this chapter you should be able to:

- Understand the value of the First Amendment with regard to journalistic activity as well as the misconceptions people hold about its applicability.

- Identify the key components of libel and apply them to potentially libelous situations.

- Apply the various defenses of libel to potentially libelous situations.

- Explain the rationale behind open meetings and open records and be able to investigate the laws governing each as they apply to your state.

- Understand the basic tenets of privacy and the ways in which reporters can violate the right to privacy.

- Define and differentiate between public and private areas as well as public figures, limited-purpose public figures and private individuals.

- Discuss issues related to confidentiality and press shield laws.

THINKING AHEAD: THE LAW IS YOUR FRIEND

The concept of media law often fills students with anxiety over court-case memorization and broad-sweeping legal decisions. Legal precedents and case law are important aspects of journalism, although very rarely will you have to cite a specific decision during the course of a reporting assignment.

The law is fraught with contradictions, conundrums and general confusion, as it isn't created once, but rather as a giant patchwork quilt that does its best to cover important aspects of life and keep up with a rapidly changing world. To

that end, what the law deems important in one state might be less concerning in another state. Understanding what you can and can't do as well as where you should or shouldn't be will prevent officials from restricting your access to events and documents.

This chapter will examine the various aspects of media law, including topics of open access, libel and invasion of privacy. What you will get here should help you find your legal footing and perhaps pique your interest for that higher level law course.

BRITTA PEDERSEN/AFP/Getty Images

A protester holds a poster during a demonstration in support of freedom of the press in Berlin, a reaction to a treason investigation against two writers of the news blog Netzpolitik. The case centers on the blog Netzpolitik.org (Net politics), which earlier this year published documents on plans by Germany's domestic security agency to step up internet surveillance.

UNDERSTANDING THE FIRST AMENDMENT

The **First Amendment** to the Constitution reads as follows:

Congress shall make no law respecting an establishment of religion, or prohibiting the free exercise thereof; or abridging the freedom of speech, or of the press; or the right of the people peaceably to assemble, and to petition the government for a redress of grievances.

That's five freedoms (or six, depending on if you see one or two freedoms under religion) the Founding Fathers gave to us in a tightly written, 45-word paragraph. The concepts of "speech" and "press" are crucial to our work as journalists, and we need to take those responsibilities seriously. The writers of the Bill of Rights didn't throw those in there because they were looking for something to fill space. They saw the ability to get information from people and convey it to a larger audience without government interference as crucial to the functionality of this country.

Since its introduction, the First Amendment has been interpreted and analyzed in a variety of ways that widen its protections in some cases and limit it in others. The amendment is a living thing that constantly evolves, and as a journalist, you need to be aware of how it works and what it does and doesn't do for you.

MISCONCEPTIONS ABOUT THE AMENDMENT

People often get in trouble when they think of the First Amendment as a sword instead of a shield. They convince themselves that "freedom of the press" provides them with access to areas that are off limits, allows them to publish material without thinking about potential ramifications and generally act like numbskulls in public. Even those people who see it as a shield can get into trouble once they realize the amendment isn't bulletproof. Here are some of the bigger misconceptions associated with the First Amendment:

NO ONE CAN STOP YOU FROM PUBLISHING ANYTHING YOU WANT

The First Amendment clearly notes, "Congress shall make no law," which was later extended to all forms of government. However, the government isn't the only body or organization that can prohibit you from publishing things. Corporations that own your newspaper or magazine can prohibit certain things from being published. The Federal Communications Commission has a say in what can and can't be done on television news. Even certain web platforms place specific rules and regulations on content in their user agreements.

NOTHING BAD CAN HAPPEN TO YOU AFTER YOU PUBLISH

The ability to publish without governmental prohibition isn't as great as it sounds in some cases. People erroneously equate "free press" and "free speech" with "consequence-free press" and "consequence-free speech." Whatever you publish can run afoul of the law, and that can lead to some negative outcomes. If you publish incorrect information that harms someone, you can end up on the wrong side of a libel suit. If you enter a private area without permission, someone might sue you for invasion of privacy or trespassing. Even if you publish accurate information, you could still be harmed in the "court of public opinion," with readers turning their backs on you. The First Amendment doesn't protect you from every potential harm, so you need to be careful with what you publish.

PROFESSIONAL JOURNALISTS ENJOY STRONGER PROTECTIONS THAN OTHER PEOPLE

The United States doesn't consider journalists to be a special class of the citizenry. Every John and Jane Q. Public has the same rights and responsibilities as the journalists at the top publications in the country. The benefit of this is that we have many more opportunities for an engaged and informed citizenry. The drawback is that any yahoo with an internet connection and a Twitter feed can land himself of herself in a lot of trouble without even knowing it.

THE FIRST AMENDMENT IS CLEAR AND ABSOLUTE

The amendment is neither of these things, as the government has limited speech and press during times of war, as it did with the **Sedition Act** during World War I and with the **Smith Act** during World War II. Courts have limited speech with time, place and manner restrictions, prohibiting people from doing certain things at certain times in certain areas. Although the phraseology of "Congress shall make no law" sounds like a rock-solid judgment from on high, plenty of people have found out the hard way that the First Amendment is open to interpretation.

LAW ACROSS MEDIA PLATFORMS: LEVELS OF PROTECTION

Throughout this chapter, most of what we talk about involving freedom, access and rights applies to all citizens of the United States. That said, the laws that govern media vary from platform to platform and have continued to evolve. This is why a full understanding of media law is crucial to reporters.

Traditional print publications, such as newspapers and magazines, enjoy the broadest freedoms under the law, as those inalienable rights were codified in the **Bill of Rights**. The Founding Fathers determined that an unfettered press would lead to an informed citizenry and thus a healthy and robust society. It was for this reason that they declared in the First Amendment that the government may not stand in the way of the press to gather and publish information under most circumstances.

Chip Somodevilla/ Getty Images

Alt-right blogger Jason Kessler waits for protesters to quiet before beginning a news conference in front of City Hall Aug. 13, 2017 in Charlottesville, Virginia. Kessler, who helped organize the Unite the Right rally one day earlier, blamed Charlottesville government officials and law enforcement for failing to protect the First Amendment rights of the rally's participants, a collection of white supremacists, neo-Nazis, Ku Klux Klan members and alt-right supporters.

Television and radio stations are overseen and licensed by the Federal Communications Commission, which can establish rules and guidelines for broadcasters. The FCC cannot censor news content, as that would be in clear violation of the First Amendment, but it can place restrictions on content based on issues such as indecency and profanity. It can also react to citizen complaints regarding the "rigging or slanting the news," or otherwise producing intentionally false content.[1]

The FCC's level of oversight regarding a particular station is determined based on how the content is disseminated. Broadcast channels that use public airwaves are the most heavily governed, because the broadcast spectrum is viewed as a limited public resource. The FCC also oversees cable and satellite stations, but these outlets have a wider degree of latitude in terms of content, in part because of the unlimited number of channels available on which they can operate. Additionally, the public airwaves can arrive in a person's home simply by turning on a television, while cable and satellite programming requires people to subscribe to a service and actively bring the content into their homes.

The current battle over censorship rests with the internet, which contains aspects of both print and broadcast. The internet currently receives protections more akin to those enjoyed by print products, although the government has made several efforts over the years to curtail free speech online. The **Communications Decency Act of 1996** was the first and most well-known effort to place restrictions upon online content. The act was proposed in reaction to the proliferation of pornography online and sought to apply broadcast indecency regulations to the internet. This would have extended the FCC's oversight to websites and would have punished indecent speech that would have otherwise been protected by the First Amendment.[2] In 1997, the Supreme Court determined in Reno v. ACLU that the anti-indecency provisions were unconstitutional.[3] Other similar efforts followed, including the **Child Online Protection Act**, but for the most part the internet has emerged unscathed.

BEN STANSALL/Getty Images

This picture taken on July 14, 2011 shows WikiLeaks founder Julian Assange holding a legal document as he addresses a press conference in central London. The whistleblowing website WikiLeaks said Oct. 24, 2011 it was suspending publishing classified U.S. diplomatic files to focus instead on fundraising "to ensure our future survival."

REPORTER'S PRIVILEGE

Journalists in the United States are not licensed as they are in other countries, and as such they do not tend to receive rights not bestowed upon the general citizenry. For example, anyone is allowed to attend a public meeting and report on what happened during the event. Any citizen can be sued for libel if the actions of the accused fall within the parameters of libel (see the section on libel later in this chapter).

One term that indicates that reporters do get special rights is "**reporter's privilege**," which states that journalists cannot be compelled to testify or disclose information about confidential sources in court. The constitutionality of this privilege came before the Supreme Court in the 1972 Branzburg v. Hayes decision, in which the court held that reporters could not use the First Amendment as a defense against testifying before a grand jury.

In the case, the Louisville Courier-Journal's Paul Branzburg witnessed people making and using hashish in the process of reporting on a story about drug use. He was subpoenaed and ordered to name his sources. The court ruled 5-4 that Branzburg and two other journalists who had been subpoenaed in separate cases did not have a reporter's privilege. However, the court did establish that this was limited to the facts of these cases and that a subsequent case could provide cause to prevent a reporter from testifying.

The courts have generally created a balancing test between the reporter's right to protect sources and the law's desire to obtain information. Legal expert Ashley Messenger notes that the courts usually examine three criteria to determine if a reporter's privilege exists:

1. Has the person subpoenaing the journalist tried to get the information sought from the journalist in all other reasonable ways before resorting to a subpoena?

2. Does the reporter possess information that is relevant and crucial to the case at hand, or is this a "fishing expedition?"

3. What kind of case is this and is there an overriding public interest in this information? Messenger notes courts are more likely to grant privilege in civil cases than criminal ones.[4]

According to the Reporters Committee for Freedom of the Press, 31 states and the District of Columbia have passed "**shield laws**" that give journalists an explicit level of reporter's privilege. Those laws vary from state to state, so understanding exactly who receives protection and under what circumstances requires some due diligence on your part. For a full list of the states and what level of protection you can receive, go to https://www.rcfp.org/reporters-privilege.

LET THE SUNSHINE IN: RULES FOR TRANSPARENCY AND ACCESS

Congress passed the Government in the **Sunshine Act** in 1976 as part of a series of laws intended to increase transparency at the federal level. This act dictated that, with rare and specific exceptions, federal meetings should be open to the public for observation. Officials who supported the act surmised that if government business was conducted in the "sunlight," politicians would conduct themselves in a way that best served the people to whom they were accountable.

Each state also has a series of laws meant to provide members of the public with access to the machinations of their governmental bodies. The rules that govern each state vary from the federal rules and from one another, but all forms of government are held to some standard of openness. One

Chip Somodevilla/Getty Images

Charlottesville Mayor Mike Signer (C) takes a seat before the start of a "community recovery" town hall meeting. Rules regarding the "openness" of events like these are important for journalists to understand.

key thing noted in many of the state laws is the phrase "all persons are entitled," which makes it clear that these rules serve everyone, not just journalists.

Although the term "sunshine laws" means different things to various people, the rules of most concern to journalists tend to fall into one of two areas: open meetings and open records.

OPEN MEETINGS

Laws that govern the gathering of public officials are meant to give citizens an opportunity to see how politicians represent the best interests of their constituents. Governmental bodies are thus required to meet in public, provide an agenda in advance of their meetings and keep minutes of those events. The federal government and the states vary on how they meet these and other requirements. For example, the state of Oregon requires that "all public bodies provide reasonable notice to the public for meetings," noting that special meetings require at least 24 hours' advance notice to the public and the media. Texas, however, requires that governmental bodies "must provide 72 hours notice including an agenda for all public meetings." In the state of Washington, the legislature is exempted from the state's open meeting law, while in New York, the legislature is specifically included in the law. (For a full list of the states and the laws that govern their open meetings, go to https://ballotpedia.org/State_open_meetings_laws.)

Each state also allows these bodies to close all or some of the meeting to the public, but they must announce in advance that they are closing the meeting and provide a legal rationale for closing it. Although the rules vary from state to state, closed meetings can take place to discuss things such as personnel matters, property purchases and collective bargaining strategies. That said, meetings are presumed to be open, and the burden rests on the governmental body to take the steps necessary to close the meeting and justify the reasoning behind its closure.

OPEN RECORDS

The goal of having federal and state open record laws is to provide people with the most transparency possible with regard to the actions of the governments that oversee them. Most governmental agencies generate a lot of paper, which includes interoffice memos, budgetary assessments and procedural documents, as well as a lot of electronic communication, including email and text messages. The federal government operates under the Freedom of Information Act (FOIA) and provides any member of the public with the opportunity to request and examine the records of federal agencies. In most cases, these documents are available to the public, with a few notable exceptions.

Each state also offers its citizenry the opportunity to examine and request copies of documents generated by governmental bodies. The "sunshine laws" that govern the release of these records vary from state to state, so it is important to understand the rules of the state you work in as well as any state from which you wish to request records. However, the underlying premise of these laws is standard across the board: People have the right to know what is going on in their government. These documents can be crucial to reporters, as people can often forget or lie, but documents have a knack for telling the truth. (A larger review of how to request documents is included in Appendix C.)

THOUGHTS FROM A PRO ➡ CHARLES N. DAVIS, DEAN OF THE HENRY W. GRADY COLLEGE OF JOURNALISM AND MASS COMMUNICATION, UNIVERSITY OF GEORGIA

© Charles N. Davis

Charles N. Davis has spent a lifetime as an advocate for open access to governmental procedures. He currently serves as the dean of the Henry W. Grady College of Journalism and Mass Communication at the University of Georgia. Before that, he spent 14 years as a faculty member at the University of Missouri, where he also served as the executive director of the National Freedom of Information Coalition and the Freedom of Information Center.

Davis, who has published several books on acquiring public records and journalism in the information age, said that beginning reporters must understand the importance of access.

"It's really difficult when you are just starting out and someone in a position of authority walks up to you and says, 'You can't be here,'" Davis said. "Can you be there? Is your reporting taking place in a public forum? A limited purpose public forum? Do you leave, or stand your ground? It's an intimidating situation, and one in which you need to know your rights, so you can gently and civilly push back if you are in the right."

Reporters who know their rights will do much better in the field than those who don't, Davis said, especially when faced with people who don't want the media covering them.

"As a reporter, I encountered situations where those I was covering mistakenly thought I had no legal right to be there, and it was on me to know better," he said. "In the heat of the moment, you need to have a good grasp of your legal standing to be on site."

On the opposite side of the spectrum is the issue of privacy, which Davis said is another huge issue facing journalists today. Although the two issues seem mutually exclusive, Davis argues that these journalistic needs can and should coexist.

"Public officials have done a most effective job of convincing the public that it protects their privacy by removing whole categories of information from public scrutiny," he said. "I reject that premise. What happens instead is that information that once belonged to the public becomes the exclusive property of government, and that reduces our sovereignty as people with each exemption. It's a delicate balance, and I am no absolutist, but I have watched as whole classes of records are removed from the public with little thought as to the reduction in public scrutiny and accountability."

To improve transparency and accountability, Davis said journalists need to educate record keepers about the importance of open records. In addition, journalists need to make open record requests part of their standard reporting.

"The biggest single issue with access, day to day, is a lack of training on both sides of the ball: those entrusted with access know little about the ins and outs of FOI law and are far too often hunkered down in a defensive mode, devaluing the democratic importance of transparency . . ." he said. "On the other side of the equation, journalists don't use FOI laws nearly as often as they should. They are up against deadlines, crushing realities with regard to time management and just getting through the day, I know . . . but

(Continued)

(Continued)

man, the stories that just sit there for want of a simple FOI request! Newsrooms need to regularize FOI requests as part of the daily workflow. Reporters need to get themselves into a 'documents state of mind'—constantly thinking about what records might be out there."

ONE LAST THING:

Q: If you could tell the students reading this book anything you think is important, what would it be?

A: "What I always remind student journalists is that the law is the floor of human behavior—it is what you can do, and often not what you should do. So much exists in the extralegal domain of good, old-fashioned reporting. How persuasive can you be? Have you asked the right questions, of enough people? Have you exhausted every angle, talked with every single person who might be able to help you get to the truth? The law is not an excuse for not doing the work."

Each state has specific rules about who must consent to the recording of conversations. Look up the rules pertaining to your state before you inadvertently break the law.

finwal/iStock.com

RULES FOR RECORDING

The Reporters Committee for Freedom of the Press notes that federal law allows the recording of calls and other electronic communication as long as at least one person involved in the communication is aware of the recording. In addition, 38 states have adopted similar "**one-party consent**" rules, which allow you to record someone without their consent. The other 12 states require that all parties involved in a phone call or other similar discussion consent to the recording. In almost no circumstance can you record a call to which you are not a party, a concept often referred to as wiretapping. (You can find a full listing of the states and their laws on recording on the committee's website: http://www.rcfp.org/reporters-recording-guide/state-state-guide.)

In many cases, you might be better off just asking your source if you can record the call or the conversation. It can inspire trust and provide a mutually respectful environment for your discussion. (We will talk more about the "can" vs. "should" approaches to things like this in Chapter 13 on ethics.)

THE BASICS OF LIBEL

The term **libel** is frequently misunderstood and misapplied. Libel refers to the publication of false, defamatory statements that can harm a person's reputation. The harm can come in a variety of ways, such as financial losses, persistent ridicule or societal hatred.

Reporters often harm people's reputations when they reveal shady business practices, criminal activity and some truly stupid public behavior. This can lead people to feel aggrieved and looking for some form of payback, and this often takes the form of a lawsuit (or at least the threat of one).

Legal expert Ashley Messenger outlines seven key elements that a plaintiff (the person bringing the suit) must demonstrate[5] to win a libel suit:

1. The statement is defamatory.

2. The statement is false.

3. The statement is a factual, as opposed to opinion-based, assertion.

4. The statement clearly identifies someone.

5. The statement is published.

6. The defendant acted with the requisite level of fault.

7. The plaintiff suffered damages.

Singer Courtney Love found herself at the center of several "Twibel" suits due to her use of Twitter to attack other people.

This is a difficult, but not impossible, burden to meet for people hoping to win a lawsuit. Some of the elements are easier to understand than others, so for the sake of simplicity, we will review the defenses of libel, hitting on the more crucial elements outlined above. Before we get into those defenses, it is important to look at the aspect of publication, because it has taken on new meaning thanks to the variety of media platforms available to professional journalists and the general public.

The courts have defined publication as the sharing of information with someone other than the plaintiff in the libel case. Some people erroneously believe this means the material has to be printed in a newspaper or a magazine in order to qualify as being "published." However, as long as the material is sent to a third party, a court may determine the material meets the publication standard. For example, if you printed a single sheet of paper that listed false and defamatory statements about your professor and shared it with your classmates, you might meet the standard of publication. The same could be true if you posted it to a campus kiosk where students frequently go to learn about events at the university. It's also worth noting that the republication of someone else's false statement is viewed as publication in many cases.

The bigger concerns come in the digital realm, where a single tweet or post can go viral in hours or even minutes. Courts have held that publication is not limited to the "dead-tree" versions of publications and that material shared via social media sites, like Twitter and Facebook, or posted on blogging sites can meet the publication standard. For example, in the wake of the death of music legend Prince, musician Sinéad O'Connor wrote on her Facebook page that Prince had often used drugs throughout his career and that he "got his drugs over the decades" from actor Arsenio Hall. In May 2016, Hall filed a $5 million defamation suit against O'Connor, stating that her claims were absolutely false and damaging.[6] In February 2017, O'Connor publically retracted her claims, and Hall said he would drop his suit.[7]

The concept of "**twibel**," a term referring to potentially libelous statements made via Twitter, has also found its way into the courts recently, thanks to actress and musician Courtney Love. In January 2014, Love won a case in which she was accused of defaming her former attorney with a tweet. Rhonda Holmes sued Love for $8 million after Love's tweet alleging that Holmes had been "bought off" during her investigation into the estate of Love's late husband. The jury found

HELPFUL HINTS ➡ WHEN SOMEONE TELLS YOU, "I DON'T LIKE THIS! I'M SUING YOU!"

Just because someone is screaming at you and threatening to sue, it doesn't necessarily mean that person is right. Don't let fear of a screamer force you to change your story before you know all the facts.

Angry phone calls and hostile emails go with the territory in journalism. People aren't thrilled when their misdeeds are made public or when a story fails to do what they wanted it to do. In some cases, people will say or do something without giving it a second thought until a media outlet makes it public and the person receives unexpected backlash.

All of this usually leads people to threaten a journalist with something along the lines of "I'll sue you!"

Lawsuits can be scary, and flustered journalists can react poorly in these situations. This can take the form of an angry rebuke or a quick backpedal with a promise to "fix it." To help you deal with threats and anger, here are a few quick pointers:

- **Remain calm:** Just like when you are in the field, a panicking reporter is a useless reporter in this situation. You need to realize that the threat of a lawsuit is just that: a threat. It is highly unlikely that the person will sue you at all, let alone sue you successfully. However, you should take every call or email like this seriously and keep your wits about you while you do.

- **Determine the problem:** Just because someone doesn't like something, it doesn't necessarily follow that they have grounds for legal action. The key thing is to determine what has upset this person so you can figure out your best course of action. For example, if a caller says something in the story is wrong, you can determine if there is a factual error or if the person just disagrees with a source in your story. This will help you see if you need to run a correction or if you need to explain how reporters gather information from sources.

- **Don't make a promise you can't keep:** When a person is yelling at you on the phone about how you screwed something up, the "fight or flight" instinct can kick in pretty quickly. You might feel like the best way to get out of the situation is "flight," where you apologize profusely for everything and assure the person everything will be fixed right away. This can lead you to make promises you can't keep, such as changing a story, pulling something off the web or something else to make this person back off. In other cases, you might go into "fight" mode, where you push back at the caller with some anger of your own. This can further enrage the person and lead to even worse consequences if your publication eventually has to correct an error or apologize for a story. You probably won't be the final arbiter of how your publication will deal with these situations, so don't promise action when it's not yours to promise. The only thing you should promise is that you will do your best to look into this and inform your superiors.

- **Get contact information:** You will almost certainly need to do a bit of digging before you can solve any problem. Even if the problem isn't yours to solve, you want to make sure you have the contact information from the person who raised the issue. With email, this is easy enough, as you can forward the complaint to the reporter involved in the story (if it's not you) or to your editor and the person's email address is right there. In the case of a phone call, make sure you get the person's name and number so you or someone else at your office can get back to him or her as needed.

that although Love's statements did have the potential to harm Holmes' reputation, the plaintiff did not prove that Love knew the statements she made were false.[8]

A second set of legal battles between Love and fashion designer Dawn Simorangkir has also codified social media as a danger zone for libel claims. Simorangkir sued Love over claims of defamation made via Twitter in 2009. Although Love settled the suit for $430,000 in 2011, the issue reemerged when Love repeated her statements in 2013 on the social media site Pinterest.[9] In 2015, Love settled with Simorangkir again, agreeing to pay her $350,000 over the Pinterest statements.[10]

These outcomes should make it clear that every word you type and share with others has the potential to get you into trouble. With that in mind, you should use your best judgment every time you present information to an audience.

DEFENSES AGAINST LIBEL

As we have discussed throughout the book, good reporting and meticulous recordkeeping can keep you out of trouble most of the time. That said, even if you do take care with your approach to content, people can still become disgruntled and threaten to sue you. With that in mind, here are some crucial defenses for you:

TRUTH

Truth is the silver bullet of defenses against a libel claim. In most cases, defamation is easy to prove, or at least it can be interpreted easily. It's highly unlikely that people would debate that being accused of murder didn't defame someone. Thus, the first big stop on the road to a libel suit is the issue of factual accuracy.

Absolute privilege allows officials acting in an official capacity to say pretty much whatever they want without fear of a libel suit. Journalists operate under qualified privilege and can quote these people with a similar level of protection.

As much as the mayor might dislike that you reported he had stolen funds from the city to buy a Rolex, if you are right, he doesn't have much ground on which to stand from a libel stand-point. The law dictates that not only must the plaintiff demonstrate that the information published is false, but that it is substantially false. In other words, it is the responsibility of the person suing you to show how the inaccuracy is at the core of the defamation. If you made a few minor grammar or spelling errors in the piece, those aren't enough to demonstrate falsity.

This is why checking your facts, verifying content with your sources and otherwise nailing down the accuracy of information is crucial to your job as a reporter. If you know you have the right stuff, you can feel a lot better about your odds of winning.

OPINION

The line "You are entitled to your own opinion, but not your own facts" applies nicely when discussing the issue of libel. Courts are required to determine if something is factually based, as opposed to being an opinion, before they can act on a claim of libel. If you wrote, "Earl

Aside from the key defenses against libel, journalists would do well to understand the ways in which fault and damage apply during a defamation suit.

According to the Digital Media Law Project website, fault is determined based on the degree to which a publisher did something or failed to do something prior to publication with regard to the potentially libelous statements.

The DMLP site notes that fault generally falls into one of two categories: **negligence** and **actual malice**.[11] Negligence is the easier of the two standards to meet, and it applies to private individuals suing for libel. This standard requires only that the media outlet did not do everything reasonably necessary to determine the truth of the defamatory statements. Sloppy reporting, poor research and other similar snafus can fall into the area of negligence.

Actual malice is the harder hurdle to clear, and it applies to **public figures**, such as famous athletes, movie stars and well-known recording artists. This standard requires that a plaintiff show that the defendant published the information even though he or she knew it was to be false or that he or she acted with reckless disregard for the truth. In short, for a person to win a suit under this standard, the plaintiff has to show that the defendant either knew or should have known the libelous content was wrong but didn't care and published it anyway. (For more on how to determine who is and isn't a public figure, visit www.dmlp.org.)

Damages are equally crucial and somewhat difficult to calculate in some libel cases. The amount of money provided to the plaintiff is often a function of how much the person lost as a result of the libel and how egregious the actions of the defendant were. Courts often discuss the issue of damages in terms of **compensatory damages** and **punitive damages**. Compensatory awards are used to help the plaintiff recover specific losses while punitive damages are meant to punish the defendant.

Attorney David Berg notes that compensatory damages in a defamation case usually fall into one of two areas: calculable damages and incalculable damages.[12] The first type of damage is often called special or economic damages, and these damages have a specific price tag attached to them. If a libelous statement costs a person his job, the loss of salary and benefits can be calculated based on past, present and expected future earnings. The same thing is true for a business owner who can show a drop in his revenue in the wake of a libelous statement.

Incalculable damages are those that lack monetary specificity and are often called pain and suffering damages. These damages can include things like emotional distress, anxiety, loss of reputation and more. The courts don't have a way of determining exactly how much money damaged reputations and sleepless nights are worth, and thus it is up to the jury to make a "best guess" in these areas. Berg notes that this often comes down to the likeability of the plaintiff and the actions of the defendant.

For example, a holistic healer won a $1 million judgment from KSTP-TV in 2011 after the Minnesota station aired a story accusing her of having a role in a client's suicide attempt.[13] Susan Anderson stated that she was ambushed by a KSTP reporter, who accused her of "de-prescribing" anti-anxiety medication for one of her clients. The client also alleged that she tried to kill herself after Anderson weaned her off of the medication. Anderson's suit noted that the woman's own doctor reduced the medication, and the station found no proof of a suicide attempt. Even more, the woman had a long history of mental illness, which the station should have considered prior to airing the story. The station lost the case, and the jury awarded Anderson $100,000 in lost earnings and $900,000 damage to her reputation.

Watson committed murder and spent 20 years in prison as a result," that has elements that could be checked for factual accuracy, such as the conviction, the charge and the length of his term. However, if you were to write, "Earl Watson is a vile and evil person," this would lean toward opinion, as the terms "vile" and "evil" are vague and lack the ability to be proved or disproved.

In a similar vein, hyperbolic language is often protected as well. **Hyperbole** is language that is so over the top and unbelievable that no one could really take it seriously. So, if you published an article that noted, "Professor Nick Jones is so stupid they had to burn down his elementary school to get him out of third grade," most people would understand this to be a lousy joke and clearly an unbelievable statement.

PRIVILEGE

Officials constitute a majority of the sources you will use as a reporter. Everyone from the mayor to the fire chief can count as an official you could quote, and like any other person, those officials occasionally make mistakes. The concept of **absolute privilege** allows officials to speak out as a part of their job without fear of libel concerns. This often applies to things like state senators issuing declarations from the floor of the Capitol and statements judges issue from the bench. Police and fire officials are granted similar standing in some states, and sworn statements made in open court fall under this standard as well.

Journalists operate under **qualified privilege**, which allows them to report these statements in their publications without fear of libel. The statements should be attributed to the source and be germane to the topic if journalists wish to receive the strongest protection against libel. This is why relying on official sources, accurately quoting those sources and attributing that information to them is crucial during the reporting and writing processes.

INVASION OF PRIVACY

Aside from libel, journalists can find themselves in legal trouble if they invade people's privacy. The law in its various forms has determined that people have a general right to be left alone, which can seem to create a problem for reporters who often have to interact with members of the public. Not every interview is at risk of creating legal turmoil for reporters, but several aspects of privacy should be considered during news gathering and information publication.

Who is at fault and how seriously that person has damaged a plaintiff is often at the core of libel suits.

INTRUSION

People can expect certain levels of privacy in certain settings. If you enter those areas or engage in surveillance practices, your actions could constitute an **invasion of privacy**. However, understanding

CONSIDER THIS ➡ DRONES: JOURNALISM FUTURE OR JOURNALISM FAD?

Drones have a great deal of potential as a journalism tool, but as a new technology, the rules and values associated with them remain nebulous at best.

University of Nebraska–Lincoln professor Matt Waite founded the Drone Journalism Lab in 2011 to determine how these unmanned probes could influence the future of journalism. In the years since then, other universities and professional organizations have launched their own efforts to explore news-gathering options with these devices.

As **drone journalism** is still in its infancy, legal and ethical standards pertaining to this concept remain relatively nebulous, especially with regard to privacy concerns. In an interview with the Columbia Journalism Review in 2016, Waite noted both the importance of drones in covering topics like natural disasters as well as the way in which they could invade people's privacy.[17]

The ownership of low-level airspace, especially the space above someone's home, has become a concern for governmental officials. Although the Federal Aviation Administration claims the right to regulate all air-based traffic, this hasn't proved to be the case for unmanned aircraft that operate between 1 and 500 feet above the ground.[18] Some cities are trying to ban drones, while some private citizens have taken even more extreme measures. For example, Stephen Loosey of Norfolk, Virginia, shot down a drone that was hovering over his backyard. Loosey told police he was concerned that the drone was recording his children while they played on a trampoline.[19]

The Federal Aviation Administration placed restrictions on drone use for commercial purposes in 2013, but promised licensing and exemptions by the end of 2016. In an article for the Nieman Lab, Waite said early versions of the proposed regulations looked promising for journalists, while noting that a full version of the rules have yet to emerge.[20]

As the government continues to shape and mold the rules associated with drones, journalists will have to consider to what degree drones are valuable news-gathering tools. Previous breakthroughs in recording, portability and access have all given journalists an edge in capturing content. However, some breakthroughs have become little more than interesting toys that lack the reporting power of more traditional methods.

who has what rights in which situations can become tricky, and you need to take care in your approach to news gathering.

People engaging in public acts, such as city parades or protest marches, place themselves in the public eye and thus have limited claims of invasion of privacy. Although people are not required to speak with you or give you their names, they cannot stop you from talking to other people or taking photos of anyone involved in an event like this. However, there are places in which people have reasonable expectations of privacy, such as a public bathroom, where cameras and recording devices have been deemed to constitute a clear violation of people's rights.

Places like malls and stores fall into a quasi-public environment, as they are both open to large groups of people and also privately owned. Management or ownership representatives can ask you to leave and have the right to do so. In most cases, it is beneficial to obtain permission before you go there, especially if the story is on a sensitive topic, like an armed robbery at the store or a kidnapping at the mall.

Privately owned places provide the highest level of protection against intrusion. Entering a private area to get a story or a photo can fall into an area of the law called trespassing. Journalists don't have the right to enter a home or a hospital room to get information, regardless of how important that information might be. Posted "No Trespassing" signs can legally prevent you from getting close enough to request permission to enter the area. In many cases, reporters can walk up to a home and ring a doorbell to request an interview with a limited amount of fear. However, if the owner of the home declines your request and asks you to leave, it is in your best interest to do so.

TV personality John Oliver mocked the coal industry and several major mine owners during his show "Last Week Tonight." One coal magnate, Bob Murray, sued him for a number of things, including false light. A director with the ACLU has called Murray's suit "plain nuts."

FALSE LIGHT

Information that is true but paints someone in an unfair or misrepresentative context can put you into as much trouble as reporting factually inaccurate information. A claim of **false light** indicates that the information associated with the plaintiff gives people the wrong impression of him or her and is thus damaging. An example of this came out of the Braun v. Flynt case, in which Jeannie Braun sued publisher Larry Flynt in the 1980s over the inclusion of a picture of her in the pornographic magazine Chic.[14] Braun was employed at a Texas amusement park and as part of her job, worked with a diving pig named Ralph. A photo of her, taken as a promotion, featured her in a bathing suit, feeding Ralph from a baby bottle. Chic editors obtained a copy of the photo and ran it next to photos of seminude women and stories about sexual acts. The court ruled that a reasonable person could infer that Braun approved of her inclusion in the magazine and that the image represented some sort of sexual connection between her and the pig.

A recent case involving false light ended with one of the largest internet defamation awards—$38.3 million—when a coin-making company attacked a Los Angeles businessman online. Ross Hansen and Steven Firebaugh of Northwest Territorial Mint LLC were found guilty of building websites that accused real estate investor Bradley S. Cohen of fraud and misconduct.[15] The sites compared Cohen with jailed financier Bernie Madoff, who pleaded guilty to running a multimillion-dollar Ponzi scheme. The site contained photos of Cohen and Madoff next to each other and also stated that Cohen was a convicted racketeer. The information about the crimes was later discovered to be about a different Bradley S. Cohen. The mint filed for bankruptcy as a result of the suit.[16]

Although these seem a bit outside of what you might face as a reporter, false light can be a serious concern if you aren't keeping an eye on the accuracy of content or how you present it. For example, if you photograph someone standing nearby while a KKK march is taking place, a caption could lead to a false-light concern:

> Willie Metcalf watches with KKK supporters as the Klan performs its annual "White Pride Days" protest Wednesday in Springfield.

Metcalf might have been watching the parade and there might have been KKK supporters around, but the caption implies he's watching with fellow white supremacists. When that turns out to be false, you can be in a lot of trouble.

PUBLIC EMBARRASSMENT OF PRIVATE PEOPLE

Accuracy remains the watchword of journalism, but in some cases, factually accurate material can still harm people. As noted above with the issue of libel, private people get more protection against invasion of privacy than do public figures. The goal of open access and "the public's right to know" is often weighed against the people's right to be left alone.

Consider this as an example: A fire seriously damages a dorm on the campus of a public university, costing a large number of students everything they own. In an attempt to help the students, the student government uses an emergency fund to purchase clothing and toiletries for the fire victims. Since the student government can't just hand out money, officials collect a list of clothing items and sizes as well as preferred toiletries and purchase them for the students. In doing so, the student government uses public funds and creates a public record of who asked for what.

The student newspaper makes a request to get the documents related to purchases with the intent of publishing stories like "Boxers, Briefs or Thongs: Guess Who Wears Each in Smith Hall?" and "Size Matters: Check Out Who Wears the Biggest Pair of Pants in the Dorm!" This information is about public money, but it would clearly involve the embarrassment of private people. A court examining whether to require the university to release this information would have to weigh the value of the information against the likelihood that it would harm private people.

To determine what information is of public interest and who gets protected from these kinds of disclosures, courts have to determine the status of the people involved. Public figures, such as mayors, professional athletes and TV stars, get the lowest level of protection, while private figures, such as school janitors, homemakers and regular college students, get the highest level. In between sits the **limited-purpose public figure**, a category that includes people who have placed themselves into a public situation for a specific purpose. A good example of this would be a private citizen who organizes a "Save Our Simians" group and petitions the city council to stop plans to remove all the monkeys from the local zoo. Although this person has entered the public eye and has made herself known to the media, it doesn't follow that every detail of her life is now fair game for disclosure through the media.

12

LAW AND THE MEDIA

THE BIG THREE

Here are the three key things you should take away from the chapter:

1. **The law is fluid:** Although the First Amendment seems clear and the concept of a free press seems simple, the law pertaining to what you can and can't do is almost always changing. The introduction of digital media has forced courts to apply aging standards to new platforms or break new ground in unpredictable ways. Good reporters should always keep an eye on what's happening in the field of law as it relates to media operations.

2. **Be careful all the time:** You can get in just as much trouble in a 14,000-word investigative series as you can in a 280-character tweet. Whenever you publish, whether it's a short post to a social media site or an extended piece on your own website, you are operating as a publisher and assuming a risk. The defense "It was only Twitter" won't get you very far if you libel someone.

3. **Know your rights:** As a reporter, you will need to go places that other people wish you wouldn't and cover things some people hope you won't. Those people will likely try to prevent you from entering areas you have a right to enter or photographing things you clearly should be able to shoot. The better you know what your rights are, the less likely you are to be intimidated in the face of people who are willing to violate the law so they can feel more comfortable.

KEY TERMS

absolute privilege   221
actual malice   220
Bill of Rights   211
Child Online Protection Act   212
Communications Decency
   Act of 1996   212
compensatory damages   220
drone journalism   222
false light   223

First Amendment   210
hyperbole   221
invasion of privacy   221
libel   216
limited-purpose public
   figure   224
negligence   220
one-party consent   216
public figures   220

punitive damages   220
qualified privilege   221
reporter's privilege   212
Sedition Act   211
shield laws   213
Smith Act   211
Sunshine Act   213
truth   219
twibel   217

DISCUSSION QUESTIONS

1. Of the five freedoms listed in the First Amendment, how many have you availed yourself of? Which ones are they? Which one mattered the most to you? The least? Why?

2. What do you see as the positive and negative aspects of drone journalism? Do you see this as a fad or as something that will be important in telling valuable stories in different ways? Support your position.

3. How far would you go to protect a source that told you something confidentially or anonymously?

4. One key element of libel law is the concept of "publication," which means sharing the potentially libelous content with someone other than the offended party. Given the widespread use of social media, like Twitter and Facebook, how often do you think about issues like libel before you "publish" your content? How concerned are you now and going into the future about this topic and the potential fallout from your actions?

WRITE NOW!

1. Review your social media feeds, such as Twitter and Facebook, and examine them for potentially libelous statements you or your friends made. Select two or three posts or tweets you think have the potential for libel, keeping in mind that these items have already met the "publication" standard. Walk through the remaining standards Ashley Messenger outlined for successful libel suits and see how likely you think it would be that this post could lead to a solid suit.

2. Explain the two levels of fault associated with libel, including the definition of each, to whom each applies and which standard is easier to demonstrate. Also, explain the two forms of damages, including the definition of each and how each one applies in a libel suit.

3. Review the example in the book that discusses the public embarrassment of private people. When it comes to the records the student paper is seeking, would you release them? Why or why not?

Visit edge.sagepub.com/filaknews to help you accomplish your coursework goals in an easy-to-use learning environment.

13

ETHICS

LEARNING OBJECTIVES

After completing this chapter you should be able to:

- Determine why ethics matter both during individual journalistic efforts and as a set of overriding principles for the field on the whole.

- Understand specific ethical paradigms along the ethics continuum, including the golden mean, the categorical imperative, the principle of utility, the veil of ignorance and the principle of self-determination.

- Define and explain various elements of journalistic ethics, including honesty, accuracy, diversity, independence and compassion.

- Apply ethical standards as you approach your work in the field of journalism.

THINKING AHEAD: JUST BECAUSE YOU CAN, IT DOESN'T MEAN YOU SHOULD

In the previous chapter, we discussed the issue of law and how it pertains to our work within the field of media. At the risk of oversimplifying things, the law tells us what to do and what not to do as well as what punishments and rewards we can expect if we break or adhere to those laws. **Ethics**, on the other hand, lack the rigidity of legal dictates and rely more on the formation of moral codes that guide a person's actions. They vary from field to field and even among disciplines within a given field. An extremely simple way to view ethics is to see them as things that tell us "right" and "wrong," as opposed to "legal" and "illegal."

Ethics establish a social contract between journalists and media users, thus allowing both parties to understand the value of journalism and how it can benefit society. Journalists

essentially promise to find information of relevance and value to the audience and report it without bias or malice. Audience members understand that the content is created with the best of intentions and that errors or oversights are unintentional. The readers and viewers also understand that reporters are attempting to be objective and fair in their work.

This chapter will outline the basics of ethics as they pertain to journalism and explain why media ethics matter to journalists and the audience. The chapter will also examine a series of ethical codes that media organizations created to help guide journalists in their daily work. By finding similarities within these codes, the chapter will outline some basic ethical elements that can help you as you enter the field.

Bliznetsov/iStock.com

How you go about gathering information is almost as important to the public as the information itself.

WHY ETHICS MATTER

Ethics create a relationship that is mutually beneficial so that each person with whom you interact or for whom you create content gets a proper sense of who you are and why you act the way you do. Credibility is at the core of every ethical standard, and as a reporter, each action you take requires you to determine how much that action adds to or detracts from your credibility. If you get a story in a dishonest way, you might give your readers an important piece of information, but you now may have a source who will never trust you again. If you cut a shady deal with a source to get crucial information, your readers might view you and your work with suspicion from that point forward.

Credibility is perhaps the most fragile element of journalism, and without it, you will cease to be an effective reporter. To that end, you need to determine to what ethical standards you will meet and how your actions will create a stronger or weaker bond between you and your publics.

BASIC APPROACHES TO ETHICS

As mentioned earlier in the chapter, professions, disciplines and organizations have varying ethical standards. How comfortable you are with those standards will determine how strongly attached you feel to those groups. If you feel the standards of your workplace or social club run counter to your personal ethics, you might consider disassociating from that group. If you feel like your standards mirror a group's ethical code, you will feel more comfortable as a member of that group.

You will determine your ethical standards based on your own moral compass and your overall sense of right and wrong. Even then, you won't be able to find a perfect philosophy that captures all of your beliefs and values. Ethics usually operate on a spectrum of behavior and this makes it difficult for people to clearly define their own specific code. However, scholars like Joseph R. Dominick have noted a few ethical typologies that capture specific points on the ethical continuum.[1] Here are some ethical standards he outlines in his book on mass media:

THE GOLDEN MEAN

This standard attempts to find a middle ground for all of the people involved in an ethical dilemma in the hope of creating the most good for everyone. This approach seeks to balance needs and wants against potential negative outcomes for any one group involved in the situation. An example of this is when news organizations balance the right of people to know something against the privacy rights of individuals. The **golden mean** seeks a "sweet spot" for a decision where compromise leads to shared quality outcomes.

THE CATEGORICAL IMPERATIVE

This form of ethical behavior is often misinterpreted as "the golden rule," in which you should do unto others as you would have them do unto you. However, the **categorical imperative** is more nuanced and requires people to use their conscience to determine what is right and wrong before taking action. This means that if you believe it is acceptable to misrepresent yourself to someone, it is acceptable for people you meet to misrepresent themselves to you. The goal of this approach is to have all people act in the ways in which they would like everyone to act during all interactions with others.

THE PRINCIPLE OF UTILITY

The goal of the **principle of utility** is to create the highest net benefit in each ethical interaction. This means that you should attempt to minimize harm or maximize gain for the most people in any situation. **Utilitarianism** measures the consequences of an action and then determines the ethics of the action.

The veil of ignorance suggests that justice is blind to outside influences such as money, power and prestige.

This form of ethical approach would mean that if a story led to a massive public benefit, then individual negative outcomes are acceptable. For example, you publish a story revealing that Company X has dumped toxic waste illegally and tainted the city's water supply. As a result of your story, the city launches a major effort to clean up the water and sue the company, thus saving nearly 100,000 people from a serious illness. However, as a result of the cleanup and the suit, the company goes bankrupt, and all 100 people in your city who worked there lose their jobs. A utilitarian view would be that this loss of jobs was acceptable because the positive outcome outweighed the negative outcome significantly.

THE VEIL OF IGNORANCE

The approach to this philosophy is to avoid making exceptions based on specific situations or special circumstances. The **veil of ignorance** demands that all people be treated the same, no matter what. Therefore, if you find out that a player on the local college football team was arrested on suspicion of assault, whether that player was the star running back or a backup kicker shouldn't factor into your decision to run or hold the story. Either you run the story or you don't, regardless of the person's prominence. Dominick simplifies this approach nicely when he notes, "Justice is blind."

THE PRINCIPLE OF SELF-DETERMINATION

The goal of this ethical philosophy is to treat all people with respect and avoid treating them as a means to an end. In this approach, people have rights that need to be respected, and therefore, the relationship between the media and the public must be mutually beneficial. A reporter can't break the trust of a source just to get a story. A website can't publish an irresponsible story that destroys a person's reputation just to improve the financial position of the publication. People who espouse this form of ethics support and respect everyone's sense of **self-determination**.

TENETS OF JOURNALISTIC ETHICS

Various journalism groups subscribe to certain ethical codes and provide them for reporters, photographers and broadcasters as a baseline for their respective fields. The National Press Photographers Association, the Radio Television Digital News Association and the Society of Professional

Journalists each lists a set of ethical ideals for its members, along with a set of specific dictates to guide working journalists in their actions. Although each group has its own medium-specific elements outlined in each code, several common themes run through all three ethical codes. Below is a synopsis of the primary tenets outlined in those codes and some examples of how to meet them:

HONESTY

All three codes discuss the concept of "truth" at length in a variety of ways. RTDNA's code lists its first section as "truth and accuracy above all," while SPJ dictates that journalists should "seek truth and report it." NPPA notes, "Photographic and video images can reveal great truths," and "Be accurate and comprehensive in the representation of subjects." The photographers' code also states that members should not manipulate images and should strive to be "unobtrusive and humble in dealing with subjects."

Some people reflexively dislike the news because it often does not reflect their own worldview. As a result, the concept of "fake news" has emerged as a go-to argument for information that does not jibe with the ideas of the readers. To better reach all viewers, even those who disagree with your content, you must rely on heavy levels of strong fact checking and honest reporting.

The purpose of striving for honesty is to create a bond between you and your sources as you attempt to gather information in the reporting process. You can't lie to a source or hide information from a person just so you can get information you wouldn't have access to any other way. As much as your duty is to your readers, you can't sacrifice honesty with your sources as a means to that end. Consider these premises:

BE UPFRONT IN YOUR REPORTING

Sources often fear reporters, because of prior poor interactions or a general sense that only bad things can come from agreeing to work with "the media." Some of these concerns are well founded: Whistleblowers open themselves up to retaliation if they inform on their company or organization. Crime victims will likely fear additional victimization if they publicize their situation. People engaged in illegal activities put themselves at risk of arrest if they help reporters understand how criminal enterprises work. Not only should the sources know these risks, but you should know and acknowledge them as well.

Journalists must demonstrate honesty in interacting with sources, regardless of the situation. Student journalists occasionally tell sources that a story is "just for class" in order to get a nervous source to talk. Reporters sometimes obfuscate the purpose of a story to get a source to agree to an interview or to reveal a specific piece of information. Journalists will occasionally use undercover tactics, such as using a hidden recorder or assuming a false identity to get information that isn't readily available. Even worse, some journalists have knowingly taken material from another source and used it without crediting the source, an ethical violation known as plagiarism.

A member of the hackers collective Downsec Belgium, accused of cyber attacks on government sites, wears a Guy Fawkes mask ahead of the start of the trial against Downsec Belgium at the Brussels correctional court on Feb. 28, 2017 in Brussels.

The NPPA code notes that photographers should "treat all subjects with respect and dignity." The SPJ code also states that journalists should "avoid undercover or surreptitious methods of gathering information unless traditional, open methods will not yield information vital to the public." RTDNA's code goes even further, stating that "deception in newsgathering, including surreptitious recording, conflicts with journalism's commitment to truth." In short, you need to lay all your cards on the table when you deal with your sources. Don't lie or cheat to get a story, because it will undercut the credibility of your story and your reputation.

KEEP YOUR PROMISES

You don't have to be a journalist to understand the importance of keeping your word. Even little kids understand the sacred bond between people that is sealed with a promise or even a "pinkie swear." When that trust is violated, kids have no compunction whatsoever about wailing, "BUT YOU PROMISED!" Just like that child who feels cheated, sources are equally likely to express exasperation when you say one thing and do something different.

Reporters should avoid explicit promises to sources, especially those they lack the power to keep. Front-line editors can overrule writers, and executives can overrule lower editors. In addition, you might find that a promise made to a source could clash with your organization's rules and regulations. As much as you need to be upfront with sources regarding your intentions as a reporter, you need to be doubly honest in terms of what you can and can't guarantee.

The SPJ code of ethics explicitly states that journalists should be cautious when they make promises, but they should keep the promises they make. The other two codes make similar references to holding yourself to high professional standards and striving to be responsible to all parties associated with your story.

BE FAIR

This aspect of fairness is both easy and complex in today's media world. In terms of simple fairness, you need to provide people with an opportunity to speak on their own behalf, especially if others have spoken against them. Many stories include accusations or criticism levied against people in the public eye. As noted earlier, journalists are duty-bound to speak truth to power and shine a light into the dark corners of the public. However, not every complaint is fair or accurate. This is why the SPJ code dictates that journalists should "diligently seek subjects of news coverage and allow them to respond to criticism or allegations of wrongdoing."

Allowing a source to respond is a simple concept, because journalists often hear that there are always two sides to a story, much like there are two sides to a coin. In reality, stories are more like diamonds, in that they have multiple facets, each of which illuminates the whole through a specific angle. This means that you can't just look at one angle of a piece and expect clarity or value. As the RTDNA code of ethics notes, "For every story of significance there are always more than two sides. While they may not all fit into every account, responsible reporting is clear about what it omits as well as what it includes."

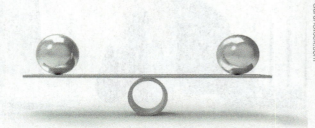

Remaining balanced and providing equal treatment to sources is crucial to many ethical codes.

This is where the complexity of fairness comes into play. In adhering to a fairness standard, you need to think about the varying points of view associated with each story. NPPA's code notes that journalists should "work to show unpopular or unnoticed points of view." SPJ also espouses this approach, arguing that journalists should "support the open and civil exchange of views, even views they find repugnant." If we don't allow this free exchange of ideas, we become the biased media others accuse us of being. The goal of quality journalism is to provide an open set of opportunities for people to state their opinions and thus allow the readers to make their decisions.

However, media experts are now pushing harder to demonstrate that "fairness" does not equate to "neutrality" with regard to viewpoint. For example, David Uberti wrote in the Columbia Journalism Review that media outlets are entering a "new normal" when it comes to covering news in the wake of Donald Trump's ascendency to the presidency. Uberti noted that while some journalists try to keep neutral in their coverage, others want to push back against what they see as unwarranted attacks against the field.[2] Journalist Christiane Amanpour, who was honored in 2016 with a lifetime achievement award from the Committee to Protect Journalists, called on journalists to "recommit to robust fact-based reporting" in the age of **hyperpartisan** news and negative attacks on the press. During her acceptance speech, she stated that the media "got itself tied into knots trying to differentiate between balance, objectivity, neutrality and, crucially, the truth." With that, she argued that false equivalencies and equal time for the sake of balance only undermined the purpose of journalism. "I believe in being truthful, not neutral," she said.[3]

ACCURACY

Journalists view accuracy as their primary professional value. The RTDNA code places "truth and accuracy above all," while the NPPA code dictates that journalists should "be accurate and comprehensive in the representation of subjects." SPJ notes that "ethical journalism should be accurate and fair." When journalists fall short on accuracy, they open themselves to accusations of sloppiness and bias, both of which undercut their credibility.

It might seem unfair that journalists have to be right all the time and that one fatally flawed piece can undo the credibility built with 100 accurate ones. However, the contract between the public and journalists says that readers can turn to the media for fair, balanced and accurate content each day, without fear. When a reporter violates that contract, it's a problem not only for that one journalist in that one story but for the field as a whole.

When journalists use inaccurate or hyperbolic rhetoric to "sell" a news piece to readers, they essentially take part in the fake-news phenomenon. It might lead to more people liking a story who are predisposed to believing whatever falsehood you are perpetuating. It might even help draw more clicks or likes. However, in the end, inaccurate content breaks the bond between journalist and readers, and that bond never fully heals. You can help promote accuracy in a few key ways:

When you get a story from a source, you should verify that information to make sure you aren't inadvertently spreading false information.

VERIFY INFORMATION

The famous line in journalism about **verification** is, "If your mother says she loves you, go check it out." The central premise of this is to never assume something to be true without checking on it. Verification requires you to micro-edit your copy carefully, checking on spellings, dates, places and word choices. It also requires you to look at the bigger picture, such as the overall feel your piece presents to the readers and the degree to which it is properly representative of reality.

You need to verify the facts you publish, relying on trustworthy sources to assure you that you aren't misleading your readers. The codes all put this front and center: SPJ notes that journalists should "take responsibility for the accuracy of their work. Verify information before releasing it. Use original sources whenever possible." The NPPA also stresses that journalists should "be accurate and comprehensive" in their work. Perhaps the most interesting approach is that of the RTDNA's code, which starts its section on truth and accuracy with this explanation: "The facts *should* get in the way of a good story [emphasis in the original]. Journalism requires more than merely reporting remarks, claims or comments. Journalism verifies, provides relevant context, tells the rest of the story and acknowledges the absence of important additional information."

This might seem like a tall order, but you can do it. Start with the basics of verification: Look at every fact in a story and assume you were wrong about it. Then find a way to prove you are right as you use trustworthy digital or print sources. Look carefully at each letter in a name and check each name each time it is mentioned. Check addresses to make sure if you called something "Maple Street" it wasn't actually "Maple Avenue." When you publish someone's age, verify it with internet databases or by doing the math from that person's date of birth.

Then, move into the bigger verification part of the process: intention and tone. When you interview a source, you get the idea of what that person felt about a given topic. Do the quotes you selected and the paraphrases you wrote reflect that point of view accurately? If you aren't sure, go back through your notes and pick out more concrete quotes. If you can't make that work, go back to the source and ask for clarification. Don't assume you know what is right. Be sure.

AVOID MISINFORMATION

Sources who complain about accuracy often note a reporter's use of misinformation as a point of contention. For them, accuracy isn't always about proper spellings or factual verification, but rather the intent and the tone of the piece. Journalists often hear the argument "That might be what I said but it's not what I meant." This can frustrate reporters and sources alike, because both sides want the most complete story presented, and neither side feels this happened if a source is complaining about intent.

Unless you have a special "X-Men" power that allows you to read minds, you will probably have a situation or two when you put forth your best

When you have to retract a story due to problematic reporting, you can seriously undermine your credibility.

interpretation of a source, only to fall short in the source's estimation. However, you should strive to actively avoid misinformation, which includes the manipulation of words, images and tone. Misinformation also includes the use of vague statements, innuendo or other approaches to content that fails to provide the most accurate story possible.

Attributing information to a source can help you avoid those vague comments or overly generalized statements that lead to misinformation or create a lack of trust between you and your readers. One of the few absolutes contained in the SPJ code of ethics relates to telling your public from where your information originated: "Always attribute." Both the SPJ code and the RTDNA code stipulate that the source matters as much as, if not more than, the content the source provided. The RTDNA also notes, "Attribution is essential. It adds important information that helps the audience evaluate content and it acknowledges those who contribute to coverage." SPJ tells journalists, "Identify sources clearly. The public is entitled to as much information as possible to judge the reliability and motivations of sources."

The RTDNA also notes that "responsible reporting includes updating stories and amending archival versions to make them more accurate and to avoid misinforming those who, through search, stumble upon outdated material." The code further states that "scarce resources, deadline pressure and relentless competition do not excuse cutting corners factually or over-simplifying complex issues." A similar statement exists in the SPJ code: "Provide context: Take special care not to misrepresent or oversimplify in promoting, previewing or summarizing a story."

DIVERSITY

The media often provide people an opportunity to see things they would otherwise never see. The newspapers, magazines, television programs and websites open windows for people to view and experience life beyond their own part of the world. This can help diversify their perspectives and broaden their sense of humanity.

Journalists have a responsibility to provide readers and viewers with a broad array of experiences and to avoid overly simplified caricatures of people, groups, organizations and nations. As we try to help people make sense of their world and their place in it, diversity can take a back seat to self-interest. To help provide meaningful diversity, the codes note the following items:

REJECT STEREOTYPES

From a psychological standpoint, your mind is a cognitive miser: It really doesn't want to do hard things. To help it make sense of a continual stream of changing information, it creates quick ways to access information to make it part of what you see and do over and over. These shortcuts become mentally fixed images that allow you to create shortcuts. For example, when you first started driving, you had to think through each aspect of the process: Start the car, apply the brake, shift into gear, look in various directions, turn the wheel, apply the gas and so forth. After you have gotten used to these practices, they become almost reflexes, and those reflexes can transfer to other situations. In other words, if you frequently drive a Toyota Corolla, you probably can drive a Honda Civic, even though they are different cars made by different manufacturers.

This may seem shocking to you, but this process of creating and storing shortcuts is known as stereotyping. In the cases of knowing how gas pedals and turn signals work, a **stereotype** can be helpful, but when they are applied socially, they can lead to biases, prejudices and discrimination. This is why journalists strive to avoid negative stereotypes of people based on race, gender, ethnicity, creed, sexual orientation and other similar traits.

For example, if a woman in her 60s is running for mayor of a small town, a news story on her might describe her as "a spry grandmother of three," thus drawing attention to her gender and status as a grandmother. It's highly unlikely that a newspaper article would refer to a male opponent as "a spry grandfather of three," thus creating a double standard. In 2013, the New York Times faced criticism of this nature for its obituary on Yvonne Brill, an incredible rocket scientist who helped revolutionize satellite placement in space. The opening paragraph noted that she "made a mean beef stroganoff, followed her husband from job to job and took eight years off from work to raise three children."[4] The second paragraph mentioned her important contributions to the scientific community.

These images from the coverage of Hurricane Katrina demonstrate how word choice can lead to stereotyping behaviors.

Another famous double standard came during the post–Hurricane Katrina floods of 2005, when residents of the Gulf Coast were struggling to stay alive in the wake of the disaster. Numerous media outlets captured the chaos of people fending for themselves, seeking dry land and foraging for supplies. In one example, Getty Images put out a photograph with the caption: "Two residents wade through chest-deep water after finding bread and soda from a local grocery store. . . ." The Associated Press provided a similar image noting: "A young man walks through chest deep flood water after looting a grocery store. . . ." Critics quickly pointed out that in the "finding" photo, the subjects were white, while the "looting" photo featured an African-American man. In short, the verbiage indicated that the African-American man was participating in criminal activity, while the other two people were merely fortunate to "find" things.[5]

RTDNA notes in its code of ethics that stereotyping and bias create problems that journalists must avoid. "Journalism challenges assumptions, rejects stereotypes and illuminates—even where it cannot eliminate—ignorance." The SPJ code demands that journalists "avoid stereotyping. Journalists should examine the ways their values and experiences may shape their reporting." The NPPA goes deeper, noting that photographers should "avoid stereotyping individuals and groups. Recognize and work to avoid presenting one's own biases in the work."

GIVE VOICE TO ALL

Diversity isn't simply an issue of race, culture or creed, but one that involves the ability to provide a wide array of people the opportunity to speak on issues of importance. Journalists often find themselves quoting public officials, corporate leaders and other "important" people who have influence and power. Although these people have value and importance, they should not be the sole source of information for stories, nor should their interests trump those of people who have less money or stature.

BREAKING NEWS

Dickinson, Texas
5:12 PM CT

CNN
NEWSROOM

Ana Cabrera ✔
@AnaCabrera

🐦 Follow

A powerful moment on @CNN just now -- a flood rescue with @edlavaCNN

3:21 PM - Aug 27, 2017

💬 679   🔁 5,409   ♡ 11,591

Journalists need to exude compassion in order to best reach and serve their readers. This is especially true in a time of crisis.

Journalists have the ability to focus attention on issues and provoke public reaction. This important responsibility carries with it the understanding that all people should have equal access to the media's power to alert the public about crucial issues. SPJ notes that journalists should "give voice to the voiceless" when telling stories, and the NPPA code notes that journalists should be "comprehensive in the representation of subjects." These dictates note the importance of the media to seek information that provides myriad perspectives for public consumption through the use of diverse sources.

COMPASSION

Negative journalistic stereotypes emerge from a sense that reporters do not care about anything but the story. Journalists often find themselves in unpleasant situations that yield negative interactions with the public. In the middle of shootings, fires, floods and other disasters, journalists arrive to ask potentially difficult questions of people who are suffering as a result of these incidents. Negative news tends to permeate the nightly newscasts and leads to the most hits on major news websites. Scandals, fights and accusations become the resting pulse of the news, and long-held newsroom phrases like "If it bleeds, it leads" don't do much to help people understand who we are and why we do what we do.

Journalists know we have to ask difficult questions in awkward situations. We have to speak truth to power, cover incidents as they emerge and even intrude upon people's grief. However, the ethical codes of these organizations help provide journalists with a sense of how to behave compassionately and caringly in situations that require a special touch.

THINK BEFORE YOU ACT

Journalists often have to bother people at some of their worst moments in life. This can lead to all kinds of problems. As Kelly Furnas noted during his discussion of the Virginia Tech shooting and its aftermath, people might want to talk about these moments, and it's not up to you to make the choice for them. However, when you do ask someone about a particularly painful act, you have to know that you might provoke the wrath of a wounded individual.

What you ask is not nearly as important as how you ask it or why you want to know it. For example, you are sent out to cover a fatal accident in a small community. The crash involved a man who was drunk and survived the incident and a woman who leads the local Mothers Against Drunk Driving chapter, who died.

You might want to ask a husband who just lost his wife in that crash to explain his emotions at that point. The "why" is to give people a good sense of how important this woman was to the community or her overall place in the heart of her family. However, how you ask that question

CONSIDER THIS → THE TROUBLE WITH TWITTER: JOURNALISTS AS PRIVATE CITIZENS

If you had a dime for every stupid, insensitive or otherwise vexing comment posted to Twitter, you'd never have to work another day in your life. The social media outlet is filled with horrible spelling, angry attacks and otherwise troubling tweets.

Public figures give up some of their rights to be left alone when they enter the public sphere. People hang on their every word, even if those words are delivered 140 characters at a time via Twitter. When President Donald Trump, the Pope or a major athlete tweets, it can spark a massive news cycle in which pundits parse every character. When your third cousin whom you follow on Twitter only because he followed you says something provocative or ill informed, you tend to let it go, thinking, "Well, that's another good reason not to attend the family reunion."

For journalists, this line between public and private can lead to some sticky situations. A piece on the website Axios lists more than a half dozen situations in which a journalist either apologized or lost a job as a result of a problematic tweet.[6] These situations included a Denver Post reporter who was fired after tweeting that he was uncomfortable with a Japanese driver winning the Indianapolis 500 on Memorial Day and a New York Post reporter who lost his job after comparing Trump's inauguration to 9/11 and Pearl Harbor.

"Regular people" have also lost their jobs as a result of a problematic tweet, as we noted earlier in the book. Stories about people ranting about their jobs, inadvertently dropping F-bombs from official business accounts or showcasing their drug use have landed on Twitter and thus landed people in the unemployment line.[7] What is unknown, however, is the proportion of these cases that cost people jobs to the cases of companies saying, "Well, that's just Carl being Carl."

Journalists use Twitter like they use other media platforms: to relay information to an interested audience. However, the newspaper, television station or website does not own a journalist's Twitter account, and many organizations do not require the same level of editing and approval for tweets that they do for pieces disseminated via legacy media. Even more, journalists don't always tweet while "on the clock" and often banter with followers more like people having a chat at a bar than a source speaking to a reporter. The comments are often off the cuff and instantaneous, and thus can come across as gruff, crude or worse.

Media outlets often want to disassociate themselves from the controversy when an employee says something out of turn on social media, so a quick axe to the career of a journalist can seem the right way to go. Journalists, of all people, should know that opening one's mouth (or tweet) in public can lead to some serious consequences. However, it is unclear where the line is between a headache-inducing tweet and a fireable offense. How media outlets and journalists negotiate these situations in the future is something to keep an eye on.

will determine a great deal about the answer you get. "How do you feel about this?" is perhaps the worst question you can ask at this point, as it's pretty clear that the person will have predominantly negative emotions and will have difficulty articulating them. A similarly stupid question can be "Don't you find it ironic that your wife was killed by a drunken driver?" You can get at either of these issues with much better questions if you put your mind to it, so stop and think before you open your mouth.

The RTDNA code tells journalists "shying away from difficult cases is not necessarily more ethical than taking on the challenges of reporting them. Leaving tough or sensitive stories to non-journalists can be a disservice to the public." SPJ also notes that journalists should "weigh the consequences of publishing or broadcasting personal information" of private individuals. In both of these statements, journalists are told to go get the story when the story needs to be told, but to think about the broader ramifications of their choices.

BE HUMAN

SPJ ethics committee Chairman Andrew Seaman (see "Thoughts From a Pro" later in this chapter) notes that journalists get a reputation as being uncaring and for lacking empathy. Journalists often pursue stories with determination and vigor, which some mistake for a lack of common decency. This is why compassion and humanity remain crucial ethical elements of media professionals who want to serve the public trust and retain credibility.

Although all people deserve dignified treatment from journalists, all three codes dictate that media workers should show additional care in special circumstances. SPJ notes that journalists should "show compassion for those who may be affected by news coverage. Use heightened sensitivity when dealing with juveniles, victims of sex crimes and sources or subjects who are inexperienced or unable to give consent." NPPA and RTDNA also push for special consideration for victims of crime, tragedy and particularly vulnerable individuals. In addition, the NPPA code argues that journalists should "intrude on private moments of grief only when the public has an overriding and justifiable need to see."

INDEPENDENCE

Journalists often operate under the moniker of "the **Fourth Estate**," a term attributed to 18th-century British politician Edmund Burke. In Thomas Carlyle's book "Heroes and Hero Worship in History," Carlyle quotes Burke discussing the importance of the press by saying that beyond the three estates of Parliament, "there sat a fourth Estate more important far than they all."

The First Amendment to the Constitution establishes both this level of importance in the United States as well as the implication that government cannot interfere with the press itself. The ability for the press to remain unfettered as it seeks truth was crucial for the Founding Fathers, as they hoped the free exchange of ideas would lead to an informed and engaged citizenry.

Outside of the legal issues, however, resides the ethical question of how journalists should ethically

The independence of journalists reaches back into the history of media.

cyano66/iStock.com

© Andrew Seaman

As the chairman of the Society of Professional Journalists' ethics committee, Andrew Seaman finds himself working to educate people about the value of quality journalism and how it can help establish trust between readers and journalists.

"I think one of the biggest challenges within journalism is that we have a lot of people who are on the fringe of traditional journalism," he said. "A lot of people assume there is journalism happening in all the media they read, but that's not quality journalism. A lot of things use elements of journalism, but they don't meet journalistic standards."

Seaman, a senior medical journalist for Reuters in New York, said that journalists have a responsibility both to act ethically and to help the audience members understand the importance of ethical, quality journalism.

"Years ago, we used to see good media literacy programs." he said. "When papers became less profitable, I doubt those programs survived or thrived and I think that hurt media literacy in this country. . . . I think in the code there's a place where it says you have to educate people about the role of the press otherwise people won't understand it and they won't understand what good information is and how to use it. When people are seeing all this information and they don't understand what is and what is not factual, we have problems."

The ethics committee spent a good amount of time working to address fake news, digital proliferation and other similar issues during a recent revision to the code, which hadn't been updated since 1996.

"When the code was last revised in 1996, there wasn't a lot of digital media," he said. "Obviously we've had Facebook and Twitter and things like that since then. . . . We decided that digital media and social media are ubiquitous and if you look at our previous code, we don't talk about print and broadcast but rather underlying elements of journalism. So what we did going in was to agree we wouldn't call attention to Facebook or Twitter specifically, because wherever journalism occurs, we still expect journalists to meet basic standards in regard to the information that is being sent out."

The ethical code also received additional strengthening in regard to **transparency** and veracity, Seaman said.

"We strengthened language around attributions," he said. "We said 'Always attribute' because we were seeing a lot of people doing aggregation work and it turned out the information was plagiarized or lacked attribution. . . . We strengthened some of the things people needed to see strengthened."

The ethical standards of the SPJ code help create stronger, better journalism, Seaman said, noting that its tenets can improve not only the quality of the content, but also media organizations' finances.

"People are being told that there's not enough money to support good journalism," he said. "Good journalism is good business. You just have to look at some of the court cases that have popped up recently like (the judgments

(Continued)

TENETS OF JOURNALISTIC ETHICS

(Continued)

issued against Gawker and Rolling Stone). If you look at Gawker over the years, you can see this coming."

In the Gawker case, in which former professional wrestler Hulk Hogan sued over the website's publication of a sex tape involving him and a friend's wife, Seaman said attorneys spent several days going through the SPJ code of ethics to condemn Gawker. Seaman said SPJ didn't like the use of the code as a legal cudgel, but noted that ethics can shape good journalism that leads to better outcomes for everyone.

"When you disregard fact checkers and when you have poor editorial oversight, you'll get into trouble," he said. "Now, they have these multimillion dollar judgments against them. When I travel around, I hear the same thing: 'We don't have the money we need,' and I think, 'If you did quality journalism and told your investors that this is just worth the money. Just give us a while and

we'll do better,' I think we would see journalism improve and succeed. I think there is a future out there for good journalism."

ONE LAST THING

Q: If you could tell students anything about anything you think is important in the field or in life or whatever, what would it be?

A: "I think that when it comes down to journalism, stripping away the code and everything else, I think every religion has their version of the golden rule. If you're not sure what to do, ask yourself, 'How would I like to be treated if I were on the other end of this pen?' I think sometimes journalists get a reputation for being cruel or uncaring and that's unfortunate. I think if we were better at empathy it would work out better for everyone."

operate to reflect their independence and trustworthiness for their audience. The law, for instance, says the government can't tell journalists they must print something, but journalists have to rely on their own set of ethics when they decide if they want to publish something that might make a legislator happy or might upset someone else in power.

Journalists are expected to provide information of value to the public without allowing undue influence to change what they write or how they write it. Consider these areas of interest when you examine the issue of independence:

AVOID CONFLICTS OF INTEREST

You need to serve the public interest in your work as a reporter. To do this, you need to keep away from things that could jeopardize your ability to be fair and impartial. A **conflict of interest** means that you have two incompatible outcomes vying for your loyalty, leading you to sacrifice one to the benefit of the other. For example, say you were asked to award a prize to the best college newspaper in a stack of submissions that included your own publication. Your goal of being fair would be compromised by your feeling of loyalty to your own staff. The RTDNA code dictates, "editorial independence may be a more ambitious goal today than ever before. . . .Still, independence from influences that conflict with public interest remains an essential idea of journalism."

It's not just impropriety you need to fear but also the appearance of impropriety. In the example above, you might decide to give your paper the top prize because you thought it was the best. The rest of the people who submitted to the contest would likely question your judgment and argue that you chose it because it was your paper. On the other hand, you might decide to award the prize to another paper, leading your own paper's staff members to wonder if they didn't win because you didn't want to look like you were favoring the publication.

Conflicts often present themselves to reporters who spend time working a specific beat or living in a particular area. As a government reporter in a small town, you might have several friends who sit on a city council or county board, which could lead to a perception of favoritism. An entertainment reporter might know people in promising local bands, leading to the question of why those bands got coverage while others did not. In cases where a conflict of interest emerges, it is best to both disclose the potential conflict and then find a way out of the situation. The SPJ code makes this clear for you: "Avoid conflicts of interest, real or perceived. Disclose unavoidable conflicts."

You can't be someone else's puppet if you want to serve your readers. Avoid being manipulated whenever you conduct business as a journalist.

Journalistic ties can also limit you personally when it comes to your ability to take part in various activities available to regular citizens, such as owning a side business, running for office or taking part in a protest. The NPPA code places special emphasis on active participation in events as a media professional: "Avoid political, civic and business involvements or other employment that compromise or give the appearance of compromising one's own journalistic independence."

RESIST BEING MANIPULATED

It's hard to be impartial if you find yourself taking sides on an issue. This is why many organizations work hard to find ways to curry favor with reporters through a variety of manipulative activities. A movie company might offer you a "press junket" where they will fly you to the set of a film, put you up at a hotel and give you access to the actors, all for free. The idea is that if you get all this free stuff, how can you write a negative review on the film? In a similar vein, researchers found that embedded reporters who covered the Iraq War were more positive in their coverage than those reporters who were not under the protection of the military. The question in the title says it all: "Can you criticize a soldier and then have breakfast with him in the morning?"[8]

The SPJ code outlines the ways in which manipulation can occur and how journalists should react:

- "Refuse gifts, favors, fees, free travel and special treatment."

- "Be wary of sources offering information for favors or money."

- "Deny favored treatment to advertisers, donors and any other special interests, and resist internal and external pressure to influence content."

The RTDNA code goes even further in this regard, noting that outside of access opportunities to cover events with other working reporters, journalists should shun all "freebies" that serve as enticements for current or future favorable coverage. The code makes specific mention that these rules should apply even when journalists are "off duty or on their own time."

Students walk past the Phi Kappa Psi fraternity house on the University of Virginia campus on Dec. 6, 2014 in Charlottesville, Virginia. Rolling Stone magazine issued an apology for discrepencies that were published in an article regarding the alleged gang rape of a University of Virginia student by members of the fraternity.

In terms of photography and broadcast, manipulation can occur at multiple levels, and thus the code dictates that journalists avoid being manipulated as well as manipulating content itself. "Resist being manipulated by staged photo opportunities," requires that photographers do their best to represent truth as opposed to whatever is set before them. For example, in 2003, President George W. Bush pitched his economic plan during a press conference in St. Louis. As part of his speech, which focused on "Strengthening America's Economy," he was surrounded by boxes bearing the stamp, "Made in the U.S.A." The problem was these boxes were made in China and merely had the origin labels covered up. Journalists there called out the event organizers, who blamed the issue on an "overzealous advance volunteer."[9]

ACCOUNTABILITY

As discussed throughout the book, journalists are held to a high standard that requires the pursuit of perfection each time they create content. No matter how hard journalists try to meet that standard, errors will occur. Stopping errors before publication is like catching sand in a sifter: No matter how hard you try, you can't grab everything. This is why the ethical codes of professional journalists help you understand what to do when mistakes happen. The actions listed here will provide accountability and help sustain credibility in the face of errors:

ACKNOWLEDGE MISTAKES

Few people like making mistakes, and even fewer like having someone point out those errors. Some errors, like misspelling someone's name or placing an event at an incorrect address, can make you feel stupid or sloppy. Other errors, like the "journalistic failure that was avoidable" in the case of Rolling Stone's 2014 "A Rape on Campus" story,[10] can undermine a journalist, a source, a publication and even a whole part of journalism.

When a reader or viewer tells you that your story has an error, you need to fully investigate that person's claim. Not every accusation of falsity bears out upon scrutiny. However, if you find out the person's claim is correct, you need to admit and acknowledge your error. The RTDNA code states, "Ethical journalism requires owning errors, correcting them promptly and giving corrections as much prominence as the error itself had." In most cases, your media outlet will have a process outlined for verifying claims of inaccuracy, admitting errors occurred and correcting the record. This will help guide you in your approach to fixing the mistakes you made.

It might seem counterintuitive that telling people you made mistakes will make them trust you more. However, journalists and researchers have found that audience members trust people more when they acknowledge and correct their mistakes.[11] This is why SPJ states simply and clearly: "Acknowledge mistakes and correct them promptly and prominently."

EXPLAIN YOURSELF

As much as the audience has "the right to know" when it comes to the actions of public officials, it also has the right to know how your media outlet has addressed errors, lapses in judgment or anything else that can cut into your credibility. Accountability requires that journalists not only find and fix errors but explain what was done, why it was done and how it was done. This isn't about weaseling out of the consequences for these mistakes, but rather as a way to help assure the readers you take ethical concerns seriously. As the RTDNA code notes, "Effectively explaining editorial decisions and processes does not mean making excuses." Instead, the code notes, the explanations should come at the end of a reflective and honest examination of what occurred and how the publication plans to reestablish trust with the audience.

In 2003, the New York Times found itself at the center of a scandal after journalists at a Texas newspaper alerted a Times editor about a case of potential plagiarism. While investigating this accusation, the Times found dozens of cases of plagiarism and fabrication in the work of Times reporter Jayson Blair. A team of journalists reevaluated all of Blair's work, and on May 11, 2003, the Times published a front-page story of more than 7,000 words explaining what went wrong with this reporter and his coverage.[12] The story noted that at least 36 of the 73 stories the team analyzed contained errors or other serious problems.[13] The Times also dedicated more than 6,000 words inside the paper to correct the errors in Blair's stories. The work of the Times in this case reflected a simple edict in the SPJ's code of ethics: "Expose unethical conduct in journalism, including within their own organizations. . . .Abide by the same high standards they expect of others."

THE BIG THREE

Here are the three key things you should take away from this chapter:

1. **Ethics matter:** If you treat ethics as either something you have to "deal with" as part of your job or ignore them, you put yourself at risk of violating the trust of your audience. You might get away with that for a little while, but eventually readers and will wise up and view you with suspicion. If you don't care about your readers and viewers, it is unlikely they will care about you or your work.

2. **View ethics holistically:** You have to take all of the elements of your approach to ethics into consideration each time you create content. In some cases, certain issues may emerge as primary, such as compassion or fairness. However, you can't consider one element of your ethical code in a vacuum. You need to look at how your actions touch on the varying elements of your ethical approach to journalism as you complete your work. You also have to be willing to look back on what happened as a result of your efforts, in hopes of improving your work and codifying your ethical standards.

3. **Choose wisely, adapt accordingly:** Your ethical philosophy should reflect your moral code and your approach to your work. It is more important to adopt specific ethical tenets you can support than it is to choose a cookie-cutter philosophy you can easily spout off as needed. However, as you gain experience in the field, you should revisit your approach to ethics and adjust your thinking as needed. Your ethical paradigm should best represent your sense of right and wrong, so make sure it does that at every stage of your career.

KEY TERMS

categorical imperative 230	hyperpartisan 234	transparency 241
conflict of interest 242	principle of utility 231	utilitarianism 231
ethics 229	self-determination 231	veil of ignorance 231
Fourth Estate 240	stereotype 236	verification 235
golden mean 230		

DISCUSSION QUESTIONS

1. Do you feel it is important to have a written code of ethics for journalists? Why or why not?

2. Some people in journalism argue that people have a right to know everything about everyone. Others believe it's better to miss a story than to create a problematic or uncomfortable situation. From an ethical standpoint, where do you fall on this spectrum? What is at the core of your feelings on this topic?

3. What makes a source ethical and credible in your mind? What have people or organizations done to make you trust them more often than not? What have others done that make you extremely distrustful of them?

4. What do you think formed your approach to ethical behavior? How did you start to think about this topic? Do you believe that your ethics will remain unchanged as you continue in the field of journalism, or do you see yourself altering your approach to ethics as you get deeper into your career?

WRITE NOW!

1. Briefly explain each of the five ethical approaches and philosophies discussed in the chapter. Then, explain which one of these is most in line with your approach to ethics. Also, note which philosophy you feel least comfortable with.

2. Review the six tenets of ethics that reside in the various journalistic codes we examined in this chapter. Of the six, which ones do you feel are the most important in establishing a bond of trust with your readers? Which ones are least important in your mind? Explain the reasons behind your thought process.

3. Find a topic that interests you and seek out a story on that topic from several sources that you believe to be what Christiane Amanpour might call "hyperpartisan." Compare and contrast how each site presents the information on the topic, including word choice, sensationalism, source material and more. Then find a story on this topic from a news source you trust. Which of those partisan sites best mirrors the story you trust? What concerns you about the stories that don't mirror your views? Discuss issues of accuracy and fairness as well as you summarize your findings.

Visit edge.sagepub.com/filaknews to help you accomplish your coursework goals in an easy-to-use learning environment.

APPENDIX A:
USING FOCII TO BUILD YOUR LEADS

The five interest elements outlined earlier in the book (fame, oddity, conflict, immediacy and impact) all can play a role in not only what makes your story interesting but also in how you should shape your lead. Let's delve into some leads that focus on the FOCII and see how each element can help you build a lead:

FAME

When you have an element of fame, you want to use a name-recognition lead to get that element as close to the front as you can:

> **BAD:** Several concertgoers injured earlier this year in Philadelphia have filed suit against rapper Snoop Dogg, after he enticed fans to move toward the stage where a metal rail collapsed, causing the injuries.

This lead buries the name that might draw people's attention. Get the name to the front:

> **BETTER:** Rapper Snoop Dogg acted negligently when he told concertgoers to move toward the stage, where a metal railing collapsed and injured several people, a lawsuit filed in Philadelphia this week states.

Whenever possible, focus on the famous person, place or thing:

> **PERSON:** President Donald Trump announced Monday he has a creative plan to combat an increasing terrorism threat against the United States.

> **PERSON:** Big State University Chancellor John Robarts resigned Tuesday after an FBI sting caught him stealing campus computers and filing reports that blamed custodial staff for the missing items.

> **PLACE:** Graceland, the estate of deceased rock 'n' roll star Elvis Presley, is under a health advisory this week after several visitors to the home contracted Legionnaires' disease during their stay.

PLACE: The Washington Monument, which has been under renovation for damage suffered in a 2011 earthquake, will not reopen for at least two more years, officials announced Monday.

THING: A copy of "Stadium Events," the rarest game ever released for the original Nintendo Entertainment System, sold for a record $38,000 at auction Tuesday.

THING: One of only four known home movies that captured the assassination of President John F. Kennedy has been donated to a Dallas museum, officials there said Tuesday.

ODDITY

When you have a weird situation, focus on the oddity with an interesting-action lead:

BAD: Charles Manowar, 43, was charged Wednesday in Obalaba County Court with 12 counts of burglary and 12 counts of endangering domesticated animals.

BAD: Thomas Joseph, 22, was arrested Wednesday in the Oakton Regional Bank on suspicion of attempting to steal money after hours.

BETTER: A 43-year-old Obalaba County man, accused of stealing parrots from people's homes by stuffing them in his pants, was charged Wednesday with burglary and endangering domestic animals.

BETTER: A 22-year-old Oakton man injured himself so severely while attempting to steal money from a bank after it closed, he had to call 911 on himself, police said Wednesday.

If you have the reporting to make it work, a narrative lead can also work to make things more interesting:

Nate Kazmark didn't recognize the partygoer limping out of the bathroom and heading to the front door, but Kazmark said he recognized the sound coming from the man's pants.

"I heard 'OUT! OUT! OUT!' in Darwin's voice," he said. "She always makes that sound when she wants me to open her cage and let her fly around the house. I had no idea who invited this guy to my party, but I could tell he had my parrot."

Kazmark said he confronted the man, who squirmed as his pant leg moved and continued to scream, "OUT! OUT! OUT!"

"I almost had to tackle the guy and depants him to get him to stop and let my bird go," he said. "Then we hung onto him and called the cops."

Charles Manowar, 43, was arrested on suspicion of stealing parrots from people's homes during parties by stuffing them in his pants. Police said Manowar has done this at least 12 times before, but had never been caught.

The call to the 911 center was among the most polite Jane Longwire said she ever received in her 25 years of service.

"The young man on the other end said, 'Excuse me, ma'am. I don't want to be a problem, but I have really hurt myself and I can't get to a hospital. Could you please send an ambulance, but no police cars?'" Longwire said.

According to the call transcript, the man said he cut his arm after breaking through a glass window, severely burned his leg trying to cut metal with an acetylene torch and now had his arm stuck in a metal vault.

"I asked him for his address and when I pulled up the screen, I saw it was the bank," Longwire said. "I asked him if he was trying to steal from the bank and he said, 'Yes, ma'am, but I guess I'm not really good at it.'"

Longwire continued the call for five minutes, which was when the police arrived and arrested Thomas Joseph of Oakton. The 22-year-old is accused of burglary and damage to private property.

Oddities also include rarities like the first, last or only instance of something:

FIRST: Sir Edmund Hillary, the first person to summit Mount Everest, disliked the danger associated with climbing and distained the "commercialism" of today's Everest climbs, a posthumous biography released Tuesday revealed.

FIRST: The first-ever marathon in which racers run entirely on a frozen river is in jeopardy of cancellation because of unseasonably warm weather, event organizers said Thursday.

LAST: Eugene Cernan, the last human to set foot on the surface of the moon, died after ongoing health issues, NASA officials said Monday.

LAST: The Class of 2018 at Beakton Memorial Academy will be the last group to graduate before the district closes the school because of low enrollment, Superintendent Clare Minker said Friday.

ONLY: Johnny Vander Meer, the only pitcher to throw back-to-back no-hitters in the major leagues, will be featured during a special event at the Baseball Hall of Fame this fall.

ONLY: Kentucky's only abortion clinic will remain open after a federal judge granted it a temporary stay Friday.

CONFLICT

When you have a situation with multiple people, groups or sides that want incompatible outcomes, you should focus on the conflict. In many cases, this means writing a lead that incorporates the specific conflict and how each side sees it. That means more than telling the readers that conflict exists:

BAD: The city of Springfield held a meeting Tuesday where city administrators and business officials disagreed about the future of Snapper Lake.

In this case, we don't know what the core of the disagreement is or why we should care as readers.

BETTER: While city officials say Bark-A-Lot Enterprises polluted Snapper Lake and should pay for its clean up, company administrators said the city's shortsighted environmental polices led to the lake's horrific condition.

A narrative lead with a good nut graph could also focus on the conflict:

Bark-A-Lot Chairman Rich Docker held a Mason jar filled with green sludge, candy bar wrappers, used tissue and rusty bolts in his right hand as he addressed the city council Monday.

"This is what you have allowed to happen to Snapper Lake over the past 50 years," he told the council. "To say that our one, accidental spill of pet treats has caused all of this is beyond ridiculous."

Alderwoman Jenna Jibense, whose district includes the dilapidated lake, quickly stepped forward and cut him off.

"It wasn't the only time you polluted," she said in a firm tone of voice. "It's just the first time we caught you."

The city and the company have been at odds over what caused the body of water to fall into such a horrific condition and therefore, who should pay to clean it up. Monday's meeting was the first step the city took toward seeking restitution from the pet-food giant that has a plant roughly 200 feet from the lake's shores.

IMMEDIACY

The word "news" has the word "new" built right in, which means newer items matter more than older ones. You should look for ways to focus on the newest aspects of an ongoing story with a second-day lead:

> **BAD:** The trial of Milton Newton, the philanthropist accused of stealing $6.4 million from a nonprofit group, began March 3, and three months later, the jury has yet to render a verdict, despite two weeks of deliberation.

The first time element in there is a date, meaning we are at least a week away from when something happened. The next time element tells us that the mention of the date is three months old, which makes this even worse. Then, we have a third time element that tells us something has been happening for two weeks.

When you have a problem with a time element, look for ways to freshen up the lead with a more recent time peg and then weave the older information deeper into the body of the story.

> **BETTER:** The jury in the Milton Newton case remained deadlocked Monday after two weeks of deliberating if the area philanthropist stole $6.4 million from a nonprofit group.

You can also approach a "story update" based on when you did your most recent reporting:

> Police said Monday they are no closer to catching the man who robbed six gas stations this month than they were when the crime spree began.

ONE MORE NOTE

When it comes to immediacy, newer is better, but that doesn't mean that the time peg should be the first thing you see. In most cases, people put the time element at the front of the sentence for fear of creating misplaced modifiers like these:

> **BAD:** Gov. Jim Smith said he wants to eliminate homelessness Wednesday during a speech on the steps of the Capitol.
>
> (Sounds like he's going to have a busy Wednesday.)

Or you can run into a problem of having back-to-back proper nouns when the time element is out of place:

> **BAD:** A 23-year-old man will spend the rest of his life in jail after he was convicted in Wabeno Court Wednesday of trying to run his elderly neighbor over with a snowmobile.
>
> (As opposed to the other branch named Wabeno Court Thursday?)

To fix that problem, people tend to move the time element to the front of the lead, creating sentences like this:

BAD: Wednesday, three people died and two more were injured when a cement truck slid off an overpass and crushed a minivan on Interstate 192, police said.

The main problem placing the time element at the front of the lead is that you have now told your readers that the most important thing in the most important sentence in your story is when something happened. On rare occasion, that can be true in some cases, such as historical events:

Twenty-five years after being declared killed in action, a U.S. Marine who fought in the Iraq War was found alive and well Friday.

Fifty years after he ended the 1960 World Series with a one-of-a-kind home run, Bill Mazeroski was honored at PNC Park with a bronze statue commemorating the moment.

In most cases, however, putting the time element up front is a dodge. The best way to avoid a misplaced modifier and keep the focus where it belongs is to place the time element next to the verb it should modify. You should also use this as an opportunity to reevaluate your verb choice to make sure you are focusing on the right aspect of the story in your lead:

BETTER: This state must do more to take care of its homeless population, Gov. Jim Smith said Wednesday on the steps of the Capitol.

BETTER: A 23-year-old man attempted to kill his elderly neighbor with a snowmobile and therefore should spend the rest of his life in jail, a Wabeno County jury decided Wednesday.

BETTER: Three people died and two more were injured Wednesday when a cement truck slid off an overpass and crushed a minivan on Interstate 192, police said.

IMPACT

This interest element answers the biggest question readers tend to have: "Why should I care about this?" The level of impact can be presented through quantitative or qualitative measures. Qualitative measures examine the severity of the impact, such as death or property loss. Quantitative measures examine how many of something is impacted.

QUALITATIVE: Six people died and five were critically injured as a result of Tuesday night's tornado, which swept through the heart of Springfield County.

QUANTITATIVE: Nearly 54,000 homes lost power Tuesday as powerful thunderstorms downed electrical lines and burst transformers throughout Springfield County.

Impact also matters more when it is brought down to a personal level for the readers:

BAD: The city of Wishana will likely bring in $2.2 million more in revenue next year after the common council unanimously agreed Tuesday to increase fees for vehicle licenses.

The number is big and scary, but it doesn't show me the direct impact. How much will this cost me if I own a car or truck? I have no idea.

BETTER: Vehicle owners in the city of Wishana will have to pay $10 more per car, truck or motorcycle next year after the common council agreed Tuesday to increase license fees.

Although numbers will be helpful in many leads to clarify impact, using too many of them will make your readers feel like a calculator threw up on them:

LeBron James scored 14 of his 24 points in the fourth quarter on 7-of-7 shooting, leading the Cleveland Cavaliers to a 108–105 win Tuesday against the Boston Celtics and giving the team a 3–1 lead in the best-of-seven series.

Instead, pick out which numbers matter most and find ways to include information that has value without using numbers:

Behind a perfect-shooting fourth quarter from LeBron James, the Cleveland Cavaliers pushed the Boston Celtics to the brink of elimination in the Eastern Conference Playoffs with a 108–105 win Tuesday.

APPENDIX B:
RÉSUMÉS, COVER LETTERS AND MORE

Hey, kid! Get a job!

Illustration by Jason Brooks

Get "The Man" off your back and find a viable job with this collection of advice that walks you through the entire process of resume-building and job-seeking.

(Author's Note: Students often tell me that the scariest thing they deal with is trying to get a job after college. Based on those comments, I asked the good people at SAGE to let me include this "personal journey/how-to" part of the book as an appendix. I wrote it more in a first-person approach, as I thought it might help students feel like they aren't the only ones going through this. Hope it helps.)

When I was a student, I had two basic questions about textbooks:

1. How much of this do I actually have to read?

2. How much does this cost, and how much money can I get when I sell it back to the bookstore?

If you have those same questions, chances are, reading an appendix is the last thing you think about when you pick up a textbook. However, I wanted to toss together a collection of thoughts, anecdotes and suggestions to help you make that next step in your life from broke college student to somewhat-less-broke fledgling journalist.

In my own movement toward employment within the media field, I didn't find much help in the standard places I normally sought it. My mom worked for the same school district for 45 years before retiring recently, so it had been a while since she made a career move. Dad worked in a factory for almost 38 years, which was the same factory his father worked in for 42 years and his father worked in for at least 40 more. The university guidance counselors were unclear on what mattered in my field and suggested that I speak at length about my coursework and my GPA, things that got me laughed at in at least one interview.

Years later, I found that I wasn't alone in feeling like a 4-year-old kid who lost his mom at the county fair. Former students, many now in their 30s and 40s, still reach out and ask, "OK, *how* do I apply for *this* job?" Current students often note that their classes don't tell them the most important thing about finishing college: how to take the next step.

To help you do that, here are some thoughts that come from a couple decades of applying for jobs, talking to hiring managers, working with graduates seeking employment and serving as an adviser and de facto therapist for students who think they'll never get a job. My suggestions also come from screwing up (and watching others screw up) in various ways and learning from those screw-ups.

The one major piece of advice I would like to give you is the one I have told students repeatedly: Don't freak out. You will be just fine, even when it doesn't seem like that will be the case.

RÉSUMÉ BUILDING BEFORE BUILDING YOUR RÉSUMÉ

I had a great student in my upper level features-writing course, and she was ready to graduate at the end of the term. She was a smart and intuitive reporter and writer. She always had incredibly insightful quotes from her sources and extremely vivid descriptions for her profiles and scene setters. She was the kind of student anyone who valued reporting or writing would want on staff at a magazine or news publication.

Still, she was having trouble getting employers to take her seriously, and she was worried about getting a job in the field. I told her we should sit down and go through her résumé. When she sat down with me to do this, I noticed that the paper was almost blank. She had a few academic accolades, her degree and a couple years of "regular jobs" in the service industry. She looked at me and in a quiet voice said, "You were right."

What I had been right about was that I had told her for years that she needed to get some experience in the media field somewhere. As much as self-interest had me hoping she'd be at the student newspaper I advised, I told her she should consider any possible option: student television, student radio, unpaid media gigs through clubs at the school, social media jobs at the university or anything else that got her into the mix. She always told me she was either too busy or that she would, but she needed to do something else first. Now, with graduation coming down the pike, she had nothing to show employers that proved she could do the kind of media work she knew she could do.

This student wasn't unique, unfortunately, as I have had many students in my office with a bucketful of gumption, but no real-world experience. This tends to lead to limited opportunities and tragic tales of wasted youth. To give yourself a fighting chance of presenting a résumé that employers will at least consider, you need to consider doing some work in the field. Below is a nonexhaustive list of places you can go and things you can do that will help you build your résumé before you have to build your résumé.

STUDENT MEDIA

Most colleges have some form of student-run media on their campuses. Daily, weekly or monthly newspapers dot the landscape of campuses, as do student-produced magazines, websites and even yearbooks. Many of these places also have some form of student broadcast, such as traditional radio and television operations or internet-based broadcasts. These places are great outlets where you can hone your skills, pick up some work samples (bylines, clips, stories, packages or whatever else people tend to call these things) and learn by doing.

Many students ask about trying to start their own blog or run their own social media operation. These opportunities have merit in many cases, as you can learn how to use various digital platforms and interact with interested readers on important topics. However, you should consider two key factors before putting all your eggs in one of these baskets. First, journalists tend to learn through social norming in environments where other people teach them how to do things and why they must be done as such. Even as far back as 1955, scholars like Warren Breed noted that newsrooms create a social environment in which older, more experienced staffers tended to convey knowledge socially to younger staffers. Those staffers, in turn, would gain age and wisdom in this system before imparting that knowledge to the next generation of staff members. A cynic could argue the notion of "garbage in, garbage out," but social learning remains a viable way in which knowledge traverses a media outlet. A single-person, self-driven operation might make things more difficult for you as you seek employment in a standard media organization. Second, and perhaps more important, if getting hired is the goal you have in life, it's probably a good idea to road test that concept now. Apply for a job that's out there at an established student media outlet to get a feel for how this all works.

UNIVERSITY GIGS

Many universities have departments, groups and organizations that need the skills you have gathered throughout your education. However, many students skip these opportunities because they aren't exactly what they want, or they aren't news jobs or they don't pay well (or at all). Students who ignore these opportunities do so at their own peril, as these jobs can give you a chance to grow and develop your skills in a new arena.

Just because you aren't breaking news or covering a sports team, it doesn't mean you aren't getting valuable experience or improving yourself. These jobs can give you a chance to develop a social media policy and try it out on an interested and engaged audience. They can give you a chance to learn how to interview people in fields that are foreign to you, which forces you out of your comfort zone and requires you to give some more thought to interview preparation.

At the very least, if you do good work at one of these jobs, you can get a good reference from someone other than a journalism professor or a student media adviser. That can help you stand out in a giant stack of résumés.

INTERNSHIPS

The process of moving from college to the profession is a lot like a baseball player who works his way through the minor leagues before getting a chance at "the show." In that regard, an internship is like what they call a "September call-up," when professional teams get to expand their rosters and try out some of the minor-leaguers against professional competition.

Summer internships are great opportunities for employers to take you out for a test drive. They get to see how you perform in the field and determine what kind of a fit you would be if a job were to open in a year or so. Contact local and regional media outlets to see if they have internships available and what it takes to get one. Some of them are paid, while others are unpaid, but the ability to get your foot in the door and get experience at the professional level is immeasurable. (We'll talk more about how to get these gigs later in the appendix.)

REGULAR JOBS

At this stage in your career, few places looking at you as a serious candidate for an internship or an entry-level job will expect you to have multiple years of media experience. If you do, that's great. If not, trying to fill that single blank page can feel like trying to cross the Gobi Desert on foot. This is where your "regular jobs" can help you fill the space and provide the hiring manager with some insight about you.

Students have often argued that working summers as a camp counselor or serving as a part-time cashier at Wiener World has nothing to do with the media, so including these jobs is a waste of time. Although making sure the kids don't fall into Crystal Lake or keeping the condiment bar stocked doesn't attach itself to hard-hitting journalism, don't discount these experiences on your first couple of résumés. Remember, media outlets aren't just picking up a set of skills when they hire you. They are getting a human being with habits, behaviors and traits as well.

Regular jobs can show people that an organization trusted you to work well with others and complete tasks as required. Former employers can discuss your overall work ethic, your work habits and your overall value as an employee of an organization. If you are on time for work, polite to others, do good work and create a pleasant environment as a checkout clerk, a clothing store retail specialist or a member of the Camp Happy Counselors Brigade, chances are, you will replicate those behaviors in a newsroom. List the jobs until you get enough media experience to push them off your résumé.

RÉSUMÉS: "WHAT CAN YOU DO FOR US?"

I once had a conversation with a hiring manager for a major sports website, and he helped me see the issue of hiring from the other side of the table. He explained to me that the student résumés he sees are often a disaster because they focus so much on what the students have done to this point in their lives.

When I pressed him on this issue, arguing that a résumé is, if nothing else, a recounting of a person's career, he shot back at me a line that still sticks in my head:

"I don't care about what you've done," he said. "I care about what you can do for me."

That statement reminded me of the line Oakland A's General Manager Billy Beane said to David Justice in the movie "Moneyball":

"I'm not paying you for the player you were. I'm paying you for the player you are right now."

Taking these two thoughts together, the purpose of the résumé is not to recount past glories, but rather to focus on skills and talents that can help your new employer see value in you. Let's walk through the basics:

EXPERIENCE

When you outline your previous places of employment, be they high-end media internships or plain-Jane service jobs, your goal is to show how these experiences created skills for you that a future employer will value. It's not enough to say that you were an intern at a major daily newspaper or a top-20 market television news station. You need to explain what it was you did while you were there and how that translates to a new-and-improved you.

Under each of your jobs, internships and activities, list three or four bullet points that provide your future employer with a sense of the skills you gained or honed during that time period. Use strong action verbs like "wrote," "interviewed," "created," "built," and "edited" to support the underlying assumption that you did things while you were there, as opposed to fetching coffee. If you want to put in some extra effort, review each position description for each job you are seeking and pair your experience "actions" with their needs. This will help keep your résumé fresh and specialized for the jobs while also helping future employers see you as a likely fit for their position.

EDUCATION AND HONORS

You want to list your education on your résumé to let people know where you are attending school and how far into your program you are. Listing an expected date of graduation can be beneficial for hiring managers who are trying to plan their next several moves. If the manager needs a reporter to start in December and you don't graduate until May, this can be a problem. Conversely, if you apply for an internship and you don't graduate for another year, a company might want to hire you for that internship and keep you on as a part-time worker during the year as they groom you for a full-time job down the road.

Any honors you can list from your current stage of life (college) are also helpful in this area. These can be things like awards you won in student media, such as first place in feature writing at the state student media conference or academic acknowledgments, such as induction into an honor society. If you won other germane awards or participated in other organizations that might shine a positive light on you, make sure you mention those too.

COVER LETTERS 101

In the days of texts and tweets, the idea of a cover letter can seem as quaint and unnecessary as communicating via the Pony Express. Some publications require a cover letter as a matter of course and to meet specific requirements set forth by a human resources department. Other places will ask for an email or a video or some other form of introductory element that goes beyond the résumé to explain who you are and why you matter. Regardless of the format, you want to put your best foot forward when you formally introduce yourself in the hiring process. Here are a few bits of advice to help you along:

START WITH A CONNECTION IF YOU HAVE ONE

If it's an opening paragraph or an opening line in a video, you want to introduce yourself to your audience in a way that gives you an edge over any potential competition. One of the best ways to make this happen is if they already know you, which is why networking is so crucial throughout your college (and professional) career.

If you went to a journalism conference and met a recruiter for the Johnson Journal, she might say, "Hey, we have an internship this summer that you might want to consider." That connection can be helpful in pulling you to the top of the stack, if she remembers you. That's why you want to start with something like, "It was great to meet you this fall at the ABC Media conference, where we talked about potential internship opportunities. Given what you told me there, I was excited to see you had this internship available and I couldn't wait to apply."

In some cases, you won't have that connection, but you will have that "friend of a friend" connection that you can exploit for your own benefit. Professors get emails or messages from former students all the time, asking if they know of any good students that might be interested in an internship or a job. If the professor handed this off to you, this is another great way to connect with a potential employer: "Professor Smith said you were looking for a hard worker to fill your internship position this summer, and he recommended that I send you my résumé."

If you lack any specific "in" with a potential employer, consider telling the employer where you found their advertisement and why you felt compelled to apply for the opening. For example, you could explain that you read the publication frequently or that you have professors who speak highly of the writing it puts out. You could also look for a way to tie your interests to their needs. In doing this you could mention how you covered specific things such as crime or sports and that is what drew you to the company's open position for a crime reporter or a sports reporter. Look for a way to reach out and explain to the person reviewing résumés, "Hey, I'm interested in you for a good reason!"

EXPLAIN, DON'T REPEAT, YOUR RÉSUMÉ

When students take essay tests, I often advise them to go through the essay question and highlight key phrases and active verbs so that they don't miss any section. Things like "Compare and contrast the four ethical codes" and "Describe the structure of an inverted-pyramid story" call for specific actions on the part of the student. Going through and noting those requirements can be helpful when the students want to provide the most complete answer possible. If you use that same formula when you write your cover letter, you can set yourself apart from the people who use form letters to regurgitate their experience.

Go through the job posting and highlight specific things the job requires or the employer wants. This could include things like "must be proficient at social media" or "needs the ability to work well under deadline pressure." Once you highlight those elements, pick out the ones you want to discuss in your cover letter.

At this point, you don't want to repeat your résumé, but rather link your experiences to their needs and do a solid job of explaining how they connect through narrative examples. Let's say the need is "must work well under deadline pressure." You can link that to your work in student media with an example of how you did this:

> *"You noted in your position description that you need someone who works well under deadline pressure. As a news reporter at the Campus Crier, I often found myself working on tight deadlines including one case where I got a tip about the university's president resigning. In less than two hours, I managed to get the story confirmed and written. Even better, I scooped the local paper."*

Not every need will attach itself to one of your great adventures in media, but you should look for those opportunities to show people what you did and how it can be of benefit to them.

THE MONEY PARAGRAPH: WHY SHOULD THEY HIRE YOU?

After you outline your skills and traits but before you thank the person for considering your application sits the most important couple of sentences in your letter: the money paragraph. At this point, you should have made a good impression and have the person on the other end of the letter thinking that you might be a good fit. It is right here that you want to seal the deal and give the employer something to remember.

Each of us has that "one thing" that we think we're better at that most of the rest of the people in our field. We pride ourselves on our ability to work through problems, to constantly look for positives in every situation or to smooth over personnel concerns. Whatever that "one thing" is for you, hit it here with some emphasis. The goal is to say to an employer that if she is looking through your application and Candidate X's application and everything is completely equal to this point, here's the big reason why you should get the job over that other person:

"Above all else, I constantly look for new ways to reach the audience. I was one of the first reporters on our staff to integrate digital tools like Periscope and Storify into my work. I knew this was how most people in our audience got the news and now everyone else at our publication uses these tools as well. I will always look for the next best way to connect with the readers and viewers and I think this approach could really boost readership for your organization."

"LIKE A BAD DATING EXPERIENCE": THE APPLICATION PROCESS

The application process for most jobs involves a series of stages and processes that require multiple people to approve everything from the job posting to the candidate hiring. Throughout that process, human beings make decisions about deadlines for each step and how long each stage should last. Couple that with the ability for things to get lost on people's desks, at-work emergencies and the occasional personal catastrophe for the hiring manager, and this thing can drag out for what seems like an eternity.

As a candidate, you know none of the internal machinations occurring at the business to which you have applied. All you know is that you haven't heard back, and it seems like forever. Each time you check your email or voicemail can bring with it a sense of hope and anxiety and then that deflating sadness or anger. At the end of this, you can feel like someone has put you through an emotional wringer.

The only way I have ever been able to explain this to students who are dealing with this for the first time is to say it is essentially like a bad dating experience: You meet someone and express some level of mutual interest. You put yourself out there and don't hear back, so you're not sure how to feel about this because you don't know how that other person thinks. You fight the urge to send off additional texts or calls because you don't want to be annoying, but the curiosity and anxiety are killing you slowly as your insides twist into pretzels.

You send off another message and then hate that you seem needy. You still don't hear back, so now you feel angry and you've written this person off. Suddenly, you get a call two days later from the person, who is apologizing that they were unable to get back to you because of a family emergency that required out-of-state travel. The person is so happy you reached out and would really like to make all of this up to you by going out for coffee in the next day or two. . . .

And on and on it goes with the ups and downs of the process until you either end up in a relationship of some kind or you both end up going other ways.

Students who haven't gone through this tell me I don't know what I'm talking about until they go through it and then they tell me it's pretty much the best analogy available for the emotional rollercoaster that is a job search. To help you navigate the process, here are a few things to consider when going through it:

BE INTERESTED WITHOUT BEING ANNOYING

The classic 1996 film "Swingers" includes a scene in which Jon Favreau's character, Mike, calls a woman he met at a bar that night and leaves her a message. He then calls another time that night to leave a number. Then he calls another time to let her know he's interested. A fourth call tells her he just got out of a six-year relationship, so he's acting a bit weird. His next call is asking her to call him whenever she gets back because he really wants to talk to her. He then calls a few more times in which he finally says he isn't sure he wanted to date her anyway. At the end, she actually picks up the phone and it was clear she was listening all that time. She tells him to never call her again.

The point here is that a line clearly exists between showing enthusiastic interest and borderline stalkerish behavior. You want to be on the proper side of that line both in life and in the job search. That's where you need to meter out your approach to staying in touch with your potential employer.

Understand that even though your application is the number one priority for you, it might be priority 87 for the people on the other end of it. As you fret about your future, those people are likely going through the dozen other mundane tasks they need to complete every day. They might also have additional searches going that take priority over yours, or a few crises might have popped up along the way, limiting the time they can spend going through applications. It's important to you that you get hired, but it isn't necessarily a crucial part of these people's daily life.

With that in mind, you have a few things you can do to give yourself some contact options and not be known around the office as "that annoying candidate who won't leave us alone." The best opportunity for contact is after you have submitted your material. At that point, you are fresh in the employer's mind and you have an open lane to get a few crucial pieces of information.

Let's say you apply for a reporting job at the Smithville Journal. You follow the rules and submit your material electronically to editor John Jones via email. You send in the information, and in that email, you can ask John to email you back, just to make sure he got your information and that it didn't get lost in a spam filter somewhere. The next day, you get an email from John telling you that he got your information and thanks for applying. At this point, you get one more email to send back without seeming needy or weird, so make it count. You want to email him back and thank him for reaching out to you. You want to express your enthusiasm in a controlled and yet interested fashion. You also want to find out what the process looks like in terms of a time line. This is where you can get the information you need to keep from having anxiety nightmares every day for the next three months.

That email should yield a return email that fills you in on the process. If John says, "We plan to get this done in the next two weeks. We want to have phone interviews with our top candidates at that time," you now have a timeline for yourself and you should leave him alone. If he doesn't respond, give it a week and respond with a refresher email, noting that you just wanted to make sure he got your last email. That will either mentally poke him to get back to you with a "Oh, hey, sorry! I did get it and here's the process" email or it won't. At that point, let it rest. The ball is clearly in his court.

If you got the two-week timeline, don't treat it like the countdown timer on a bomb. If John didn't get back to you exactly 336 hours after your last contact, the world won't end. Many incidents can intervene that will turn that hopeful timeline into a pipe dream, so let it rest for upward of a week. A follow-up at that point is legitimate, with a "just wanted to touch base" feeling to it. Explain you don't want to be a bother, but you did want to make sure he knew you were still interested. If that yields an email with an apology and an explanation of how things have slowed, you will likely get a new timeline and this process starts all over. If you get a "don't call us, we'll call you" email, you also know where you stand and you can look elsewhere.

The biggest thing is to be relaxed in your emails and demonstrate that you like the job, but you aren't typing this desperate missive, begging for it. The more desperate and needy you seem, the less likely you are to get a second look. Many hiring managers figure that if you are this much of a pest as a candidate, you will be as bad, if not worse, as a colleague.

"I LIKE YOU. I HATE YOU. I LOVE YOU." THE SWINGS OF THE PROCESS

One of the hardest things about the hiring process from the point of the applicant is to separate the professional from the personal. Logically, you can say in your head, "Another person's résumé had more years of experience and more awards than mine did, so it makes sense that the person got the job." However, in most cases, we internalize the issue and make it about the person: "Why didn't they like me?" The rejection of our application becomes the rejection of us personally, which means something is wrong with us.

You have to find a way to put up a firewall between who you are and what you have accomplished. You're not worse than someone who has three more years of experience than you do. You're not a bad person because you haven't won a major award or garnered a major scoop. Those things might or might not come to you in time, but not having attained them at this point is not an indictment of your character.

You also want to modulate your reactions to the swings of the process. You apply and you imagine yourself working at the job, getting the salary, gabbing with like-minded colleagues near the coffee cart and becoming a seasoned pro. It's love at first sight. When the company hasn't called you back in a week or two, you start to feel disappointed and that can lead to you having the "sour grapes" approach to the job. It probably wasn't that good. The money probably wasn't that good. The coffee probably tastes like garbage. Then, you get the call that has them asking for potential times where you could do an interview. Suddenly, you're overflowing with joy, and you're counting the minutes until your phone interview.

To keep yourself on an even keel, you need to find a way to treat each step as more of a moderate movement as opposed to an emotional swing. It's great to be liked, but you're going to remain cautiously optimistic about that application. It's sad when people don't like you, but there are other fish in the sea. It's nice that they thought enough of you to do the phone interview and even if you don't get the job, the interview process is great for gaining experience.

Take it one step at a time and let it happen.

GIVE THANKS, NO MATTER WHAT

This links directly into the previous two steps: Show gratitude no matter what happens. Sure, you aren't happy you lost the internship or the job, but you don't want to leave people with a bad impression of you. Although I could make arguments about how your parents taught you to always be thankful, there is a more utilitarian reason to be grateful and pleasant: Being a jerk can come back to haunt you.

After your interview, you should send a simple "thank you" note or email to the person with whom you met. This approach can show that you are interested in the job and that you are motivated to keep the channel of communication open between you and the organization. When you find out later that you didn't get the position, you should follow up with a similar "thank you" communication as well. This one will let people know you are grateful for the time they took with you and that you don't hold a grudge about not getting the job. This is worth your time, even if you are dying inside and would love nothing more than to get a job working for one of that company's competitors so you could frequently beat the pants off those fools who didn't hire you.

Just because you didn't get this internship or job, it doesn't follow that the company doesn't like you or value you. A hiring manager might have found a more experienced person or an editor might have needed a specific skill set you don't possess. If another opportunity opens up in that company, the hiring manager might recall you as a great interview and consider hiring you for that job.

One of my students was interviewed for an internship at Company X and was passed over in favor of another one of my students. She remained professional and thanked everyone for the opportunity. A few days later, she got a call, explaining there was a different internship in another area where they thought she'd be great. She made it to the final two and was rejected again. She thanked them and offered to stay in touch in a polite and professional manner before breaking down sobbing in my office.

Three days later, another company contacted her about a different internship, and she got that one. A day later, Company X called her and offered her an internship in her area of interest that had just come up. After hearing she already had an internship, Company X offered to work around her schedule because they really wanted her to be a part of the company for the summer. In the end, she got both paid internships and got great experience (and references) from them both.

Even if Company X never offered her the internship, remaining professional was in her best interest, because we all work in a small field. The concept of "six degrees of separation," in which anyone on the planet can be linked to anyone else on the planet through no more than five other people, is true in our area of work. In reality, it's probably closer to two or three degrees of separation, so if you come off like a jerk, someone will remember you and complain about you over drinks to a colleague at another company, and you might have applied there. Don't let a small bout of anger and resentment lead to the creation of an unfair reputation.

GETTING THE JOB AND NEGOTIATING YOUR DEAL

The application, the phone interview, the weeks of waiting, the in-person interview, the week of waiting, the "checking up" phone call from the editor and the next two weeks of waiting have culminated in an actual offer.

Yes, someone out there likes you, and if your heart ever stops pounding against your rib cage, you will likely thank the person on the other end of the phone before you hang up and start screaming like a crazed hyena. In the meantime, the person passes along some congratulations and says something about sending you the formal offer and needing you to fill out a form or something, all of which is lost in the sound of blood pounding in your ears. You issue a few yes/no/thank-you answers to whatever it is you are being told, and you hang up. Before you celebrate via every social media channel you use, you need to spend some time looking at what this job will entail and what your compensation really involves, and then decide if you want to take this job.

This sounds like heresy at this point, because the euphoria of getting a job has made taking whatever is thrown your way a foregone conclusion. However, this is where you need to get grounded and really see what you are getting yourself into. You will eventually come down off of this high, and if you don't make some smart choices before you take the job, you will end up regretting it.

REVIEWING THE OFFER

Before you hang up with the employer, you want to find out how you will be receiving the formal offer. The people hiring you will need to send you some sort of documentation either via email or snail mail. Once you get that, you will be able to see what kind of hand you have been dealt. This is the time to get back into reporter mode: Do some research, ask a lot of questions and determine what you actually have in front of you.

Certain things are in almost every offer package: Salary, sick leave, vacation, health-related benefits, start date and contract renewal terms. Beyond that, other perks and caveats can crop up here and there. Some of these things are negotiable, while others are not. The variable nature of these elements can range widely based on the company, the state and other factors, such as the presence of a union. For now, let's just look at the basic things you need to work through and how to approach them:

SALARY

Money isn't everything, but it beats the heck out of whatever comes in second, so you need to understand it. Some places will hire you at an hourly rate, while others will hire you on an annual salary. In either case, you need to understand two things: How many hours are associated with your pay, and how much are you actually being paid?

Hours can vary from organization to organization and can affect your life. At some companies, full-time work is 40 hours a week, while others build in a half hour or an hour as break time or lunch. Some organizations build in a salary bump for weekend or "second-shift" work. Figure out what it is you have been given so you know what you have to do to earn your money.

Money can also vary from organization to organization, both in terms of how you are paid, what that money includes and what it can actually buy. Some places pay by the week, which can be good when you want to have a steady stream of income throughout the year. Others pay you once per month, which can force you to budget differently so you aren't broke by the last week of the month. You need to know how much you will be paid, but also how much you will get when the money finally lands in your bank account. Certain things will be taken out of your salary, such as taxes, health insurance costs and even parking costs. Taxes and medical costs can vary widely from state to state, so if you are moving from one part of the country to another, you should consider those issues when weighing a job offer or comparing multiple offers.

Buying power also varies from place to place. If you get a $35,000 offer in Youngstown, Ohio, you might be able to live very well, as that's more than $10,000 above the median income there. If you get that same offer in San Francisco, California, you are probably in serious financial trouble, given that you will make less than half of what the median income is for the city. Use some of the cost-of-living tools available to you online to figure out how much you can buy for your salary. Use online classified ads to examine the cost of housing and see where you will be able to live on your new income. The actual dollar amount is only as good as what you can do with those dollars.

VACATION AND SICK LEAVE

You need to find out how much of these precious commodities you get and when you will receive them. Some places will give you a certain amount right away and withhold a secondary chunk until you have worked there for a while. Other places will give you the whole ball of wax right up front. Many places, however, will require you to work for somewhere between six months and a year until you accrue any vacation and/or sick time. The amount and approach will vary, so figure out what you get and when you get it.

It's also instructive to find out what happens if you need time off before your vacation kicks in or what the company expects you to do if you suddenly come down with a case of the flu. Some places will let you negotiate a certain set of unpaid off days into your deal if you don't have vacation, while others have human-resources rules that dictate what reprimands you will receive if you miss work.

Finally, find out what happens to these days if you don't use them. Companies often allow you to "roll over" your sick days from year to year, with a cap of some kind kicking in if you happen to be one of those people who have great health and a lengthy career. In most cases, vacation is a "use it or lose it" proposition, so you shouldn't plan on saving up so that you can take all of June off in 10 years.

HEALTH INSURANCE AND OTHER BENEFITS

Some companies require a certain number of work hours for you to qualify for a benefits package, so you need to make sure your job meets those requirements. If you need 40 hours of work to get the health insurance, and your job calls for 37.5 hours per week, you need to figure out why. You also need to figure out how much you will be expected to pay toward your health insurance, if you need to go to specific doctors and what services will be covered. You might consider your nearsightedness to be a medical condition, but your insurance might not cover eye care. The same thing is true about dental coverage. Also, check to make sure that any preexisting conditions you have are covered. If you've had asthma since you were 5 years old, chances are you're going to need some inhalers and some doctor's visits, so make sure you are covered.

You also want to see if any other benefits exist that you didn't consider. If you have to move to take the job, see if your employer will pay for some or all of your moving expenses. Some places have discounted or free memberships to local events or local gyms. You might get free access to certain databases other people have to pay for or a free couple days off as part of the city's "Founder's Day" celebration. Don't overlook the freebies and perks when you review the deal.

UNDERSTANDING THE FINE PRINT

All of these discussions of copays and 401(k) vesting clauses can make your head swim. You might never have heard about pretax benefits or employee contribution requirements, and all of this can seem scary. If you treat these things the way you treat everything else you do as a reporter, you'll be fine.

Research the information the same way you research anything else you are reporting on. Do internet searches, read articles from trusted publications and see what other people online are saying about each thing that confuses you. The more you read, the more you will understand the main things with which you should concern yourself.

Think about it like buying a used car: When you read the reviews online, usually there are a few things people tell you to watch out for with certain brands or models of car. Those things could be specific spots where the cars tend to rust or certain noises that indicate poor maintenance. When you go to test-drive one of those cars, you don't know the quality of every screw and switch, but you know what can become problematic and you keep an eye out for it. The same basic rules apply here. For example, you might not know everything about your 401(k), but you will know to ask if the company matches your contributions, how long it will take for you to become vested and what fees are you responsible for.

If you still need more information or you aren't exactly happy with the answers you have received, do some interviewing. As a reporter, you aren't an expert on everything, so you call up experts and ask them questions when you need information. This is no different. Get in touch with knowledgeable people you trust, like family and friends, and ask them to help you understand what you are looking at here. These people can be beneficial, as you will get one-on-one help for your specific situation.

OLIVER TWISTING YOUR WAY TO A BETTER DEAL

If the money looks good and the benefits meet your needs, you are almost ready to take the job. It is here where most first-time job seekers bypass the opportunity to leverage the deal in their favor.

In general, people don't want to upset others, and they don't want to be greedy, so they will decline to negotiate. The idea many people have is that they'll take the deal and work really hard so that their boss will value them and give them more money or benefits later. As much sense as that makes, it isn't the way a job negotiation works. You will never be in a better position to get things you need than you are when you have a good deal and you are almost ready to take it.

Understand that for the most part, employers expect that you will negotiate to some degree. How hard you push and what you choose to ask for will determine an employer's reaction, but that's up to you. However, if you ask for a little more money or a few specific needs, a good employer will comply with your request, meet you in the middle or decline to do so while explaining why your request isn't possible. You are highly unlikely to blow the deal or have someone pull the contract off the table at this stage if you are polite and logical in your approach.

In short, try to be like Oliver Twist: Politely note, "Please, sir. I want some more." (And, of course, hope it turns out better for you than it did for him.)

When it comes to money, the salary is a negotiating point, so don't think it has been carved in stone. Unless your employer tells you otherwise, nothing should stop you from asking for some more money. When you ask for more money, have a number in mind and ask for a little bit more than that number. You will never get more than you ask for, and once your employer agrees to an amount, the option to ask for more is gone.

So, let's say the company offers you $26,000 and you would like $28,000. Ask for $30,000. You might get it or you might get a return offer of $29,000, which is still more than you wanted. Worst case, you can agree to "meet in the middle" at $28,000, which is what you wanted in the first place.

It also helps to have a reason why you want the money and make that part of your pitch. If you say, "I want more money," you might come across like a greedy jerk. Instead say, "I was looking at the cost of apartments near the office and they are a little pricier than I thought. I was wondering if we could move the salary figure up to X dollars to help with that." This shows that you have really looked into coming to the company and you are looking at living situations. The hiring manager will likely understand your concern and see about getting you a little more money.

Some jobs will tell you, "This is the salary and we can't negotiate it for XYZ reasons." That doesn't mean you can't get other things that will benefit you. In lieu of a salary bump, ask for an extra week of vacation or some other perk you know other people in the field get. If you have plans set up for later in the year, like a family vacation or a friend's wedding, that might not mesh with your new work schedule, see if you can get a promise to have that time put aside. Ask for a little more moving money or a promise that you can have off a specific holiday that is important to you. Whatever really matters to you, this is the time to get it.

SEALING THE DEAL

After all of this is done and you agree to the new deal, make sure you get it in writing. Have an adviser, a lawyer or someone you trust go over it with you to make sure everything is in order.

Then, sign what you need to sign, plan your next stage of life and enjoy the ride.

While the Freedom of Information Act (FOIA) covers the federal level, each state dictates how it will behave with regard to public records requests within its borders. These laws go by different names, such as sunshine laws, open records laws and public disclosures, to name a few. Inherent to all of them, however, is the idea that the law should be tailored to keep citizens in the know. You can check on any state's open records laws through the National Freedom of Information Coalition's website (http://www.nfoic.org). For the sake of an example, I've randomly chosen a state (Vermont) to unpack some of the crucial elements for you as a reporter:

Here is the state's opening statement of policy for Vermont's subchapter on access to public records:

§ 315. Statement of Policy; Short Title

(a) It is the policy of this subchapter to provide for free and open examination of records consistent with Chapter I, Article 6 of the Vermont Constitution. Officers of government are trustees and servants of the people and it is in the public interest to enable any person to review and criticize their decisions even though such examination may cause inconvenience or embarrassment. All people, however, have a right to privacy in their personal and economic pursuits, which ought to be protected unless specific information is needed to review the action of a governmental officer. Consistent with these principles, the General Assembly hereby declares that certain public records shall be made available to any person as hereinafter provided. To that end, the provisions of this subchapter shall be liberally construed to implement this policy, and the burden of proof shall be on the public agency to sustain its action.

Let's break down a few key elements of this:

1. Notice that it says "certain public records shall be made available to any person," meaning that the state is beholden to any John or Jane Q. Public who wants to see these public documents. It doesn't say "some" or "most" people, nor does this restrict it to media organizations or prohibit certain groups from having access. "Any person" means you can get ahold of any documents you see fit, as long as they legally qualify as public records.

2. The statement also notes, "Officers of government are trustees and servants of the people and it is in the public interest to enable any person to review and criticize their

decisions. . . ." Some states include the term "essential function" or "requirement of the job" that officers of the government turn these records over to the public. Unfortunately, many state agencies don't see things that way, because of fear of embarrassment or negative press. Those reasons aren't good enough to keep records out of the public eye. Some states will even make this explicit, such as Indiana, which notes, "No request may be denied because the person making the request refuses to state the purpose of the request, unless such condition is required by other applicable statute."[1] As a reporter, your job is to help the state officials and record keepers see how public access is part of their job, and an important one at that.

3. The closing line here is probably the most important aspect of the law: "To that end, the provisions of this subchapter shall be liberally construed to implement this policy, and the burden of proof shall be on the public agency to sustain its action." Some record keepers use the "possession is nine-tenths of the law" approach, meaning if they have it and you want it, you need to explain why you should get it before they release it. The law states that the exact opposite is true: You have the right to those records, and it's up to the agency to demonstrate why those documents don't fall into the category of open records. If the agency or its record keepers can't show you the point of law that allows them to keep you from having those records, you deserve them under this state statute.

WHICH DOCUMENTS ARE AVAILABLE?

What you have the right to varies from state to state as well. Some states open all governmental agencies to the widest possible inspection rules, while others use restrictive measures based on the platform of communication or the type of documents. Traditional paper records of common governmental business, such as copies of a city budget or minutes from a public school board meeting, will almost always fall under the umbrella of an open record.

The question of how to treat emails and other electronic communication has more recently become a concern to journalists and open records advocates. For example, in 2008, two Detroit newspapers sued the city to force Mayor Kwame Kilpatrick to disclose text messages he sent from his mobile device.[2] The city argued that the messages were exempt because the city leased, rather than owned, the device. The court dictated that the bulk of the messages be released, leading to several compromising issues, including Kilpatrick's conspiring with an aide to fire a deputy police chief and an extramarital affair the mayor was having.[3] That said, in San Jose, California, a case that asks if digital communication outside of state-held networks and devices constitutes a public record. In this case, an activist requested voicemails, text messages and emails sent among the mayor and city council representatives regarding a redevelopment project in the city. The request noted that all records should be turned over, regardless of whether they were on private accounts or not.[4] The city lost the first stage of that case, but won on appeal.[5] As of early 2017, the case had been appealed to the state's highest court, but remained undecided.

The law makes it clear that you have access to everything a public agency creates, unless it is specifically exempted under another part of the law. In short, you have the right to whatever hasn't been listed explicitly as not being a public document. Most of the states list items such as employee personnel records, records that would endanger someone's life, any document that would violate the state's open meeting law and any document that FOIA dictates as being nonpublic in this category. These items vary from state to state, so it is important to understand what you can and can't get. That said, it is usually best to attempt the request and make the agency tell you why you can't have the items you want. Remember, the burden is on the agency to say why the record isn't public. If the record keepers can't tell you that, you should be granted access to those items.

HOW TO MAKE A FORMAL OPEN RECORDS REQUEST

Open records requests can seem daunting if you don't know how to ask formally for the documents you are seeking. In some cases, governmental bodies and other organizations will have a specific form they want you to complete for a record request. However, in many cases, you will need to write a letter that informs the records custodian what you want. Below is an annotated sample letter for an open records request. We are keeping with the example of Vermont, but you can find sample letters at http://www.nfoic.org/state-sample-foia-request-letters for your specific state.

1. Start this letter as you would any formal letter by including your name and return address. This will also help the recipient of the letter know where to send the records if your request is successful.

2. Include the date you sent the letter. This will provide a clear start to the timeline associated with your request. Your letter will likely be stamped with an intake stamp of some kind when it arrives at the record keeper's office to help start the clock on your request. This is particularly important in states that list a specific time frame in which requests must be answered.

3. Here is where you put the name, title and full address of the record keeper.

4. Begin the body of the letter with a clear indication that this is a formal open records request. Include in this paragraph the specific state statute under which you are making this request.

5. Here is where you need to describe the records associated with your request. If you know specifically which records you want, such as the 2017 city budget, you can note it here. If you are unsure as to what records exist that pertain to your request, you should describe the information you are seeking. An example of this type of request would be something like "Any emails sent between the assessor's office and the mayor's office in 2016 regarding the property at 111 W. Main St. in Burlington." This is usually where requests run into trouble. You need to be as specific and clear as you can be, which includes listing a specific time frame for the documents, the form of the document and the topic associated with the documents. In other words, you will be far more successful asking for "Police reports written by Sgt. Bill Bates for the Smithville Police Department from May 1 to May 30 regarding

traffic stops on Whitley Way" than simply asking for "Anything officers wrote or typed this year about traffic stops." In this letter, we ask for data from two fiscal years regarding property values in the city as well as a list of assessors associated with those properties. That should be specific enough to get the request through, presuming the documents exist and are deemed public records.

6. This paragraph acknowledges that state law allows governmental agencies to charge fees for this, but it also asks that those fees be waived. If you can make a case that you are part of the news media, doing this for a greater news-gathering purpose or that you lack funds, it is more likely that you can get the fee waived. However, you should also note that you are willing to pay up to a certain amount to get this request completed. Mention that amount in your letter.

7. You should find out what your state law dictates in terms of turnaround time and mention that here. This helps establish the time frame for this request and gives the record keeper a reminder that fulfillment needs to happen in a certain amount of time. If your state doesn't list a specific number of days, or lists "a reasonable amount of time," check with open records advocates to see what best practices are in the state. That would let you note, "State law dictates that this request be answered in a reasonable time period, but best practices in this state indicate five days to be an acceptable amount of time to fulfill a request like this."

8. Before you close, you want to remind the records keeper that if any part of this is denied, he or she has to specifically cite the reason in the law for it. This prevents people from ignoring the letter or responding with something like, "I don't think you really need these records." In addition, you want to note that this person has to tell you how to proceed if you aren't satisfied with the reasoning behind the denial. The record keeper has to list an appeal process for you.

9. Add your signature and a contact number so the person can contact you to clarify any issues with the request or to inform you as to the status of it.

(1) Zoe Filak
1111 N. Main St.
Burlington, VT 05401

(2) 2/22/2017

(3) John Vickery
Assessor, City of Burlington
149 Church St., Room 17
Burlington, VT 05401

Dear Mr. Vickery,

(4) Under Vermont Public Records Law §315 et seq., I am requesting the opportunity to examine or obtain copies of the following public records:

(5)
- A listing of all real estate parcels and business personal property within the city of Burlington, including the owners' addresses, property locations, appraised values and homestead value if applicable for Fiscal Year 2017

- A listing of all real estate parcels and business personal property within the city of Burlington, including the owners' addresses, property locations, appraised values and homestead value if applicable for Fiscal Year 2016

- A listing of individual assessors associated with each property listed for Fiscal Year 2017

- A listing of individual assessors associated with each property listed for Fiscal Year 2016

(6) I would ask that any fees associated with this request be waived, as I believe this information is of public interest and will contribute significantly to the public's understanding of how assessments work in this city. Also, as I am a student journalist requesting this for a news-gathering purpose, I lack significant financial backing if the fees are prohibitive. If there are any fees associated with this request, please inform me if the cost will exceed $25.

This information is not being sought for commercial purposes.

(7) The law requires a response to this request within two days, or within 10 days for extraordinary circumstances. If you expect a significant delay in fulfilling this request, please contact me to notify me as to when my request might be fulfilled.

(8) If you deny any or all of this request, please cite each specific exemption you feel justifies your denial and notify me as to the appeal process available to me under the law.

Sincerely,

(9) Zoe R. Filak
802-867-5309

WHEN YOU HEAR BACK ON YOUR REQUEST

Once you make your request for the records, how long it will take for people to get back to you and what you will receive will vary based on the laws of your state. If you make an oral request, the record keeper can accept or reject the request the same way. This is why using a formal, documented approach is a better way to go, as you can compel the official to write out exactly what was wrong with your request and under which part of the law the record keeper used to reject it.

When you get the formal response, it has to tell you if your request was approved or rejected. If approved, it has to explain how you can get access to the documents, presuming they weren't sent along with the response, and any costs associated with the request. If rejected, the response has to explain why your request was rejected, citing specific state statutes. Many states will also require the record keeper to tell you what step you can take next if you want to appeal the decision.

In the Vermont example, the state statute lists a two-day turnaround for record keepers from the time they receive the request to their written response. The response must include a brief statement of why the request was denied and "include the asserted statutory basis for denial and a brief statement of the reasons and supporting facts for denial." It must also explain that you have the right to appeal this decision to the head of the agency.[6]

APPENDIX D:
STEP-BY-STEP EDITING PROCESSES FOR AVID, FINAL CUT AND PREMIER

(SPECIAL THANKS TO JOE DENNIS, KYLE MILLER AND JUSTINE STOKES FOR THEIR GENEROSITY.)

AVID MEDIA COMPOSER 8 USER GUIDE

(Courtesy of Justine Stokes)

CREATING A NEW AVID PROJECT

1. Open Avid Media Composer.

2. Set the folder structure to the correct local or external drive. Create a folder called "Avid Projects."

3. Set the project to match the settings of the footage you will be working with.

4. With the project you just created highlighted select "OK".

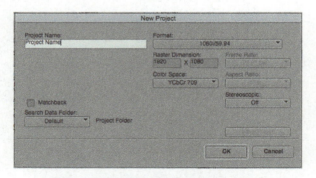

SETTING UP MEDIA CREATION SETTINGS

1. Every time you open an AVID project, you must check the media creation settings. These settings establish the file structures where various files created by AVID are stored.

2. Select Media Creation under the settings tab.

3. In the dialog box, select the Capture tab. Set the Video Drive and Audio Drive to the drive you are working in. (Never save to any other locations.) Select Apply to All. This will set the drive to each of the settings in Media Creation.

CONNECTING FOOTAGE USING LINK TO MEDIA

1. To connect footage from media cards.

    a. Highlight project bin. Select File → Link to Media. Select folder containing card footage. A bin will be created showing the media in the folder. **You have not imported footage at this point, you are only referencing the footage.**

AVID EDITING BASICS

MAKING A SEQUENCE

1. Make sure you organize your folders in the main bin window prior to editing. A nice basic bin setup will consist of bins labeled footage, sound fx, music, and sequences.

2. Press and hold COMMAND + SHIFT + N to create a new sequence.

    a. Make sure your sequence is stored in the bin you want. AVID may automatically place this new sequence in whatever bin you have selected, so be sure to move the sequence into your sequences bin.

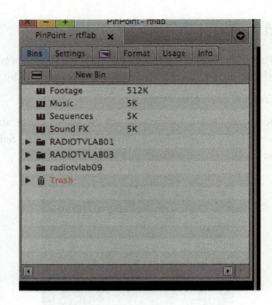

ADDING A CLIP TO A SEQUENCE

1. Double-click on a clip in your footage bin. This will load it into the preview monitor. From here you can scroll through the preview monitor and select the "in" and "out" points you want to start your sequence with.

   a. Press the "I" key to set an in point. Press the "O" key to set an out point.

   b. Press "G" to clear the in and out points.

2. Press the "V" key to splice in your clip that you set the in and out points on.

   a. Splicing a clip in before another clip will push that other clip over without deleting any of it.

   b. Press the "B" key to overwrite a clip in that you set the in and out points on. Overwriting a clip in before another clip will cause any part of the overlapping second clip to be deleted.

TOOLBARS/TRIMMING A CLIP

Important Note: If you have certain clips you do or do not want to trim, be sure to highlight or un-highlight them in the track area located to the left of the sequence.

1. To work with the clips you need to learn to use the toolbar to the left containing the colored arrows. Note, the icon on top of the menu links video with audio clips. If you wish,

click it, and this will allow you to only select an audio or video track independent from what audio or video it was originally paired up with.

a. Red Arrow Icon — Segment mode (Lift/Overwrite)

    i. SHIFT + "A"

    ii. This will allow you to select clips and OVERWRITE other clips. You can drag the clip and move it where you want, but it will delete parts of another clip if you drag the clip on top of another.

b. Yellow Arrow Icon — Segment Mode (Extract / Splice)

    i. SHIFT + "S"

    ii. This will allow you to select clips and PUSH them into other clips. This will shift any other surrounding clip to the sides.

c. Red Bars Icon — Overwrite Trim

    i. SHIFT + "D"

    ii. This will allow you to trim one side of a clip, which will ONLY DELETE parts of whatever clip you have selected for trimming.

d. Yellow Bars Icon — Ripple Trim

    i. SHIFT + "F"

    ii. This will allow you to trim one side of a clip, which will either DELETE OR EXTEND whatever clip you have selected. When you use this tool, the media after the trim you do will MOVE/ADJUST to the point of the actual trim.

2. The second way to trim involves pressing the "U" key.

a. METHOD 1 with "U" key — Drag your blue timeline indicator to a clip edge in the sequence you want to trim. Press the "U" key. There should now be a purple line in between your clips. This is known as the double roller trim feature. You can then manually drag the purple line with your mouse to where you want the trim to be.

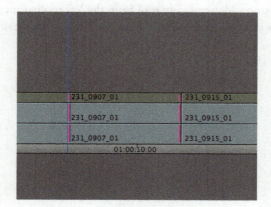

b. METHOD 2 with "U" key — Select the Red Arrow Toolbar Icon and click the clip you wish to trim. Hit the "U" key and you should have double rollers on either side of the clip.

c. METHOD 3 with "U" key — Press your mouse button down in the gray area above your sequence. Click and drag to an area in the timeline for what clips you want to trim. Release the mouse when you have your desired area and the purple line should appear on the selected clips.

HOW TO ADD AUDIO AND VIDEO TRACKS

To add an additional video track, press COMMAND + "Y". To add an additional audio track, press COMMAND + "U".

HOW TO MAKE DISSOLVES

Drag your blue timeline bar in between two clips where you wish to make a dissolve. You may also choose to select a clip area via one of the previously listed methods, such as clicking and dragging an area to get the purple trim tool. Next, navigate to the upper toolbar and select the "Quick Transition" icon.

Here you can set the duration of the dissolve by changing the amount of frames (a higher numbers results in more frame, which creates a longer dissolve).

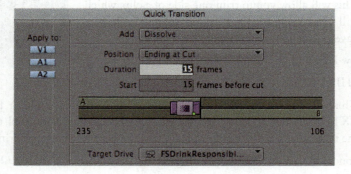

Click "Add", not "Add to Render".

Important Note: In the dissolve window, be sure to only have the video or audio tracks selected to which you want the dissolve applied.

Once the Dissolve is in your sequence or clip, you also have the ability to manually adjust its length. Select the Transition Manipulation tool from the left toolbar menu. Move your cursor over the dissolve to now change its position. You can also click on the small black circles to adjust the dissolves length.

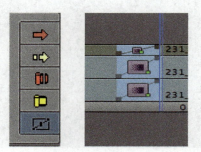

AUDIO WORK

HOW TO ADJUST AUDIO LEVELS

Navigate to the lower left-hand corner in the timeline window and click the fast menu icon.

Select Audio > Volume. You may also select waveform, which will display the audio waveform information in the timeline.

Navigate to a clip you wish to adjust audio on with the blue timeline indicator and press the apostrophe key ('). This will set a keyframe in the audio that you can adjust manually.

Important Note: You will need your audio tracks highlighted to create keyframes. Make sure no other audio tracks are highlights or other keyframes will be created in those audio clips as well.

Move your cursor over the black dot, and a hand should appear. You can now move your keyframe up and down to adjust its audio level. To move the keyframe right or left, hold down the OPTION key, click the keyframe, and drag left or right.

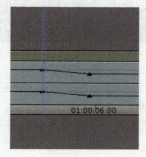

If you make your audio clip bigger for a wider range of sound levels, hold down COMMAND + "L". Press this multiple times to make the track bigger. To make the track smaller hold down COMMAND + "K".

EFFECTS

Navigate to the upper menu and select Tools > Effect Editor.

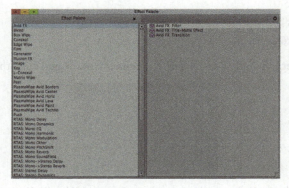

This will open up an effect bin. Select your desired effect and drag it onto the desired clip.

This will only add the effect as a preview form. Select the Render Effect button from the upper toolbar to render any effects.

ADDING TEXT

To add text select Clip → New Title. You can choose to edit your title either in Marquee or Title Tool. (Marquee is a little beefier.)

After you make your title, save it into a bin. You can then add it to a timeline just like you can a piece of video.

ADDITIONAL SHORTCUTS

1. Press and hold COMMAND while dragging with your mouse. This will act as a magnetic time bar, and your timeline blue bar will "link" to the edges of clips instead of having to zoom in to find the edge.

2. Use the "Add Edit" icon to cut a clip already in your sequence if you want to trim the clip in a certain part.

PREPARING FOR EXPORT

1. From the dialog box check the "Format" tab. Make sure it is at the correct settings for the project.

2. Check the video quality menu at the bottom of the sequence. A green and/or yellow box represents the menu. Make sure it is set to full quality (green).

3. Make sure you have no offline media. Clips in your timeline will appear RED if offline.

4. Optional step: If you have a mix of high-definition and standard-definition materials, you will need to transcode at this point to the same media type (MXF). This will rarely occur.

5. Create mixdowns. At this point you will create a video and audio mixdown. This process will render all effects and take all your clips and make one media file.

   a. Video Mixdown: Mark in and out points at the beginning and end of your sequence. Make sure you have selected all the video tracks you want included in the mixdown. Go to Special > Video Mixdown. You select your Target Bin, your Target Drive and your Target Resolution and click OK. The new sequence will appear in your bin.

   b. Audio Mixdown: Again mark in and out points for your sequence, and select the tracks you want included in the mixdown. Go to Special > Create Audio Mixdown. Select the stereo button and set the Target Stereo Track to the next available Track Number. **Select save premix so a copy of your original tracks is saved.** Click OK.

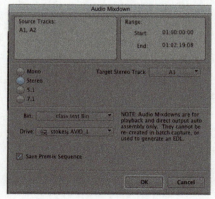

6. Create a new sequence from a mixdown. After you created the audio mixdown, it should have appeared on your timeline.

   a. Delete all other audio and video tracks, leaving only the audio mixdown. (Deselecting the track you want to KEEP and hitting the yellow extract button can do this.)

   b. Bring up the video mixdown in your source monitor and add it to your timeline. Tip: Hit home on the sequence to make sure your edit point is at 00:00:00.

   c. Play back and make sure the audio and video match.

EXPORT

1. Make sure you have cleared any In/Out points on your timeline. If you only want to export a portion of your timeline set the in and out points.

2. From your bin, right-click on the sequence you wish to export. Select export and choose your setting.

3. Select the location you wish to save the file. This should be in one of two locations:

   a. Managed Space (either individual or group/class)

   b. External Drive

   Rename the file as instructed for the project. Hit OK.

4. Once you have exported the file, make sure you playback the file in QuickTime in case there are issues.

CLOSING AVID

1. Closing a Project: Close all the bins. This will bring you back to Select Project.

2. Closing AVID: From Select Project, select Quit. From an open project, Avid Media Composer > Quit Avid Media Composer > Leave.

FINAL CUT PRO GUIDE

(Courtesy of Kyle Miller)

While you're working on stories, Final Cut Pro (FCP) saves automatically. But it's how you save your library, event and project that's key!

LIBRARIES, EVENTS AND PROJECTS

- **Library:** Make sure your library is saved to an external storage device! If not, FCP won't know where to look for your files.
  - **To begin:** Go to File-New Library-Save to your storage device.
  - **If saved:** Double-click your library in your storage device. It will then open in FCP.
  - **To double-check this:**
    - In "library properties" in the inspector (top right of screen in FCP), it should list your library name and underneath have your storage device as the location.
  - "Media" and "Cache" should default to your library (listed underneath).
  - Delete the "untitled" library underneath so files and events don't get mixed. (Right-click "untitled," then "close library untitled".)
- **Event:** Your event is where you upload all of your footage from your story. Have a folder in your storage device with your footage and in that folder, separate as much as you can into b-roll, audio, interviews, and so on.
  - **In FCP:** File-New-Event.
    - Label your event either your topic or "video story," something that you'll know what it is.
    - **Make sure the event saves back into your library!**
  - **To import your files:** File-Import-Media.
    - Click the folder with all your footage
    - **Make sure all the files are saved/added to your event!**
- **Project:** Once your library and event are created, the "project" is the timeline where you'll piece together all of your footage for your story.
  - **In FCP:** File-New-Project.
    - Label your project as "final story," or something that you'll know what it is. Your label will appear in the top left corner of your timeline just underneath the "keyword" icon.
    - **Make sure your project saves back into your event!**

EDITING

Editing in FCP gets easier with practice. Here are some tips:

- **Adding Keywords**
  - Adding keywords takes some time in the short term, but in the long term, it will really help you piece together your story. That way, you won't have to waste time hunting around for your files. I'd suggest having keywords for narration, b-roll, interviews, audio and video.

- To use keywords, select the key icon (it will turn blue), then select your video files and type in keywords to give additional labels to your footage. This will create folders in your event for those keywords and move the footage in there.

- **Selecting Files**
  - When you click on a video file in FCP, it will outline in a yellow box.
  - **If you want the entire clip:** Drag it to your timeline.
  - **If just a portion of clip:** Use the in and out points. If your timing is off when you hit the I/O keys, on the edges of the box, you can adjust its width, that is, how long you want the clip to be. You'll see the seconds adjust when you're dragging the clip. Drag the yellow box left or right as necessary, then move the clip to timeline.

- **Tools**
  - **Select:** The default tool. In this, when you drag clips to the timeline, they'll click together in chronological order.
  - **Position:** Use this if you want a clip at a specific time or need to move a clip back and forth, add a clip at a specific time, and so forth. Using this does create black space, so make sure that's deleted (it's a black box that you can highlight like a clip, but there's nothing there).
  - **Blade:** Use this to cut a clip at a certain point. Remember to go back to other tools once finished with the Blade, as you don't want to keep cutting your clips!

- **In Timeline**
  - **B-roll clips in timeline should be five to seven seconds long. Shorter, and we can't see enough of the clip to understand why it's there. Too long and it gets repetitive.**
  - Insert your narration and interviews first. Then, place b-roll on top of the narration and interviews: a connected clip.
  - Whatever the clip is on top is the clip that we will see. . .we don't see anything underneath (exception is lower thirds).
  - **Overall, avoid:**
    - Choppy edits of audio.
    - **NO BLACK SPACE!** Have b-roll over all narration and interviews. There should be clean edits of all video transitions in your story. Even the shortest black space is noticeable.
    - You will have to zoom in close to see this.
    - If using images, make sure there's no video underneath and that they're clear and in focus. If using images not your own, get permission from the user, and indicate that on screen with a caption.

- **Specific Editing Techniques**
  - **Lower Thirds**
    - Use lower thirds for all interviews. It is the "Titles" tab (T) on the toolbar.
      - Use "Basic Lower Third." Include person's name and relevant title, giving us visual information for story.
    - Lower third should appear for three to four seconds the first time we see the interviewee talking. It should not appear over b-roll.

○ **B-Roll, Narration and Interviews**

❖ Your interviewee should appear on screen. But we shouldn't see them in the entire clip. Have them appear for four to five seconds, then cut to b-roll footage.

❖ Whether you use narration or just interviews depends on what you think best tells the story; if you're unsure, I'd suggest narration. You don't need to be on camera at all. Just record narration with audio recorder.

❑ Local news stations are great for seeing how narration is used in a packaged video story.

❖ **If using narration:** Have a lead-in to your interview. It shouldn't be very detailed—you don't want to say so much that the interview is pointless—but should serve as an introduction to an interview in your story. For example:

❑ "Kyle Miller, a multimedia instructor at the University of Iowa, talks about how changes in media technology affect broadcast quality."

❑ **The general format:** Narration-Interview-Narration-Interview-Narration . . .

❖ **If using interviews:** Use the best pieces of your interview to tell the story and make sure your transitions are strong.

○ **Audio Quality**

❖ **B-Roll Volume:** You'll want b-roll volume for natural sound where it fits best in the story. For other clips, lots of b-roll sound will distract from the interview and/or narration.

❑ On clips with audio, you'll see a volume bar. Drag the volume bar down to mute the audio:

❖ **Synchronizing Clips:** If you are recording audio separately from the camera, you can then synchronize the clips in FCP.

❑ Edit this audio in Audacity or Audition, if need be.

❑ Select your audio that goes with clip.

❑ Hold "COMMAND," and select the audio file and corresponding video clip.

❑ Right click and select "Synchronize Clips."

○ It will save it into your event at the top. Drag this clip to your timeline.

❖ **Interviews:** Sometimes audio may only record in one channel (generally, whatever input you plugged a microphone cord into). To make sure we hear it in both channels:

❑ Select your interview clip.

- ❑ In Inspector: click the "Audio" tab (top center of the inspector), and click "show" in Channel Configuration.
- ❑ Instead of Stereo, click the dropdown menu to "Dual Mono."

EXPORTING VIDEO AND EMBEDDING ON WORDPRESS

When you're done with your project and need to export, you need to export to YouTube. Make sure you have an account (if you have a Gmail account, it's included).

- • There are two ways to export your video:
  - ○ **Share → YouTube**
    - ❖ Login to YouTube. In settings change video to "public."
    - ❖ Then, export it.
    - ❖ Watch the timer at the center to see when it uploads. You can't embed it until it gets to 100 percent, and this takes time!
  - ○ If direct to YouTube doesn't work, follow these alternate steps:
    - ❖ **Share → Apple Devices 1080p**
    - ❖ Click the "Settings tab" and in the "When Done" option, change from "Add to playlist" to "Do Nothing."
    - ❖ Click "Next" and save to your external storage device. Click "Save."
    - ❖ It will take a while to export. When done, log into YouTube and upload the file (make sure it's "public" not private).

- • **To embed in WordPress**
  - ○ When you're logged into YouTube, underneath your video you'll see a "Share" option. There will be a link that looks similar to this: http://youtu.be/YOyHlfYDCqA .
  - ○ **Copy this link and paste into a post. Don't just copy/paste the website URL.**

MAKING A VIDEO USING PREMIERE

(Courtesy of Dr. Joe Dennis, Piedmont College)

1. Open Premiere.

   a. Select "new project" and create name for project.

   b. Make sure "default scale to frame size" is selected under Premiere => Preferences => General

   c. Make sure Workspace is set to editing (Window => Workspaces).

2. Import all video (interviews and b-roll).

3. Edit your interview.

   a. Double click interview clip in workspace to place it in the preview screen. Press space bar to listen to your interview.

      i. Select your in point by pressing "I".

      ii. Select your out point by pressing "O".

      iii. Drag selection to the program screen.

   b. Continue editing interview by following steps above.

4. Insert b-roll.

   a. Double click b-roll clip in workspace to place it in the preview screen.

   b. Select in point and out point (see above).

   c. Drag selection to the timeline in empty track above the interview piece. To drag only the video, select the "drag video only" button at the bottom of the preview screen and drag from there.

   d. NOTE: The b-roll should be placed over all "jump cuts" in the interview. Also, punctuation is a good place to drag b-roll.

5. Insert lower third slide on the first slide.

   a. Make sure scrubber is on the first slide.

   b. Select Title => New Title => Default Still.

      i. Select "T" tool and type in name, title of subject.

      ii. Adjust font, size, color in right-hand pane.

      iii. Select arrow tool and move title to desired location.

6. Insert ending credit slide after last slide.

   a. Make sure scrubber is after the last slide (on black).

   b. Select Title => New Title => Default Still.

      i. Select "T" tool and type in © (option-G), the year and your name and email address.

    ii. Adjust font, size, color in right-hand pane.

    iii. Select arrow tool and move title to desired location.

7. Insert video transitions.

    a. Open "Effects" tab in workspace (you may have to click on the double arrow in the upper right hand corner to find the Effects tab).

    b. Go to Video Transitions => Dissolve => Cross Dissolve.

    c. Drag Cross Dissolve to desired location in timeline. Place it directly on top of desired dissolve location.

    d. Drag Dip to Black on top of ending credit slide.

8. Save file, then export as QuickTime.

GLOSSARY

180-degree rule: An approach to capturing and editing video that keeps all action on one side of a 180-degree axis to avoid "jump cuts" and disorienting video.

5W's and 1H: The staple crop of an inverted-pyramid lead: the "who," "what," "when," "why," "where" and "how" of the story a writer wishes to tell.

Abbreviation: A series of letters created through an abbreviation of a word that is pronounced letter by letter. IRS and CIA are examples of this. In broadcast, letters within an abbreviation must be separated with hyphens for proper pronunciation: I-R-S and C-I-A.

Absolute privilege: A legal standard that allows officials to make statements in their official roles without fear of libel.

Accuracy: A journalistic standard that requires content to be correct.

Acronym: A series of letters created through an abbreviation of a word that is pronounced as a single term. NATO and AIDS are examples of this.

Active media: A form of content or a media platform in which the user must interact with the material to gain information. A website would be an example of active media.

Active voice: A form of sentence structure that places the subject in a position where it is performing the action in the verb. The noun-verb-object structure denotes active voice: "Bill hit the ball."

Actual malice: A standard of fault in libel cases that requires the plaintiff to show that the publisher of the content acted with a reckless disregard for the truth.

This is the standard used for public figures in libel suits, and it is more difficult to prove than negligence.

Agenda: A formal document listing the topics slated for discussion or approval at a meeting. Public agencies must make these available to reporters and other interested citizens in advance of the event.

Ambient sound: Also called natural sound, ambient sound is the auditory elements captured as part of a broadcast story that occur naturally on location. Water rushing along a raging river and chickens clucking at a farm are examples of ambient sound.

Amphicar: A 1960s vehicle that doubled as both a car and a boat.

Analytics: A term describing how media outlets examine their audience members in terms of the content viewed, the amount of time spent on the site and the routes the readers took to arrive at the site. This allows for the systematic assessment of a digital audience.

Attribution: Information included with a quote to help readers understand the source of the content.

Audience centricity: An approach to journalism that focuses on the interests and needs of the audience while conveying content to readers and viewers. Journalists who apply this standard ask, "What do people want to know, and how would they prefer to learn it?"

Autofocus: A technique used to sharpen a frame for a still image or video shot that relies on the camera to create a specific focal point. This technique can be problematic in video shooting, as the camera may not select the proper element in the frame to sharpen or it may repeatedly attempt to focus during your shoot, thus creating awkward video.

Beat reporting: A news-gathering approach in which journalists cover areas of specific news.

Bill of Rights: The first 10 amendments to the U.S. Constitution.

Blog: A shortened version of "web log." It refers to a storytelling approach that uses short posts and bits of information logged on a website in reverse chronological order.

Boom microphone: A large audio-gathering device that attaches to a large pole and is used to gather sound from a distance.

Breaking news: An event that takes place without prior notice and requires journalistic coverage. Fires, robberies and shootings fit into this category.

Bridge: The second paragraph of an expanded inverted-pyramid story that helps move readers from the lead into the body of the story.

Broadcast lead: The introductory sentence in a broadcast story that works like a headline in text-based journalism to draw the attention of the audience members.

B-roll: Video used to provide images that showcase what the reporter is saying in the script.

Built-in microphone: An audio-gathering tool that is integrated into a digital audio or video device.

Caption: Also known as a cutline, this text accompanies a still image to explain what is happening within the photo as well as some context to explain why the image has storytelling value.

Categorical imperative: An ethical standard that requires individuals to determine right and wrong before acting and then accept those standards in others as well.

Child Online Protection Act: A federal law passed in 1998 that attempted to restrict online access by minors to material seen as harmful. The law was struck down over time, with a final defeat occurring in 2009.

Chronological approach: The telling of a story in the order in which the events of the story occurred. This is

in opposition to the inverted pyramid, in which content is arranged in descending order of importance.

Closed-ended question: An inquiry meant to induce a simple, nonelaborative answer. "Did you win the game?" is an example of a closed-ended question.

Close-up shot: Also known as a detail shot, this video approach zooms in on a small bit of action. It is useful for otherwise undetectable action, such as fingers typing on a keyboard or a doctor stitching up a wound.

Communications Decency Act of 1996: A piece of U.S. legislation passed in 1996 in an initial attempt to regulate pornography online. Section 230 of this act provides the owners of websites with legal protection against libelous comments posted there by people who don't work for the sites, such as commenters.

Compensatory damages: Real losses an individual can demonstrate during a libel case while seeking financial restitution. If a libelous statement led to someone being fired, that person can show a financial loss of salary and benefits, thus demonstrating actual damages.

Conceptual beat: An area of news coverage based on more ethereal concepts, such as multiculturalism or data-driven journalism.

Conflict: One of the five key interest elements. This element emphasizes situations in which two or more people or groups are competing for a mutually exclusive goal.

Conflict of interest: A situation in which an individual has competing and incompatible interests.

Critical thinking: As defined by the Foundation for Critical Thinking, this is an approach to analyzing and evaluating an individual's thought process with a view toward improving it.

Crop: An editing approach that removes extraneous material from the outer edges of a still image or video frame. This allows the key element of the shot to become more prominent.

Cut: A sharp transition from one shot to the next shot in video.

Cutline: See **caption**.

Data journalism: An approach to reporting in which statistical analyses provide the underlying value of the story the journalist wants to tell.

Dead art: A negative term used to describe photos that lack people, action or interaction. A photograph of a storefront or a plot of land would be an example of dead art.

Demographics: Measurable aspects of a group you hope to reach. Demographics commonly include age, gender, race, education and relationship status.

Demolisticles: A term coined by journalist Chadwick Matlin to describe postings that target people based on specific areas of interest, such as growing up in a certain area or being part of a particular group.

Digital single-lens reflex: Also known as a DSLR, this form of high-end camera uses a mirror-based system and an optical viewfinder to capture still images on a digital medium as opposed to film.

Direct quotes: Information taken from a source in a word-for-word fashion, placed between quotation marks and attributed to that source.

Drone journalism: The use of an unmanned aerial vehicle (UAV) to collect video and/or audio.

Ethics: Guiding principles that shape the actions of individuals as part of a social contract.

Event lead: A lead format used to highlight important aspects of a meeting, a speech, a news conference or another gathering. These should highlight the action of the event (the board voted to do X), as opposed to the existence of the event (the board held a meeting).

Fade: A transition technique in video editing in which one shot replaces the other by dissipating while the other shot emerges from behind. This form of transition is rarely appropriate for news coverage.

Fairness: A journalistic standard that requires reporters to provide equal standing to sources and ideas within a story as opposed to favoring one side or one individual over the others.

Fake news: A term that emerged in the mid-2010s to describe content that is purposefully false in hopes of drawing audience members through partisan ideology or shocking headlines. It is also used to describe content that individuals dislike in an attempt to discredit the material.

False light: The publication of material in such a way as to inaccurately depict an individual, thus causing harm to that person.

Fame: One of the five key interest elements. This element emphasizes the overall importance of the individual involved in the content. Subjects who fit into this interest area can be important over an extended period of time or be living out their "15 minutes of fame."

First Amendment: The first of 10 amendments outlined in the Bill of Rights. It guarantees freedom of speech, freedom of the press, freedom to peaceably assemble, freedom to petition the government for redress of grievances and freedom of religion.

Flow: The smoothness of movement among elements of a story or through questions within an interview.

FOCII: A memory device helpful in remembering the five interest elements: fame, oddity, conflict, immediacy and impact.

Fourth Estate: A term used to refer to journalists.

Frame: An action that places the subject of the shot into the viewfinder of the camera. It can also refer to the material that you selected in the viewfinder for capturing. If you frame your shot well, the subject will look natural in the image. If you don't, the source can look tiny or squished in the shot.

Freedom of Information Act: A federal law that provides access to documents and information crafted by public officials. States have similar laws known as "open-records laws" or "sunshine laws" that provide access to these types of items on a more local level. The act is intended to keep public officials honest and provide transparency in governmental dealings.

Gamer: A synonym for a game story.

Geographic beat: An area of news coverage based on a specific region of a state or city.

Geographic information: An audience characteristic media practitioners rely on to target audience members based on the audience's physical location.

Golden mean: An ethical standard that attempts to find the most good for all people involved in an ethical dilemma.

Hashtag: A social media tool that allows users to include a pound sign (#) at the front of a term to identify content on a given topic. Users can then choose to follow the hashtag to remain informed on that issue.

Hit-and-run journalism: A reporting approach in which journalists cover stories but fail to follow up on them.

Hyperbole: A statement that is so ridiculously overblown that it could not be reasonably believable.

Hyperpartisan: An extreme form of bias toward one's own viewpoint.

Immediacy: One of the five key interest elements. This element emphasizes the timely nature of content, with the newest information being seen as the most important.

Impact: One of the five key interest elements. This element emphasizes the degree to which the information will affect the audience members. It can be measured quantitatively and qualitatively.

Indirect quotes: Information taken from a source and boiled down into basic information and attributed to that source. This form of quoting is also known as paraphrase.

Infotainment: A form of media that provides entertaining content in the guise of information dissemination. Comedy shows that provide news content or viral videos meant to amuse people fall into this category.

Interest elements: Informational aspects of content that are used to draw audience members to content.

Interesting-action lead: A form of summary lead in which the author relies on the value of the "what" to draw readers into the story. These are used when oddity, conflict or impact is a key interest element in a piece of copy.

Invasion of privacy: The violation of a person's right to be left alone.

Inverted pyramid: A format of journalistic writing in which information is provided in descending order of importance. The higher a fact is in the copy, the more valuable the writer thinks it is.

Jump cut: A problematic transition between two shots often caused by a failure to vary the shots properly or breaking the 180-degree rule.

Kabob format: An approach to narrative writing that uses an anecdote or narrative thread to establish the point of the story, transitions into a nut graph and then provides several chunks of content that are segmented categorically.

Lavalier microphone: A small and unobtrusive audio-gathering device that clips onto the clothing of an interview subject.

Lead: Occasionally spelled "lede," this is the first sentence in an inverted-pyramid piece of copy. It traditionally outlines the most important facts of the overall piece in 25 to 35 words.

Libel: A false published statement that damages a person's reputation.

Limited-purpose public figures: People who aren't as famous as politicians or celebrities but have become known in relation to a specific topic or issue.

Lite-brite: A story that lacks consequence or value but amuses and entertains readers.

Loaded question: An inquiry that includes a faulty presumption or intends to trap a source into answering in an unfair way. "Senator, have you stopped beating your wife yet?" is an example of a loaded question because it doesn't offer the source a chance to proclaim innocence. "Yes" means that the senator had beaten his wife but has since stopped. "No" means that the beatings continue at the senator's house.

Localization: A story format in which a reporter covers a broader issue from a local angle. A story that explores how the Affordable Care Act will affect doctors within a newspaper's audience is an example of this form of story.

Long shot: Also called a wide shot, this type of video approach is used to showcase a lot of action within a frame to provide the viewers with a sense of place or activity.

Look room: The space in a framed shot that prevents the subject from staring directly into the outside edge of the shot. The look room should be present in the direction that the subject is looking or moving.

Manual focus: A technique used to sharpen a frame for a still image or video shot that relies on the shooter to adjust the focal point.

"Many people" lead: A lead that conveys the assumed mood of a larger group to transpose it against reality. This lead is risky because it provides an overgeneralization with regard to how people think or act without supporting it with facts or research.

Many-to-many model: The digital media approach in which content is shared socially among many publishers and consumed by many readers. In this approach, people can be both senders and receivers of content.

Media diet: The platforms and outlets that make up the information individuals consume on a daily basis.

Medium shot: A video approach that provides a smaller slice of a larger event. It is used to capture interaction between two people, the actions of a single individual or a soundbite. It is the most useful and often-used shot in broadcast.

Microblogging: A broader term for services like Twitter that allow for users to tell stories in short bursts to a social media audience.

Mini-jack port: A connecting option for input or output on a video camera.

Minutes: A formal record of statements, activities and votes that occurred during a meeting.

Mug shot: A photograph of an individual from the middle of the chest to the top of the head.

Name-recognition lead: A form of summary lead in which the author relies on the importance of the "who" to draw readers into the content. These are used when fame is a key interest element in a piece of copy.

Narrative thread: An individual or element within a story that serves as an exemplar to tie multiple elements of the article together.

Narrative writing: An approach to journalism that mimics traditional storytelling as opposed to relying on an inverted-pyramid approach. It involves scene-setting, description and less rigid structure.

Natural sound: See **ambient sound**.

Negligence: A standard of fault in libel cases that requires the plaintiff to show only that the publisher of the content did not make reasonable efforts to prevent the libelous activity. This is a standard used for private individuals in libel suits, and it is easier to prove than actual malice.

News conferences: Also called press conferences, these events allow a group or an organization to gather journalists at a single point in time.

News feature: A story format that has elements of interest for readers but lacks hard-news aspects. Coverage of a parade or a business opening would qualify as this kind of story.

Niche: A small, specialized area of information on which a media outlet might provide coverage.

Nonlinear storytelling: A web-based approach to content provision that creates self-contained blocks of content that can be consumed in any way the audience desires. This is in opposition to traditional storytelling, in which journalists determine a specific and linear path that readers must follow to consume the content.

Nut graph: Occasionally spelled "nut graf," this chunk of information sits directly between the anecdotal opening of a narrative story and the remainder of the body. Its purpose is to tell the readers what the story will explain and why the story matters to them.

Obituary: A profile story written about a person who has died.

Objectivity: A journalistic standard that requires news writers to avoid taking sides or infusing their opinions into stories.

Oddity: One of the five key interest elements. This element emphasizes rare feats, strange occurrences and "news of the weird."

Off the record: An agreement between a source and a journalist to conduct an interview in which the source will not be identified within the story.

Official source: A person who provides information to journalists as an authoritative representative of a larger group or organization, such as a police officer speaking on behalf of law enforcement.

One-party consent: A standard for recording conversations that requires only one of the people involved in the conversation to be aware of the recording in order for it to be legal.

One-to-many model: The traditional mass media approach in which one source provided content to a large audience in a one-way conduit of information. Newspapers and broadcast news reports are examples of this model.

Open-ended question: An inquiry meant to induce an elaborative answer. Interviewers often use "how" or "why" as part of the question to draw more information from a source. "How did you get the bill passed?" is an example of an open-ended question.

Pace: The speed at which a reader can move through a story based on how it is structured. This speed is also influenced by the use of punctuation and the length of sentences in the piece.

Package: A traditional news-story format in broadcast television. Reporters create these stories in advance of the newscast, and they include the voice track of the reporter, video that matches the script, two or more soundbites and a sign-off. These last between 1:30 and 2 minutes.

Pageview: A visit by one reader to a particular page on a website.

Pan: When a videographer moves a camera from side to side or up and down while recording.

Paraphrase: See **indirect quote**.

Partial quotes: A mix of direct and indirect quoting in which a fragment of information is taken directly from a source and placed between quotation marks, with the rest of the information surrounding it written in paraphrase. This form of quoting is used to place emphasis on a key element of a statement a source made.

Passive medium: A form of content or a media platform in which the user is not required to interact with the material to gain information. Television is a form of passive media.

Passive voice: A form of sentence structure that places the subject of the sentence in a position in which it is receiving the action of the verb: "The ball was hit by Bill."

Personality profile: A feature story that explores the life of an individual through in-depth reporting and observation.

Person-on-the-street interview: A type of interview a journalist conducts to get the perspective of "real people" for inclusion in a news story.

Pie chart: A type of graphic that shows the data components that create a larger whole.

Platform: A media format used to deliver content including, but not limited to, print, broadcast and online dissemination.

Post: A bit of information placed on a blog or social networking site.

Press release: A form of public relations material that is issued to the media to give them information on a specific topic.

Principle of utility: An ethical standard that attempts to create the largest overall benefit through the minimization of harm or the maximizing of gain, regardless of the impact on specific individuals involved in the dilemma.

Pronouncer: A phonetic explanation included in a broadcast script to help reporters and anchors say a word properly.

Pseudo-event: A term coined by historian Daniel Boorstin to describe an event or activity arranged for the sole purpose of drawing public attention and media coverage.

Psychographic information: A set of characteristics audience members hold, including but not limited to personality traits, values, interests and attitudes.

Public figures: People frequently in the public eye, such as politicians and celebrities. People included in this category must demonstrate actual malice in order to win a libel suit.

Punitive damages: Financial penalties a court assesses to a libel defendant to punish the person or organization for acting irresponsibly.

Qualified privilege: A legal standard that allows journalists to quote officials acting in their official capacity without fear of libel.

Question lead: A lead that asks the readers something instead of making a declarative statement. These leads are risky because they presuppose that the reader and the writer views the topic in a similar fashion.

Quote lead: A lead that uses a famous quotation or a bit of text taken directly from a story source to begin a piece of copy. These leads are often confusing or rely on cliché.

Raw video: Unedited content provided to the audience exactly as it was shot.

Reader: The simplest type of broadcast story. It has an anchor or reporter reading a script while on air. These last 10 to 20 seconds each.

Real people: Individuals who lack an official role but are affected by newsworthy events, such as a citizen protesting a court decision or a citizen whose house will be demolished to make room for a freeway.

Reporter's privilege: A term used to describe a shield law that protects journalists from having to reveal their sources in court.

Reporter's track: See **voicing**.

Rule of thirds: A guideline for framing photographs and video shots that uses a nine-panel grid to place subjects in an eye-pleasing portion of the frame. The rule dictates that the main element should reside where the lines of the grid intersect.

Said: The preferred verb of attribution, as it is nonjudgmental.

Scene setter: An opening approach in narrative writing that establishes the environment for the events to come as well as the characters who will be prominent within the story.

Script: The text of a broadcast story used to help reporters narrate a story. It also will include references to the use of video when applicable.

Secondary sources: Individuals that a journalist interviews to provide outside perspectives on the subject of a personality profile. For example, a coach would be a secondary source for a profile of a high school track athlete.

Second-day lead: A lead format used to update readers about an ongoing event or process. This format promotes the immediacy interest element, as it focuses on the newest developments on the topic.

Sedition Act: A rule of law passed during World War I that criminalized forms of speech and press that impugned the United States. It was repealed in 1920.

Self-determination: An ethical standard demanding that all people be treated with respect.

Sequencing: The ordering of video shots as part of a story.

Session duration: The length of time an individual spends on a particular website before leaving.

Shield laws: See **reporter's privilege**.

Shiny-object syndrome: A term that describes how new, shiny or fancy items easily distract people from what they are doing, regardless of the value of those new items. Think of a bird chasing a foil gum wrapper across a lawn for no good reason, and you get the idea.

Short Message Service (SMS): Also known as simple messaging service, this is another term for text messaging, referring to the way in which users can send short digital messages to one another via mobile devices.

Sign-off: A portion of a broadcast story in which a reporter signals the end of a piece by noting his or her name and the station's call sign: "For W-X-Y-Z, I'm Bill Smith."

Silos: A structural approach to teaching journalism in which students learn how skills or tools apply only to a specific aspect of the media, such as newspapers or broadcasting.

Smartphone: A hand-held mobile device that has multiple digital functions, such as the ability to record audio, shoot photos and capture video.

Smith Act: Also known as the Alien Registration Act of 1940, this law made it illegal to advocate the violent overthrowing of the United States government. It was repealed in 1952.

Social media: Digital information-sharing tools and approaches that allow people to gain information based on their interests from a variety of sources in a many-to-many media model.

Soundbite: Also known as a bite or actuality, this element of a broadcast story allows the source to speak to the audience in his or her own words on camera. This is the audio and video version of a direct quote in a text story.

Stereotype: A mental shortcut used to eliminate higher level thought processes. This can be problematic when applied to social or interpersonal situations.

Stick microphone: A handheld audio-gathering device that connects to a digital audio or video device.

Straw man: A pejorative term used to indicate the weakness in an opposing position an individual sets up for his or her own benefit in order to defeat it.

Subreddit: A specific area of a forum that is dedicated to a given topic on the Reddit website.

Summary lead: An inverted-pyramid-style lead that seeks to sum up the important elements of a piece of copy. It relies heavily on the 5Ws and 1H to determine which aspects of the piece are highlighted.

Sunshine Act: A federal law that requires governmental bodies to be open to the public in an attempt to create a higher level of transparency within the government.

Sunshine Laws: See **Freedom of Information Act**.

Super: A shorthand term used to describe text that is superimposed over video. This technique is often used to provide details about a scene or an individual.

Thematic beat: An area of news coverage based on specific topics, such as education, courts and religion.

Tracking: See **voicing**.

Topeka Test: A standard used to assess the amount and quality of the background information placed in a story.

Transparency: A journalistic standard that provides readers with the ability to see where the writers got their information and how they used it. This allows readers to form their own opinions on the matter instead of merely trusting the journalists.

Truth: The ultimate defense against a libel suit. Defamation must be false for it to rise to the standard of libel.

Twibel: A merging of the terms "Twitter" and "libel" to describe libelous acts perpetuated on social media platforms.

Unique visitor: A specific individual who views pages on a website during a specified period of time.

Utilitarianism: See **principle of utility**.

Veil of ignorance: An ethical standard demanding that all people and situations be treated equally when parsing an ethical dilemma.

Verification: A process of checking information to solidify its veracity.

Viral: A term used to describe content that spreads rapidly throughout the digital universe through social sharing.

Visit: An instance of an individual going to a website.

Voice-over: Also known as a VO. This form of broadcast story has a reporter or anchor reading a script on air while video on the topic is rolling for the audience members to see.

Voicing: Also known as tracking, this process involves the reporter recording the script for use as part of the package. Depending on the software, reporters can "track" the story into an empty file and place it into the package, or they can play the video once it is assembled and read the script on top of the video.

VO/SOT: Stands for voice-over/sound on tape and is a more complex version of a VO. This form of broadcast story operates like a VO, but includes one or more soundbites. VO/SOTs last about 35 to 40 seconds each.

Wallpaper: A derogatory term for video that doesn't enhance the storytelling of a story. This is video that only provides visual elements for the sake of having video. For example, a story on a city budget might include images of buildings or signs that feature the city's name.

Watchdog journalism: A reporting approach in which journalists inform the public about issues of importance based on the actions of public figures and institutions. Journalists serve the public trust in this approach by alerting citizens to illegal or unethical actions that governmental agencies or actors undertake.

Web 2.0: The phase of the World Wide Web in which content shifted from static content on websites to interactive content generated by users via social media.

Wide shot: See **long shot**.

Wipe: A transition technique in video editing in which one shot replaces the other in a left-to-right movement across the frame. This form of transition is rarely appropriate for news coverage.

Word picture: A visualization created by writing that allows readers to see what the journalist is describing in the mind's eye.

XLR input: A higher end connecting option for input on a video camera.

"You" lead: A lead format that uses the second-person point of view to address the audience directly. Although second-person writing is more accepted in broadcast format, text-based platforms often avoid this form of lead, as it often comes across as presumptive.

Zoom: A camera technique that closes in on the subject of the shot to make that person or thing appear increasingly larger.

NOTES

CHAPTER 1

1. Joseph Lichterman (2015, July 14). "New Pew Data: More Americans Are Getting Their News on Facebook and Twitter." Accessed at: http://www.niemanlab.org/2015/07/new-pew-data-more-americans-are-getting-news-on-facebook-and-twitter/.

2. Scott Hammond, Daniel Petersen, and Steven Thomsen (2000). "Print, Broadcast and On-line Convergence in the Newsroom." Journalism and Mass Communication Educator, 55, 16-26. Vincent F. Filak (2004). "Cultural Convergence: Intergroup Bias Among Journalists and Its Impact on Convergence." Atlantic Journal of Communication, 12(4), 216-232.

3. American Press Institute (2014, March 17). "The Personal News Cycle: How Americans Choose to Get Their News." Accessed at: https://www.americanpressinstitute.org/publications/reports/survey-research/personal-news-cycle/.

4. Will Oremus (2013, July 18). "The Rise of the Demolisticle." Slate. Accessed at: http://www.slate.com/articles/technology/future_tense/2013/07/demolisticles_buzzfeed_lists_crafted_for_specific_demographics_are_social.html.

5. Mallary Jean Tenore (2009, Sept. 15). "Koppel Criticizes Rise of Infotainment, Commentary That Disregards Facts." Accessed at: http://www.poynter.org/2009/koppel-criticizes-rise-of-infotainment-commentary-that-disregards-facts/98303/.

6. Scott Pelley (2017, March 26). "How Fake News Becomes a Popular, Trending Topic." "60 Minutes." Accessed at: http://www.cbsnews.com/news/how-fake-news-find-your-social-media-feeds/.

7. PR Newswire (2013, July 9) "National MyLife.com® Survey Reveals More Social Networks and Message Services, More Problems: Users Are Increasingly Overwhelmed, Overloaded." Accessed at: http://www.prnewswire.com/news-releases/national-mylifecom-survey-reveals-more-social-networks-and-message-services-more-problems-users-are-increasingly-overwhelmed-overloaded-214741101.html.

8. Kevin Mcspadden (2015, May 14). "You Now Have a Shorter Attention Span Than a Goldfish." Time. Accessed at: http://time.com/3858309/attention-spans-goldfish/.

9. Cathy McNamara Fitzgerald (2013, Aug. 27). "Readership Surveys: 10 Good Reasons Why." Accessed at: https://associationmediaandpublishing.org/sidebar/readership-surveys-10-good-reasons/.

10. Mu Lin (2014, May 29). "Web Analytics for Newsroom and Classroom: Essential Metrics Journalists Should Know and Use." MulinBlog. Accessed at: http://www.mulinblog.com/web-analytics-for-newsroom-and-classroom-essential-metrics-journalists-should-know-and-use/.

11. Stephen Reese and Jane Ballinger (2001). "The Roots of a Sociology of the News: Remembering Mr. Gates and Social Control in the Newsroom." Journalism Quarterly, 78(4), 641-658.

12. Samantha Schmidt and Lindsey Bever (2017, Feb. 3). "Kellyanne Conway Cites 'Bowling Green Massacre' That Never Happened to Defend Travel Ban." The Washington Post. Accessed at: https://www.washingtonpost.com/news/morning-mix/wp/2017/02/03/kellyanne-conway-cites-bowling-green-massacre-that-never-happened-to-defend-travel-ban/?utm_term=.0ae8054c3748.

13. Vincent F. Filak (2015). "Dynamics of Media Writing." Thousand Oaks, Calif.: Sage.

14. David Moye (2015, May 28). "Food Fight: Sabrina Davis Stabbed Woman in BBQ Argument Over Last Rib: Cops." Accessed at: http://www.huffingtonpost.com/2015/05/28/sabrina-a-davis-bbq_n_7455354.html.

15. "News: Weird." Toronto Sun. Accessed at: http://www.torontosun.com/news/weird.

CHAPTER 2

1. S. Holly Stocking and Paget H. Gross (1989). "How Do Journalists Think: A Proposal for the Study of Cognitive Bias in Newsmaking." ERIC Clearinghouse.
2. Richard Paul (2004). "The State of Critical Thinking Today." Accessed at: http://www.criticalthinking.org/pages/the-state-of-critical-thinking-today/523.
3. Robert Boostrom (2005). "Thinking: The Foundation of Critical and Creative Learning in the Classroom." New York: Teachers College Press.
4. Linda Elder and Richard Paul (2015). "Becoming a Critic of Your Thinking." Accessed at: http://www.criticalthinking.org/pages/becoming-a-critic-of-your-thinking/478.
5. Joe Kinchloe and Danny Weil (2004). "Critical Thinking and Learning: An Encyclopedia for Parents and Teachers." Westport, CT: Greenwood.
6. Susan T. Fiske and Shelly Taylor (2013). "Social Cognition: From Brains to Culture" (2nd Ed.). Thousand Oaks, CA: Sage.
7. Bob Baker (2001). "Newsthinking: The Secret of Making Your Facts Fall Into Place." Boston: Pearson.
8. CBS/AP (2016, March 1). "College President Resigns After 'Drown the Bunnies' Comment." Retrieved at: http://www.cbsnews.com/news/mount-st-marys-university-president-simon-newman-resigns/.

CHAPTER 4

1. Kate Fox. "The Smell Report." Accessed at: http://www.sirc.org/publik/smell_emotion.html.
2. Jane Stevens (2014). "Tutorial: Multimedia Storytelling: Learn the Secrets From Experts." Accessed at: https://multimedia.journalism.berkeley.edu/tutorials/starttofinish/.

CHAPTER 5

1. Maeve Duggan (2015, Aug. 19). "Mobile Messaging and Social Media 2015." Pew Research Center. Accessed at: http://www.pewinternet.org/2015/08/19/mobile-messaging-and-social-media-2015/.
2. Daniel Nations (2017, May 30). "What Is Social Media? Explaining the Big Trend." Lifewire. Accessed at: https://www.lifewire.com/what-is-social-media-explaining-the-big-trend-3486616.
3. John Rampton (2014, Sept. 29). "25 Ways to Grow Your Social Media Presence." Forbes. Accessed at: https://www.forbes.com/sites/johnrampton/2014/09/29/25-ways-to-grow-your-social-media-presence/#2497490362fb.
4. The Poke (2014, May 21). "The 25 Worst Best Spelling Mistakes on Twitter." Accessed at: http://www.thepoke.co.uk/2014/05/21/the-25-worst-best-spelling-mistakes-on-twitter/.
5. Geoff Weiss (2014, Dec. 5). "Sephora Mistakenly Rolls Out Vulgar Hashtag." Entrepreneur. Accessed at: http://www.entrepreneur.com/article/240530.
6. "Aurora Theater Shooting: The First Four Days of Coverage by the Denver Post." Accessed at: https://storify.com/denverpost/aurora-theater-shooting-recap.
7. "Sandy Hook School Shooting: How Newtown Was Covered." Accessed at: https://storify.com/DigitalFirst/sandy-hook.
8. Paul Mozur and Mark Scott (2016, Nov. 17). "Fake News in US Election? Elsewhere, That's Nothing New." The New York Times. Accessed at: http://www.nytimes.com/2016/11/18/technology/fake-news-on-facebook-in-foreign-elections-thats-not-new.html.
9. Craig Silverman (2016, Nov. 16). "This Analysis Shows How Fake Election News Stories Outperformed Real News on Facebook." Buzzfeed. Accessed at: https://www.buzzfeed.com/craigsilverman/viral-fake-election-news-outperformed-real-news-on-facebook?utm_term=.uyxXEVGWA#.fr8WDvZJ0.
10. Elyse Betters (2017, June 23). "What is the Point of Snapchat and How Does It Work?" Pocket Lint. Accessed at: http://www.pocket-lint.com/news/131313-what-s-the-point-of-snapchat-and-how-does-it-work.
11. Lauren Shaw and Rachel Barron (2015, Jan. 29). "The Creative and Offbeat Ways Journalists Are Using Snapchat." American Journalism Review. Accessed at: http://ajr.org/2015/01/29/creative-offbeat-ways-journalists-using-snapchat/.
12. Nisha Lilla Diu and Meabh Ritchie (2015, Feb. 9). "How Facebook Changed the World." The Telegraph. Accessed at: http://s.telegraph.co.uk/graphics/projects/youtube/.
13. Corky Siemaszko (2016, Jan. 25). "Mizzou Media Professor Melissa Click Charged With Siccing 'Muscle' on Reporter." NBC News. Accessed at: http://www.nbcnews.com/news/us-news/mizzou-media-professor-melissa-click-charged-siccing-muscle-reporter-n503871.
14. Megan Pruitt (2015, July 23). "Beginner's Guide to Periscope: What You Need to Know." Social Media Week. Accessed at: http://socialmediaweek.org/blog/2015/07/periscope-101/.
15. Cas McCullough (2015, Aug. 25). "6 Ways to Use Periscope for Your Business." Social Media Examiner.

Accessed at: http://www.socialmediaexaminer.com/6-ways-to-use-periscope-for-your-business/.

16. Anna Jasinski (2015, Aug. 12). "Periscope 101: How to Broadcast Street Journalism From Your Phone." PR Newswire. Accessed at: http://mediablog.prnewswire.com/2015/08/12/periscope-101-how-to-broadcast-street-journalism-from-your-phone/.

CHAPTER 7

1. Dennis Punzel (2016, Sept. 27). "Bucks: Team President Peter Feigin Sees Re-Energized Future for Franchise." Wisconsin State Journal. Accessed at: http://host.madison.com/wsj/sports/basketball/professional/bucks-team-president-peter-feigin-sees-re-energized-future-for/article_2edcf8d5-dcc5-51c6-a14e-ddbe432db1e0.html.

2. Mary Spicuzza and Charles F. Gardner (2016, Sept. 27). "Bucks President Walks Back Comments on Milwaukee Being 'Most Segregated, Racist' Place." Milwaukee Journal Sentinel. Accessed at: http://www.jsonline.com/story/news/local/milwaukee/2016/09/27/barrett-eager-work-bucks-after-most-segregated-comments/91162026/.

3. Susan Saulny (2009, Jan. 9). "Illinois House Impeaches Governor." New York Times. Accessed at: http://www.nytimes.com/2009/01/10/us/politics/10illinois.html?_r=0.

4. Ashley Rueff (2009, Feb. 9). "Milton Patterson: The Lone Vote Against Blagojevich Impeachment." Chicago Tribune/Huffington Post. Accessed at: http://www.huffingtonpost.com/2009/01/09/milton-patterson-the-lone_n_156625.html.

5. Edward Iwata (2004, July 8). "Enron's Ken Lay: Cuffed but Confident." USA Today. Accessed at: http://usatoday30.usatoday.com/money/industries/energy/2004-07-08-kenlay-cover_x.htm.

6. Gina Sunseri and Sylvie Rottman (2006, May 25). "Enron Verdict: Ken Lay Guilty on All Counts, Skilling on 19 Counts." ABC News. Accessed at: http://abcnews.go.com/Business/LegalCenter/story?id=2003728&page=1.

7. Scott Reinardy and Wayne Wanta (2015). "The Essentials of Sports Reporting and Writing," 2nd ed. New York: Routledge.

8. Gene Duffey (2013, Aug. 7). "Lavarnway Finds Redemption Following Wild First." MLB.com. Accessed at: http://m.mlb.com/news/article/56093818/.

9. Bob Glauber (2012, Oct. 27). "Twenty Years After Career-Ending Injury, Dennis Byrd Will Have Jersey Retired." Newsday. Accessed at: http://www.newsday.com/sports/football/jets/twenty-years-after-career-ending-injury-dennis-byrd-will-have-jersey-retired-1.4160947.

10. Associated Press. (1981, March 1). "Brett in Hospital for Surgery." New York Times. Accessed at: http://www.nytimes.com/1981/03/01/sports/brett-in-hospital-for-surgery.html.

11. Susan Svrluga (2016, May 24). "'Get off the Stage!' Crowd Yells at Commencement Speaker After She Uses Spanish, Mentions Trump." Washington Post. Accessed at: https://www.washingtonpost.com/news/grade-point/wp/2016/05/24/commencement-speaker-gets-booed-after-speaking-briefly-in-spanish-and-criticizing-trump/.

12. CBS News (2008, Feb. 7). "Six Dead in Missouri City Council Shooting." CBSNews.com. Accessed at: http://www.cbsnews.com/news/six-dead-in-missouri-city-council-shooting/.

13. Des Bieler (2016, Oct. 29). "Fan in Trump Mask Holds Noose Around Fan in Obama Mask at Wisconsin Game." Washington Post. Accessed at: https://www.washington-post.com/news/early-lead/wp/2016/10/29/fan-in-trump-mask-holds-noose-around-fan-in-obama-mask-at-wisconsin-game/.

14. Adam Nossiter and Elizabeth Paton (2016, Oct. 3). "Kim Kardashian Is Tied and Robbed of Millions in Jewels, French Police Say." New York Times. Accessed at: http://www.nytimes.com/2016/10/04/world/europe/kim-kardashian-robbed.html?_r=0.

CHAPTER 8

1. Jenna Glatzer (2004). "Make a Real Living as a Freelance Writer: How to Win Top Writing Assignments." Nomad Press.

2. Malcolm Gladwell (2004, Sept. 6). "The Ketchup Conundrum." Accessed at: http://gladwell.com/the-ketchup-conundrum/.

3. Dana Carvey (1995). "Critics' Choice." Accessed at: http://www.imdb.com/title/tt0236135/.

4. "Landlord Games." Milwaukee Journal Sentinel. Accessed at: http://projects.jsonline.com/topics/landlord-games/index.html.

5. Cary Spivak and Kevin Crowe (2016, April 23). "Former UW Star Devin Harris Behind Company That Racked Up Nearly $200,000 in Building Code Violations." Milwaukee Journal Sentinel. Accessed at: http://archive.jsonline.com/watchdog/watchdogreports/former-uw-star-devin-harris-behind-company-that-racked-up-nearly-200000-in-building-code-violation-b-376849101.html.

6. Cary Spivak and Kevin Crowe (2016, Sept. 5). "Harris' Property Firm Pays Off Taxes, Fines." Milwaukee Journal Sentinel. Accessed at: http://www.jsonline.com/story/news/investigations/2016/09/05/harris-property-firm-pays-off-taxes-fines/89774074/.

CHAPTER 9

1. Robert Papper (2012). "Broadcast News and Writing Stylebook" (5th ed.). Boston, MA: Pearson.

CHAPTER 10

1. Michael Hernandez (2013, March 5). "How to Choose a Video Camera for Broadcast Journalism." JEA Digital Media. Accessed at: http://www.jeadigitalmedia.org/2013/03/05/how-to-choose-a-video-camera-for-broadcast-journalism/.
2. Timothy R. Gleason (2015). "Photography." In V. Filak, Ed., "Convergent Journalism: An Introduction," 2nd ed., pp. 75–99. Burlington, MA: Focal Press.
3. Personal communication.

CHAPTER 12

1. Federal Communications Commission. Consumer Complaint Center. Accessed at: https://consumercomplaints.fcc.gov/hc/en-us/articles/202701094-Complaints-about-Broadcast-Journalism.
2. Robert Cannon (1996). "The Legislative History of Senator Exon's Communications Decency Act: Regulating Barbarians on the Information Superhighway." Federal Communications Law Journal, 51. Accessed at: http://www.cybertelecom.org/cda/cannon2.htm.
3. American Civil Liberties Union (1997). "Supreme Court Decision in Reno v ACLU, et al." Accessed at: https://www.aclu.org/legal-document/supreme-court-decision-reno-v-aclu-et-al.
4. Ashley Messenger (2015). "A Practical Guide to Media Law." Boston: Pearson.
5. Ibid.
6. Eriq Gardner (2016, May 5). "Arsenio Hall Sues Sinead O'Connor Over Accusation of Giving Drugs to Prince." Hollywood Reporter. Accessed at: http://www.hollywoodreporter.com/thr-esq/arsenio-hall-sues-sinead-oconnor-891136.

7. Lars Brandle (2017, Feb. 22), "Sinead O'Connor Apologizes to Arsenio Hall for Saying He Gave Prince Drugs." Billboard. Accessed at: http://www.billboard.com/articles/news/7701414/sinead-oconnor-apologizes-arsenio-hall-prince-drugs.
8. Corina Knoll (2014, Jan. 24). "Singer-Actress Courtney Love Wins Landmark Twibel Case." Los Angeles Times. Accessed at: http://articles.latimes.com/2014/jan/24/local/la-me-love-libel-20140125.
9. Simorangkir v. Cobain. Accessed at: http://www.courts.ca.gov/opinions/nonpub/B254895.PDF.
10. Eriq Gardner (2015, Aug. 27). "Courtney Love Ends Defamation Row With $350K Settlement." Hollywood Reporter. Accessed at: http://www.hollywoodreporter.com/thr-esq/courtney-love-ends-defamation-row-818025.
11. Digital Media Law Project. "Proving Fault: Actual Malice and Negligence." Accessed at: http://www.dmlp.org/legal-guide/proving-fault-actual-malice-and-negligence.
12. David Berg. "Damages in a Defamation Case." NOLO.com. Accessed May 24, 2016 at: http://www.nolo.com/legal-encyclopedia/damages-defamation-case.html.
13. Heron Marquez Estrada (2011, Nov. 8). "KSTP Hit With $1 Million Defamation Verdict." Minneapolis Star-Tribune. Accessed May 24, 2016 at: http://www.startribune.com/kstp-hit-with-1-million-defamation-verdict/133411953/.
14. Braun v. Flynt. Retrieved May 29, 2016 at: http://openjurist.org/726/f2d/245/braun-v-c-flynt.
15. Emily Field (2016, Jan. 16). "L.A. Businessman Wins Almost $40M in Defamation Suit." Law360.com. Accessed at: http://www.law360.com/articles/760728/la-businessman-wins-almost-40m-in-defamation-suit.
16. Katy Stech (2016, April 1). "West Coast Mint Files for Bankruptcy After Losing Defamation Suit." Wall Street Journal. Accessed at: http://www.wsj.com/articles/west-coast-mint-files-for-bankruptcy-after-losing-defamation-suit-1459553011.
17. Konstantine Kakaes (2016, April 21). "Drones Can Photograph Almost Anything. But Should They?" Columbia Journalism Review. Accessed at: http://www.cjr.org/the_feature/drones_can_photograph_almost_anything_but_should_they.php.
18. Jack Nicas (2015, May 13). "Drones Boom Raises New Question: Who Owns Your Airspace?" Wall Street Journal. Accessed at: http://www.wsj.com/articles/drones-boom-raises-new-question-who-owns-your-airspace-1431535417.
19. Josh Dooley (2016, April 12). "Drone Shot Down Over Norfolk." Baxter Bulletin. Accessed at: http://www

.thv11.com/features/drone-shot-down-over-norfork/129539865.

20. Matt Waite (2015, Feb. 15). "New Rules Governing Drone Journalism Are on the Way." Nieman Lab. Accessed at: http://www.niemanlab.org/2015/02/new-rules-governing-drone-journalism-are-on-the-way-and-theres-reason-to-be-optimistic/.

CHAPTER 13

1. Joseph R. Dominick (2011). "Dynamics of Mass Communication." 11th ed. New York: McGraw-Hill.

2. David Uberti (2016, Nov. 23). "A New Normal in Journalism for the Age of Trump." Columbia Journalism Review. Accessed at: http://www.cjr.org/covering_the_election/trump_media_normalization_press_freedom.php.

3. Transcript of Christiane Amanpour's acceptance speech for the Burton Benjamin Memorial Award (2016, Nov. 22). Accessed at: https://cpj.org/awards/2016/christiane-amanpour.php?mc_cid=3d31ad3066&mc_eid=4f1756f679.

4. Margaret Sullivan (2013, April 1). "Gender Questions Arise in Obituary of Rocket Scientist and Her Beef Stroganoff." The New York Times. Accessed at: http://publiceditor.blogs.nytimes.com/2013/04/01/gender-questions-arise-in-obituary-of-rocket-scientist-and-her-beef-stroganoff/.

5. Tania Ralli (2005, Sept. 5). "Who's a Looter? In Storm's Aftermath, Pictures Kick Up a Different Kind of Tempest." The New York Times. Accessed at: http://www.nytimes.com/2005/09/05/business/whos-a-looter-in-storms-aftermath-pictures-kick-up-a-different.html?_r=0.

6. Sara Fischer (2017, June 5). "Journalists Keep Getting in Trouble for Tweeting." Axios. Accessed at: https://www.axios.com/journalists-cant-avoid-twitter-misfires-2433656398.html.

7. "11 Tweets That Got People Fired From Their Jobs." Accessed at: http://emgn.com/entertainment/12-tweets-that-got-people-fired-from-their-jobs/.

8. Thomas Johnson and Shahira Fahmy (2009). "Embeds' Perceptions of Censorship: Can You Criticize a Soldier and Then Have Breakfast With Him in the Morning?" Mass Communication and Society, 12, 1, 52–77.

9. Jennifer Yuille (2003, Jan. 22). "'Made in China' Labels Hidden at Bush Event." CNN. Accessed at: http://www.cnn.com/2003/ALLPOLITICS/01/22/bush.boxes/.

10. Sheila Coronel, Steve Coll and Derek Kravitz (2015, April 5). "Rolling Stone's Investigation: 'A Failure That Was Avoidable.'" Columbia Journalism Review. Accessed at: http://www.cjr.org/investigation/rolling_stone_investigation.php?utm_content=buffer6e980&utm_medium=social&utm_source=twitter.com&utm_campaign=buffer.

11. Mallary Jean Tenore (2010, July 7). "Journalists Make Mistakes and What We Can Do About Them." Poynter.org. Accessed at: http://www.poynter.org/2010/why-journalists-make-mistakes-what-we-can-do-about-them/104195/.

12. Seth Mnookin (2005). "Hard News." New York: Random House.

13. "Reporter Who Resigned Leaves Long Trail of Deception" (2003, May 11). The New York Times. Accessed at: http://www.nytimes.com/2003/05/11/national/times-reporter-who-resigned-leaves-long-trail-of-deception.html.

APPENDIX C

1. "IC 5-14-3. Chapter 3. Access to Public Records." Accessed at: https://iga.in.gov/static-documents/0/8/2/b/082bff0b/TITLE5_AR14_ch3.pdf.

2. Reporters Committee for Freedom of the Press. "Electronic Communications Under Sunshine Laws." Accessed at: https://www.rcfp.org/access-electronic-communications/electronic-communications-under-sunshine-laws.

3. Jim Schaefer and M. L. Elrick (2008, Jan. 24). "Detroit Mayor, Aide Lied Under Oath, Texts Show." USA Today. Accessed at: http://usatoday30.usatoday.com/news/nation/2008-01-24-detroit-mayor_N.htm.

4. John Woolfolk (2013, April 11). "San Jose Fights Disclosure of Email, Text Message Records." Mercury News. Accessed at: http://www.mercurynews.com/2013/04/11/san-jose-fights-disclosure-of-email-text-message-records/.

5. Mike Rosenberg (2014, March 27). "San Jose Court: Government Workers Can Keep Messages From Personal Devices Private." Mercury News. Accessed at: http://www.mercurynews.com/2014/03/27/san-jose-court-government-workers-can-keep-messages-from-personal-devices-private/.

6. Vermont General Assembly. "Title 01: General Provisions." The Vermont Statutes Online. Accessed at: http://legislature.vermont.gov/statutes/section/01/005/00318.

INDEX

Medium shots, 182, 201, 202, 203
Meeting coverage, 117, 120, 123–124
Messaging apps, 75
Messenger, A., 213, 217
Microblogging, 81
Microphones, 176–177, 178, 183
Microsoft, 5
Mini-jack ports, 178
Minutes of meetings, 119
Mobile phones. *See* Smartphones
Monopods, 189
Mothers Against Drunk Driving (MADD), 238
Mug shots, 185
Murray, B., 223
Murrow, E. R., 2, 121

Name-recognition leads, 38–39
Narrative thread, 64–65, 65 (figure)
Narrative writing, 63
    chronological approach to story segmentation and, 67–68
    content subheadings/segmentation and, 66–68
    descriptive openings, scene setters and, 63–64
    narrative threads, kabob format and, 64–65, 65 (figure)
    nonlinear storytelling approach and, 68–71, 69 (figure)
    reader engagement, nut graph and, 65
    secondary senses, conveying story settings and, 67
    word pictures, provision of, 65–66
    See also Expanded news writing; Reporting basics; Writing process
National Action Network (NAN), 123
National Press Photographers Association (NPPA), 231, 232, 233, 234, 235, 237, 238, 240, 243
Nations, D., 76
Natural sound, 180–181
Negligence standard, 220
New York Times, 86, 245
Newman, S., 30
News conferences, 106–107, 117, 124, 126–127
News features, 99, 140
    bigger stories, extra time/effort and, 153
    fact checking/verification and, 149
    finding stories, strategies for, 141
    hit-and-run journalism and, 141
    investigative/data-driven journalism and, 149
    open-minded thinking and, 140, 142
    See also Beat reporting; Personality profiles; Reporting basics; Watchdog journalism
News values, xii, 2, 7
News writing. *See* Breaking news; Expanded news writing; News features; Newspapers; Writing process
Newspapers, xi, 2
    beat reporters and, 23
    choice of news outlets, historic lack of, 4
    First Amendment rights/protections and, 211

lead construction, 5Ws/1H and, 37, 37 (figure), 38
lead construction, circle diagram for, 38, 38 (figure)
lead problems, solutions for, 40–43
leads, types of, 38–40
press releases, construction of, 35–37
readership self-interest question and, 36–37
what matters most question and, 35–36
See also Expanded news writing; Inverted pyramid format; Reporting basics; Writing process
Niches, 2, 4, 81, 84
Nixon, R. M., 152
Nonlinear storytelling, 68
    audience choice and, 68, 71
    buffet approach and, 3, 70, 71
    democratization of information, Internet platforms and, 68, 71
    nonlinear vs. nonsensical writing and, 69–70
    order/clarity, key elements of, 70
    self-contained segments, construction of, 70
    story webs, visualization of, 68, 69 (figure)
    user-controlled navigation, understanding of, 69–71
    See also Expanded news writing; Narrative writing; Writing process
Northwest Territorial Mint LLC, 223
Note-taking process, 104
"Notebook emptying" problem, 46
Nut graph, 65

Obama, B., 3, 23, 27, 104, 124
Obituaries, 5, 109–110, 237
Objectivity standard, 13, 121, 158
Oddity interest element, 14, 60, 249–251
Off-the-record interviews, 105
Official sources, 9
Oliver, J., 223
On-the-record interviews, 105
One-party consent standard, 216
One-to-many model, 2, 75
1H. *See* 5Ws/1H
180-degree rule, 162
Open-ended questions, 113, 150
Open meetings rule, 214
Open records rule, 214

Pace considerations, 161–162
Package development for the web, 200
    adaptations for web distribution and, 204
    audio bites online and, 196, 198
    audio track, manipulation of, 200–201
    digital tools and, 203
    error checks and, 205
    fade technique and, 203
    gimmicky transitions, avoidance of, 203
    graphics, use of, 203, 205